Ordinary Families,
Extraordinary Lives

Ordinary Families, Extraordinary Lives

Assets and Poverty Reduction in Guayaquil, 1978–2004

CAROLINE O. N. MOSER

BROOKINGS INSTITUTION PRESS
Washington, D.C.

Library of Congress Cataloging-in-Publication data

Moser, Caroline O. N.
  Ordinary families, extraordinary lives : assets and poverty reduction in Guayaquil,
1978–2004 / Caroline O. N. Moser.
        p.   cm.
  Includes bibliographical references and index.
  Summary: "Longitudinal account of five families strategically accumulating assets to
escape poverty in Guayaquil. Captures the causes and consequences of these
developments through economic data and anthropological narrative, within the broader
context of political, economic, and spatial changes in Ecuador. Covers such issues as
housing, employment, family dynamics, violence, and emigration"—Provided by
publisher.
  ISBN 978-0-8157-0327-3 (pbk. : alk. paper)
  1. Saving and investment—Ecuador—Guayaquil—Case studies. 2. Guayaquil
(Ecuador)—Social policy—Case studies. 3. Poverty—Ecuador—Guayaquil—Case
studies. 4. Poor—Ecuador—Guayaquil—Case studies. 5. Poverty—Government
policy—Ecuador—Guayaquil—Case studies. 6. Economic assistance, Domestic—
Ecuador—Guayaquil—Case studies. I. Title.
  HC79.S3M67 2009
  339.4'3092286632—dc22   2009030942

9 8 7 6 5 4 3 2 1

Printed on acid-free paper

Typeset in Adobe Garamond

Composition by Circle Graphics
Columbia, Maryland

Printed by R. R. Donnelley
Harrisonburg, Virginia

Front cover: photo by Brian Moser

Dedicated to

Señora Emma Torres

Dirigente, Comité Barrial Indio Guayas, Guayaquil

and to the four who made this book possible

Peter, Titus, Nathaniel, Brian

Contents

Acknowledgments

Indio Guayas has been a fundamental part of my life for more than thirty years while researching and writing about the remarkable lives of its community members, culminating in the completion of this book. So many people have helped me along the way—my friends and neighbors in Indio Guayas itself, academic colleagues, research assistants, funders, friends, and family—as I moved between universities, development agencies, and think-tank institutions, across oceans, and through different life-cycle stages. To each and every person who has supported me on this extraordinary personal journey I would like to express my profound thanks. While it is not possible to acknowledge by name all those who have influenced me or helped me, I would like to mention a few upon whom my research and the culmination of this work have depended.

My deepest gratitude, first and foremost, is to the heroic families in Indio Guayas. Central to my efforts has been Emma Torres, the community leader who made the research possible in 1978, continued to do so until this present day, and to whom this book is dedicated. I want to express my thanks to her wonderful family, who welcomed me into their home as a friend and then *comadre.* I also particularly wish to thank the four women in the community who so openly shared their lives with me—Carmelina, Aurora, Amelia, and Rosa, their husbands, and families—whose names, as well as those of others in the community, have been turned into pseudonyms in the book so as to protect their identities. In addition, I remember with affection their inspirational sons and daughters now in Barcelona who continued the same tradition of Ecuadorian hospitality taught to them by their parents in Indio Guayas. Finally, without the team of community researchers, including Ana Rosa Vera, Josefina Tomala, Carmita Narboa, and Amelia Vinneza, I would not have been able to undertake the survey questionnaires in the last two stages of the research. Particular thanks are due to Lucy Zavalla, who not only worked alongside me in Indio Guayas but also accompanied me to Barcelona and introduced me to her friends and old schoolmates.

Colleagues in different institutions in diverse places at changing points in time have provided intellectual inspiration, guidance, and invaluable support. Amartya Sen, Alison Scott, Diane Elson, and Richard Webb served as crucial external advisers to the 1992 World Bank research project. In Ecuador Diego Carrion, Gaitán Villavicencio, Father Frank Smith, and Fernando Carrion supported me on my constant revisits to Guayaquil while Gioconda Herrera, Alicia Torres, and Xavier Andrade kindly shared their research publications.

In the United States, Michelle Adato, Ruth Alsop, Ray Boshara, Robert Buckley, Mayra Buvinic, Charles Call, Michael Carter, Marty Chen, Anis Dani, Frank DeGiovanni, Patricia Fagen, Clare Ferguson, Paul Francis, Estanislao Gacitua-Mario, Miguel Garcia, Lawrence Haddad, Jesko Hentschel, John Hoddinott, Michael Jacobs, Steen Jorgensen, Ravi Kanbur, Peter Lanjouw, Santiago Levy, Roza Makonnen, Kate McKee, Deepa Narayan, Andy Norton, Manuel Orozco, Janice Perlman, Alejandro Portes, Bryan Roberts, Michael Sherraden, Pamela Sparr, Peter Ward, Michael Woolcock, and Cecilia Zanetta all assisted in shaping my understanding of poverty and assets.

In the United Kingdom, Tony Addison, Jo Beall, Tony Bebbington, Robert Chambers, Sylvia Chant, Fiona Clark, Sarah Cook, Alison Evans, Rosalind Eyben, Alan Gilbert, Howard Glennister, Meia Green, Alicia Herbert, Jeremy Holland, David Hulme, Caren Levy, David Marsden, Simon Maxwell, Cathy McIlwaine, Diana Mitlin, Maxine Molyneux, Ronaldo Ramirez, Denis Rodgers, Michael Safier, David Satterthwaite, Hubert Schmitz, Alfredo Stein, Nadia Taher, John Turner, and Patrick Wakely have likewise sharpened my research ability.

Scattered across the world, the following individuals have influenced my work: Angelica Acosta, Maruja Barrig, Lourdes Beneria, Arjan de Haan, Eivor Halkaer, John Harriss, Elisabet Hellsten, Norman Long, Francie Lund, Alison Mathie, Julian May, Sue Parnell, Marni Piggott, Pilar Ramirez, Alfredo Rodriguez, Mauricio Rubio, Ismail Serageldin, Andrés Solimano, Richard Stren, Maria Eugenia Vasquez, and Vanessa Watson.

While I was living in Washington, D.C., Monique and Lewis Cohen, Elunid and Julian Schweitzer, Moustafa Mourad, Alison Cave and Monty, and the late Sally Yudelman provided friendship and support. Cathy McIlwaine and Lee Drabwell, Sukey Field, Monica Hicks, Marylla and Julian Hunt, Nathaniel, Olya, and Savva Moser, Diane and Ken Rochelle, Ben and Sue Shephard, Maud and the late Ken Sollis did likewise while I was in the United Kingdom. Titus, Ingrid, Tage, Kaia, and Sebastian Fossgard-Moser generously shared their home through a snowbound Calgary Christmas while I was in the last stages of drafting this book.

At the Brookings Institution in Washington, D.C., Carol Graham and Lael Brainard kindly invited me to become a Research Fellow, allowing me to undertake the final stage of this lengthy research process. Navtej Dhillon, Amanda Amarh, Janet Walker, and Chris Kelaher all provided invaluable support. Over the last thirty years, at different stages, Michael Gatehouse, Helen Garcia, Annalise Moser, Jennifer Doleac, Kathryn Lankaster, and James Pickett all dedicatedly grappled with fading questionnaires and data entry problems. Sue Shephard, Erika Avila, and the late Hanka de Rhodes transcribed or translated diaries and interviews. Anastasia Bermudez, Ralph Kinnear, and Nicholas Scarle provided research assistance, and the editorial support of Starr Belsky is gratefully acknowledged.

Since the mid-1980s, when he first sat in my kitchen in London, Mike Cohen's vision in encouraging me to examine economic adjustment processes at the microlevel and to keep returning to Guayaquil has been a crucial element. In Andy Felton I finally discovered an economist prepared to collaborate with an anthropologist; without this interdisciplinary approach, the asset index would not have been developed.

Over the years a range of financial grants has supported this research. The original visit in 1978 was undertaken as part of background research for a Granada Television film; a small summer grant from the London School of Economics helped me return to Ecuador in the early 1980s. The 1992 study was one of four cofunded by the World Bank, the Netherlands Ministry of Development Cooperation, the United Nations Children's Fund (UNICEF), the Swedish International Development Authority, and the United Nations Center for Human Settlements (HABITAT)–World Bank Urban Management Program. Both Theo Kolstee and Richard Jolly played a significant role in ensuring this support. Finally, the completion stage of this research, involving fieldwork in Guayaquil and Barcelona as well as analysis undertaken while I was at the Brookings Institution, was funded by a grant from the Asset Building and Community Development program of the Ford Foundation. I would like to gratefully acknowledge vice president Pablo Farias for his sustained commitment to this research and its associated development of an asset adaptation approach to poverty reduction.

Above all I would like to thank my family. I would like to acknowledge my mother, Lorna Wilmott Shephard, who inspired me with her intellectual curiosity, and my father, Rupert Shephard, who taught me the virtues of perseverance and to take the long view of life. Brian Moser first introduced me to Indio Guayas, collaborated in the first research stage, and has very generously provided his photos from 1978 for this book. My sons Titus and Nathaniel coped with their parents' recklessness in taking them out of a London school to live in Indio Guayas—an experience that profoundly affected their lives. Finally, Peter Sollis has been with me on so much of this journey, selflessly giving his time, enthusiasm, and intellectual support, not only during the years in Guayaquil itself but also through the protracted process of bringing this book to fruition, sustaining me with his encouragement and meticulous editing, as well as some of the later photos (the rest are mine). It is these four men who ultimately made this book possible. To them, above all, I owe a great debt of gratitude.

Caroline Moser
Manchester, England

Prologue

"Most people have come here because they are in the same state as me. I have two children, but many have five, six, up to eight children. Salaries are so low they don't cover food, let alone rent. We are all poor; you cannot describe it any other way. Anyone who has money would not come here; only those who are poor and really in need."

—Marta

With these words Marta, leader of the local community committee, introduced me to her neighbors in Indio Guayas in 1978. These were poor households—only one in five lived above the poverty line—squatting in bamboo-walled houses in a mangrove swamp on the periphery of Guayaquil, Ecuador. Recently arrived, they were young, upwardly aspiring families who had taken advantage of free waterlogged land to build and own their homes and were living without basic services such as electricity, running water, or plumbing, or social services such as health care and education. Yet thirty years later Indio Guayas was a consolidated settlement with reduced levels of poverty and less than one in three households considered poor.

This book describes how households living in this typical third world urban slum community relentlessly and systematically struggled to get out of poverty while simultaneously contesting with the authorities to provide both physical and social infrastructure. Over a thirty-year period, households spanning two generations steadily built up "portfolios" of assets, accumulating human, social, financial, and physical capital, with their day-to-day struggles involving success stories as well as tragic disasters and failures.[1] Such documentation of the minutiae of daily slum reality lacks the immediacy of sensational drama that instant global communication increasingly demands. However, while tabloid stories may relieve our daily monotony, they poorly approximate reality. Behind the mundane slum routine of ordinary families lie extraordinary lives. The challenge is to portray the amazing fortitude and determination of people who have not only survived but quietly brought up their children; relentlessly striven to prosper in the adverse conditions of an urban slum, a fluctuating economy, and a crisis-ridden government; and tried to give the next generation better opportunities in the far more complex world of the twenty-first century.

This prologue briefly introduces the main themes running through this book and outlines the structure of its contents. The first theme is the issue of poverty itself, with its reduction being one of the most relentless development challenges of the past fifty years, as highlighted by global poverty reports (World Bank 1990, 2000) and the UN Millennium Development Goals (United Nations General Assembly 2001). It is this changing debate on the nature, measurement, and contextualization of poverty that informs the book.

What do we mean by *poverty*? Robert Chambers maintains that poverty often becomes "what has been measured and is available for analysis" (2007, p. 18). He argues that by focusing only on readily available data, development analysts have often constructed a flawed conceptualization of poverty that ignores information not easily gathered and quantified.[2] Equally, such analyses fail to include interpretations of poverty, deprivation, and exclusion grounded in the agency and identity of the poor themselves.[3]

This book addresses such limitations by going beyond the measurements of income or consumption poverty to introduce as a central focus an asset accumulation framework. This identifies the range of assets that households, and individuals within them, accumulate, consolidate, or at times lose through their erosion. At the same time, it is important to recognize that while the measurement of assets can help identify overall asset accumulation trends, it cannot provide explanations of the underlying social, economic, and political processes within which such accumulation occurs. To identify how and when different assets are accumulated, this book, of necessity, broadens the focus to tell the story not only through statistics and numbers but also through the lives of individuals and families. This requires an understanding of the social relations within families, households, and communities as well as their structural relationships with external actors (see Harriss 2007a).

A second theme relates the contrast between short-term static "snapshots" and longitudinal studies of poverty. Snapshots can only capture a single point in time. Poverty, however, is dynamic and constantly changes along with both internal life cycles and external circumstances, such as natural disasters, government policy, and social forces. The longitudinal study presented here provides the opportunity to go beyond a short-term diagnostic of poverty levels or asset portfolios to document longer-term factors. It identifies the agility of individuals and households in detecting opportunities and taking advantage of them when responding to changing macroeconomic conditions—whether it is the Ecuadorian structural adjustment programs of the 1980s or the globalization-linked dollarization of the late 1990s. A longitudinal study not only incorporates changes in poverty levels and asset portfolios but also includes the evolution of subjective perceptions of well-being, including intergenerational differences. In the case of mothers and daughters, these relate to changes in gender power relations and perceptions of empowerment; from the perspective of fathers and sons, it includes the positive upward mobility expectations of less-educated fathers versus the rising aspirations and growing despair of their better-educated sons.

This book tells the story of how poor households struggled to get out of poverty and accumulated assets. Just as Oscar Lewis focused on a single day in the lives of five families when he conceptualized poor households as living in a "culture of poverty" in urban Mexico in the 1960s and 1970s (Lewis 1966; Lewis and others 1975), so too the present narrative about Indio Guayas is focused through the voices of five women and their families, but in this case over a thirty-year period. This highlights a third theme that relates to the agency of individuals—community members and leaders alike—in achieving such outcomes. Associated with this is their contestation and negotiation with the range of state, civil society, and international agencies that assist, rather than effect, poverty reduction or community consolidation. In a context of changing delivery systems, the sequence of priorities negotiated by the community is important in achieving successful outcomes. For instance, the strength of community social capital has a direct impact on the accumulation of other assets, in part because a socially mobilized community is better able to negotiate political concessions.[4] The Guayaquil study also tracked sons and daughters who had migrated to Barcelona, Spain. This permitted a comparison of differences in opportunities between an economically static city with rigidities in socioeconomic and political power structures, such as

Guayaquil, and one where political change and an economic boom are eroding such inflexibilities and opening up dramatic new prospects, as is the case
in Barcelona. Here the next-generation migrants are rewarded for what they
do rather than which school they went to or which social contacts they have.
A focus on institutional structures contributes to understanding the underlying reasons for different mobility trends, namely, why some households succeed in getting out of poverty, others do not, and yet others get out but fall
back into poverty again.

A further theme relates to the fact that this is an urban story. Only recently
has this environment become a focus of attention. With rural poverty deeper,
broader, and long considered a more intractable problem (Lipton 1977; Corbridge and Jones 2005), it is only with recent demographic shifts in the scale
and velocity of urbanization in the South in past decades, as well as new evidence on levels of urban poverty, that the challenges posed by urban poverty are
being reconsidered.[5] By 2007 the turning point had passed worldwide, with
more people living in cities than rural areas; by 2030 a predicted two-thirds of
the world's population will live in urban areas (United Nations 2008). This
includes not only the burgeoning global megacities but also the more typical
small and medium towns. In an urban world, the critical question concerns the
extent to which such "exploding cities" create economic opportunities both for
rural migrants as well as for the urban-born.

In the light of globalization, another important theme is increasing the
understanding of urban poverty and challenging the pervasive, persistent, and
embedded stereotypes and myths about urbanization. In particular, these stereotypes relate to oversimplifications about urban poverty and the slums or informal settlements where the poor live.[6] In the 1970s urban slums were popularly
perceived as "hotbeds of revolution" (Eckstein 1977), and that perception has
changed little since then. Today many such slums are described as "streets without joy," where the daily violence associated with economic exclusion provides
incipient links to the "urbanization of insurgency" and the "urban war on terrorism" (Davis 2006; Beall 2006). In an age of media hype and celebrity development specialists, it is common to associate "global poverty" with violent urban
slum wars and even terrorism, as claimed by the U.S. government's 2002
National Security Strategy, which cited poverty as one of the root causes of the
terrorist impulse (Broad and Cavanagh 2006).

While poverty does not necessarily breed violence, neither are there quick
fixes and instant solutions that reduce it. The search for new solutions to end
the age-old problem of poverty, as well as more recently recognized issues

such as vulnerability, inequality, and exclusion, is extensive. As donor aid has expanded to include not only funding from established international financial institutions, bilateral donors, and nongovernmental institutions but also the new philanthropy of private sector donors, so too has its focus shifted more to quick-fix, top-down, results-focused solutions. Current popular answers range from cash transfer safety nets for the poor through integrated social protection programs (Levy 2006; United Nations Development Program [UNDP] 2006; Barrientos and Hulme 2008; Farrington and Slater 2006), to sector-specific interventions designed to eradicate specific diseases (Gates Foundation 2008), to spatial experiments in model villages or leadership academies where celebrities rather than local communities identify the development solutions they consider appropriate (Sachs 2006).[7]

An important policy theme in this book is that upward socioeconomic mobility is not the simple story many practitioners would like. Along the way are changes in perceptions, aspirations, and expectations that relate to the contextualization of poverty in time and place. A short-term focus tends to deny endogenous processes and to maintain that history does not matter. The work presented here shows that achieving "the end of poverty" is more complicated than is recognized by those promoting sector-specific, top-down solutions. Not only are local institutions and social actors critically important, so too is the agency and empowerment of individual women and men embedded within households and communities. By fashioning cross-cutting solutions to establish homes, mobilize for infrastructure, educate family members, identify opportunities in the local economy and abroad, and deal with violence within the family and community, many households successfully transition out of poverty with minimal support from external agencies.

Overall, this volume seeks to show how a more sophisticated understanding of the complexities of poverty, as well as an understanding of asset accumulation, can contribute to counterbalancing some of the predominant ideological stereotypes regarding global poverty. These include those promoted by Easterly (2006), who maintains that international development aid has failed, as well as those sponsored by Sachs, the guru of decontextualized, quick-fix experimentation solutions in twelve villages in rural Africa.[8] Despite constraints in representing the agency of individuals, households, and communities, this book identifies the huge creativity, pride, and resilience of poor communities, which contribute not only to their local economies but also to the social mobility of cities. Such characteristics and achievements are exemplified in the thirty-year history of Indio Guayas as presented here.

Organization

This volume combines the econometric statistical measurements of poverty levels and asset indexes for Indio Guayas between 1978 and 2004 with the individual and household narratives associated with the processes of accumulating different assets. As mentioned above, this story is told mainly through the lives of five women neighbors, including the community leader, Marta, and their families over three generations. The life cycle stories of small families that originally invaded the swampland and now have complex multiple-generation families that still live in the community, as well as second-generation members living elsewhere in Guayaquil and in Barcelona, are presented within the context of broader political, economic, and spatial changes in the city of Guayaquil as well as in Ecuador as a whole. The simultaneous examination of these interrelated levels presents challenges in terms of structure and content. To address such complexity, the book is divided into three parts.

The first part of the book comprises two chapters. Chapter 1 sets the context by introducing the families in Indio Guayas—the main protagonists in this story—as well as describing my involvement with the community over the last thirty years. Here I document my efforts as an anthropologist to understand changes in the community, while making such information accessible to academics and development practitioners whose discourse has changed fundamentally over this thirty-year period. Chapter 2 briefly outlines the theoretical background to the research, discussing conceptual approaches to poverty reduction and asset accumulation as part of ongoing debates concerning the "technification" of poverty (Harriss 2007a), and analyzing social relations within both local and broader contexts (Green 2006). The chapter describes the theoretical shift from the asset vulnerability framework, developed in the 1990s, to the asset accumulation framework (and its associated index) as a measurement tool. It describes the quantitative results from the 1978–2004 panel data set; this includes changes in household income poverty as well as in the accumulation of human, social, financial-productive, and physical capital assets over the same period. Analysis of the relationship between household assets and income mobility shows that the most common route out of poverty for most households is a gradual accumulation of a range of assets as opposed to a dramatic change based on one asset.

There are limitations to such quantitative data. For instance, they cannot identify why some households are able to accumulate sustainable assets and others are not. Equally, they cannot address the causes of intergenerational mobility. For example, is it the external context or household attributes or both that affect outcomes? Household and individual asset accumulation potential depends on a complex interrelationship between numerous factors. These include the original investment asset portfolio, the broader opportunity structure in terms of the internal life cycle, social relations both within households and in the community, and the external politicoeconomic context and wider institutional environment. Such complexities consequently are often better understood by combining qualitative narratives with econometric measurements.

The second part of the book, therefore, turns to the longitudinal contribution of different household and community capital assets to well-being outcomes. Chapters 3 to 6 describe the sequential and interrelated accumulation of different assets, contextualized in terms of broader changes. Chapter 3 details the process of acquiring a home of one's own, with physical capital the first asset prioritized, contextualized in terms of the changing spatial development of Guayaquil. Chapter 4 shifts to the contestation for physical infrastructure undertaken with political parties in the 1970s and early 1980s, and highlights the importance of community social capital. Chapter 5 examines the significance of community leadership and empowerment in the mobilization for social services from international institutions, which had consequences both for health and education, thus affecting the human capital of individuals and households. Both chapters 4 and 5 point to the importance of intracommunity gender relations for political negotiation within the changing political context. Chapter 6 shifts from the community to households and focuses on the thorny issue of employment and financial-productive capital.

The third part turns to the implications of households and intrahousehold relations for moving out of poverty. Chapter 7 examines the changing structure of households over the last three decades in terms of the increasing importance of household social capital to confront the repeated financial and economic measures that for the past twenty years have had serious implications for the poor. This is complemented by chapter 8, which turns to intrahousehold issues and the significance of changing gender relations. Chapter 9 compares the asset accumulation choices of the first generation with those of their sons and daughters, showing how patterns differ between generations and how first-generation choices have affected the second generation. The chapter also looks at comparative intergenerational aspirations. Chapter 10 provides a further comparison, this time between the income mobility of the second generation still living in Guayaquil versus those living in Barcelona. Chapter 11 concludes by discussing the worrisome growth of insecurity and violence in the community. Finally, chapter 12 outlines the components of an associated asset accumulation policy, drawing on the results of the Guayaquil research. By way of reference, these twelve chapters are complemented by three appendixes: appendix A describes the fieldwork methodology; appendix B elaborates more extensively on the broader economic and political context; and appendix C (coauthored with Andrew Felton) explains the econometric methodology developed for the asset index.

The challenge this book undertakes is to document the extraordinary resilience of the households in Indio Guayas in their daily lives over the past thirty years. Any "analytical" or "conceptual" framework ultimately is an artificial construct and only useful if it helps unpack the complexity of the lives of this community over three decades. How closely does the reality defined by outsiders coincide with that of the residents of Indio Guayas? Ultimately, that is the litmus test of a book such as this.

Ordinary Families,
Extraordinary Lives

1

Introduction to Indio Guayas and the Study

This chapter sets the scene for this thirty-year story by introducing the households and families in Indio Guayas that are the main social actors, summarizing the changes they have experienced over the thirty-year period. It highlights how the similarity between their socioeconomic characteristics and economic circumstances in 1978 enabled them to be considered what scientists term a natural experiment. By 2004 differentiation was more visible between those that had made it out of poverty and those who had not. The causes and consequences of this change are the main theme this book seeks to address.

Marta and Her Neighbors in Indio Guayas

In 1978 Marta, a twenty-six-year-old dressmaker; her husband, Jesus, a tailor aged thirty-nine; and their two young daughters, Adriana and Ana Maria, bought a ten-by-thirty-meter plot of waterlogged mangrove swamp from a professional squatter in Cisne Dos, one of a number of neighborhoods (*barrios*) in the parish (*parroquia*) of Febres Cordero. This particular neighborhood, soon to be named Indio Guayas after its community committee, is an eleven-block area (*manzana*) located on the southwest edge of the city, about seven kilometers from the central business district. Indio Guayas, at the far end of the parish, is bounded by two wide "artery" roads, the *Calle* (street) 25 and Calle 26, and stretches from

Calle F to Calle Ñ, and runs up to one of the estuaries (*estero*) of the River Guayas. Ecuador's largest city, chief port, and industrial center, Guayaquil is located on low-lying land 160 kilometers from the Pacific Ocean where two rivers converge. In 1978 the city had a population of 600,000, with the poor living in inner-city slums, known as *tugurios,* or in squatter settlements, called the *suburbios,* on tidal swampland.

Anxious to escape the high rents in the city center, Marta and her family left the relative comfort of a shared multifamily house for the suburbios, which housed a third of the city's population. In the early 1970s, when she, along with the first homeowners, arrived in the area, it was a mangrove swamp, which professional squatters sold off as ten-by-thirty-meter plots (*solars*). Her family quickly erected a very basic bamboo and wood housing structure above the water, and began the challenge of living a life lacking not only permanent dry land but also all basic services such as electricity, running water, and plumbing, as well as social services such as health care and education.

Settling around them on the same "street," the Calle K, were other young families equally eager to take advantage of the possibility of invading or buying cheap plots from land speculators. Directly across the perilous wooden walkway was Mercedes with her husband, Claudio, another tailor as well as an informal dental technician, and their two young children. To the left of Mercedes lived Carmen, a laundrywoman, and Alonso, a skilled builder, and their three daughters. Lidia and Salvador and their four children lived on the other side. Among others settling nearby was Alicia, also a washerwoman, a thirty-six-year-old single mother with seven children who lived four doors down from Marta. A few doors away in the other direction from Marta were two brothers, both tailors. Walter lived with his wife, Eloisa, and two sons, and two doors down was the bachelor household of Alvaro, who would later marry Yasmin and have three children. Among other neighbors forming this close-knit community were Diego and Andrea Ortega (whose son Mateo would later go to Barcelona).

When these families first arrived, there were no roads; houses were connected by hazardous wood and bamboo catwalks (*puentes*). This isolation meant that the women were forced to rely on previously unknown neighbors; they quickly developed complex social networks for mutual aid while the men, in turn, formed close drinking relationships.[1] Many of these connections were formalized through a godparent relationship (*compadrasco*). Figure 1-1 shows women's and men's social networks in the Calle K in 1978. These stopped halfway down the street, reflecting the fact that "communal" catwalks were only constructed by half the group of neighbors, preempting contact with those living further down the street. There the networks were not as dense; among these

Figure 1-1. *Gender-Based Reciprocity Networks in the Calle K, Indio Guayas, 1978*

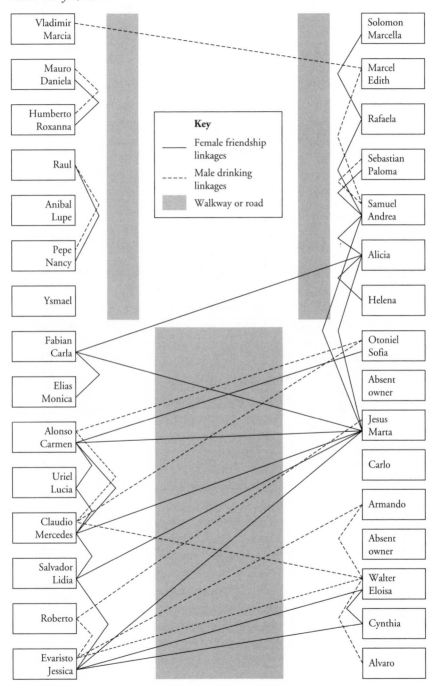

less cohesive neighbors there were a multitude of small individual catwalks rather than one collective catwalk.

The neighbors quickly formed a highly cohesive self-help committee that covered the eleven-block area, and they soon elected Marta president. Throughout the 1980s and 1990s, as described in chapters 4 and 5, the committee, with broad support from the community, lobbied government authorities and political parties as well as international agencies to acquire basic physical and social infrastructure.

Indio Guayas as a "Natural Experiment"

When they first settled in Indio Guayas, these neighboring households were surprisingly similar, not only in their living conditions but also in their ages, life cycle, household structure, and professions, despite minor differences in terms of family size and marital status. Many of the men were craftsmen such as tailors or carpenters, while the women were domestic servants, washerwomen, or dressmakers. Both men and women were also involved in informal sector retail selling. Indio Guayas was a homogeneous community in nearly all respects, including initial household endowments as well as the external political and economic context in which they lived.

The nearly identical household circumstances of this young population of settlers, struggling to make their way in the city and many just starting families, provided the conditions for a "natural experiment."[2] In 1978 more than 80 percent of households were below the income poverty line, two-thirds of households were nuclear families, both women and men had a mean age of thirty years, the average household size was nearly six, the average age of children was seven years, and the average number of working members per household was one and a half. The adults had little education and few assets other than the same amount of land provided by the municipality. This unique set of circumstances allows one to pose compelling questions: What has happened over time? Have they all succeeded in getting out of poverty, and if not, why not?

Indio Guayas Thirty Years Later

Thirty years later, Indio Guayas was a stable urban settlement. The level of infrastructure provision was attained through a remarkable process of community contestation in which Marta's leadership, along with the support of neighbors such as Lourdes, Claudio, and Alicia, was critical for success. Families no longer lived in bamboo houses but rather in cement block houses. They were no longer connected by dangerous walkways but instead lived on paved roads built on solid land, and the neighborhood had physical infrastructure such as running water, lighting, and sewerage. Development was not limited to utilities but also included social infrastructure such as schools and clinics. The city's rapid spatial expansion during this period meant that Indio Guayas was no longer on the periphery. By 2004 many of the children of the original settlers had also formed families of their own and were living on their parents' plots within the community, elsewhere in Indio Guayas, or in other parts of Guayaquil, or had migrated abroad, particularly to Barcelona.

After this lengthy time period, Indio Guayas emerged as a relative success story in terms of income poverty reduction. By 2004 fewer than one in three was poor, and all residents lived in permanent settlements with land titles and physical and social infrastructure. Nevertheless, there had been winners and losers in terms of income poverty. Households had moved in different directions. Some, such as Marta and Jesus, Carmen and Alonso, and Alvaro and Yasmin, had moved steadily upward and gotten out of income poverty.[3] Some, such as Claudio and Mercedes, and Walter and Eloisa, had moved upward and then downward, while others, such as Lidia and Salvador, and Alicia, remained stuck in income poverty.

An examination of assets, however, reveals a more complex story than the measurement of purely income-based poverty levels. For instance, in the 1970s the trust and collaboration that formed the social relations in the community (identified as its social capital) were essential for the acquisition of social and physical infrastructure by all households.[4] From 1985 to 1995, welfare benefits and child care based on community services using women's voluntary labor were provided first through the United Nations Children's Fund (UNICEF) and then through Plan International. Thus community social capital continued to be important. However, in the following decade, as a consequence of both the acquisition of such infrastructure and the demise of the community welfare support programs, the importance of the community organization declined.

Yet it was social capital that initially helped households to accumulate the physical capital required for home construction, acquiring land titles, and filling in their plots with earth. Over time, as households incrementally upgraded their houses and replaced bamboo walls with cement blocks and earth, or replaced wooden floors with cement, the value of this physical asset increased. From 1978 to 1992, housing, the first critical asset that households sought to accumulate, grew fastest. During the 1992–2004 period, once housing was established, parents made trade-offs between their children's human capital or their own consumption, either investing in their children's education as a longer-term strategy for poverty reduction or spending on "luxury" consumer durables including DVDs, TVs, and occasionally even computers. Over time, households became more differentiated not only in terms of poverty levels but also in terms of asset ownership, with interesting patterns of income mobility and asset accumulation and an associated relationship between them.

By 2004, for instance, while Alicia was still income poor, she was asset rich in terms of human capital. Having put most of her nine children through secondary school, her family was finally upgrading the house and acquiring consumer durables. On Mother's Day in 2005, her children joined together to buy her a washing machine. One of her daughters, Reina, commented, "Our mother spent thirty years as a washerwoman so as to support us. Surely this is the best way we can repay her." In contrast, Lidia was both income and asset poor, and her wayward husband was unemployed. They relied on small intermittent financial support from her children (none of whom finished high school) and unpredictable remittances from one daughter, with much of the money spent on alcohol.

Turning to the next generation, we find that by 2004 adult sons and daughters were better educated but also had greater expectations and aspirations to match. They faced new and increasingly daunting challenges in a globalized context where few good employment opportunities would present themselves. Nearly half still live on the family plot and benefit from the assets accumulated by their parents. Household social capital had increased over time, particularly among poorer households. Low wages, the high expenditure on human capital (health and education) associated with privatization of social infrastructure, and increasing demand for conspicuous consumption left households needing more income earners than before.

Others of the next generation, such as the sons and daughters of Lidia and Salvador, had left to acquire homes of their own, repeating their parents' experience but this time squatting on the hills that form the city's new periphery. Despite their better education, they had been insufficiently economically mobile to make it to the gated communities (*cuidadelos*) where the new middle class lived. A third group had migrated abroad. These included Marta's nephew, Gonzalo, and Diego and Andrea Ortega's son, Mateo, both of whom had gone to live in Barcelona, where the employment opportunities, labor rights, and access to financial capital such as mortgages all contributed to far more rapid asset accumulation than that of their peers in Guayaquil. In Barcelona there were greater opportunities as well as higher levels of socioeconomic mobility.

Despite the upward economic mobility of her family, Marta still identified herself as poor. This highlights the limitations of both income poverty and asset measurement, and raises the question: Whose perception of poverty are we, or should we be, talking about? Ultimately, poverty is a relational concept, not an absolute level. Marta's situation must be contextualized within the broader economic, political, and social structure of Guayaquil, which in many ways has remained constant over the past thirty years. Thus, while Marta knew she was not as poor as many of her neighbors, her daughters nevertheless lacked employment commensurate with their educational level. Although Ana Maria had a university degree in industrial psychology, she had become an underpaid administrative secretary at the local state secondary school in Indio Guayas, while Marta's other daughter, Adriana, scraped by selling clothes and cosmetics informally in the local neighborhood in between fixed-term contract jobs with the local government.

For the next generation, merely escaping poverty may not be sufficient since inequality and exclusion represent powerful development challenges in their own right. In Indio Guayas increasing alienation, associated with higher educational levels and a lack of decent wage employment due to the stagnant Guayaquil economy and inflexible broader social and political structures, has exacerbated perceptions of exclusion for the next generation. In some cases this has resulted in a dramatic rise in violent robbery, theft, and drug dealing, with insecurity and growing fear affecting all households.

The story of the pioneers who created Indio Guayas tells us that "getting out of poverty" is closely linked to the accumulation of different assets, with successful accumulation strategies varying according to circumstances. However, while the history of asset accumulation illustrates individual, household, and community "pathways out of poverty," ultimately the fundamental question remains as to how well rising expectations can be met without accompanying changes in the broader economic and political context. In this instance, the state, despite an oil boom economy, has fundamentally failed to generate adequate economic opportunities for the majority of the better-educated next generation.

The National and City-Level Context of Indio Guayas

Long-term changes in income poverty and assets need to be examined in terms of internal life cycle factors such as changes in household headship, age, and number of children. However, these considerations cannot be divorced from the external structural macroeconomic and political factors operating during different phases of Ecuador's history as well as the stages in Guayaquil's spatial development. These factors provided the broader context within which poverty reduction and asset accumulation occurred. (See time line summary in appendix B, figure B-1.)

The geography of Guayaquil is an important starting point. Guayaquil is Ecuador's largest city, chief port, and major center of trade and industry. Along with Quito, the highland capital, Guayaquil is one of the country's most important cities. This lowland coastal town was founded by the Spanish in 1537, some 160 kilometers upstream from the Pacific Ocean at the confluence of the Daule and Barboyo Rivers. Guayaquil's growth stemmed from its optimal location for receiving tropical produce, transported from the hinterland by river craft, for transfer to seagoing vessels for export. Consequently, the city's development was closely linked to Ecuador's primary, export-oriented economy, making the city dependent on shifts in the world market structure (MacIntosh 1972).

Before the dramatic 1970s oil boom, Ecuador was primarily an agricultural exporter with most of its wealth and power base on the coast. Late nineteenth-century industrialization and associated urbanization resulted from the coastal cultivation and export of cacao. By 1920 this accounted for more than 70 percent of the country's exports. The linked influx of wealth created a market for industrial products in Guayaquil, and early industrialization included the manufacture or processing of basic commodities, such as starch products, milk, rice, beverages, and clothing. The Ecuadorian banana boom began in 1933. Facing little competition, Ecuador was soon the primary banana producer worldwide. Between 1945 and 1956, its banana exports constituted a fifth of the global market (Gerlach 2003, p. 30). The urban population increased dramatically as a result of the economic prosperity, which again was strongest on the coast; between 1942 and 1962, the coastal population doubled, and Guayaquil's 5.8 percent a year growth throughout the 1950s transformed it into the economic hub of Ecuador.

The discovery of oil in the interior in the 1970s marked a crucial turning point for Ecuador. Oil revenue funded industrialization and stimulated economic development just as the banana boom was winding down. One major consequence was a shift of both economic and political power from Guayaquil and its coastal merchant class to Quito, where the central government was located. This allowed Quito more overt control over the economy and society, as well as strengthened the military at the expense of the traditional oligarchy (Gerlach 2003, pp. 35–36).

Turning to the more recent past, we can loosely divide the last three decades during which this research was undertaken into three periods, each of which was distinguished by different macroeconomic development models, national political conditions, and changes in policy approaches by government institutions, donors, and nongovernmental organizations (NGOs). (See appendix B for a detailed description of the broader context.)

Guayaquil in 1978: Optimism in a Buoyant, Expanding Economy

At the time of the first fieldwork in 1978, Guayaquil was experiencing rapid economic and industrial growth. Associated with this were increasing in-migration, a high level of urbanization, and the expansion of low-income settlements on the city's periphery (Santos Alvite 1989). In 1978 the city had a population of around 1 million, with 30 percent of its annual growth produced by in-migration, mainly mixed-race people (*mestizos*) from the surrounding littoral departments but also a limited number of indigenous people (*serranos*) from the highlands. During the 1970s Ecuador also emerged from military rule and experienced a political democratization process that included the establishment of new democratic parties such as Izquierda Democrática (Democratic Left). The democratization process prompted municipal reforms that gave mangrove land to the poor in Guayaquil and provided the opportunity for community-level committees to lobby and contest the local municipality to acquire physical infrastructure.

1978–92: Economic Stagnation from Structural Adjustment and Stabilization Policies

The second period from 1978 to 1992, corresponding to the years between the first and second panel data, was marked by macroeconomic structural adjustment policies, a decline in state social sector provisions, and the increasing presence of international development agencies. During nearly a decade and a half, repeated political change accompanied the inability of successive governments to adequately address mounting economic crises. Guayaquil's economic growth was fundamentally affected by the impact of both international oil price changes and internal natural disasters. The 1970s policy of low taxes also exacerbated the effect of the end of the oil boom. While oil revenue was dwindling, voters had become accustomed to artificially cheap public services (such as gas and electricity) subsidized by the government and to paying lower taxes. As foreign currency dried up in the 1980s and domestic demand also fell, the predictable result was heavy inflation and a new economic crisis. Industrial and basic commodity production declined after 1982.[5] With impending elections, the Febres Cordero government went on a spending spree and further reduced social services that it was unable to fund. Ultimately, the fallout from its misguided macroeconomic policies prompted the Ecuadorian government to commit to a structural adjustment program designed by the World Bank and International Monetary Fund (IMF).

1993–2004: Recovery from Late 1990s Dollarization Crisis and Dramatic Out-Migration

The third and most recent period, from 1992 to 2004, was one of globalization and dollarization, characterized by financial crisis, increased involvement of the private sector in providing social services such as health and education, and rapid expansion of international migration as an alternative safety net for many households. This final period was again one of economic turmoil during which political instability increased and the country failed to make good on the economic reforms implemented in the 1980s. In the first part of the 1990s, successive governments pursued strategies to promote and augment economic growth. They eliminated many subsidies favoring the rich, such as those for gasoline, while maintaining those that helped the poor, such as those for electricity and cooking gas. Dollarization brought hyperinflation to a halt, though not immediately (Solimano 2002). Perhaps more important, confidence in Ecuador's banking system was restored.

My Home Away from Home in Indio Guayas

Just as Indio Guayas and the broader context in which it is situated have had a complex history over the past thirty years, so too has my involvement with the community. In most anthropological studies, this description is usually relegated to a methodological appendix or footnote; yet the manner in which researchers become involved in communities, the methodologies they use, and the ways in which they retain long-term relationships with community members all fundamentally influence the research process. They are basic to understanding a researcher's identity as well as the agency of the different members of the community that inform the study. For this reason, this section describes in some detail my relationship with the community.

Over the past thirty years I have spent varying lengths of time on ten different occasions in Indio Guayas. I first lived there between September 1978 and April 1979 with my then husband, Brian Moser, and my two sons, Titus and Nathaniel, who at that time were aged eight and six, respectively. Our initial objective was to make a TV documentary film for Granada Television, a U.K. independent television company. Community leader Señora Marta Perez provided our entry point into the community by quickly grasping our commitment to make a film that would provide the inhabitants of a third world slum community with the opportunity to describe their daily lives. It would document their resourcefulness and courage in overcoming difficult and dangerous living conditions as well as their ingenuity in bettering their lives by collectively mobilizing to challenge Hanne Muse, the city's mayor, to provide running water for the community. The film, entitled *People of the Barrio,* was shown on British television in 1981 and challenged the perceptions of sensational misery in slum films of the time, such as Louis Malle's *Calcutta.*[6] Equally, it debunked the prevalent stereotype of third world urban slum dwellers as being caught in a "culture of poverty"—with an autonomous dynamism and self-perpetuating transmission mechanisms (Lewis 1961, 1966) and being marginalized by wider structural constraints, not only spatially but also politically, economically, and socially (Perlman 1976; Roberts 1978; Quijano 1974).[7]

A U.K. newspaper article written to promote the film reflected popular perception when it described our experience as follows:

> [Caroline and Brian's] idea was to move away from the prevalent shock-horror approach to the portrayal of Third World Slums, the filming of undernourished inhabitants in conditions so humiliating that they seemed less human beings than cyphers at a peep show. What better way than to become slum dwellers themselves, to experience at first hand the way people managed to cope with extreme poverty? . . . It was living next door to people rather than looking at them from outside and above that helped the Mosers to realize that slums were "neither hotbeds of revolution or hell-holes of despair."[8]

To make the film, we accepted the invitation of Marta to build our own four-by-eight-meter bamboo house on part of her plot.[9] As a family we were widely welcomed since it was unheard of for foreigners to enter allegedly dangerous communities such as Indio Guayas, let alone live there; put our children in the local school with sixty children in a class; and learn to live without any basic services.[10] My identity as a wife and mother had significant implications in terms of my access to different community members. It meant I made very close friendships with the women, who taught me to cook using kerosene, lent me water when my supply ran out, and showed me how to deal with potentially rabid dog bites by applying soap and water. This experience provided the roots of friendships that have continued to this day.

As a wife I was not taken seriously by the men, who, with a few marked exceptions (such as local tailors, whose petty commodity production I spent time studying), treated me with the same irreverence they tended to show their partners or wives. This would set a pattern that has persisted. Although I returned in 1981 as a divorced woman, this did not change men's attitudes toward me. The rules of the game were established, only to be broken by one or two audacious men who now saw the potential that I might be sexually available and flirted subtly with me, particularly at community parties. When Peter Sollis, my new partner and then husband, first appeared in Indio Guayas, it took time for him to be accepted. He was subject to considerable scrutiny and comparison with Don Brian, who along with one of my sons has continued to remain in contact

with the community. While living there in 1986 and 1992, Peter formed friendships with men in the community, particularly Jesus, Claudio, and Alvaro. In
this way he, too, became accepted as part of this extended English family.[11]

Despite my friendship with the women on Calle K, this is not a book about
the lives of women but about the lives of families and households. Nevertheless,
because of my gendered identity, the voices documented in this study are primarily those of women—in particular, the women already mentioned earlier in this
chapter, namely, Marta, Mercedes, Alicia, Carmen, and Lidia, along with their
respective families. All close neighbors, they are the central protagonists of this
story and provided much of the detailed narrative.[12] However, many other
social actors contributed important insights to my understanding of Indio
Guayas. My gender stereotype had less significance when I talked with second-
generation young men, not only in Guayaquil but also in Barcelona, and was
offset by their affectionate memories of my now adult sons. In contrast, because
I knew their mothers well, some of the daughters—while polite—were more
guarded in expressing opinions.

My academic training included a graduate diploma from the University of
Manchester, where I studied in a unique department that had joined together
the disciplines of anthropology and sociology. My commitment to combining
qualitative anthropological research with quantitative surveys began then, and
was first implemented in a study of market sellers in Bogotá, Colombia (Moser
1976). Thus, from my first visit to Indio Guayas, I adopted what more recently
has become known as a "mixed method" approach (Kanbur 2003). In my case
this meant combining anthropological techniques—such as participant observation and interviews with "key informants"—with three quantitative sociological
household surveys undertaken in 1978, 1992, and 2004. The surveys provided
the important quantitative panel data set. From 2004 onward I also used participatory urban appraisal (PUA) techniques (see Moser and McIlwaine 1999).
In Barcelona a sample survey was complemented by PUA and taped interviews.
Finally, in writing this book, I have incorporated entries from diaries and field
notes, extracts from the extensive transcripts associated with the film, and other
interviews undertaken during the 1978–2005 period. (See appendix A for
details of the fieldwork methodology.)

Influence of the Indio Guayas Study

Over the past thirty years, learning about the opportunities and constraints confronting community members—both in terms of changes in their life cycles and
in the broader context in which they lived—has inductively informed my own

research agenda as well as influenced my contribution to wider development debates. In turn, changes in focus and emphasis along the way also have been influenced by broader academic debates and my own professional development.

In the 1970s informal sector employment (Moser 1978, 1981), housing, and land (Moser 1982) were important in the analysis of the Indio Guayas research, not only because this was the early period of invasion and settlement consolidation in the community but also because they reflected my own academic work as a young lecturer in an academic urban planning department (the Development Planning Unit, University College London). By the early 1980s, I had become involved both intellectually and politically in the early gender and development debates, developing the concept of gender planning (Moser 1989b, 1993). When I next undertook fieldwork in 1982, community leader Marta, along with her committee, was deeply involved in complex negotiations with the newly formed Izquierda Democrática political party to exchange votes for infrastructure works. Given my interests, I focused particularly on changing gender roles and social relations in community management and politics (Moser 1987).

While I was a lecturer in social policy in developing countries at the London School of Economics in 1988, a study undertaken collaboratively with Peter provided the first opportunity to understand the social and economic impact of macroeconomic structural reform programs on households, particularly on women (Moser 1992). As a consequence of this pathbreaking research, I was offered the opportunity to undertake a further, more comprehensive study and to engage with policymakers. In 1990, therefore, I joined the World Bank and broadened the research to include community studies in three other cities as well as Indio Guayas. One unexpected research finding was increased levels of both social and economic violence and associated levels of fear and insecurity. These results from Indio Guayas informed a decade of subsequent research on urban violence in other contexts (Moser and Holland 1997; Moser and McIlwaine 2004; Moser and Winton 2002). Returning once again to Indio Guayas in 2004, I was confronted by the new phenomenon of international migration and its impact on the community, which has provided yet again a new focus for my research.

It is only since 2007, with the support of a Ford Foundation grant, that I have had the opportunity to pull together all the pieces of the puzzle, to move from a sequence of "snapshots" of reality at different points in time to examining the thirty-year period in its entirety. This has posed challenges in terms of the analytical framework for this final study. Although in each previous stage research results were analyzed within an ongoing development debate (as reflected in the publications cited above), this is not a book about development debates. For this reason I have chosen not to undertake a detailed analysis of the data—which range over a quarter of a century—in terms of the specific development debates existing at the time they were collected.[13] Rather, since poverty and assets, and the associated policy issue of poverty reduction, have been the overriding theme throughout my association with the Indio Guayas community, this book uses as its underlying theoretical framework the changing poverty debate over the past two decades, incorporating as appropriate the empirical results from different stages.

Narrative Econometrics: A "Qual-Quant" Methodology

As a small study that combines qualitative, participatory, and quantitative methodological approaches, the research presented here has been challenged by the criticism that it is neither statistically robust nor representative. However, justifying complementarities between quantitative and qualitative data is by no means a new problem.[14] For instance, some forty years ago, pioneering "applied" social anthropologist Max Gluckman (1968) and sociologist Clyde Mitchell (1968) introduced the concept of "apt illustration." Closely linked to "situational analysis," it was an important anthropological research tool used in two definitive studies to justify to colonial administrators the importance of qualitative research in explaining the complex political, economic, and social phenomena associated with rapid rural-urban migration in Southern Africa.

Thirty years later, in the middle phase of the Guayaquil research, I also faced similar problems when as a World Bank staff member, I undertook a study on the "social impact" of structural adjustment reforms in four poor urban communities in four different regions of the world. These included not only Guayaquil, Ecuador, but also Lusaka, Zambia; Budapest, Hungary; and Metro Manila, the Philippines (Moser 1996, 1997, 1998). To address the issue of robustness and representativeness, the four-city project implemented three identical research tools in all four communities, with built-in monitoring mechanisms to cross-check consistency in implementation (Moser, Gatehouse, and Garcia 1996; Moser 2003).[15] This ensured uniformity both in the fieldwork methodology and in the data analysis across all communities. The results highlighted similarities and differences in individual-, household-, and community-level vulnerability in the context of economic crisis in four communities in very diverse countries, and identified the manner in which a household's management of its complex asset portfolio influenced its capacity to cope (Moser 1998).[16]

At the time, the effects of adjustment policy were highly contested: while the World Bank maintained the essential macroeconomic necessity of such measures, the NGO community lobbied against them, arguing that they exacerbated rather than alleviated poverty (Ribe and others 1990; Development GAP 1993). In hindsight, it was somewhat dangerous territory for an anthropologist since even economists themselves were having methodological problems with the causality and associated quantitative measurements of the social impact of macroeconomic adjustment measures (World Bank 1995b). Nevertheless, my research results were summarily dismissed by many, particularly economists, on the grounds that they were neither representative at the national level nor robust in terms of cross-country comparisons. At best it was concluded that they provided interesting case study or "anecdotal" information on community and household coping strategies in crisis situations.[17]

While the results from "microstudies" such as this were never designed to be representative at the national level, they nonetheless provided important data on the complexity of daily life in poor communities that elude quantitative national level household surveys. However, in seeking to actually measure changing poverty levels among households in Indio Guayas, rather than anthropologically ascribing to them the status of a low-income community, I unwittingly entered into the "hegemonic discourse on poverty" where the "constitution of poverty as a research agenda (has become) predetermined by the policy agenda of the international development institutions and the World Bank in particular" (Green 2006). Or, as Escobar has commented, poverty is "an entity brought into being through the institutions established to describe, quantify and locate it" (1995, pp. 21–22).

In designing the research methodology for the final phase of this thirty-year study, it might have been more straightforward to have continued as before. Perhaps perversely, I have chosen to build on earlier cross-disciplinary combined methodologies, now further legitimized by Ravi Kanbur's conceptualization of the "qual-quant" divide (Kanbur 2003), and to push the envelope even further through the elaboration of narrative econometrics.[18] Andrew Felton, an economist, has worked with me not only to combine qualitative and quantitative research results but also to introduce the econometric measurement of the quantitative data. Narrative econometrics seeks to combine the econometric measurements of change in asset levels with in-depth anthropological narratives that identify the social relations within households and communities that influence well-being, thereby contributing to the identification of the associated causality underpinning economic mobility. By using this approach, I seek to bridge the divide in current debates about the limitations of measurement-based poverty analysis that disregard context and therefore "cannot address the dynamic, structural and relational factors that give rise to poverty" (Harriss 2007a; Green and Hulme 2005).

Have I succeeded in bridging this divide? This is the challenge addressed in the following chapters, first by providing the econometric results, and then by combining them with the narratives that come from the perceptions and analyses of community members in Indio Guayas. Does this ultimately provide different answers from static snapshots? The following chapters will tell.

2

Grappling with Poverty: From Asset Vulnerability to Asset Accumulation

"We used to live in the center. We came because they demolished the house where we used to live and the owner gave us a part of the zinc roofing and wood. We are poor and how can we pay the rent? Besides, the rooms are tiny, and they now cost 1,000 or 2,000 sucres. So we bought the plot and made the house. One buys the material little by little to finish it. When I first came I could not walk on the bamboo walkways [puentes], over the water [because] my head would just spin."

—Aida, 1978, two weeks after she moved from the
city center to the periphery of Indio Guayas

In 1978, Aida, a local resident in Indio Guayas, identified her family as poor. At the same time she described how her family, even in the midst of considerable vulnerability, was starting to accumulate an important asset, housing. This chapter introduces the relationship between poverty, vulnerability, and assets. The first part describes two frameworks that focus on the assets of the poor. These have been developed sequentially over the past ten years on the basis of inductive research in Guayaquil.[1] The "asset vulnerability framework" was closely associated with research on the social and economic impacts of macroeconomic structural adjustment reforms that dominated the 1990s. It is briefly described as background for the more recent "asset accumulation framework," which is linked to the current context of globalization and provides the frame-

Box 2-1. *Definition of the Most Important Capital Assets*

Physical capital: the stock of plant, equipment, infrastructure, and other productive resources owned by individuals, the business sector, or the country itself.

Financial capital: the financial resources available to people (such as savings and supplies of credit).

Human capital: investments in education, health, and the nutrition of individuals. Labor is linked to investments in human capital, health status determines people's capacity to work, and skills and education determine the returns from their labor.

Social capital: an intangible asset, defined as the rules, norms, obligations, reciprocity, and trust embedded in social relations, social structures, and societies' institutional arrangements. It is embedded at the microinstitutional level (communities and households) as well as in the rules and regulations governing formalized institutions in the marketplace, political system, and civil society.

Natural capital: the stock of environmentally provided assets such as soil, atmosphere, forests, minerals, water, and wetlands. In rural communities land is a critical productive asset for the poor whereas in urban areas land for shelter is also a critical productive asset.

Sources: Bebbington (1999), Carney (1998), Moser (1998), Narayan (1997), and Portes (1998).

work for the thirty-year longitudinal study of Indio Guayas.[2] The second part of the chapter then turns to the overall research results to compare the 1978, 1992, and 2004 panel data in terms of both changing levels of household income poverty as well as the accumulation of a range of assets.

Poverty, Vulnerability, and Asset Accumulation Frameworks

What do we mean by an asset? Generally, it is identified as a "stock of financial, human, natural or social resources that can be acquired, developed, improved and transferred across generations. It generates flows or consumption, as well as additional stock" (Ford Foundation 2004, p. 2).[3] Popularized by the livelihoods framework, the concept of assets or capital endowments includes both tangible and intangible assets.[4] The capital assets of the poor are most commonly identified as physical, financial, human, social, and natural (see box 2-1). In addition to these five assets, which are grounded in empirically measured research (Grootaert and Bastelaer 2002), additional intangible asset categories are in the process of being developed. These include "aspirational" (Appadurai 2004), psychological (Alsop, Bertelsen, and Holland 2006), and political assets, most commonly associated with human rights (Moser 2007; Ferguson, Moser, and

Norton 2007).[5] These intangible assets illustrate the growing importance of thinking outside the box and moving beyond well-established categories of capital assets.

The 1990s: Poverty and Asset Vulnerability

The first framework, described here as background, identified the relationship between assets and vulnerability, and was rooted in the poverty alleviation or reduction debate of the 1990s. This debate arose as a critique of the World Bank's 1990 World Development Report on poverty (World Bank 1990) and reflected a resurgence of interest in poverty reduction by major multinational and bilateral aid agencies during the 1990s.[6] The surrounding discussion introduced a "new poverty agenda" (Lipton and Maxwell 1992), which questioned the current measurement of poverty. At the time the prevailing theories on poverty measurement were categorized into two "polarized" alternative approaches (Baulch 1996). The first was a conventional, objective approach that identified income or consumption as the best proxy for poverty (Ravallion 1992). This was usually measured through large-scale, random sample household surveys, with a preference for using consumption expenditure rather than income as being more stable over time (Lipton and Ravallion 1995). The second was a subjective, participatory approach, which rejected the income-consumption approach as a narrow reductionist view that served the technocratic needs of development professionals but failed to address the complex, diverse, local realities in which the poor live (Chambers 1992, 1995). The participatory approach used multiple, subjective indicators of poverty status that emerged out of the poor's reality, collected through participatory techniques (see Chambers 1994a, 1994b, 1994c).

This debate led to recognition of the multidimensionality of poverty, redefinition of the meaning of poverty, and elaboration of new poverty reduction strategies. Heavily influenced by Sen's work (1981) on famines and on entitlements, assets, and capabilities, as well as the work of Chambers (1989) and others on risk and vulnerability, an extensive literature differentiated between poverty as a static concept and vulnerability as a dynamic one, and focused on defining concepts such as assets, vulnerabilities, capabilities, and endowments. In addition, the literature included policies to address the impacts of livelihood shocks by focusing on the assets and entitlements of the poor. Underlying the focus on vulnerability were the issues of risk and insecurity. Insecurity was defined as exposure to risk, with vulnerability the outcome of a decline in well-being.

The so-called new poverty agenda produced a proliferation of approaches, a "bewildering confusion of competing intellectual frameworks and alternative paradigms using similar words in different ways" (Longhurst 1994, p. 17). In deconstructing different overlapping analytical concepts and operational approaches to poverty reduction, I developed a framework, based on empirical research in Guayaquil, that focused specifically on the relationship between vulnerability and assets.

The Asset Vulnerability Framework

In developing an asset vulnerability framework in the 1990s, three issues were of particular importance. First was the differentiation between poverty and vulnerability. Capturing the multidimensional aspects of changing socioeconomic well-being in poor communities required identifying both *levels of poverty* and *types of vulnerability.* Thus I argued that although vulnerability was often used as a synonym for poverty, the two were not identical. Poverty measures were fixed in time and static whereas vulnerability was a more dynamic concept and therefore better able to capture change processes as "people move in and out of poverty" (Lipton and Maxwell 1992, p. 10). Although poor people were usually among the most vulnerable, not all vulnerable people were poor, a distinction that facilitated differentiation among lower-income populations.

In such fields as disaster management, epidemiology, and food security, vulnerability had been specifically defined.[7] Over the years, however, its meaning had expanded considerably to include a range of elements and situations of "livelihood security," including exposure to risks, hazards, shocks, stress, and difficulty in coping with contingencies (Longhurst 1994, p. 18). It also included people's subjective perceptions of their poverty, that is, what it means to be poor (Chambers 1995). Definitions of vulnerability required two dimensions: its sensitivity—the magnitude of a system's response to an external event—and its resilience—the ease and rapidity of a system's recovery from stress (Blaikie and Brookfield 1986).

In the 1992 Indio Guayas study, vulnerability was defined as "insecurity and sensitivity in the well-being of individuals, households and communities in the face of a changing environment, and, implicit in this, their responsiveness and resilience, to risks that they face during such negative changes" (Moser 1998, p. 3). Environmental changes that threatened welfare could be ecological, economic, social, and political, and could take the form of sudden shocks, long-term trends, or seasonal cycles. With these changes often came increasing risk and uncertainty and declining self-respect.[8]

The critical relationship between vulnerability and asset ownership is a second issue of operational significance. Analyzing vulnerability involved identifying not only the threat but also the resilience or responsiveness in resisting—or recovering from—the negative effects of a changing environment. The means of resistance were identified as the assets and entitlements that individuals, households, or communities could mobilize and manage in the face of hardship. Vulnerability was therefore closely linked to asset ownership. The more assets people had, the less vulnerable they were; the greater the erosion of people's assets, the greater their insecurity.

As with vulnerability, conceptual confusions and overlapping categories in the extensive literature on entitlements, assets, and endowment reflected not only a rapidly developing debate but also the divergent objectives of different researchers in the field. Thus Sen (1981), in his entitlement approach, distinguished between ownership endowments (such as land and labor) and exchange entitlement.[9] Swift (1989) analyzed vulnerability and security as a function of assets, which he classified as investments (human investments in education and health, and physical investments in housing, equipment, and land); stores (food, money, or valuables such as jewelry), and claims on others for assistance (including friendship and kinship networks and patrons in the community, government, and international community).[10] Finally, Maxwell and Smith (1992), in identifying the risks to food entitlement, classified five sources of entitlements as productive capital, nonproductive capital, human capital, income, and claims.[11]

Contributing to the extensive asset-vulnerability debates, but with a clear emphasis on an urban perspective, I made a first effort at classifying assets that were appropriate for the urban poor. This classification included well-known tangible assets, such as labor and human capital, prioritized in the 1990 World Development Report on poverty (World Bank 1990); but as an initial attempt to think outside the box, I broadened it to include less familiar assets such as housing and largely invisible intangible assets such as household relations and social capital. I argued that the ability to avoid or reduce vulnerability depended not only on initial assets but also on the capacity to manage them and to transform them into income, food, or other basic necessities.

The third and final issue of operational relevance was the categorization of coping, survival, and response strategies. These concepts were not new; since the 1970s they had been integrated into anthropological, urban, third world "shanty town" ethnographies. The role of economic, social, and political networks of reciprocal exchange as critical mechanisms for survival in marginalized contexts was highlighted in numerous "classic" Latin American slum studies done in such urban areas as Mexico City (Lomnitz 1977; Eckstein 1976) and Ciudad Guayana (Peattie 1968).

In the 1990s Indio Guayas research, I concluded that the poor were strategic managers of complex asset portfolios. The multifaceted nature of asset portfolios highlighted the limitations of using unidimensional indicators for coping strategies to measure those "complexities which need to be understood before they can be simplified for policy-making and implementation" (Davies 1993, p. 68).[12] Different household capital assets contributed to well-being outcomes, with the associated capacity to manage assets cushioning households and limiting the impact of shocks. Some strategies, however, had unanticipated, negative effects such as increasing inequality, conflict within households, and levels of violence, crime, fear, and insecurity in local communities (Moser 1996, 1998).

The 2000s: Opportunities and Asset Accumulation

By 2000 the impact of a decade of research on the "new poverty agenda" had produced a dramatic paradigm shift in the focus of poverty studies and associated poverty reduction policies, which had important implications for my analysis of changes in Indio Guayas in 2004. Again, a brief summary of the main influences is useful. This can be most succinctly summarized by a comparison between the poverty reduction strategies formulated in the 1990 and 2000 World Development Reports (World Bank 1990, 2000; Moser 2001). In 1990 the World Bank attacked poverty with the so-called two and a half legs of labor-intensive growth and human capital, with safety nets as the poor relation.[13] In contrast, the 2000 World Bank poverty reduction strategy identified three equally important legs, namely, opportunity, empowerment, and security.

As Green observes, "Poverty viewed from this perspective is not merely a matter of reduced income or consumption but amounts to a state of relative powerlessness, and exclusion from decision making processes" (2006, p. 1111). Risk and vulnerability are at the core of the associated operational social protection framework (World Bank 2000; Holzmann and Jorgensen 1999), which uses a threefold typology of risk to distinguish between idiosyncratic and covariant risks; while microlevel idiosyncratic risks affect individuals or households, mesolevel covariant risks affect groups of households and communities, and macrolevel risks affect regions or nations.[14] The operational risk management framework associated with this typology distinguishes between reducing risks, mitigating risks (with livelihood diversification and insurance the two key mitigation strategies), and coping with shocks (Moser and Antezana 2002).

Recognition of poverty as "multidimensional" deprivation—not just lack of income but also a lack of capabilities, assets, entitlements, and rights—resulted in further research to better understand the causes of persistent poverty, which includes those who are chronically poor, considered most vulnerable and therefore most likely to be multidimensionally deprived (Barrientos, Hulme, and Shephard 2005; Sabates-Wheeler and Haddad 2005). This included the identification of "poverty traps," with the distinction between stochastic or structural poverty traps assisting in identifying the underlying individual and broader causal factors for the persistence of poverty from one generation to the next (Adato, Carter, and May 2006; Carter and Barrett 2006). A further focus was on inequality, the theme of the 2006 World Development Report (World Bank 2005), with inequality traps referred to as "structures of economic, political and social difference that serve to keep poor people (and, by extension poor countries) poor" (Woolcock 2007, p. 5; Rao 2006).

Since 2000 the World Bank's revitalized leadership in promoting poverty reduction has included establishing robust and systematic ways of representing, analyzing, and theorizing about poverty (Green 2006, p. 1109), a trend that has both positive and negative consequences.[15] Its operationalization at the country level through poverty reduction strategies, participatory poverty assessments, and monitoring procedures now makes developing country governments accountable, if reluctantly, for attacking poverty. At the same time, the social construction of poverty as the target of international assistance means that the World Bank, along with the bilateral donors and UN agencies that follow its lead, now has a vested interest in poverty as a policy objective. The outcome has been a tendency for these institutions to define the content of the agenda and methodology for studying poverty as well as the issues that are identified as priorities for the poor.[16] Thus scientific knowledge is seen to hold the key to solving the poverty problem (O'Connor 2001).

This has "decontextualized" and "technified" poverty and, as critics argue, has reduced the problem of poverty to the characteristics of individuals or households, abstracted from class and other power relations.[17] Summarizing the main position of a complex debate by Green and Hulme (Green 2006; Green and Hulme 2005) and others, Harriss argues that

> poverty becomes a tangible entity, or a state that is external to the people affected by it: individuals or households fall into it, or are trapped in it, or they escape from it. It is not seen as the consequence of social relations or of the categories through which people classify and act upon the social world. Notably the way in which poverty is conceptualised separates it from the social processes of the accumulation and distribution of wealth, which depoliticises it—and depoliticisation is of course a profoundly political intellectual act. . . . Poverty is a kind of social aberration rather

than an aspect of the ways in which the modern state and market society function (2007a, p. 5).

Poverty is seen not only as a problem of the poor but also as their responsibility. The work on U.S. welfare poverty by O'Connor (2001) has been instrumental in highlighting the fact that by locating the crux of the poverty problem in the characteristics of the poor, researchers have, however unintentionally, opened up their research to a conservative interpretation of poverty. With arguments reminiscent of Oscar Lewis's "culture of poverty" (1966), this interpretation emphasizes the economic responsibility of individuals. Thus the failure to achieve, and hence poverty itself, is interpreted as an individual's problem and not a consequence of the wider structure. This conservative position supports the perception that poverty is a moral failure that justifies punitive welfare interventions. In the same way, the Millennium Development Goals are defined in terms of the characteristics of the poor instead of the changing context of the global economy and the larger political structures within which they are produced (O'Connor 2001).

This critique of the World Bank's hegemony on framing the discussion about poverty calls for inclusion of an analysis of social relations and of the structure and relationships embedded in the broader political power environment within which such relations exist. Anthropological studies have consistently demonstrated the social construction of categories and the importance of social relations as the bedrock of inequality. Such studies have argued that poverty is a social relation, not an absolute condition. Poverty is not a thing to be attacked but rather the outcome of specific social relations that require investigation and transformation (Green 2006, pp. 1115–24). Thus the focus needs to shift from the characteristics of the poor to the social relations that keep them poor.

The Asset Accumulation Framework

This kind of critique has important implications for the development of an asset accumulation framework. First it calls for more than a technical analysis that identifies levels of asset accumulation in terms of correlations between individual and household characteristics and poverty levels. Second, it emphasizes the importance of context, that is, the analysis of the political economy in processes of accumulation and the associated distribution of economic resources and political power. This requires recognition that assets exist within social relations. Social processes, structures, and power relationships—linked to concepts of social capital, networks, and exclusion—all mediate access to assets and the accumulation of their value. Finally, it calls for an understanding of links between local asset accumulation processes and wider processes of capitalist accumulation (Harriss 2007a).

As discussed in chapter 1, I have opted for the middle ground between quantitative measurements of asset accumulation and a qualitative emphasis on social relations. The methodology of "narrative econometrics" measures processes of asset accumulation not in isolation but within the social relations and institutions that exist in households, communities, and the broader political and macroeconomic structure.

Back in 1978 the important linkages between poverty and physical assets such as housing were also obvious to a new pioneer settler such as Aida, even though she did not articulate them as assets. Revisiting the 1990s asset vulnerability framework during the final stage of this longitudinal study of Indio Guayas has required me to investigate not only the protection of assets associated with vulnerability but also to identify the accumulation of assets linked to opportunities. At the same time, developments in the theoretical literature have challenged me to move beyond the measurement of assets to their contextualization in terms of the social relations that are embedded in the narratives of the poor.

BACKGROUND: ASSET-BASED APPROACHES. Assets are not simply resources that people use to build livelihoods. As Bebbington (1999) argues, assets give people the capability to be and act. Thus the acquisition of assets is not a passive act but one that creates agency and is linked to the empowerment of individuals and communities. The concept of asset accumulation draws on theoretical and policy-focused literature on asset-based development approaches. While closely connected to issues of asset vulnerability, asset-based approaches are concerned more specifically with assets per se and their associated accumulation strategies. Assets are identified as the basis of agents' power to reproduce, challenge, or change the rules that govern the control, use, and transformation of resources (Sen 1997). At the same time, asset accumulation requires a match between endowments and opportunities. This reflects not only deeply rooted structural and cultural constraints (such as gender stereotyping) but also appropriate matches in labor market opportunities (Osmani 2008).

A review of current asset-based approaches (Moser 2008) shows that there is no single analytical asset framework. For instance, the asset-based research of Adato, Carter, and May (2006) and Carter and Barrett (2006) has sought to address the causes and dynamics of longer-term, persistent structural poverty, primarily in rural Africa and Asia. This group of U.S.-based economists, together with their partners in the South, has drawn on longitudinal data to identify "dynamic asset poverty." They distinguish between "deep-rooted persistent structural poverty" and "chronic and other forms of poverty that the passage of time will alleviate." Their research differentiates between "churning" or stochastic poverty (the regular descent into or elevation out of poverty due to short-term shocks) and structural mobility associated with the gain or loss of productive assets. It identifies poverty traps, defined as a critical minimum asset threshold below which households cannot take advantage of positive changes or recover from negative changes in circumstance (Carter and Barrett 2006).

In fact, one of the best-known asset-based approaches originates from the United States. First developed by Michael Sherraden (1991), it is based on two premises: first, that the poor can save and accumulate assets, and second, that assets have positive social, psychological, and civic effects independent of the benefits to income (Boshara and Sherraden 2004). Sherraden distinguishes between assets (identified as the stock of wealth in a household) and income (the flows of resources associated with consumption of goods and services and standard of living). He argues that welfare policy has been constructed mainly in terms of income and proposes that it should be based on savings, investment, and asset accumulation.

Sherraden's research in the United States has shown that saving and accumulation are shaped by institutions, not merely by individual preference. The poor are not only asset poor but have few institutional structures within which to accumulate assets. For impoverished welfare recipients, asset accumulation is not encouraged and sometimes not even permitted: for example, the "asset test" associated with means-tested income transfer programs prevents the accumulation of more than minimal financial assets. In contrast, an extensive range of asset-based policies exists, operating mainly through the tax system (such as homeownership tax benefits and 401(k) plans). Thus asset-based welfare policy is designed to promote and institutionalize asset accumulation through a progressive (meaning greater subsidies for the poor), inclusive (U.S. asset inequality is largely racially based), lifelong, and flexible approach (Sherraden 1991, pp. 7–9).

A number of asset-based approaches in both the North and South have extended the asset-building concept beyond individuals and households to incorporate community assets. They have also shifted from a somewhat Northern top-down concern with the problems of apathy in an alienated, welfare-dependent population to a bottom-up, demand-driven approach. Foremost among these is the Ford Foundation's Asset Building and Community Development program, designed to "reduce poverty and injustice" (Ford Foundation 2004). Building on the work of Sherraden, Sen, and others,

Ford's asset-building framework proposes that when low-income people gain control over assets, they gain the independence necessary to resist oppression, pursue productive livelihoods, and confront injustice (Ford Foundation 2004). The program proposes that an asset offers a way out of poverty because it is not simply consumed but rather is a "stock" that endures and can be used to generate economic, psychological, social, and political benefits that foster resilience and social mobility. This approach highlights inequalities in asset distribution across race, ethnicity, and gender, and supports initiatives to build assets that communities can acquire, develop, or transfer across generations. It includes financial holdings, natural resources, social bonds and community relations, and human assets such as marketable skills.

COMPONENTS OF THE ASSET ACCUMULATION FRAMEWORK. The asset accumulation framework developed from the empirical evidence in Indio Guayas has two components. First is the conceptual framework of an asset index, an analytical tool for understanding the processes of asset accumulation. Second is an asset accumulation policy, an associated operational approach for designing and implementing sustainable asset accumulation interventions. This chapter introduces the first component, an asset index, as the analytical framework for the analysis of the Indio Guayas empirical data. The final chapter of the book turns to the second component, an asset accumulation policy, and discusses its usefulness and appropriateness as a long-term poverty reduction solution, in the light of findings from Indio Guayas presented in the intervening chapters.

While the 1970s and 1980s research emphasized income poverty, and the new wave of pro-poor policy supported by the World Bank (World Bank 2000) and the UN's Millennium Development Goals changed the focus to consumption, asset accumulation shifts it even further by connecting it to production. This identifies the link between individual and household enterprises, labor market participation, assets, and poverty reduction. Whereas both income and consumption poverty data are static, backward-looking measures, an asset-based approach offers a forward-looking, dynamic framework that identifies asset-building thresholds and measures movement into and out of poverty. As an integrated approach, the latter includes the links between different assets and their transformative potential through effective risk management, seeking to identify and promote mechanisms that strengthen opportunities and reduce constraints. In focusing on how the poor construct their asset portfolios, this approach recognizes the importance both of individual and collective agency and of links between asset accumulation and the social and economic contextual processes relating to security and political stability.

AN ASSET INDEX. An asset index quantitatively measures the accumulation or erosion of different assets. It uses techniques developed to aggregate ownership of different assets into a single variable, building on the asset index methodology of Carter and May (2001), Filmer and Pritchett (2001), and Kolenikov and Angeles (2004), as well as earlier on asset vulnerability research in Indio Guayas (Moser 1997, 1998). Appendix C provides a detailed description of the econometric methodology used to develop the index.

In creating an index from the longitudinal panel data set, Andrew Felton and I found that the components constituting different assets were not always ideal, since it was the data that determined what could be measured. Components were based on the information available in all three panel data sets, and since the original study in 1978 did not specifically focus on assets, the scope of the asset index was restricted. This constraint was particularly pronounced for the components of social capital and employment. Yet this problem is not exceptional; a review of the existing literature shows that to date, most indexes are limited to the measurement of household durables and housing-physical assets (see appendix C). The fact that the asset index developed in this study is more extensive than most others in terms of breadth of measurement means that this study makes a unique methodological contribution to the literature.

Table 2-1 shows the components of the asset index for Indio Guayas. There are four types of capital assets: physical, financial-productive, human, and social capital. Physical capital is split into two subcategories: housing and consumer durables. Financial capital is extended to incorporate productive capital, while human capital is limited to education because of a lack of panel data on health. Finally, social capital is disaggregated in terms of household and community social capital. A fifth type of capital, natural capital, is commonly used in the livelihoods literature (Carney 1998). This includes the stocks of environmentally provided assets such as soil, atmosphere, forests, water, and wetlands, and is more generally used in rural research. In urban areas, as in this study, where land is linked to housing, it is more frequently classified as physical capital. However, since all households acquired a plot of similar size in 1978, natural capital is not included in this asset index.

This fourfold asset index provides a diagnostic tool to examine the long-term investment choices households make. It categorizes the range of assets that households held, the processes by which each accumulated or eroded over time, and the relative importance of different assets in terms of intergenerational poverty reduction. The index also shows the way in which different tangible assets such as physical, human, and financial capital were accumulated at different points in time and the interrelationship between them. Of all the capital

Table 2-1. *Asset Types, by Index Categories and Components*

Capital type	Asset index categories	Index components
Physical	Housing	Roof material
		Walls material
		Floor material
		Lighting source
		Toilet type
	Consumer durables	Television (none, black and white, color, or both)
		Radio
		Washing machine
		Bike
		Motorcycle
		VCR
		DVD player
		Record player
		Computer
Financial-productive	Employment security	State employee
		Private sector permanent worker
		Self-employed
		Contract or temporary worker
	Productive durables	Refrigerator
		Car
		Sewing machine
	Transfer-rental income	Remittances
		Rental income
Human	Education	Level of education:
		Illiterate
		Some primary school
		Completed primary school
		Secondary school or technical degree
		Some tertiary education
Social	Household	Jointly headed household
		Other households on plot
		"Hidden" female-headed households
	Community	Whether someone on the plot:
		Attends church
		Plays in sports groups
		Participates in community groups

Source: Moser and Felton (2007).

assets, by far the most difficult to discuss sequentially or "measure" in such a way is the intangible asset of social capital—both at the household and community level. As discussed in chapter 4, this is also the most contested concept of the different capital assets. The very limited components of this asset category are intended as the basis for exploring the complex structures of social relations that elude measurement.

Social capital at both the household and community level is the "glue that holds it together" (Serageldin and Steer 1994), that fundamentally determines the processes of accumulating all other assets. At the household level, for instance, consensus and agreement among male and female adult partners in young families—to invade swampland and take advantage of free land to own their own home—determined their successful acquisition of a free good. At the community level, collective mobilization for physical infrastructure occurred through the formation of a suburbio-wide Frente Lucha Suburbana (Front for the Suburbio Struggle, known as "the Frente"). This contestation of the dominant political structures resonates with and predates what Appadurai (2001, p. 29) has more recently identified as "deep democracy," with the politics of the Frente associated with negotiation, long-term pressure, and accommodation rather than with confrontation or threat of political reprisal.

In subsequent chapters the microlevel narrative detailing the perceptions and analyses of members of the community underscores the index measurements of asset accumulation and associated poverty reduction over the three decades. However, before turning to such narratives, the second part of this chapter sets the scene by providing the overall poverty and asset accumulation trends.

Intergenerational Poverty and Asset Accumulation Trends in Indio Guayas

Have households become richer or poorer over the nearly three-decade period, and which assets have they had most success in accumulating? Is there a direct relationship between the two? This section briefly describes the longitudinal panel data on poverty and asset trends in Indio Guayas from 1978 to 2004. As mentioned in chapter 1, such an analysis is situated within the broader economic context of the three points in time when the surveys were undertaken. These were summarized as the 1975–85 oil boom and democratization process, the 1985–95 collapse of the oil economy and associated structural adjustment policies, and the 1995–2005 globalization and dollarization crisis. Associated with each were changes in the labor market and a highly unstable governance structure at both the local and national level.

This section first describes household income poverty levels and associated changes in inequality and mobility during these three different periods. An asset index then tracks trends relating to the accumulation of the four capital assets over the same period, showing the relationship between income poverty and asset accumulation, as well as the link between household assets and income. This overview thus provides a background for subsequent chapters that focus on specific assets and the underlying factors, both structural and in terms of household life cycles, that have affected the well-being of households in Indio Guayas.

Changes in Income, Poverty, Inequality, and Mobility in Indio Guayas

How was poverty measured? Per capita household income levels were used, building on research using the Ecuadorian poverty line (Moser 1996, 1997).[18] Households were divided into three categories: nonpoor, poor, and very poor. A household was considered nonpoor if its income was at or above the poverty line; it was poor if its income was below the poverty line but at or above half of the poverty line; and it was very poor if its income was below half of the poverty line. A monthly per capita income of 84,243 sucres was defined as the World Bank's 1992 poverty line for urban Guayaquil, Ecuador (Moser 1996, p. 87). In year 2000 dollars, this translates into a real per capita poverty line of $50.52 a month, based on the International Monetary Fund's international financial statistics data on consumer price index and exchange rates.[19]

In 1978, when there was optimism in Guayaquil's buoyant expanding economy, Indio Guayas was predominantly a poor community, with less than one in five households classified as nonpoor and half classified as very poor (table 2-2). They were poor because they were young families in small households, the income earners were mainly unskilled and semiskilled workers, and most of the women earned little if anything as they balanced child care and work while living on the city's periphery.[20] How did this measurement of poverty relate to the perceptions of community members themselves? In 1978 they all saw themselves as poor but with aspirations to get out of poverty that reflected optimism about the future.

The period between the first and second panel data, nearly a decade and a half, included repeated political changes that accompanied the inability of successive governments to address adequately the mounting economic crises. By 1992 the macrolevel economic crisis was reflected in the poverty levels of Indio Guayas households. Poverty had increased, with only just over one in ten households now above the poverty line (see table 2-2). Although families were larger and therefore had more income earners, they also had more mouths to feed.

Table 2-2. *Distribution of Household Poverty Status in Indio Guayas, 1978–2004*
Percent

Poverty category	1978	1992	2004
Very poor	51.0	56.8	31.4
Poor	33.3	31.4	29.4
Nonpoor	15.7	11.8	39.2
Total	100.0	100.0	100.0

Source: Moser and Felton (2007), from panel data surveys for 1978, 1992, and 2004.

The period between the second and third panel data was likewise one of national level economic turmoil, with both economic recovery from the dollarization crisis and dramatic out-migration influencing the local situation in Indio Guayas. In 2004 the total number of poor households in the panel data had declined. During the period between 1992 and 2004, life cycle changes also helped some households rise out of poverty. Many children had grown up and begun working. Some had moved out of the family home, with those migrating abroad often remitting income back to their parents (all issues explored in subsequent chapters). To summarize the panel data, they show that over the twenty-six-year period, the overall number of nonpoor households doubled. However, regardless of this reduction in poverty, the majority of Indio Guayas residents were still below the poverty line in 2004 (table 2-2).

POVERTY IN INDIO GUAYAS VERSUS AT THE URBAN OR NATIONAL LEVEL. Poverty line comparisons are highly contentious, given the incompatibility of data sources. Nevertheless, the 1978–92 Indio Guayas sample survey went to great lengths to assess representativeness and concluded that in 1992 "poverty levels were higher than in the country as a whole or in Ecuador's urban areas generally" (Moser 1997, p. 28). Since the poverty level results for the sample survey are remarkably similar to those for the larger 1978–92 study, findings for that period are also applicable to the panel data.

The 2004 panel data results from Indio Guayas reflect national trends for coastal areas, which show a slow decline in poverty levels, despite increasing poverty at the national level. The 2004 "Ecuador Poverty Assessment" (World Bank 2004), for instance, calculated that the poverty level for Guayaquil declined from 38 percent in 1990 to 34 percent in 2001, while the national poverty level increased from 40 to 45 percent, respectively. Absolute numbers of poor increased by about 54 percent in Guayaquil during that period, but the total number of poor that lived in Guayaquil remained stable at about 14.5 per-

Table 2-3. *Real Monthly Income Summary Statistics, 1978–2004*
Year 2000 U.S. dollars

Statistic	1978	1992	2004
Mean	150.74	202.79	332.62
Median	145.45	157.72	232.92
Standard deviation	89.69	147.9	271.29
Minimum	14.54	0	563.71
Maximum	407.27	34.94	1,327.67

Source: Moser and Felton (2007).

cent of the city's population whereas it increased from 10 to 26 percent of the population for the urban coastal region in general. Thus, while still predominantly poor, communities such as Indio Guayas have fared better than the poor at the national aggregate level.

INEQUALITY AND INCOME MOBILITY IN INDIO GUAYAS. While poverty declined over the longer term, levels of inequality increased, particularly in the latter period (see table 2-3). The percentage of households categorized as poor over the entire research period was fairly consistent. However, between 1992 and 2004, numerous household shifts occurred, from very poor to poor and from poor to nonpoor. The data show that increasing inequality was driven by households at the top of the income distribution rising faster than those at the bottom, with the Gini coefficient increasing during each time period, rising from 0.322 in 1978 to 0.375 in 1992 and 0.416 in 2004. The 2004 measure was close to that for all of Ecuador (0.437), reflecting a gradual process of differentiation among households in this "natural experiment," such that after nearly thirty years, it had become more representative of the entire country (United Nations Development Program 2004).

Rising levels of income and inequality were also accompanied by a great deal of income mobility. This study utilizes Carter and May's distinction (2001) among four mobility categories: stable not poor (those remaining above the poverty line in both 1978 and 2004); stuck in poverty (below the poverty line in 1978 and 2004); and upward and downward mobility (moving into or out of poverty between 1978 and 2004).

As shown in table 2-4, between 1978 and 1992 most households were stuck in poverty, with the mean per capita income staying roughly the same. However, during at least one of the two intersurvey periods, twenty-three households (45 percent) experienced upward mobility and eleven (22 percent) experienced downward mobility; four households were upwardly mobile in both

Table 2-4. *Frequencies in Household Income Mobility Categories in Indio Guayas, 1978–2004*

Units as indicated

	Households					
	1978–92		1992–2004		1978–2004	
Mobility categories	*Number*	*Percent of total*	*Number*	*Percent of total*	*Number*	*Percent of total*
Stable, not poor	2	4	1	2	3	6
Upward	4	8	19	37	17	33
Downward	6	12	5	10	5	10
Stuck in poverty	39	76	26	51	26	51
Total	51	100	51	100	51	100

Source: Moser and Felton (2007).

periods; and only one household was downwardly mobile in both periods. Aggregate trends obscure the fact that there was considerable household income mobility. Although the majority of impoverished families in 1978 remained so in 2004, with less than half able to rise above the poverty line, nevertheless, overall conditions in the community can be said to have improved because more families climbed out of poverty than sank into it.

The households living on Calle K, introduced in chapter 1, provide a microcosm of the mobility trends, as well as an increasing differentiation as a result of changing external circumstances as well as internal household dynamics. Marta, the community leader, and her tailor husband Jesus, were income poor in 1978 when they first arrived with their two young daughters. By 1992, despite the worsening macroenvironment, they had moved out of poverty and maintained this upward mobility through 2004. In contrast, Lidia and Salvador remained stuck in poverty throughout the same period, falling into the very poor category from 1978 to 2004. Both households suffered serious negative shocks. Salvador left Lidia and had a relationship with another woman for most of the 1990s, reducing her status to that of female household head. Marta's husband became ill, and after eight years of expensive treatment, he died in 2002, leaving her a widow.

Although household characteristics may be significant, it is nevertheless important to look beyond income if differences in poverty dynamics are to be understood. For example, Marta and Jesus invested heavily in human capital through the education of their daughters and informally adopted son. In the

1990s Jesus, using his wife Marta's networks to political leaders, was able to leave his job as a tailor and become a waged employee, as a night watchman in a government institution. Parental income was used to expand the house, accumulating financial capital through rental income and the establishment of a microbusiness. By 2004 all three children had achieved some level of tertiary education, still lived on the family plot, and were contributing to the family income.

In contrast, none of Lidia's children finished high school, so the income from their unskilled jobs contributed far less than that of Marta's children. Equally, Salvador was not a successful earner. When the building boom collapsed in Guayaquil in the 1990s, he became a street seller. Most recently, he became unemployed when new municipal legislation pushed sellers off the streets into fixed markets. Lidia fared no better, with a series of low-paid cooking jobs while trying to raise five children. This illustrative comparison between the changes experienced by two families points to the need to move beyond income and to deepen the examination of household asset accumulation patterns. Overall trends are summarized in this section, while subsequent chapters focus on each asset in turn.

Patterns of Asset Accumulation

Longitudinal analysis of changing income poverty levels identifies who remains stuck in poverty, who gets out of poverty, and who falls back into poverty. While this is one measure of well-being, comparable data on asset accumulation provide additional insights into household well-being while raising additional questions. Do asset accumulation data provide a better understanding of household well-being than income poverty measures? How far is asset accumulation associated with income mobility? Answers to such questions require examination of the way stocks of assets are accumulated over time, the contribution of different assets to household mobility, and their relationship to income poverty.

Analysis of the overall trends in asset accumulation between 1978 and 2004 highlights the ways in which households in Indio Guayas accumulated different types of assets at varying rates. Based on the asset index methodology, figure 2-1 shows that households invested heavily in housing capital when they first arrived in Indio Guayas; adequate housing was an obvious first priority when they invaded swampland and lived under very basic conditions. When such needs were met, households accumulated other types of capital, both for production and consumption purposes. Housing capital accumulation then leveled off and was replaced by the accumulation of consumption capital. Education and financial-productive capital increased fairly steadily between 1978 and 1992

Figure 2-1. *Household Asset Accumulation in Indio Guayas, Guayaquil, Ecuador,*
1978–2004

Standard deviation

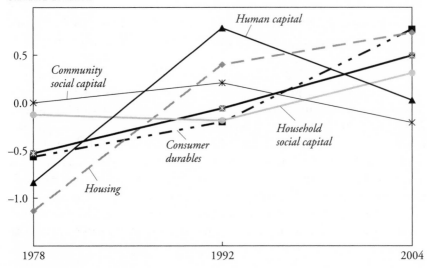

Source: Moser and Felton (2007).

though education capital declined between 1992 and 2004. This reflected the
fact that most children of the fifty-one households had completed their education. Financial-productive capital continued to rise during this last period.
Finally, while community social capital actually fell between 1992 and 2004,
household social capital rose.

HOUSEHOLD ASSETS AND INCOME POVERTY REDUCTION. Analysis of the
relationship between income poverty and asset accumulation helps identify
whether particular assets were more helpful than others for moving households
out of poverty. Households in Indio Guayas accumulated assets in a sequenced
process. Regardless of income poverty level, they first accumulated housing capital although it was not in itself significant for getting them out of poverty.
Investment occurred especially during the 1978–92 period and then trailed off
from 1992 to 2004. Because settlers first lived under such basic conditions,
there were enormous incentives to incrementally upgrade. Bamboo walls, for
instance, had to be changed after seven years, so it made economic sense to
replace them with concrete blocks.

Although financial-productive capital grew steadily over time, there were
important differences by poverty category. In 1992 a considerable gap existed

Table 2-5. *Household Asset Portfolios, by Mobility Categories, 1978*[a]

1978 level of capital	Housing	Consumer durables	Per capita human capital	Per capita financial capital	Number of household members
Stuck in poverty	−1.692	−0.581	3.157	−0.083	6.115
Upward	−1.556	−0.498	3.155	−0.137	6.824
Downward	−1.232	−0.197	3.160	−0.091	4.400
Stable, not poor	−1.534	−0.725	3.251	−0.497	2.333
Total	−1.592	−0.524	3.162	−0.126	5.961

Source: Moser and Felton (2007).

a. Values refer to level of assets in standard deviations, calculated using polychoric principal components analysis as described in the text, relative to the entire 1978–2004 sample.

between the poor and nonpoor, reflecting the devastating economic conditions in that year. However, by 2004 the poor (not counting the very poor) actually achieved greater levels of financial-productive capital than the nonpoor. This was because poor people were more likely to rent out part of their houses to lodgers and received higher levels of remittances, compensating for the fact that they had less secure jobs and fewer productive durables.

Differences among households regarding consumer durables illustrated diversity in priorities over time. While all households made sacrifices to reach a certain standard of housing, after this had been achieved, some cut back to invest in consumption items. The purchase of consumer durables did not lead to poverty reduction; rather it was an indicator of household priorities after escaping poverty. Between 1992 and 2004, nonpoor households shifted their spending to consumer durables, while poor and very poor households restrained their consumption in favor of housing.[21] Indeed, very poor households invested more in housing between 1992 and 2004 than did the nonpoor. Similarly, patterns of investment in housing and consumer durables differ over time by income level, with wealthier households having higher levels of total physical capital. However, the gap was wider for consumer durables than for housing, especially by 2004 when all income groups converged in terms of acquiring housing (see appendix C, figure C-3).

It is also useful to identify whether those poor who moved out of poverty started out with more assets. In fact, the average starting level of households experiencing upward mobility between 1978 and 2004 shows that they did not necessarily start out with higher levels of capital than households that remained stuck in poverty (see table 2-5). But households that remained nonpoor between 1978 and 2004 began with significantly higher levels of financial-productive

Table 2-6. *Household Asset Accumulation, by Mobility Categories, 1978–2004*[a]

Change, 1978–2004	Housing	Consumer durables	Per capita human capital	Per capita financial capital	Number of household members
Stuck in poverty	2.597	0.858	0.418	0.162	2.962
Upward	2.555	1.752	1.088	0.253	0.176
Downward	2.688	0.775	–0.126	0.360	4.000
Stable, not poor	2.725	1.655	–0.403	0.599	2.000
Total	2.599	1.195	0.542	0.226	2.078

Source: Moser and Felton (2007).
a. Values refer to number of standard deviations increase of assets measured.

capital and fewer resident family members than those that started out nonpoor but descended into poverty. Households that experienced upward mobility acquired significantly higher levels of human capital and financial-productive capital than households that remained stuck in poverty. Moreover, households that were nonpoor in 2004—both those that were stable and those that were upwardly mobile—acquired far fewer additional household members than households that ended up in poverty (see table 2-6). Ultimately, for many households it was the slow appreciation of the entire asset portfolio rather than one asset in particular that ensured long-term upward mobility. Household size and dependency ratios were important but were not a determinant of mobility alone.

ASSET POVERTY LINES AND STRUCTURAL VERSUS STOCHASTIC POVERTY. Can asset ownership complement income data to serve as a predictor of long-term welfare? Any measurement of asset poverty requires the use of asset levels either to estimate income directly or its approximation using a binary poverty status variable. Carter and May (2001), for instance, use an asset poverty line to complement income poverty lines and distinguish between structural and stochastic poverty. They define the structurally poor (or nonpoor) as those whose income and asset poverty levels match whereas the stochastically poor (or nonpoor) are those whose income and asset poverty levels do not match. Among the stochastically poor, their income level is below their assets; among the stochastically nonpoor, their income is above their assets. Carter and May argue that income is more subject to stochastic shocks than assets are. A household may have low income because of temporary factors such as job loss or illness. A household that is structurally poor, on the other hand, has income below the poverty line and lacks the assets to lift itself above that level.

Table 2-7. *Categorization of Actual and Expected Household Poverty Levels,*
Indio Guayas, 1978–2004

Number

Actual poverty level	Expected poverty level		Total
	Not poor	*Poor*	
Not poor	Structurally not poor	Stochastically not poor	34
	13	21	
Poor	Stochastically poor	Structurally poor	119
	4	115	
Total	17	136	153

Source: Moser and Felton (2007).

In the Indio Guayas study, an asset poverty line was estimated by regressing income on the levels of assets for each time period.[22] This made it possible to calculate for each household whether it was expected to be above or below the income poverty line based on the assets it owned. This was called its "expected" poverty level. If a household was poor according to its income and assets, then it was categorized as being in structural poverty; however, if a household was below the income poverty line, but its assets indicated that it should have been above the income poverty line, it was considered to be in stochastic poverty. Table 2-7 shows the number of instances in Indio Guayas of each type of poverty, structural or stochastic, throughout the entire time period. It indicates that most poverty was structural in nature; in addition, many of the households that were above the poverty line appeared to be stochastically nonpoor.

The stochastically nonpoor are vulnerable to falling back into poverty. Of the eleven households that were stochastically nonpoor in 1978 or 1992, only three of them were above the poverty line during the next sample period. Although this sample is too small to draw statistical inferences, the generally negative outcomes of the stochastically nonpoor complement the anthropological insight that low levels of assets do not lead to sustainable income.

In 2004 most of the stochastically poor were elderly people who had remained in the family home, unable to earn sufficient income themselves but having some financial capital from family income support. For instance, Adolfo, a clothing seller, and Roxanna, a domestic servant, arrived in 1971 and raised six children, all of whom completed some secondary education. By 2004 all the children had left home except Thelma, who was in her first year of university studies. Although their other five children lived in other areas of Guayaquil, they did not support their parents, so the couple lived off Adolfo's meager earnings. By contrast, stochastically nonpoor households tended to be populated by people with poor job prospects but who were propped up by a large number of working children. All of them had low levels of consumer durables, which is usually a good indicator of poverty status, as well as low levels of financial capital. These were households with many people working but few prospects.

From the Econometrics to the Narratives

The complexities associated with household asset accumulation in Indio Guayas, Guayaquil, and the relationship between asset accumulation and poverty reduction provide a starting point for this story. The narrative econometrics methodology combines narratives of people's lives with econometric asset indexes. Together, they show how a highly homogeneous community, which provides a natural experiment, has changed over time into a heterogeneous, lower-income settlement. For some this has meant increased prosperity while for others, who have remained poor or descended further into poverty, it has resulted in greater inequality and insecurity. Focusing on the relationship between asset accumulation and income poverty, the data show that households make crucial choices in managing complex asset portfolios at different stages of their life cycles. Housing is the first-priority asset, and while it does not necessarily get households out of poverty, adequate housing is generally a necessary precondition for the accumulation of other assets.

There are no magic solutions in terms of specific assets contributing to poverty reduction. Both income and assets matter. Moreover, a longitudinal study such as this shows that poor people also consider it important to accumulate assets. Over time those who do best consolidate slowly—first human capital, followed by financial-productive capital. They often make trade-offs in the process, investing in their children's education before acquiring consumer durables. Important differences among households exist; those that do best make their assets work for them. They purchase assets with their income and then generate more income from those assets. In this complex process of getting out of poverty, some succeed while others who start as poor or nonpoor fall further into poverty. The analysis of poverty continues in chapter 9, where intergenerational poverty levels (between one generation and the next) are examined to identify whether the second generation has been better able to escape poverty and accumulate assets than their parents were.

Overall, as this chapter shows, this is a community that has slowly but surely improved itself at the aggregate level. Is the story now complete? The problem is that at this point the story cannot differentiate why some households do better than others. In addition, it cannot identify to what degree community-level actions also played a fundamental role in the changes in Indio Guayas over the past thirty years. If econometric measures of the rate of accumulation from the panel data provide half the story, what else is required to explain the household differences and the collective assets accumulated, such as land and physical and social infrastructure? The following chapters demonstrate how anthropological narratives can contribute to addressing some of these unanswered questions. Since housing was the first asset accumulated, the next chapter, inspired by Virginia Woolf's famous *A Room of One's Own* (Woolf 2002), begins the Indio Guayas story by describing how households struggled to acquire "a home of one's own."

3

A Home of One's Own: Squatter Housing as a Physical Asset

"At first we lived in the mud and we walked on the catwalks (puentes). I lived without four walls. But little by little I built my first little house."

—Lidia

In this way Lidia, a member of one of the families who by 1978 had settled in the Calle K in Indio Guayas, described the primitive conditions in which she first lived. Under very similar circumstances to those of her neighbors, she and her husband Salvador had acquired a ten-by-thirty-meter plot and, over the mangrove swamp water, built a modest house with a wooden floor, bamboo walls, and zinc roof. To acquire their own home, the couple together with their three young children had left their rented, tugurio (inner-city slum) accommodation. Accompanying them were Lidia's mother and her brother, who had bought the plot from a professional squatter. Living next to them were Mercedes and Claudio, who had moved directly from a small village in the nearby rural area of Guayas; on the other side was another young couple, Carmen and Alonso, who had obtained their own plot after living for four years in their parents' rented accommodation.

Alicia, with her seven children, acquired her plot and small house by swapping a more valuable plot she had owned nearer the city center in Cristo Consuelo. Her husband had abandoned her and the house had fallen down, so moving to Indio Guayas gave her both her own home and some cash. Finally, in contrast, Marta and Jesus owned a home in the city, but it was such an over-crowded multifamily space that they came to Calle K to get away from family disputes, first buying plots in an uncleared mangrove swamp before invading a cleared but unoccupied plot. With them came three of Marta's younger brothers and sisters. Marta described their new situation in glowing terms: "It was nice here, and besides, everything was new. At high tide it seemed like Venice, all the houses touching the water. One enjoyed it because one had never had it before."

The narratives of these five families begin in the 1970s when they first acquired their plots and incrementally began to accumulate housing—the land as well as the physical house structure—as an asset.[1] By 2004 the same five families still lived on their plots, all with formal land titles (*escrituras*). However, during the intervening thirty years, upgrading and housing improvements varied considerably from family to family.

Lidia's home, with minimal improvements apart from the block walls and cement floors that all families had built, reflected the family's dire situation. In 1978 the house had caught fire and been rebuilt (see below); in the 1980s her mother and brother had moved away after a family quarrel, thereby reducing her household's income. This was exacerbated in the 1990s when Salvador abandoned her to live with another local woman, and Lidia had to struggle to keep going. By 2004 eight people in two households were sharing the single-story small house. Some walls were still made of bamboo, and the plot had not been completely infilled, so stagnant water continued to collect in the patio. Salvador—who had returned after his lover threw him out—Lidia, and a son and his girlfriend shared cooking space with her daughter Dora, her two children, and a cousin lodger.

"I have my house because of Señora Marta's support. Little by little I constructed it." Thus commented Alicia, whose struggle to improve her house had benefited considerably from the support provided by Plan International that Marta and the Indio Guayas committee managed (see chapter 5). Over the years as she acquired roofing, septic tanks, and other housing materials, she recruited her sons' and sometimes even her ex-husband's labor to slowly convert her dwelling into a solid, larger, block and cement house, with the back patio infilled with earth. During the 1980s when eighteen family members lived in the house, she sold a four-by-thirty-meter section of the plot to address a family financial crisis. In 2000 her daughter Sylvia left her husband, and she constructed a separate bamboo house at the back of the plot. When this caught fire, the local evangelical church, Huerto de Olivos, helped out with building materials (see chapter 9). By 2004 the plot contained nine people living in two separate households: Alicia plus four of the remaining children in the front house and Sylvia and her three sons in the back.

The high demand for builders meant that Alonso, a skilled builder, earned well in 1978. With his wife Carmen's earnings as a washerwoman, they were income nonpoor. Yet their house was extremely basic, lacking side and back walls and a proper roof. By 1992, when the building boom had ended and the household had more mouths to feed and educate, the household income had hardly improved, and the family had sunk into poverty. By 2002 the state of their house led Carmen to migrate to Spain, leaving her elder daughters to look after the family. Two years later the household had moved out of both asset and income poverty as a result of Carmen's remittances from abroad. Her $20,000 earnings remitted over four years were a "positive" shock, providing family income support and the funds to upgrade and expand the family home, resulting in separate sleeping quarters for four of her five children in a two-floor, block and cement constructed house—the dream Carmen had always had (see chapter 10).

Of all five families, Marta and Jesus were most successful in improving their housing stock and also in transforming it into a productive asset. From the time of their arrival they had operated home-based enterprises, starting with Jesus's tailoring and Marta's dressmaking. When Jesus found work at the docks and Marta began to devote all her time to her voluntary job as president of the community committee, they turned half of their front room first into a computer café and then, when that failed, into a Nintendo play center for young men. Household savings were used to incrementally improve the housing fabric, turning it into a solid block and cement, three-floor building, while allocating separate space within the house as well as on the plot to their two daughters and their growing families. By 2004 there were thirteen people living in five separate households on the plot, two of them paying rent. Marta, now widowed, shared the original house space with her adopted nephew Emilio; daughter Adriana and her family of three lived in a separate house next door, while Ana Maria and her family of three lived upstairs. The top floor apartment as well as a small room in the back patio were rented out.

How did these five families, along with all their neighbors in Indio Guayas, gain access to such an asset: the unvalorized "free" land on the city's periphery? Their experience was not unique but rather part of an extensive "invasion" of the mangrove swamps that occurred in the 1970s as young Guayaquil households sought to acquire their own homes. As described in chapter 2, housing was not only the most important component of physical capital but also the first asset accumulated.[2] Although housing did not get all households out of poverty, for various reasons it was a precondition for the accumulation of other assets. First, shelter reduced the physical vulnerability of the homeowner's family as well as the socioeconomic fragility of extended household members, who often stayed during times of adversity. Second, over time it provided a mechanism through which additional income could be generated; options included home-based enterprises, rent (from rooms or separately built apartments above the original house), and cash from subdivisions. Finally, for many of the next generation, the original plot continued to provide shelter for them as adults with their own families, with houses extended (upwards or outwards) or separate structures built in the same plot.

This chapter describes how the *moradores* (inhabitants), as the first settlers in Indio Guayas were known, acquired "a home of their own" and over the subsequent thirty-year period consolidated it. As the narratives of the five families in this chapter show, households that started off with equal access to plots ended up with very different housing conditions in 2004. Chapter 9 returns to the importance of housing as an asset by identifying cross-generational transfers to adult sons and daughters in a context where, with "free" land no longer available, they faced a very different housing situation.

Contextual Background:
Guayaquil's Urbanization and Spatial Development

It is important to examine the housing process in Indio Guayas within the broader structural context of rapid urbanization and the associated Guayaquil land market during the 1970s, as well as in terms of Latin American state housing policy during this period.[3] As mentioned in chapter 1, during the 1970s Guayaquil experienced rapid economic growth, increasing in-migration, a high level of urbanization, and the expansion of low-income settlements on the city's periphery (Santos Alvite 1989). At this time Guayaquil was a medium-size urban center with commercial activity focused around the forty gridiron blocks that had broadly formed the Spanish colonial city (see figure 3-1). On the edge of this area were the tugurios, consisting of rental rooms in either subdivisions of decaying middle-class houses or purpose-built tenements that accommodated up to fifteen people per room in appallingly overcrowded and unsanitary conditions. A few of the buildings dated from before the 1890s when the last of a series of fires swept through the city.

To the north, separated on higher, hilly ground, were the predominantly middle- and upper-income areas while to the west and south, stretching

Figure 3-1. *Guayaquil and Indio Guayas*

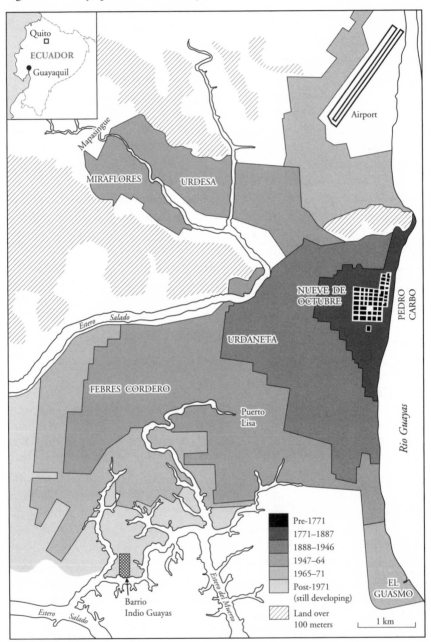

Source: Adapted from MacIntosh (1972).

toward the river estuaries that bounded the city, was an area of tidal swampland with little commercial value in its natural state and that provided the predominant area for low-income expansion. This area, known as the suburbios, grew far faster than the rest of the city: in 1950 it contained 12 percent of the population, rising to 60 percent by 1975 (Departamento de Planeamiento Urbano 1975).

The suburbios constituted an extensive heterogeneous spatial area in terms of housing structure, type of tenancy, density of population, and provision of services. The older, more consolidated parts were virtually indistinguishable from the tugurios, with upgraded brick and cement housing, high population densities, a rising incidence of rented accommodation, and some services (but no sewerage).[4] A transitional zone gradually gave way to kilometer after kilometer of small, bamboo and timber houses standing on poles above the mud and polluted water. The houses were interconnected by a complex system of catwalks (puentes), linking them to the nearest solid land, in some areas as far as a forty-minute walk away. The furthest extreme of the suburbios, which stretched to the River Estero Salado and its tributaries, was where Indio Guayas was located and had a much higher incidence of ownership, lower population densities, and virtually no services (see figure 3-1).

Migration and Housing Shortage

In 1978 the city had a population of around 1 million, with 30 percent of its annual increase the result of in-migration, mainly mestizo (mixed-race) migrants from the surrounding littoral departments but also a limited number of indigenous people from the highlands. This was reflected in the histories of Indio Guayas families. A typical migrant pattern was that of Claudio and Mercedes, now living opposite Marta. They first met while working in a small village called Pedro Carbo, in the nearby canton of Guayas, where he was a tailor and she a nursemaid for a "rich" aunt. Setting up together, they first rented accommodation there before moving to Guayaquil in 1976. Alicia was also from Guayas, in her case from Mangla Alta near St. Helena, where her father was director of a music band. She came to Guayaquil at age fourteen, along with her brother. Others such as Marta and Lidia came when very young. In Lidia's case she moved from Quito where her father was a policeman and her mother a domestic worker. In contrast, Salvador and Jesus were both Guayaquil born.[5]

Claudio summarized the motivation of many when he described his reasons for migrating:

> I lived in the country with my family, my father and my mother, in Canton Santa Helena, Guayas. They still live in the country and work in

agriculture. But one looks for a new life, new adventures, taking a chance. Because life in the country is hard, very hard, and as a young man one wants to dress a little better. Living in the city, there are more opportunities to study. In the country there are none. But in Guayaquil if you don't learn, it's because you do not want to."

Coinciding with the economic oil boom and rapid urbanization was a construction boom in the city center. Many old inner-city houses were destroyed to make space for new offices, banks, shops, and apartment blocks. Consequently the city's lower-income population confronted a housing shortage; rents increased and housing densities reached the level where conditions in rooms were unsanitary and overcrowded. Because prices were prohibitively high, Aida, for instance, moved to the furthest edge of the *estero* (estuary), building her home in very deep water.

Like Aida's family, most of the urban poor were effectively excluded from the conventional public and private housing markets (Banco Ecuatoriano de Vivienda 1975, p. 7), and as in other Latin American cities such as Lima, Caracas, and Mexico City, "invasions" were the principal manner in which the low-income population in Guayaquil obtained housing. More than half (55 percent) of the respondents to the 1978 survey had lived in rental accommodation before coming to Indio Guayas, most often in the inner-city tugurios, 88 percent living in one room.[6] Just under half (44 percent) had not previously rented but stayed with relatives, not only when arriving in the city but also when first setting up house with a partner. So it was not just the expense of inner-city rental accommodation that forced people out into the suburbios; some had been forced, or "chose," to live with relatives as a short-term strategy while saving to buy their own plot. This was the case with Marta:

> We moved here because the house where Jesus lived was not his only. Four families lived on one property in two houses. Half of one of them belonged to Jesus's father; it came to him as an inheritance from his father's mother. So it was a piece of one house that belonged to Jesus's father and another piece to his uncle and so on. And it was very crowded. There were problems with several families; one couldn't hang one's washing because someone would knock it down. The people fought all the time, and it was really ugly to see people getting drunk, having fights, and insulting each other. We lived there for nine years until Adriana was five. I told Jesus that we couldn't go on living like that now we had a daughter and had to look to the future because that house would never belong to us.

Broader Context: The Latin American Housing Policy Debate

The potential for Guayaquil families to acquire "self-help" housing through invasion reflected a fundamental shift in housing policy that occurred across Latin America during this period. In the 1950s and early 1960s, the proliferation of squatter and shanty settlements was seen as a failure of conventional housing programs to satisfy low-income housing demand. Government officials identified these makeshift settlements as temporary reception areas in spatially "marginal" locations for recently arrived migrants, who were "unintegrated" into the city (Bonilla 1970; Leeds 1969). "Squatter settlements were seen as zones of total social breakdown: policy-makers equated the problem of marginality with that of substandard housing; marginality was seen as something to be physically eradicated, a manifestation that had a simple cure" (Perlman 1976, p. 103). At the time government responses often involved the bulldozing and clearance of whole settlements labeled as "public eyesores" and a form of "urban cancer."

However, by the late 1960s, the formative work of John Turner (1968, 1969) and others led to the recognition that self-help housing was in fact a rational response by low-income populations to the growing shortage of conventional housing. The moradores of Indio Guayas benefited from the ensuing policy shift that swept across urban Latin America in which squatter settlements were now viewed as a viable alternative solution. Here the poor could incrementally build their own homes within their income constraints, allowing them the "freedom" to decide on size, standard, and style according to their individual family needs (Turner 1972). Although the upgrading process could take ten years or more, subletting and home-based enterprises were seen as mechanisms that could be utilized to increase the homeowner's income. Widespread acceptance by international agencies and national governments that the process of self-help housing did not represent a problem and might even be a solution to the housing situation meant that numerous national and local governments, including the municipality of Guayaquil, shifted from formal housing policies to "self-help" alternatives (Ward 1978, p. 38).

The Politics of Land Ownership in Guayaquil: Housing as a "Free" Asset?

In Guayaquil, as in many other rapidly urbanizing Latin American cities, land ownership historically varied according to the terrain, in keeping with Gilbert and Ward's comment, "Where land has limited alternative use values or is publicly owned, squatting tends to be more common" (1978, p. 298).[7]

For centuries the higher land to the north and south of the commercial center had been owned by a few families. Some were land speculators who had sold off plots for middle-class housing or industrial estates. In these areas squatting by the poor was actively discouraged, with the police deployed to remove any who tried to gain access to land in this way. By the 1970s however, invasions had begun to occur on private land in northern areas such as Mapasingue and Duran, and on partly municipal land in Guasmo in the south. By the end of the twentieth century, when the sons and daughters of Manuel and Lidia and others of the next generation were buying land from professional invaders, this process would even begin to occur on private agricultural land on the small mountainous hills in the far north of the city.

The lowland mangrove swamp to the west and southwest of the city had a different, very complex history during the fifty-year period when it was gradually turned into land through incremental infilling (primarily with quarried rocks and rubble and, to a much lesser extent, with the city's garbage). In 1880 the land fronting the river, known as the Barrios Suburbanos, was originally bought by the Guayaquil municipality from the Banco de Crédito Hipotecario for 14,500 pesos (Estrada Ycaza 1973, p. 23).[8] During the 1940–70 period, different types of invasion occurred on the municipally owned suburbio land, processes dominated by politics.[9]

First were the politically motivated, organized land invasions, tending to occur near election time. As Lutz (1970, p. 60) observed, "When a political party wins an election but cannot deliver on promises on jobs, housing and improved standards of living, it may 'give away land it doesn't own.' " The first large-scale, block-by-block wetland invasions, which occurred during the Second World War, were promoted initially by the political party of Velasco Ibarra and later by the Concentration of Popular Forces party (Estrada Ycaza 1977, p. 231). During the 1960s, self-help campaigns to make the mangrove swampland habitable were encouraged by two politicians, first Carlos Guevara Moreno and after him Assad Bucaram, as a strategy to enlist supporters for their terms as mayor of Guayaquil.

The financial interests of landowners encouraged a second type of invasion, namely, taking over valueless land to raise its compensation level on expropriation. This apparently occurred on five sizable suburbio areas owned by landowners who covertly hired professional barrio leaders to organize invasions on their own land. Leaders helped invading squatters demand infill, electricity, bus lines, and other services that increased the value of the formerly unusable land. However, when local barrio leaders demanded that the municipality expropriate the land, the latter could not afford to pay (Lutz 1970, p. 61). A third type of invasion was that of "professional squatters," who opened up new land for low-income, self-help housing by clearing the mangrove swamp and "selling" off individual plots, charging for their labor.[10]

No overall survey of suburbio land at the level of Guayaquil exists, nor are there any detailed descriptions of the processes of plot acquisition and incremental house construction. From the sources available, it would appear that the first two types of organized invasions were more common in the suburbios before 1967 while the third type, the professional squatters, predominated when the moradores invaded Indio Guayas.[11]

The year 1967 proved to be a turning point in terms of suburbio land ownership. As part of the complicated history of Indio Guayas, in 1950 thirteen hectares had been mistakenly declared unsettled (*terrenos baldíos*) and sold by the Parroquia Urbana of Ayacucho to five private individuals. However, in 1967 the national government issued a new decree (number 151) that declared the 1950 sale invalid, and the land was returned to the municipality.[12] The enactment of this legislation was influenced by powerful political pressure from the Concentration of Popular Forces party of Assad Bucaram. Although this decree reaffirmed the rights of the municipality, its control over the mangrove swamp "land" was limited in several ways.[13]

First, the municipality was required to sell land for 5 sucres per square meter to the existing occupier, provided he or she had been there one year or more, owned no other property in the city, and the plot (solar) was not larger than 300 square meters. Second, all the so-called shore zone (*zona de playa*), which the state had given irrevocably to the municipality, was to be donated to settlers with more than one year's occupancy.[14] This gave settlers the right to invade Indio Guayas. In 1974 a municipal ordinance for the allocation of plots laid out the process for the acquisition of legal title to the land. This ordinance established an Office for the Distribution of Solars to allocate and administer titles to the land, as well as prohibiting the invasion or occupation of empty solars located in the *zona de donación* (donation zone). However, the process for acquiring permanent title was highly complex, involving several government offices (Moore 1978, p. 190), and by 1978 only 2,000 out of an estimated 60,000 titles had been distributed, with the entire process taking decades to complete.

The Invasion Process in Indio Guayas

Indio Guayas was settled through plot-by-plot squatting by poor people desperate to take advantage of the opportunity to acquire a home of their own. All the 1978 panel data households were plot owners.[15] Both individuals and groups cut back the mangrove swamp and marked out the area, acting primarily for personal profit. For example, Don Cecilio Valdez, an ex-leader of the banana ship loading union and later president of a neighboring committee, recalled with nostalgia the hazardous task of wading through mud, water, and mangroves to position white flags on the end of long poles, meticulously ensuring that the gridiron layout was correct.[16] Since individuals had the "right" to own a plot, so-called professional squatters were careful to "advise" others how and where to acquire plots, with the financial payments they exchanged labeled as "tips" so as to circumvent any illegality.

The inhabitants of Indio Guayas identified seven different ways to acquire a plot, with clear distinctions between paid and unpaid possession. The 1978 survey reflected the panel data set, identifying that the most common method of acquisition for nearly one in three households was to purchase a plot from a professional speculator. One in five paid a professional squatter to cut down the mangrove and put in a few perimeter poles, while one in ten bought a plot with a house already built. This last method was more likely in the longer-established blocks where the owner moved to another area of the suburbios or sold the plot for speculative reasons.[17] Other less common methods included cutting the mangrove without paying, a means of acquisition used by less than one in five (14 percent).

There were also three types of "invasions": group invasion without payment (1 percent), individual invasion with payment (6 percent), and individual invasion without payment (9 percent). Such invasions in reality referred to the occupation of plots "owned" by others who neither had lived on the plot nor built on it. Although the invasion of empty plots was prohibited by the 1974 municipal ordinance (Saavedra and Loqui 1976, p. 153), the lack of legal titles meant that de facto ownership was obtained through possession. Thus those who did not live on their plots were liable to lose them since it was nearly impossible to evict an individual once he or she had invaded (see chapter 4).

Acquisition of the Plot

How did the moradores find a plot and move to the community? Potential inhabitants heard about vacant plots through their families (30 percent) or friends (44 percent). This was a lengthy process during which an extended family settled over time. First to arrive was often the eldest son with his nuclear family. After a few months, or even a year or two, he would acquire a second plot in the same street or slightly further out, move to the new plot, and bring in his mother or siblings to the older plot, transferring the title to their name. In this way extended families settled in close proximity. In addition, one in ten individuals joined their kin in the suburbios directly from the countryside, thereby bypassing the rented accommodation stage discussed above. The 1978 survey identified that in the Calle K, one in four (26 percent) households had kin living in the same street, of which two-thirds (68 percent) were extended family, while half (54 percent) had kin in the survey area. The widespread availability of plots during this early period meant that families often had complex histories of plot acquisition, as the history of Marta's household illustrates:

> Adriana's godfather had a mistress who had relatives around here, and they told her there were plots of land for sale, and to come and choose one. I came with Jesus and chose five plots. I always had the idea that I couldn't be the only one to have a place, that my brothers and sisters had to have something as well. It was on the 25th and LL. Mr. Hurtado was clearing the land, and he said, "I can sell you the plots if you pay me for clearing of the land." So we agreed and came walking with the mud up to our knees. They cost 400 sucres each. So we gave the man 2,000 sucres to clear the land.
>
> It was frightening there because our house was in the middle of jungle. So I knocked the house down to come over here where the land was cleared. We took over the plot as squatters because it was vacant. I chose this plot for myself, this one for Lourdes, and that one for Roberto. We came at night, because I was terrified that the owners would come and take my house away from me. Until one day I ran into the owner who said she needed her place. So I said if she needed the place, she should have built and lived in it; that I needed a house and I was living in it, so how much did I owe her. But she said she didn't want to be paid, that she wanted her plot. So I said, "If you don't want to charge me anything, I will not pay you anything." And I didn't pay her anything. She came back once and insulted me, and that was all.

Constraints on Moving to Indio Guayas

Plots, once acquired, were not always occupied immediately but often held as a future investment to be occupied when infrastructure had reached the area. The distance from the city center, lack of electricity, running water, sewerage, and especially roads all deterred families from living on their plots. As Alicia commented, "There was nothing here then, nothing. It was very difficult to walk on the walkways (puentes). There was no light, no water. We came in through the overgrown mangrove swamp on walkways. I was very afraid, but I had to do it numerous times."

Women were most reluctant to move because of the dangers to children posed by the perilous system of catwalks, the additional burden of domestic responsibilities under such primitive conditions, and the very real fear of loneliness. It was often the men who persuaded the family to move, even though it was the women who bore the brunt of the hardship; the distress experienced by many in the early months and years was considerable. Initially, walking on catwalks was so frightening that many crawled on hands and feet, venturing out as infrequently as possible. The logistics of acquiring water from the tankers, or food from shops up to two kilometers away, were time consuming and physically grueling, with women recounting stories of hazardous wading through mud to acquire necessary provisions. As Aida described it:

> The life on the catwalks was terrible. To live on the catwalks without light, without water, without anything was excessively terrible. To live in the hope that friends from outside would help to get water was terribly difficult. Often there would not even be a drop of water to drink. Because if one wanted to eat, one would have to bring the tank of water from over there, and they charged so much for bringing it here in canoe. When my husband had time, he sometimes carried it. I did not carry any because I was afraid, because those catwalks were very high, and they would often collapse. Women would fall off, and they would injure themselves, they would get sticks stuck in them and get gangrene. Two women got mangrove sticks stuck into themselves and they died.

Purchasing the Plot

Almost three quarters of the households (74 percent) occupied their plot the same year they acquired it, suggesting that the lack of legal title acted to reduce large-scale speculation and limited the length of time an owner could risk owning but not living in a plot. Certainly, Marta benefited from this situation by taking over unoccupied plots for her immediate and extended family. De facto ownership by occupation meant that it was very difficult for absentee owners to guard their plots by "lending" them to others since the person, once installed, might simply claim the plot. Similarly, the very low incidence of renting in Indio Guayas was a direct result of the same phenomenon occurring with rented accommodation.[18]

With plot sizes varying, data from the 1978 survey showed that half of the households bought their plots for less than $24 (1978 U.S. dollars; see Moser 1982, p. 176). While this was obviously an economic outlay, more than half managed to buy their plots with personal savings; a further 15 percent purchased with money lent by family or friends, and only 13 percent used formal credit agencies (employers and loan or credit companies). Prices for the later arrivals at the very edge of the Estero Salado were less than those of resold plots in upgraded areas. This indicates that land valorization depended not only on the supply and demand of uncleared swampland but also on infill and infrastructural provision (see chapter 4).

The vast majority of the panel data households acquired their plots in the earlier years of the 1970s, with 1974 identified as the average year overall. Few (7 percent) "purchased" plots from family members, with the vast majority buying from a third person; nearly half (42 percent) bought from local people they could name; and one in five (21 percent) purchased from local, "unknown" persons. A few professional sellers, such as Don Cecilio mentioned above, had sold more than three plots, but most sellers only sold one or two. In Indio Guayas this was predominantly a small-scale income-earning opportunity in which local community members made small profits by illegally acquiring an extra plot or two when they first arrived, clearing it of mangrove, and holding it speculatively for a period of time before selling it off to later arrivals.

Longitudinal Consolidation of Housing as an Asset

Acquiring a plot and moving to Indio Guayas was the first critical stage in the housing process. Over the next decades, households consolidated their housing in a number of ways. The acquisition of land titles improved their security, upgrading their houses increased the value of housing while enhancing living conditions, and finally, strategies for using housing to generate income included the establishment of home-based enterprises, renting, and even selling off some of the plot to raise income. This section describes some of these consolidation trends.

Acquiring a Land Title

Once the plot was acquired, the next stage was to obtain a land title (escritura). Not only was this essential to ensure security, but it was also linked to asset accumulation strategies such as home-based enterprises, renting, and collateral for credit. Although the municipal decree provided the normative framework to claim the right to tenure, the process itself was very lengthy. In 1978 only 2 percent of households possessed a legal plot title; in 1992 this had increased significantly to two out of three households (61 percent), rising again by 2004 to four out of five households (80 percent). Intriguingly, a lower percentage of nonpoor households held legal titles in 1992 and 2004 (50 and 75 percent, respectively) than did poor (69 and 80 percent, respectively) and even very poor households (59 and 88 percent, respectively). It may be that basic necessity drove the poorer families to be the most eager participants in community mobilization efforts to claim legal land rights.

Despite this increase in land title acquisition, some thirty years after invading the mangrove swamp, one in five of the original squatters still had not received the legal deed and was still in the process of legalization (*en tramite*), or had acquired one of a number of nonlegal documents. This would seem inexplicable until the complexity and costs of the process are understood. According to local community members, the procedure comprised ten different stages, with the acquisition of a range of legal documents required at each stage (see table 3-1). Formal costs amounted to the equivalent of between two and three months' minimum salary ($363), but in practice the process could cost up to six months' salary ($745) in order to "pay" the relevant personnel to complete the process. Hernando de Soto (2000) has written extensively about how South American legal systems act as a development constraint, and that it is the poor who are particularly disempowered. Thus, though a legal framework is necessary, it does not automatically facilitate the acquisition of land. In practice, such legal frameworks can impede access to legal resources because individual households are often incapable of successfully negotiating their way through the system's labyrinthine complexities.[19]

The Process of House Construction

House construction was a time-consuming process that occurred in distinct stages between 1978 and 2004. The vast majority of moradores (84 percent) bought their plots without a house, and even those who bought it with an existing structure were soon forced to upgrade, expand, or alter it. Contrary to the popular conception of self-help housing as a process lasting an extended period, in Indio Guayas two-thirds of the inhabitants built their *original* houses within a three-month period, using savings accumulated before plot acquisition. The brief construction time was possible because of the relatively low cost of a basic living structure in the tropical climate characterizing Guayaquil. Reflecting this process, six weeks after first living on the water on a basic platform with plastic sheeting for walls, Aida commented, "The house will be finished in two or three months. One buys the materials little by little to finish it. It depends what my husband makes selling toilet rolls around the city center. Every week he buys lumber and boards; last Saturday he bought two sheets of zinc. This week he wants to buy bamboo for the fence."

Table 3-1. *Stages in Obtaining Legal Deed for Land Title in Indio Guayas, 2004*[a]
Year 2004 U.S. dollars

Process	Issuing institutions	Cost	
		In theory	*In practice*
1. Legalization: Documentation required			
—Identity certificate of household head and spouse if married	Dept. of Civil Registration	6	15–20
—Certificate of voting for household head and spouse if married	Electoral tribunal	6	15–20
Make solicitude			
Inspection of size of solar←[b]			
Social and technical report on family situation←	Dept. of Land, Municipality	Free	100–300
2. Purchase of document of estimation of legalization	Municipal Office	5	5
3. Take out a property registration form: to show that person does not own any other solar	Office of Registration of Property (previously the Palace of Justice)	15	30
Documentation required: Certificate of identity of all adult household members	Dept. of Civil Registration	6 per adult	15–20 per adult
4. Put all documents in a yellow folder with band (bincha)	Legalization Office, Dept. of Land, Municipality	15–20	20–30
Documents required: —As in 1 above			
—Birth certificate of all sons and daughters	Dept. of Civil Registration	5 per child	5 per child
5. Municipal approval: Approval in three council sessions (these take place before elections and at the Annual Festival of Guayaquil)	Dept. of Land, Municipality	No payment	No payment

(continued)

Table 3-1. *Stages in Obtaining Legal Deed for Land Title in Indio Guayas,*
2004[a] (Continued)
Year 2004 U.S. dollars

		Cost	
Process	Issuing institutions	In theory	In practice
6. Pay the value of the plot (this also requires contacting the Central Bank to verify that it has then paid the fee)	Central Bank	Depends on plot size: 10 × 30 = 30	30
7. Send the minutes of the award			
Notarize the deed	Notary Office of the canton	200	200
8. Write in to the Property Registration Dept.	Property Registration Dept.	50	50
9. Buy evaluation of value in kind (*especie valorado*)	Dept. of Cadastral Survey, Municipality	5–10	10–15
10. Deliver filled-in documentation	Dept. of Cadastral Survey, Municipality	No payment	No payment
Total cost		363[c]	745[d]

a. As identified by community members.
b. Arrow (←) indicates that exchange is from issuing institution to plot owner; in all other cases, it is from plot owner to issuing institution.
c. Minimum for two-adult, one-child household.
d. Maximum for two-adult, one-child household.

Houses were built with varying amounts of paid labor. More than half were built by the individual homeowner with construction done on weekends, during periods of unemployment, or after work. John Turner's description (Turner 1972) of the resilient poor who joined together to build each other's houses was inapplicable in Indio Guayas, where the utilization of unpaid kin or neighborhood labor was not common.[20] Paid labor was usually employed in the first, most crucial stage when the mangrove foundation poles on which the whole house rested were sunk into the mangrove swamp and joined together. Many of the professional squatters who had cleared the swampland were also builders and carpenters working in small crews, involved not only in digging foundations but also in constructing entire houses for a prenegotiated price in three to five days, with intense competition for this work among the large number of construction workers living in the area.[21]

As described above, plots left unoccupied were often invaded overnight.[22] This prompted households to quickly erect the wooden stilts and then add the bamboo walls, wooden floors, and corrugated iron roofs. The most important building materials were standardized. In 1978, 86 percent of houses had corrugated iron roofs, 76 percent had split-cane walls, and 82 percent had wooden floors. The house was built on top of an intricate foundation made from thick mangrove poles, which did not rot in water. Still, houses were nevertheless unstable—bamboo walls could easily be split by the knives of thieves—and the building materials rapidly deteriorated.

The combination of bamboo walls and the use of kerosene and candles for lighting meant houses were a fire hazard. Lidia and Salvador suffered a serious disaster when their house caught fire. Three of the children were badly burnt, and the house required rebuilding. As I wrote in my diary for Friday, December 23, 1977:

> The kids were in bed and we were wrapping Christmas presents when there was the most terrifying noise—dog barks and screams—we rushed out the front door to see a horrifying sight—flames licking away inside Salvador and Lidia's bamboo house opposite. People were shouting, throwing water and sand, banging down the door, with the sound of children screaming and the weeping of people watching. I stood rigid, but Brian rushed out with our small half-filled water tank. There was a lot of confusion as the house filled with people and the crying, burnt children were brought out. Lidia was in a total daze while Danilo, her eldest son, was burnt all over and in a bad way—with people pouring water over him. The fire was quickly put out, and in the darkness we realized the children must be taken to hospital. I got hold of Chris, a visiting volunteer, and in what seemed like two seconds, he and I were in the front of the Land Rover, Marta, Mercedes, Lidia, and the burnt, whimpering, and crying children in the back—we raced as fast as possible to the Hospital del Suburbio, ramming into the emergency entrance with the three children.
>
> The cause of the fire was a kerosene light put by the side of their bed when they went to sleep, which ignited the mosquito net and then quickly

set alight the vast amounts of plastic sheeting used for walls, flapping in the wind. The whole family would probably have been killed had not Denis (Lourdes' husband), Alonso, Alvaro the tailor, and others been drinking and noticed the flames. A most horrifying day in all sorts of ways—and one I will not forget.

Incremental House Upgrading: Econometric Findings on Housing as an Asset

Bamboo-walled houses had a life of six to ten years, and so the second stage of the housing process was undertaken as soon as resources were available. Upgrading the original houses took the next three decades to complete, such that the community was heavily involved in house construction, with family members—along with professionals—acquiring building skills. For instance, women made small repairs to their houses as they lived in them, while children fixed the roof when the rain came in or patched the bamboo walls with newspaper to keep out the wind. The daily movement of building materials brought in on donkey carts, pickup trucks, or bicycles served as a constant reminder that construction and repair was a way of life for the community.

This incremental process of house improvement started with infill to turn the tidal mangrove swamp below the house into solid land. Once this was accomplished, houses were reconstructed with more permanent materials: wood floors were replaced with cement, and bamboo walls were replaced with brick or breeze blocks. This process is reflected in the econometric findings on housing, based on four indicators: type of toilet, light, floor, and walls (for further econometric elaboration see appendix C). With indicators ordered in terms of increasing quality, the data show a high degree of correlation among households. The rarest type of housing asset to own was a flush toilet, and it was only in 2004 that most households acquired one, although many people had connected to the main electrical grid and upgraded their floors and walls to concrete or brick by 1992.

The number of households that had achieved the maximum measured level of housing, in terms of the asset index, increased from 0 percent in 1978 to 24 percent in 1992 and 47 percent in 2004. Thus there was a slightly greater shift upward in the average level of housing stock, and in equality of housing stock, between 1978 and 1992, than between 1992 and 2004. These increases demonstrate the importance households placed on shelter and security as by far the most important priority when first arriving in Indio Guayas.[23]

Table 3-2. *Types of House Improvement, 1992–2004*
Number of households

Improvement	1992	2004	*Additional improvements 2004*
None	10	14	0
Reconstructed, same size, same materials	5	3	0
Reconstructed, same size, better materials	11	4	0
Reconstructed, larger, same materials	7	5	0
Reconstructed, larger, better materials	17	18	1
Extended	0	3	1
New roof	1	2	2
Cement floor	0	1	1
Iron door	0	1	2
Total	51	51	7

Source: 1992–2004 panel data.

While the econometric data provide an important starting point, beyond building material upgrading, the indicators do not reflect complex changes in house structure and size. Table 3-2 shows the different investments households made in housing. When houses were rebuilt, either the same size or larger, the most important trend related to the use of better materials.

Changing Plot Size: Housing as an Income-Generating Asset

By law, households invading the suburbios had the right to own a ten-by-thirty-meter plot, with the panel data showing that the average plot size in 1978 was 268 square meters, just short of the maximum 300 square meters allowed. Equally by law, they were not permitted to subdivide it. However, households treated their land as an asset and, as Alicia's story illustrates, sold off portions of it to address economic crises and augment income. Consequently, over time subdivisions occurred, as shown in the way plot sizes decreased with each survey, from 211 square meters in 1992 to 192 square meters in 2004. Despite this decrease, some thirty years later the average plot was still sufficiently large for extensive densification, providing adequate accommodation for more than half of the next generation still living on the same plot (see chapter 9). Indeed, the limited increase in the value of the suburbio land market was an important reason for the high level of stability of the Indio Guayas community stretching over this long period.

Nevertheless, by 2004 land as an asset was becoming more important, with increasing differentiation not only in plot size but also in upgrading. Not all households had achieved the same level of housing improvements. To summarize the differences between the five families in terms of the housing indicators, at one end of the continuum was Marta and Jesus's house, which by 2004 was a large three-storied structure and way beyond what the housing asset index indicators measured. Claudio and Mercedes' house, as well as Alicia's, met the indicators, while Salvador and Lidia's fell far short and was in a serious state of disrepair, with no real improvements made apart from replacing bamboo with basic block walls. The outlier was Carmen and Alonso's house, finally being totally reconstructed very late in the day on the basis of remittance earnings (see chapter 10).

To explore these differences, the focus of the following chapters goes beyond housing itself to identify the way in which other assets, such as the social relations embedded in social capital at both the household and community level, as well as human capital, were critically linked to the increasing value of housing as an asset in Indio Guayas.

4

Social Capital, Gender, and the Politics of Physical Infrastructure

"We must fight. Above all I want the women, the housewives, to help us, to come with us wherever we go to get the services we need. Why? Because you are at the heart of your home. You are the ones who suffer the actions of your husbands. The woman is a slave in the home. The woman has to make ends meet."

—Marta, president, Indio Guayas Committee 1978,
addressing a community meeting

"Twenty-five years ago this was a challenge for me. They elected me president of the Indio Guayas committee, and I had an enormous responsibility. We did not have houses; soon we constructed them of bamboo and wood. We did not have infill; we did not have water, light, a school, a college. I had to take responsibility for all these basic necessities."

—Marta, president, Indio Guayas Committee 2004,
recalling her work

These two comments made twenty-six years apart by Marta, president of the Indio Guayas barrio committee throughout this period, describe different stages in the struggle (*lucha*), as it was called, for infrastructure. As a young woman, shortly after arriving in Indio Guayas, she highlighted the importance of women's support for the mobilizations being planned; as a grandmother more

63

than a quarter of a century later she reflected back on the responsibility she had assumed to ensure that both physical and social infrastructure were acquired.

Turning from household priorities centered on the acquisition of plots, this chapter and the next address the most important community-level concern—the lack of basic physical or social infrastructure—and describe the complex multifaceted contestation processes needed to acquire it.

Why were poor slum dwellers forced to challenge the state to deliver infrastructure automatically provided by the municipality or the private sector to the upper-class neighborhoods on the other side of town? Class interests, government budgets, and political priorities all played their part in a common urban Latin American story in which the state's failure to prioritize poor, marginal areas for infrastructure development resulted in the formation of local neighborhood (barrio)-level committees such as the Indio Guayas Committee (IGC), which embarked on a lengthy process of negotiation and contestation with a range of state, private, and international institutions until, thirty years later, it had finally acquired the community's basic needs. This achievement required long-term collaboration that was only possible because of the trust and cohesion embedded in neighborhood social relations. In such a drawn-out process, local women played a critical role. It also required strong leaders. While local committee presidents in Cisne Dos were both men and women, in the case of Indio Guayas, the leader was a woman called Marta. Therefore this extraordinary story of the struggle for infrastructure is also her personal story, one that reflects the gendered nature of mobilization.

This chapter focuses on the 1970s and early 1980s, the first phase of mobilization, which coincided with a buoyant oil boom–linked economy and rapid urbanization process. At the political level, it marked the return of democratic government and the formation of new political parties that offered a concrete opportunity to petition local government officials and political party representatives for physical infrastructure in return for votes.[1] Physical infrastructure included not only electricity, water, and sanitation but, above all, earth infill *(relleno)*, both to create land for roads and to place underneath houses constructed on mangrove swamp. Chapter 5 turns to the period of the late 1980s through to 2004, when Ecuador experienced a series of economic crises and an accompanying decline in the importance of national-level patronage politics. To negotiate for social services—including health care, school improvements, and safety net support—barrio committees, such as the IGC, turned their attention directly to international nongovernmental organizations, like Plan International, and United Nations agencies, such as UNICEF.

Processes in Indio Guayas
in Terms of Broader Conceptual Debates

In this section, the history of contestation and negotiation in Indio Guayas is positioned within ongoing theoretical debates about community participation and urban social movements. It also briefly discusses the complexities in defining community social capital, the capital asset of particular importance in this chapter and the next. Finally, this section concludes by examining the gendered nature of social capital.

Community Participation, Social Movements, and Social Capital

The important role that local community-level organizations play in urban development processes—whether by bottom-up self-help, contestation, or protest, or through top-down community participation in local-level interventions—has long been widely acknowledged (Skinner 1983; Roberts 1978). However, just as the forms of mobilization have changed, so too has the extensive global political debate associated with them. In the 1970s and 1980s, an important distinction was made between community participation as a *means* for delivery agencies to improve project results and achieve "development on the cheap," or as an *end* in itself that resulted in the empowerment of communities (Oakley and Marsden 1984; Moser 1989a).[2]

In Latin America the concept and practice of community development were heavily influenced by the radical left-wing arm of the Catholic Church, particularly in Brazil, where the writings of Pablo Freire influenced a new generation of activists in the 1970s. Residential-level protest and struggle, in which communities organized to confront the state about the lack of local services, was articulated in terms of the "crisis of collective consumption" (Castells 1978). As in Guayaquil, this was the inevitable consequence of the state's inability to provide adequate services to the rapidly expanding peripheral urban settlements. A major debate concerned the extent to which the point of residence, rather than the point of production (traditionally where broad class alliances were linked together in political struggle), provided the basis for urban social movements (Castells 1983; Friedmann 1989).[3] Women played a crucial role in many of these political struggles. For instance, in the Madres de la Plaza de Mayo protest in Argentina, women in their gendered roles as mothers, wives, and grandmothers opened up one of the few avenues for public political protest during an oppressive military dictatorship (Walton 1998; Navarro 1989).

By the late 1980s and 1990s, the conjuncture of neoliberal macroeconomic adjustment reforms, widespread processes of political democratization, and the end of the cold war all served to reduce and change the nature of protest in Latin America (Pearce 1998). Among the poorest people, structural adjustment packages in cities such as Guayaquil were associated with bottom-up coping strategies for community-based family welfare provision (Moser 1992). This period in Guayaquil, as in other parts of the world, was also marked by the increasingly important role of civil society organizations (including, but not limited to, NGOs), which incorporated issues of rights and citizenship and the "deepening" of democracy at both the local and international level (McIlwaine 2007; Appadurai 2001).[4]

Measuring Urban Social Movements: Social Capital as an Intangible Asset

The concept of social capital is closely linked to what constitutes civil society. As Fukuyama notes, "An abundant stock of social capital is presumably what produces a dense civil society, which in turn has been almost universally seen as a necessary condition for modern liberal democracy" (2001, p. 11).

Although rarely identified as such, social capital can be usefully viewed as the latest concept in a lengthy endeavor, by academics and practitioners alike, to understand, measure, and operationalize the cohesion and trust assumed to be embedded in poor communities. Defined as the "rules, norms, obligations, reciprocity, and trust embedded in social relations, social structures, and societies' institutional arrangements that enable its members to achieve their individual and community objectives" (Narayan 1997, p. 50), social capital is generated by and provides benefits through membership in social networks or structures at different levels, ranging from the household to the marketplace and political system (Portes 1998, p. 6).

In fact, social capital is the most contested form of capital (Bebbington 1999; McIlwaine and Moser 2001), with a range of competing, overlapping interpretations. Based on the seminal theoretical work of Coleman (1990), Bourdieu (1993), and Putnam (1993), it was popularized by a World Bank study that demonstrated the contribution of social capital, along with widely recognized human capital, to economic development (Narayan and Pritchett 1997). Subsequently, the World Bank used it to incorporate social development concerns into the dominant economic discourse of the institution through such issues as participation, empowerment, social inclusion, and the role of local associations in development processes (Bebbington and others 2006).[5] As part of a broad critique, Harriss (2002) argues that the concept has been "technified," and as with measuring poverty (described in chapter 2), this has had the affect of "depoliticizing development." "Social capital for some implies social exclusion for others" (Harriss and De Renzio 1997, p. 926), insofar as it can be inclusive or exclusive in nature, and therefore it is not necessarily beneficial for all involved.[6]

To measure the level of collaboration in Indio Guayas, which was crucial to effective mobilization for infrastructure rights, this study incorporates the concept of social capital as one of the four capital assets identified in the asset index. This also allows for comparisons between social capital and other types of assets in terms of processes of accumulation or erosion over time. However, mindful of the widespread critique of the concept, this study does not take social capital as a decontextualized starting point but rather uses an extensive anthropological narrative to delineate the community trust and cohesion embedded in the mobilization processes undertaken by the IGC within a changing political context. This description is underpinned by the quantitative econometric data on social capital. As described in chapter 2, the study differentiates between two types of social capital: household social capital, identified in the longitudinal panel data on changing intrahousehold structure and composition (further discussed in chapter 8); and community-level social capital, discussed in this and the following chapter.

One potentially negative dimension concerns the impact of violence on social capital. Fear and insecurity can erode social capital when, for instance, community members cease attending community meetings held at night for fear of attack (Moser 2004). But violence can also generate "perverse"—versus productive—social capital, usually premised on the use of force and violence (Rubio 1997; Moser and McIlwaine 2004).[7] Equally important, but less visible, is the way in which community organizations manage to control relentless internal and external conflict that threatens to erode institutional cohesion—an issue explored in this chapter.

Gender and Social Capital

Since women played such a crucial role in IGC mobilizations, it is also necessary to contextualize gender within broader urban social movement debates. In the 1970s literature on residential-level struggle, the role played by women was mentioned descriptively and in passing (Castells 1978; Singer 1982). If analyzed conceptually, the role of women was described in terms of feminist consciousness, on the assumption that low-income women developed an awareness of the nature of their subordination and their strategic gender needs through consumption-based struggles (Kaplan 1982; Castells 1983). Two decades later the critical importance of women as "community managers," involved in a range of residential-level mobilization, was widely acknowledged, even if these were movements of women led by men (Logan 1990; Moser 1993).[8] Above all, it was the "male bias"' identified in structural adjustment programs that heightened awareness of the wide array of roles played by women in poor communities (Elson 1991). Such programs implicitly assumed that processes carried out by women in such unpaid activities as caring for children, preparing meals, and nursing the sick, as well as in "participatory" programs, would continue regardless of the way resources were allocated. Along with increased labor market participation (see chapter 6), women acted as "shock absorbers" in economic crisis (Barrig 1991; Moser 1992).

More recently it has been argued that gender has been displaced from efforts to integrate social capital into development policy (Molyneux 2002, p. 169). In the 1990s the emphasis on political and economic changes decreased as the burden of delivering social welfare shifted from slimmed-down states to civil society. Yet in their eagerness to mobilize social capital for their poverty relief or community development programs, NGOs (and governments) did not adequately consider, or problematize, how central women were to its function. Since the concept of social capital includes little analysis of the social relations within organizations, the effect of gendered power relations on the inclusion or exclusion of certain actors with respect to aspects of social capital has remained invisible (Radcliffe 2004). In contrast, the longitudinal evidence from Indio Guayas, both in this chapter and the next one, clearly demonstrates the political agency and identity of women in a protracted mobilization process, and the way it had implications for their empowerment as gendered actors, both in the community and within their homes.

Econometric Data on Social Capital in Indio Guayas

In measuring intangible assets such as social capital, it is important to recognize the value of "surrogate indicators" (Bebbington 1999, p. 2036), such as types of community participation, as components of social capital. The Indio Guayas longitudinal panel data measured community social capital in terms of participation levels in social organizations, with the asset index using three simple components: whether or not a household member participates in a community group, a church, or a sports clubs (see appendix table C-7). Not only are these very limited representations of community social capital, but quantitative data were only available for 1992 and 2004.[9] Such quantitative data therefore can only provide support in confirming the detailed anthropological narrative that identifies the long-term trends. Community social capital was an asset that grew in importance with the mobilization for physical and then social infrastructure;

however, it subsequently declined, in contrast to a trend of increasing household social capital.

The econometric data, even though modest in scope, show that this was the only asset that unambiguously declined. During the 1992–2004 period, the number of people (mainly women) who participated in the community committee declined from 31 percent to 14 percent. Acknowledgement of church membership (which is different from church attendance) also declined during the 1992–2004 period, from 71 percent to 47 percent, while membership in a sports club grew from 10 percent to 14 percent (see appendix table C-7). The latter trend partly reflects the fact that in 2004 the questionnaire was broadened to go beyond formal sports club attendance to include the informal football and volleyball groups that spontaneously appeared on weekends on the local streets, once they had been paved. These gatherings provided important male networking and socializing opportunities, often accompanied by alcohol and, more recently, drug consumption. Closely associated were informal gangs or male groups of different age cohorts, ranging from ten to forty years of age (see chapter 11 and appendix C).

Origins of Popular Participation in Indio Guayas

In the suburbios of Guayaquil, community-level mobilization was neither automatic nor immediate, and the development of what Castells (1978) terms an urban social movement was influenced by both internal and external factors. The rest of this chapter describes the origins of community participation in Guayaquil and then recounts the history of the formation of the IGC. The committee's functions are described in relation to the struggle for infill, with a further brief mention of mobilization for water and electricity. The chapter ends with an evaluation of the successes and limitations of political mobilization, including a gender-based analysis of its implications for political leaders.

External Political Context

External factors relating to the broader political and economic context of Guayaquil and Ecuador included the 1970s oil boom economy and the fundamental political upheavals and shifts from military to democratic government, in which different factions sought to control the new wealth. Such a shift was not new; Ecuador had a long history of "fragile" democracy. But the transition to civilian rule was unusual in that civil society groups were included in the negotiations over the type of civilian regime (Isaacs 1993).

Democratization also allowed political space for the formation of new political parties and associated grassroots mobilization efforts. In anticipation of upcoming political activity, Juan Pendola, Guayaquil's mayor from 1973 to 1976, set up a broad alliance of barrio community committees from the suburbios, naming it the Frente de Lucha (Front for Struggle). Of particular relevance to the IGC was the Izquierda Democrática (the Democratic Left, or ID), a new, center-left political party established in 1972 (with support from the Social Democratic Party in Germany) by the sierra-based politician Rodrigo Borja and his colleagues, who wanted to "modernize" Ecuador. To establish its political base, the ID reached out to regional technocrats involved in community development. One such person was the Guayaquil-based politician Raúl Baca Carbo, who formally joined the ID in 1977 and provided the necessary legitimacy and networks for the ID to win the support of poor suburbio communities. To better communicate its commitment to assisting these communities, the ID co-opted Mayor Pendola's Frente de Lucha, reconstituting it as the Frente Lucha Suburbana (Front for the Suburbio Struggle), subsequently referred to as the Frente in this text. This alliance of some twenty local barrio committees provided an important coalition that strengthened the capacity of the suburbio poor to identify their basic needs and to negotiate with a variety of social actors to obtain them.

The ID failed to win the 1979 election due to poor organization, unclear messages to its potential voters, and untrustworthy local leaders (Menéndez-Carrión 1985, pp. 407–13). Nevertheless, it represented an important nationwide political movement that would prove enduring in Ecuadorian politics, and with Rodrigo Borja finally elected president of Ecuador in 1986, it contributed to changing the predominant economic development policy discourse to include social policy. This then was the broader political context within which the formation, successes, and failures of the IGC occurred.

Internal Context: The Building Block of Trust and Cohesion

Within Indio Guayas trust and cohesion developed out of the common experience of living in an insecure physical environment during the early settlement period. Indeed, the first stages often began during the process of finding a plot. As Marta explained:

> I came once and saw the plots were vacant. Mrs. Ortega lived here, and I used to bring her bread, and sometimes meat; she used to give us water, so we became friends. She said, "Why do you live so far away? Come around here, this place is vacant." So they backed me, and so did

Segundo's mother. They were the only two families living here; all this was uninhabited.

For many women, moving to the suburbios was also the first time they had left their parents' home, and because it frequently forced them to give up paid work, it meant they became increasingly financially dependent on their male partners. While families recognized the positive aspects of homeownership—it enabled money previously spent on rent to be used for house building, education, and consumer goods—they also identified a negative side. Previously, it was close family or kin who most often shared hardships. In the suburbios, women in particular became more aware of the importance of different forms of solidarity and support. Women neighbors thrown together soon recognized the need to intervene to improve the situation. Even water was a scarce commodity; when the water tanker failed to arrive, they discussed in groups how to share what they had. When a child was killed falling off the catwalk, women gathered to console the grieving mother. Commiserating together, the women became aware that this was a collective rather than an individual problem. As Marta observed in 1978:

> In this area where we are now, two little children died. A man also died by being electrocuted. He was making the light connection when the tide was in, there was lots of water, and he got caught and died. There were some terrible cases that happened here. When we saw it was extremely difficult to live under these conditions, that's when we decided to get organized in a committee.

In the early years, socioeconomic differences between neighbors were not visibly marked. All lived with their young children in rudimentary bamboo houses; previous experience or their men's occupations were largely irrelevant when they tried to survive under the same hazardous conditions. However, awareness of common suffering did not always provide sufficient motivation for common action—particularly among women living in a society that placed great emphasis on the submissive, dependent, and mothering role of women (*hembrismo*), in contrast to the dominant, aggressive, and fearless role of men (*machismo*).[10]

Influence of the Broader Political Context

Barrio self-help committees possessed Guayaquil-level knowledge of procedures for petitioning for services in return for votes, and this knowledge catalyzed popular participation in the newly settled communities. Since the 1940s the city's politics had been characterized by a system in which populist parties bought votes from barrio-level committees in return for the provision of infrastructure. However, until the late 1960s, such committees were short lived, forming before elections and disbanding soon afterwards. It was only in the late 1960s, when the post-Guevara Cuba tremors shook liberal Latin America, that these committees took on a more "institutionalized" form. At the international development policy level, particularly in the United States, slums were identified as potentially threatening "hotbeds of revolution." The desire to prevent unrest resulted in extensive urban aid, such as the Community Development Program of the U.S. Agency for International Development (USAID), which focused "above all on politically tense yet economically vital areas for U.S. interests" (Mayo 1975, p. 132).

In Guayaquil this new aid strategy took the form of President Kennedy's "Alliance for Progress" program, accompanied by assistance from a variety of church, student, and middle-class women's organizations, which briefly flooded the suburbios with dispensaries and clinics. As a condition of a large USAID grant for squatter community improvement, the Guayaquil Municipality had to create a Department of Community Development (DCD) whose purpose was to assist communities to "fight for infrastructure." The 1972 Plan 240 to infill the mangrove swamps was organized around local barrio committees. By 1976 the project had terminated for lack of funds, with most committees disbanded or existing only in name; nevertheless, the experience gained with local organizing was easily replicated, as and when the need arose.

Formation of the Indio Guayas Barrio Committee and Its Leaders

As Marta explained, the barrio committee started as a splinter group of another committee, because of discontent with the incumbent leadership:

> The first committee here was terrible. All the president did was steal money and swindle the people. Many presidents live off their members. They don't care if anyone dies or drowns. But to be a leader one must be truly human and also to live here. Because otherwise how does one know what the needs are? I was experiencing that reality living here. I made the people understand that we would not achieve anything if we stayed in that committee and that we should organize ourselves, whoever might be the president. So one evening we met in my house, some thirty of us from this area, and we organized the committee. My brother-in-law Denis became president. But as he too was lax, he did not like to fight if he met any problem. I was vice-president, so later I became president.

The IGC was formed on September 15, 1975, by a group of neighbors who had already collaborated building communal catwalks.[11] That evening in Marta's house they also agreed on the name of Union de Moradores Indio Guayas, chosen "in honor of the Indian who struggles to have a better deal and to take the name of our noble Province that welcomes equally all those that come in search of a better life" (Committee Indio Guayas 1986).

Copying the DCD model, the committee comprised fifteen elected officials, including the president, four named officials, and nine representatives. In reality, a core group of three or four made all important decisions, both because of the time constraints and the frequent necessity for rapid action, which made it difficult to get fifteen people together.

Although women urged their neighbors to form a committee, they were not automatically elected as leaders. They joined committees out of desperation over their living conditions, moving into leadership positions when they became frustrated with incumbent male presidents. Even so, in 1978 the majority of presidents were men, although through the 1980s and 1990s, those headed by women increased. In Cisne Dos, four out of twenty committees were headed by women in 1976, increasing to eight in 1982.[12] Men and women were attracted to the position for different reasons. All emphasized a commitment to "help the community," reflecting the official DCD line that if community work was to avoid corruption, it must be unpaid and voluntary. Yet, in reality, it was arduous and costly, with obvious economic interests involved. When the president was a man, this was recognized as "work," allowing men to be transparent about personal motivations. Professional squatters used the position to legitimize "advising" overnight invasions of unoccupied land for remunerative tips; shopkeepers and artisans used it to increase clientele in the neighborhood.

In contrast, women were expected to be selfless, working to improve living conditions for their families. For this reason their motives for becoming president were more complex than men's, changed over time, and were more open to accusations of corruption and conflicts with other women as well as husbands. Marta explicitly recognized her own personal needs when she said:

> I wasn't born to slave away at the sewing machine. I do believe that a woman has to do the cooking and cleaning, but not to be stuck at home all the time with nothing else. We must get some profession, do something for the community and also work. They probably think that I order my husband around, that I am very overbearing. But I am not; it's merely that the woman has the same rights as the man. Because if he wants to go out, so do I—not to get drunk, but to have a good time.

While many men leaders had prior organization experience in trade unions, women did not.[13] Nor did women presidents necessarily have prior exposure to politics through their parents or spouses. Their life histories showed that those who had suffered difficult childhoods were more likely to involve themselves in residential struggle, out of a determination that their own children, particularly their daughters, should not suffer in a similar manner. Marta, for instance, was the eldest daughter of a woman who had six children by five men, most of them short-term relationships. One was murdered in a fight, others simply walked out, and the children were brought up in abject poverty. Marta had the responsibility for her brothers and sisters while her mother worked. She started working at age twelve and at fifteen married Jesus, some thirteen years older than she was, who provided the resources for her to train as a dressmaker. Even when married, she retained responsibility for her siblings. Obviously, not all childhood experiences had similar repercussions. Nevertheless, personal pain and suffering can be as important as external political struggle in developing an awareness of the nature of oppression. As important as "class consciousness," then, was the gradual development of a consciousness of gender oppression and the subordinated position of women.

Regardless of the composition of elected officials, women members took responsibility for most day-to-day work. Strict societal norms concerning women working alongside men, to whom they were not related, often caused malicious gossip or marital friction. Women therefore often preferred to work with other women such that committee composition was influenced by the gender of the president. Thus, when the IGC was formed with Denis as president, it comprised eight men and four women. A year later when Marta took over, there were eight men and seven women, but by the 1980s there were nine women and five men.

Functions and Responsibilities of the Barrio Committee in Indio Guayas

The eminent Chilean urbanist Alfredo Rodriguez, while living in political exile in Guayaquil in 1978, commented, "The suburbios are good business for everyone."[14] Figure 4-1 diagrammatically represents how people living in areas such as Indio Guayas were left to cope on their own with concerns that did not yield economic benefits for the city; this included policing, churches (with one or two exceptions), and almost all social and physical infrastructure. At the same time, community members had to go out of the area to access such needs, either individually, as in the case of health services and higher education, or collectively, as with the acquisition of physical infrastructure. Simultaneously, individuals and institutions with different interests came into the area, some to

Figure 4-1. *Flow Chart of Institutions and Individuals into and out of Indio Guayas*[a]

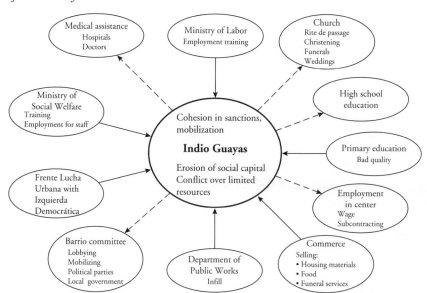

Source: Based on author's field notes.

a. *Dashed line:* community goes outside Indio Guayas; *solid line:* services coming into Indio Guayas.

extract economic or political gain—funeral service providers, traders, and a multitude of politicians—or to ameliorate the hardships of suburbio life, as was the case with small NGOs and the occasional church group.

The IGC had responsibilities both "internally"—within the area—as well as "externally"—mobilizing service delivery agencies, the mayor, or political parties. Table 4-1, entries extracted from my daily fieldwork diary, lists the range of issues in which the IGC and its community were involved during a four-month period between October 16, 1977, and February 11, 1978. It provides a glimpse of the extensive internal and external processes in which Marta and the IGC were involved. It also highlights the high levels of conflict and violence associated with contestation and negotiation. The scarcity of resources within the community, as well as politically motivated allocations made in an intentionally partial manner, meant that conflict management and negotiation skills were always needed in interactions both within and between barrio committees.

Table 4-1. *Events and Issues Handled by Indio Guayas Committee and Community*[a]

Issue	No. of events	Actors in barrio	Actors outside barrio	Examples of conflict or negotiation
Invasion	5	Marta, Mercedes, and acquaintances invaded lots		Dispute between owners against invader; physical attack with machetes; woman in hospital; problems with arrival of infill
Death of baby	1	Marta and committee members		Conflict over money allocated for the purchase of a wreath
Lot allocated for community center	3	Ramirez (rival barrio leader) and Marta	Ministry of Labor social workers; municipal department–DCD	Threat to take over artisan school; documentation acquired from DCD to show Ramirez he could not get access to the community plot
First Communion	1	IGC committee, Umberto	Sister Lucia, Archbishop Mons. Bernardo Echeverría	Conflict between Marta and Umberto because archbishop not aligned with ID
Infill	11	Marta, Valdez; two mobilizations of 200–300 in buses; ID pays off bulldozer driver and two local sharks; local women's affiliate to IGC	Ledesma; provincial council officials; municipal subsecretary of public works; ID party (Cevallos); Joaquin Carbo from DCD; infill contractors	Threats to storm office with 200 if infill gets diverted (power of force); Marta walks around to ensure bribes not paid to divert patio infill to other communities or for feeder roads
Electricity	1	Valdez, Umberto; 200–300 mobilized	Electricity company	Large-scale mobilization
Ministry of Labor social workers	3	Marta and IGC	Sr. Lucia, Guadalupe López (social worker), Raúl Franco (Argentine sociologist)	Conflict between IGC and Sr. Lucia over working in community
DCD	2	Marta	Joaquin Carbo, DCD	Conflict over who gets infill

Event	No.[a]	Participants	External actors	Notes
School director sacked	2	IGC; Valdez and bus mobilization	Plan International, Ministry of Education	Director sacked for embezzling money donated by families through Plan International
IGC barrio meetings	8	Marta, IGC, and community members		Negotiation over invaded plot; Frente to join ID; information about property documents; affiliation to ID in exchange for infill
Political meetings of Frente	4	Marta, Umberto; at home of Gabriela de Mata; other potential presidents	Scrutiny of other political parties	Strategy discussion over land agency; criticism of Sr. Lucia's links to Febres Cordero; conflict over lack of payment by ID
IG/Frente support to ID	21	Marta, Valdez, Maria Claudia, Umberto; political mobilizations (four busloads); ID establishes base in Indio Guayas with Frente	ID party (Cevallos, Ledesma, and Borja); governor of Guayas	Conflict about Maria Claudia taking principal role; affiliation to ID; Marta absent from discussion after dispute with Jesus; ID linked to infill; competition from Febres Cordero's party; Lola and Valdez leave Frente
Land agency	1	Marta, Sonia, Rivera, Gabriela de Mata		Discussion of lack of police protection
Denouncement as member of CIA or CP[b]	1	Ramirez, Brian, Caroline, Marta	Military, marines, police	Conflict between Ramirez and Marta over the community center lot
Other political parties try to enter community	2	Ramirez, Umberto	Two groups of leftist students, Sixto Duran, wife of Febres Cordero, Febres Cordero	Big discussion over party platforms; Marta fed up with Umberto's opportunistic behavior
National referendum	1	All adults in community	Hospital of suburbio voting site	Not enough booths, so many failed to vote

Source: Author's fieldwork notes.

a. From October 16, 1977, through February 11, 1978.

b. CIA, U.S. Central Intelligence Agency; CP, Communist Party (nonspecific).

Internal Functioning of the IGC

When first founded in 1975, the IGC was primarily concerned with internal barrio responsibilities. Aside from support to members at times of personal crises, such as an unexpected death or imprisonment, its most important function was to maintain social order in a peripheral area lacking a police station or any law enforcement services. Particularly in the early years of settlement consolidation, the primary responsibility was to mediate and settle invasion disputes. Even in 1978, when the majority of owners were occupying their plots, I documented five invasion-related negotiations (see table 4-1).

Chapter 3 describes how plots unoccupied on acquisition, held for speculative purposes or as a future home to be lived in when infrastructure had reached the area, were susceptible to overnight invasions. In the ensuing negotiations, the community favored the invader over the absentee owner because of the desire to increase permanent settlement density. This related directly to the trade-offs between votes and politicians' resource allocation systems, which meant that densely settled areas with larger populations had greater negotiating power than those with few inhabitants. In fact, the community even abetted clandestine invasion to assist the process. While a barrio president often might gain financial benefit for providing a tip-off about an unoccupied plot, the principal motive was the need to have as many people as possible living in the area.

The invasion itself was carried out at night when a family would occupy the plot and rapidly construct a rudimentary shelter. Most absentee owners paid a local resident to keep an eye on the plot, so news of the invasion rapidly reached them. The owner rushed to the scene and attempted to oust the new occupants, during which abuse and violence frequently occurred. Local leaders were called in to arbitrate informally the invasion dispute. Generally, this was a cash compensation payment to the absentee owner for the loss of the plot rather than eviction of the new occupant, which the leaders had neither the power to effect, nor the wish to do so. Negotiations were often protracted, with the invader ensuring that a family member was permanently in residence. Although the price ultimately paid bore some relation to market value, it more often reflected the financial resources of the invader, with the old owner desperately trying to get as much compensation as possible.

My diary for October 25, 1977, described one such negotiation and mediation incident:

> Two women came to see Marta about their two adjoining plots on the Calle N, which two young men, their wives, and families had invaded. The women are two of three sisters both living in the center, with the

third one out here, affiliated with the IGC for two years, and "gradually" building their houses with the sister living on a nearby plot keeping an eye on the others. When she tried to get them off, the young men attacked her and her son with machetes and stones. She's now in hospital, and her sisters have come to Marta to sort it out.

Five of us went out there, the two women, Marta, Sonia, and I, walking for over half an hour on perilous catwalks to get to the half-built structure. There were too many people, including us, on the catwalk, with people shouting and dangerously jumping. A vicious argument ensued; one young man brandished a machete, while the wives and children cowered behind plastic sheeting walls. The young man said that Valdez (the neighboring committee president) had given permission for them to move there, while one woman shouted that she was the plot owner. Marta intervened, saying it had to be sorted out at a barrio meeting on Saturday. People shouted their opinions, the catwalk swayed under their weight, and the exchange finally ended because of the fading light. We came home by moonlight. Goodness knows how they negotiate the catwalks at night. Marta said, "I know they are the owners, but they are not living there—I would prefer to have the plot occupied," as she later negotiated the payment of 1,000 sucres to each woman.

External Functions of the IGC

The IGC's most important external function was to address the infrastructure problem. As in other urban contexts, this was a highly complex reciprocal process that required committees to be co-opted by political parties that exchanged services in return for votes and political support (Sepulveda 1977).[15] The resurgence of local and national political activity associated with democratization (described above) offered self-help groups, which had been dormant under the military government, the opportunity to obtain infrastructure. This led Marta and her committee to mobilize for infill, as did other suburbio barrio committees in the Frente de Lucha. As Sonia, a member of the committee, described it:

> Marta said we must make a big demonstration; we must get all the people out. And Valdez said, "If they make any trouble for you, knock Pendola's [the mayor of Guayaquil] door down with your feet, and you will see that they will give you something." And so it was. We came along the catwalks, Valdez along one side and Marta on the other side, going all around calling all the people to come to the city hall. We went in seven buses packed

with women and children; people full of mud, without shoes, because they had to go around like that. We went around ten in the morning. Mayor Pendola was real mad; he said that the police must evict us from there. And we didn't budge. "We want infill," everyone was shouting. We were happy because like that we could achieve something.

By 1978, when intense political activity took place during the run-up to national elections, and different political parties sought to obtain patronage, the IGC still had not obtained infill for most roads off Calle 25. Since Indio Guayas, as well as the surrounding communities, had not spatially existed when the previous elections occurred, committees were as yet not politically co-opted. When the new Izquierda Democrática party sought to establish its political base in this new "popular sector" of Guayaquil, the party, under its skillful local leaders Xavier Ledesma and Carlos Cevallos, persuaded the IGC, together with twenty other local committees, to reconstitute themselves as the Front for the Suburbio Struggle (Frente Lucha Suburbana, or Frente).[16] The marriage was one of mutual convenience rather than of political conviction, in which both sides recognized their relative power; the outcome of a negotiated discourse was an informal agreement in which the community would deliver election votes in return for the provision of infrastructure.

This decision was based on a remarkable level of "urban savvy" (Anderson 2003), a knowledge of how urban institutions function, possessed by community leaders such as Marta, Don Umberto (an IGC committee member and also president of the Frente), and Don Valdez, president of the neighboring committee, Defense of the Suburbios Number One (Defenso del Suburbios Numero Uno). The fact that the city's mayor, engineer Raúl Baca Carbo, aligned himself with the ID (as did his nephew, Joaquin Carbo, head of the department responsible for improving suburbio conditions) was crucially important. During the 1978–85 period, the IGC, along with other members of the Frente, engaged in a reciprocal process, maintaining its commitment to the same political party over the years as it finally acquired not only patio and street infill but also electricity and water services, as well as social infrastructure. This continued into the mid-1980s, by which time the IGC decided that the ID had not delivered sufficiently, so it shifted its allegiance to a series of other political parties.

Acquisition of Infill

During 1978, in the run-up to the first democratic elections, a complex, time-consuming political contestation process occurred to obtain infill, the first infrastructure priority for households once their houses were built. Table 4-1 shows that over one four-month period alone, Marta, together with other social actors both inside and outside the community, was involved in an infill-related event every two days on average; while 16 percent of these activities were contestations directly connected to infill, almost half (48 percent) were related to political commitments, ranging from IGC meetings and Frente political gatherings to participation in political party rallies and public assemblies. The political commitments included running community meetings for ID candidates, attendance at party headquarters briefings, the mobilization and organization of busloads of supporters for political gatherings, and extensive barrio-level canvassing to ensure that people signed up as party members. To launch itself as a political party, the ID was required to have 10,000 people affiliated. As part of that process, it held citywide events, with Indio Guayas community members attending, as documented by a local Guayaquil newspaper:

> Last night there was a massive concentration in the Huancavilca Coliseum in which the Provincial Executive Committee was established under the leadership of Xavier Ledesma Ginatta. The multitude came from diverse barrios in the port and populations of the province. Rodrigo Borja Cevallos, candidate for ID for the Presidency, said, "We are the party of young people who have the right to open the way to power and mould with their hands a new society in which they wish to live." Ledesma stated that the party of the pueblo was born in the same way as ID, with a massive meeting up of people who desired a new flag, a sincere word, and a strong yearning to forever bury cheap lies. "The province of Guayas is paralyzed through the fault of our worst enemies; the administrative and economic centralization that has submitted us to the worst bureaucracy in Ecuador's history," he said in the first large gathering that the party has had in the city.[17]

The acquisition of infill in return for political support was a complex process involving diverse interests. As figure 4-2 shows, Marta and the other leaders first negotiated with Carlos Cevallos, the ID Coordinator for the Province of Guayas. He in turn briefed the ID's regional director, Xavier Ledesma. Both he and Rodrigo Borja, the ID's Quito-based presidential candidate, then leveraged Guayaquil mayor Raúl Baca Carbo's public affiliation with the ID. Baca Carbo then ensured that his nephew Joaquin Carbo, director of the DCD, included infill to this area of Cisne Dos in his work plan. Joaquin used the Guayaquil Municipality's Department of Public Works to manage the process, mixing "three straight projects with four political ones" to hide the fact that it was a political deal. Two additional sets of players in the project had to be negotiated

Figure 4-2. *Flow Chart of the Politics of Infrastructure Allocation*

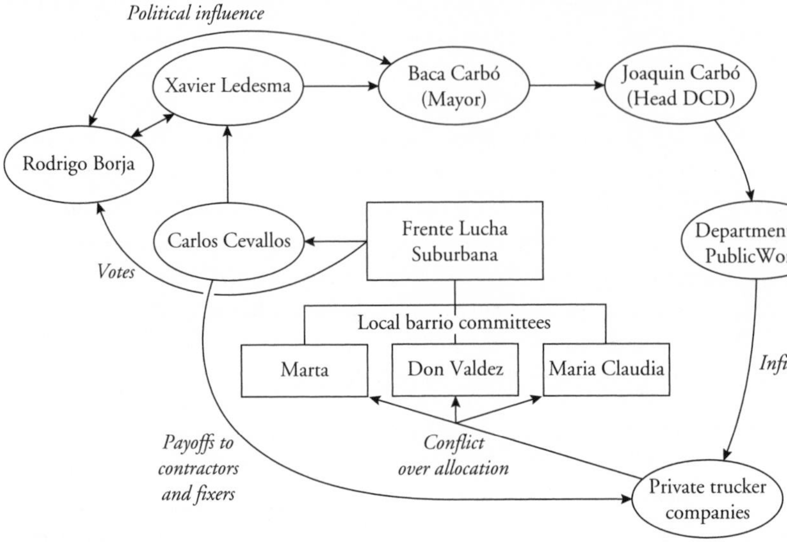

Political influence

Xavier Ledesma

Baca Carbó
(Mayor)

Joaquin Carbó
(Head DCD)

Rodrigo Borja

Carlos Cevallos

Votes

Frente Lucha
Suburbana

Department of
PublicWorks

Local barrio committees

Marta

Don Valdez

Maria Claudia

Infill

*Payoffs to
contractors
and fixers*

*Conflict
over allocation*

Private trucker
companies

Source: Based on author's field notes.

with before the infill got to the area, with frequent opportunities for derailment through bribes and handouts: first were the officials in the Department of Public Works who had responsibility for the job, and second were the private contractors hired to do it.

Although the municipality had used garbage for infill in some suburbio areas (as occurred in Plan Piloto), this practice had met with considerable local resistance, and subsequent infill was primarily done with rocks, stones, and gravel.[18] These materials came from private stone quarries to the north of the city, whose owners benefited both from selling crushed stone as well as from selling the resulting flattened hillsides for residential development. Infill required earthmovers and trucks, generally subcontracted from large companies, and political party affiliation was a major procurement criterion. Truck drivers who finally delivered the rocks were also open to bribes to divert loads from their scheduled destination. To ensure that barrio committees in other areas did not get access to infill, up to 200–300 people from Indio Guayas and neighboring barrios organized "spontaneous" demonstrations to present a petition to the Department of Public Works. In addition, Marta and other leaders walked the neighborhood, monitoring that truckers followed orders.

Ultimately, Carlos Cevallos himself came to Indio Guayas and paid off bull-dozer drivers, to control where the infill went and to prevent local "sharks" from diverting it for their own homes.

Without a transparent implementation plan, conflict was widespread as the allocation of street infill proceeded. Each time one street was finished, a crisis occurred until it was clear which one was next. Since the legitimacy of a barrio president's leadership was linked to the acquisition of infill, some leaders, worry-ing that it would not reach their areas, threatened to resign, form a new com-mittee, and join a new party. Equally, the arrival of infill increased conflict over invasions and multiplied the number of committees wanting to join the Frente in order to get access to infill. Some Indio Guayas members left the committee over concerns that community leaders had gained financial reward as well as infill for their own houses. The infill struggle in 1978 was only the start of a lengthy process that continued over the next two decades.

Acquisition of Physical Infrastructure from 1978 to 2004

Community mobilization did not stop with the successful acquisition of infill. Indeed, it motivated the IGC to undertake further negotiations with local offi-cials and politicians to provide electricity and piped water, the next priority in basic needs.[19] Contestation, following a similar pattern to that for infill, required constant motivation by the president. In her 1980 New Year speech at the Indio Guayas community meeting, Marta highlighted the difficulties ahead:

> We begin this New Year with the determination to go on fighting for the social needs of the suburbios. We need to join the demonstration to the Electricity Company and the Municipality. . . . We don't want twenty people, we want thousands—that's why we have been organizing as the Frente. There are people here who have an I-don't-care attitude, who don't want to participate but want to receive the benefits. The work will be done when people start to participate, when they decide to fight for their rights. We want everyone's participation, because unity has always bought us gains. Politics has worked for us, we have got things done, so we are going on with the fight for our demands."

In the case of both electricity and water services, longitudinal quantitative data demonstrate the incremental nature of acquisition. A private company first installed street lighting on the infilled main roads in 1976. Households quickly set about "pirating" electricity from the roadside connections into their houses, with extensive lengths of cable the only asset required. In 1978,

24 percent of households had no electricity at all and used candles or kerosene lamps, while the majority (76 percent) obtained it by illegal connection. To successfully run such a system required collaboration between committees. Don Valdez, the neighboring committee president, had the nightly task of climbing up a ladder to the top of a power pole on Calle 25, turning off the main switch so that the system did not overload (at peak usage hour), and then turning it back on after 9 pm.

Legal household electric connections were obtained in 1979, after two years of intense political activity. By 1992 all households had electricity, of which 76 percent had a legal connection while the remainder still tapped into it illegally. This free riding caused conflicts between those households paying for the service and those pirating it. By 2004 there had been a considerable resurgence of pirated electricity by households disconnected by the electric company due to nonpayment; 4 percent of households had no electricity, 35 percent had electricity via an illegal connection, and only 61 percent had a legal connection to the main electric line. This situation was the consequence of increasingly high costs for electricity, nonpayment of bills, and subsequent service termination, as well as the imposition of a large fine by the electricity company for failure to pay.

In 1978 100 percent of households purchased water from a private transport cooperative that owned forty-four tankers and had monopoly control over the price, hours of delivery, and prioritization of clients to whom it delivered water (PREDAM 1976, p. 55).[20] The profits were considerable since tankers filled up free from municipal supplies located at five points designed to serve the suburbio area of the city.[21] Households were vulnerable to the vagaries of supply, particularly during shortages (when vendors gave priority to factories and higher-income areas) and winter months (when vendors disliked entering the area because of the poor road quality). The availability of piped water, first introduced into the community during 1983–84, around election time, was again associated with community-level cohesion in support of the ID party.

By 1992 the panel data showed that only 35 percent of households purchased their drinking water from tanker trucks, a dramatic decline; 43 percent obtained their water through their own connection to the main water line; and the remaining 22 percent used both sources. However, households dependent on water mains had to cope with a reduction in water quality.[22] Finally, by 2004, 94 percent of households had their own main connections, with only 6 percent getting water from tankers.

Limitations of Mobilization and Suburbio Political Leadership

The successful delivery of physical infrastructure in return for active political support (and the tacit agreement for votes) was an arrangement that depended on complex trust agreements, both internally within the community as well as externally with the political party. Here the distinction between "bridging social capital" (weak ties linking individuals who are merely acquainted in a horizontal pattern) and "linking social capital" (based on vertical ties between the poor and those with influence in formal institutions) may be a useful one (World Bank 2000, p. 128).[23]

In Indio Guayas the bridging social capital was the cohesion among neighbors necessary to sustain the barrio committee. The most important tension was gender based; even in the 1970s, when the community lacked physical infrastructure and both male and female family members joined the committee, it was the women who regularly participated. Male participation was unreliable, often occurring only after pressure had been applied by both the committee and female community members. Political party leaders, administrative officials, and barrio men all saw this as naturally women's work because, as was widely stated, "Women have free time while men are out at work." This was a convenient myth, hiding the fact that most women were involved not only in domestic and child-rearing work but also in income-earning activities, mainly home based (see chapter 7). Women, therefore, made considerable sacrifices, risking jobs and neglecting children, in order to participate; those with very young children experienced the greatest constraints on community-based involvement.

Women also frequently rationalized that committee work should be left to them because of their gender-ascribed roles: just as domestic work in the home was their responsibility, so too was the improvement of family living conditions through community mobilization. The lack of reliable participation by the majority of men was jokingly dismissed as laziness, selfishness, and irresponsibility, stereotypical male behavior associated with the domestic arena. Men allowed their wives to participate, as long as they could see the benefits for the family, and their own domestic comforts were not disturbed. This was the arena where tension often developed, exacerbated by the fact that mobilizations required women to travel in groups outside the barrio, often at night.

Linking social capital, the vertical ties between community leaders and political parties, involved complex, tense political juggling on both sides; while the ID was concerned that the community would not deliver the support necessary for it to get elected, the community leaders, whose sustained legitimacy depended on continuing to deliver works (*obra*), were anxious that this would be captured by other communities. ID political leader Xavier Ledesma placed the blame on infighting among the twenty-two organizations constituting the Frente, rather than on the politician's tactic of playing one committee against the other.

When I interviewed Ledesma in 1982, he commented, "Fighting between community leaders is the most dangerous thing. It causes confusion for the people and destroys the base. The leaders must cooperate and work together and not just fight for their committee's infill."

Don Umberto, Frente director but also a member of Indio Guayas, while publicly agreeing, summarized the tense conflict when he said, "Cooperation is a joke; these are no more than words. The Frente committee is meant to be run not just by leaders but with the active membership of people who contribute to the political party by working across committees. But in reality every committee has to fight for itself, fighting tooth and nail to get the infill it can."

The ID, in setting out to be a "new party for new men," maintained that it would not collude with established patronage systems. While Ledesma admonished local leaders, stating that "a political party costs money," community leaders—though reluctant to voice publicly such self-interest—expected to be rewarded for their unpaid time and effort. Indeed, community members assumed they had received payoffs, which was a source of conflict. Consequently, the alliance was always fragile; as the Frente came to recognize its political power, its leaders shopped around and were open to wooing from other political parties. As shown in table 4-1, Don Umberto, much to Marta's wrath, welcomed right-wing candidate Febres Cordero (Ecuador's president from 1984 to 1988) to the community, while Sister Lucia, a local nun, accompanied the president's wife on another occasion. Leaders such as Don Valdez threatened to change parties, while others, such as committee member Lola, did so by joining Bucaram's populist Partido Roldosista Ecuatoriano party.

The so-called fickleness of local barrio leaders can be contextualized within an elite political system that effectively excluded working-class leaders from access to political positions. This was particularly true for women leaders, such as Marta, trying to cross class and gender boundaries to move into an elite men's world. These women's actions entailed heavy costs at both the personal and professional level. Personally, as women leaders became more powerful, they were increasingly distanced from their female neighbors (see chapter 8). In addition, they had to cope with marital criticism and local abuse. To address this problem, women leaders behaved in a scrupulously "respectable" manner, were always accompanied by kin or a woman friend when traveling outside the suburbios, and did not dress provocatively. Publicly, they justified their participation in terms of a concern for their children's needs rather than personal ambition.

Barrio women leaders were co-opted by political parties because of their ability to organize the rank-and-file community members, the majority of whom were women. Moreover, women leaders were more reliable, committed, loyal, and less fickle than men in changing allegiance from one party to another. As Xavier Ledesma also commented in 1982, "The women from the suburbios are fabulous. They are the real leaders and critical to the Party. They commit themselves with real passion to the work, while the men play around. In the Frente Marta is the epicenter. They all work around her. But she has to learn to think with her head as well as with her heart."

Opinions such as this reflected attitudes in a political party that used women leaders for their local power while failing to take them seriously as people. As Rodrigo Borja, also interviewed in 1982, commented:

The openings are there. Women simply don't take advantage of them, and don't want to go into politics. From birth they are taught to respect men and not to be independent. So they are not prepared to fight. That is why there are no women in the National Congress, and only a few at other levels. But when a woman is in politics, she is stronger than the men. When a woman has power the men say that she is very dangerous and they don't like her.

Although barrio women leaders were politically co-opted, it was very difficult for them to achieve elected political positions. Of the four political levels in the Ecuadorian political system—barrio leader, activist in political party, elected municipal councilor, and elected national congress representative—local barrio men sometimes reached the third level but rarely lasted more than one term; their lack of financial resources undermined their survival in a system of political payoffs. Women rarely reached the third stage. The furthest that Marta reached, in 1984, was to run as a Frente principal representative (vocal principal) in the ID internal elections, but she was beaten by a male candidate from another Guayaquil suburbio. By then she had recognized that her power lay in, and not beyond, the suburbios. Reflecting on her political career in 1982, she commented:

I don't know if I want to stand as a councilor. Politics just causes problems in my home and with everyone here. Men like playing around, but I know what I can do well. I can get things done. Look how many people have got water around here. I got the water, not only in Indio Guayas but all over. I am a leader not because I am that capable but because the people have confidence in me, because they see I will fight for what I believe in. That's why I know this is where my power is, here in the suburbios.

Thus, along with other local barrio leaders, Marta cut her formal affiliation to political parties, such that when in 1988 Borja did become president of Ecuador, Indio Guayas and other local Frente communities in Cisne Dos were not an important, vote-winning constituency. By then Marta and her committee had recognized, that to "get things done," they needed to negotiate with a very different set of social actors—the international development agencies. If political struggle was so difficult and achieved at such a price in terms of personal family and community relationships, what drove Marta and other leaders to continue this struggle? And were they as successful once they moved outside the established rules of political contestation? The next chapter addresses these issues in describing the second decade of community mobilization.

5

Leadership, Empowerment, and "Community Participation" in Negotiating for Social Services

"Sofia, Alicia's baby daughter, had diarrhea for days. She was dehydrated and listless with sugared water and herbal remedies not helping. Jessica said she was so thin that like Alicia's previous baby, she might die. But with six other children to feed and no paternal support, Alicia did nothing—she simply couldn't pay. I arrived, and as Sofia's godmother, agreed to accompany Alicia through the process and help by paying. So on Monday we went by bus to see a private doctor in the center, leaving the kids locked up at home. It took three hours of our time (as did each trip), and cost 30 sucres for a five-minute consultation, during which the doctor prescribed Chilean apples to reduce the diarrhea. They cost 20 sucres for four, while the bus roundtrip cost 4.80 sucres. We returned on Friday, another three hours, 30 sucres, some vitamins and instructions to get a stool test done. On Monday we paid 20 sucres at the laboratory for papers plus a small test bottle. On Wednesday we took the sample to the lab, returning Friday morning for the results, followed by another doctor's appointment. A further 30 sucres, amoebas diagnosed, and a chemist's prescription provided. The diagnosis time was two weeks; Alicia's lost five workdays as a washerwoman. The total medical costs were 174 sucres, while Alicia's weekly earnings were 150 sucres."

—Caroline Moser, field notes, January 1980

This salutary experience overturned any misconceptions I might have had about a "culture" of poverty (Lewis 1966). The problem was not Alicia's "cultural" ignorance or apathy; rather it was the overwhelming structural constraints facing her. In 1980, although three government health facilities provided services for the entire suburbios area, the quality of care was very poor, and lack of resources meant that none provided free services.[1] With only four private doctors in the area, the majority of residents had to travel out of Cisne Dos for health care. Like most of her neighbors, Alicia only took curative action as a last-ditch measure when a medical crisis occurred, rather than allocating resources to the preventative health care so essential for human capital.

As far as education in Indio Guayas was concerned, the following diary extracts from October and November 1977 reflect some of the ambivalence I felt when my elder son, Titus, was taken out of his state-run primary school in London to attend the local state school in the barrio:

> [October 20] Titus went off to school for the first time at 7.30 a.m., so cheerful and gallant in his new yellow shirt and smart tight green trousers that Jesus had made for him. Brian left him sitting there along with sixty others in his class. He spent the whole morning writing four words 100 times, and came home at 12 a.m. [October 25] Titus bravely goes to school and finds nothing happens. The teachers arrive late, bang on the wall to talk to each other, and sell biscuits to the kids at a profit in break-time. [October 27] He had a terrible fight with some boy who kept on trying to push him off his two inches of bench. He's still endlessly copying out numbers—twenty, thirty, forty, hundreds of times—bored stiff. [November 7] Titus's non-progress is most worrying; he goes through a daily fight to keep his desk and bench space—he's doing no work at all except the dreadful copying, which is all they do.

The Othón Castillo School on Calle 25 was constructed on infilled land and had sand floors, cane walls, and a zinc roof. Anthropologically, his experiences provided me with hands-on knowledge of the local educational system; however, as a mother I was concerned about the quality of the teaching he was receiving. As the only state school in the area, it was oversubscribed, with sometimes more than seventy children in a class. The teachers all lived outside the area and traveled into the suburbios daily to teach at the school.

My preoccupations with the school's limitations were widely echoed by many mothers in the community. Marta, whose children also attended the school, saw this as both an individual and structural problem, commenting at the time:

I believe for that school to be at a good level, everyone has to be changed because they are all complete scoundrels. Money is collected every week for toys for the children, and the teachers take the money for themselves. The school's patron is Tom Castillo, a newspaperman now settled in the United States. Four months ago I was with his wife in the school when he gave me 8,000 sucres for toys and 8,000 for zinc. I bought the zinc, and the teachers have the money for the toys but think it is all for them.

By the early 1980s, inadequacies in both the health care and state education systems had become a very real preoccupation for Marta, other Frente community leaders, and the community at large. Indeed, mothers in particular considered that the area was healthier before infill and running water arrived, because of the tidal movement and perceived cleanliness of truck-delivered water. As Carmen commented just after the suburbios were hit by the first-ever outbreak of dengue fever, "The running water is not very healthy. It is half water and half dirt. Before, everywhere was cleaner because the tide washed away the rubbish and the sea breezes kept everyone cooler. There were no mosquitoes then."[2]

While negotiation for physical infrastructure, described in the previous chapter, had been with the ID political party and its powerful municipal level allies (see table 5-1), addressing the pressing problem of social infrastructure required community organizations to move beyond the municipality to the national level. When their lengthy contestation with the national level Ministries of Health, Education, and Social Welfare failed, leaders in the Frente had to change their tactics and acquire a range of new skills to undertake different types of negotiation with international donors and international nongovernmental organizations (INGOs).

During the 1980s and 1990s, in a far more difficult political and economic climate than the 1970s (see appendix B), the Frente committees embarked on health and preschool education programs with UNICEF, and later with an extensive cross-sector, community-based program via Plan International (Plan), an INGO. Both organizations had entered Ecuador to address the pervasive poverty and improve human capital through community-based service delivery programs, and had chosen to work in the suburbios of Guayaquil. Table 5-1 summarizes the impressive range of social infrastructure, as well as some physical infrastructure, acquired through this collaboration during successive national governments.

This chapter describes the very different negotiation processes undertaken, first with UNICEF and then with Plan. As a community leader, Marta welcomed these programs because of her frustration with the short tenure of many

Table 5-1. *Physical and Social Infrastructure Programs and Implementers in Indio Guayas under Various Governments, 1975–2002*[a]

Year	Program	Area or committee	Political or international actors	Government ministries
1975–79—Supreme Council of Government (junta)				
1975	Indio Guayas Committee (IGC) formed	Carlos, president		
1976	Marta becomes president of IGC	Marta, president		
1976	Stage I infill	Areas of Cisne Dos		Juan Pendola, mayor
1977	Legal status acquired (*persona jurídica*)	IGC	Xavier Ledesma, Carlos Cevallos (ID)	Ministry of Welfare and Labor
1977	Frente Lucha Suburbana (Frente) formed	Marta, director	Ledesma, director ID Guayas	
1977	Stage II infill	Cisne Dos		Baca Carbo, mayor
1978	Stage III infill	Cisne Dos		
1979	Legal electricity connections	Frente (3-year mobilization)		Empresa Electrical Engineers
1979–81—Jaime Roldos, president (CFP)				
1980–86	Health centers and *hogares comunitarios* (PHC); DCD	Frente	UNICEF; Carlos Cevallos; Xavier Ledesma (1D)	Louis Alfredo Cevallos, Ministry of Health; Carlos Castillos, regional coordinator
1980	Primary school improvements	Agreement with IGC	Plan Padrino (later Plan International)	Ministry of Education; Inez Cruz, inspector
1980	Integral land infilling program (Decree 249)	Cisne Dos		

Table 5-1. *Physical and Social Infrastructure Programs and Implementers in Indio Guayas under Various Governments, 1975–2002*[a] *(Continued)*

Year	Program	Area or committee	Political or international actors	Government ministries
1981–84—Osvaldo Hurtado, president (DP-UDC)				
1983	Community center completed	IGC ("United we are more" appeal)	Support from Plan International	
1983	Main roads paved	Cisne Dos		Ministry of Public Works
1980–84	Land titles (Decree 2740)	Frente	Xavier Ledesma, provincial deputy (ID)	
1983	Water pipelines	Frente (5-year mobilization)	Lucho Ramirez (ID)	Department of Water; Lucho Ramirez, engineer
1984–88—Leon Febres Cordero, president (PSC)				
1984	Othón Castillo School completed	Calle 25 and Calle K	Leon Febres Cordero and Plan International	Ministry of Education; Guido Sambrano, subsecretary
1985	Agreement signed with Plan	IGC along with other committees	Plan International (Henry Beder, director)	
1987	Nonconventional programs	Committees in Cisne Dos		Ministry of Social Welfare and Education
1987	Program of Muchachos Trabajadores			INFA; Louis Alfredo Cevallos (ex UNICEF)
1987	Adult education courses		CECIM	Sylvia Leon, coordinator

(continued)

Table 5-1. *Physical and Social Infrastructure Programs and Implementers in Indio Guayas under Various Governments, 1975–2002*[a] *(Continued)*

Year	Program	Area or committee	Political or international actors	Government ministries
1988–1992—Rodrigo Borja, president (ID)				
1989	Community basic health care (SAFIC); community crèches	One in Cisne Dos	Plan International	Ministries of Health, Welfare, and Education
1992	Sewage pipes laid (not completed)	IGC		Ministry of Sewerage
1992–96—Sixto Duran, president (PUR)				
1992	Garbage collection initiated	Cisne Dos		Municipality
1996–2004—Six presidents, two juntas				
2000	Public lighting	Indio Guayas		Municipality and electricity company
2002	End of Plan programs	Cisne Dos	Plan International	

a. Abbreviations: DCD, Department of Community Development; CECIM, Comité Ecuatoriano de Cooperación con la Comisión Interamericana de Mujeres; CFP, Concentracion de Fuerzas Populares; DP-UDC, Democracia Popular–Unión Demócrata Cristiana; ID, Izquierda Democrática; INFA, Instituto Nacional de la Ninez y Adolescencia; PHC, Primary Health Care; PUR, Partido Union Republica; PSC, Partido Social Cristiano; SAFIC, Salud Familiar Integral Comunitaria.

NGOs and politically aligned groups, whose transiency and offers of quick-fix solutions constantly undermined community members' long-term perspectives. In addition, she recognized that continued community participation in the Indio Guayas committee depended on rolling out new projects, commenting in 1992, "If you want to keep the committee functioning, you have to keep looking for projects."

In depicting the programs, this chapter describes their impacts on both leaders and community members. Positive outcomes included the strengthening of the leadership capacity of community leaders as a result of the complex negotiation processes, as with UNICEF. Increased financial independence and an associated "empowerment" of local women also derived from participation in the home-based child care (*hogares comunitarios*) program. However, there were also negative consequences, particularly for community social capital. Acceptance of Plan's model of community participation was required to guarantee long-term service delivery. It also meant, however, that Plan's long-term presence created a welfarist dependency; when Plan pulled out in 2002, after twenty-five years in Indio Guayas, the barrio committee's importance had declined, and community social capital, as measured in the 2004 asset index, was reduced.

Community Leadership and the UNICEF Primary Health Care Project

Although the Frente committees began lobbying the Ministry of Health in the late 1970s for accessible, cheap, and effective community-based health programs, using the same methods they had employed with the political parties, their struggles were unsuccessful until UNICEF chose Cisne Dos as the location for one of its first urban Primary Health Care (PHC) projects.[3] Introduced in the early 1980s, the project was intended to bring important health benefits to Indio Guayas through a participatory approach to service delivery.

UNICEF's choice of Cisne Dos was influenced by the fact that the Frente had been identified as a "solid community organization" that would act as the local counterpart to ensure community participation (UNICEF 1985b). The PHC project, just one component of a pilot program pioneering UNICEF's integral approach to urban basic services, assumed that the Ecuadorian government would take it over (and provide the necessary resources) once it was up and running.[4] In the PHC project, community participation was central to an integrated package that also included preschool community facilities and home-based care for children (hogares comunitarios).[5]

Despite its focus on community participation, the project had a top-down design, with UNICEF first involving Frente leaders at the "negotiation" stage.[6] Women leaders, such as Marta, particularly wanted the project and therefore set no conditions on participation. In fact, Marta saw the project as "theirs," something to which the community was entitled, and presented it at the barrio-level meeting as work (*obra*) the president had successfully obtained. In turn, local women not only identified potential community health promoters but also facilitated access to their homes so that their children would be checked and weighed. Eight Frente committee presidents, including Marta, accepted the project, which covered about 42,000 people, with Marta, by then Frente president, designated as coordinator.

Agreement on the characteristics of "community participation" in the project showed the resourceful way in which community leaders worked with the demands of the international agency to ensure that the project was implemented. At the same time, this process provided an important learning experience that served them well down the line. As with many participatory projects, the issue of remuneration was a fundamental tension. Frente presidents were not paid for their work, even though their endorsement was essential for project success. Although the presidents nominated the two female health promoters for each sector, UNICEF's technical team and Ministry of Health personnel made the final decision. Promoters signed a contract with the community committee and were paid a stipend fixed below the minimum wage, with terms and conditions drawn up by the ministry. This followed UNICEF's philosophy that health project promoters worked for the "good of the community," not just for income, and that Frente presidents were responsible for disbursing the promoters' stipends monthly. By investing responsibility for quality control and monitoring in the community itself, principally through the community leadership, UNICEF expected "community participation" to be ensured.

The PHC project began implementation in May 1981. In 1985, after four years of progress, a crisis occurred over the payment of promoters, which led to termination of the project in 1986. This occurred as UNICEF shifted the project's management to the Ministry of Health, at which point four promoters demanded to be incorporated into the Ecuadorian Social Security Institute and paid a minimum wage. Although promoters had entered the project knowing that only a stipend would be paid, Don Valdez, Marta's neighboring community leader, took on their cause, and as a trade union leader, argued that once this became a regular Ministry of Heath program, promoters should be treated like other public employees.

Frente leaders such as Marta were given responsibility for the associated social security payments since the promoters' contracts were with them. With community leaders unclear if they had the right to "'fire" the promoters causing trouble, the situation became more complicated in 1986 when Frente leaders were accused of using the project politically to generate ID support and financial benefit. Reflecting on this accusation in 1992, Marta commented, "We are in politics, but we did not use the PHC politically, since this was a community program." Eventually, tired of "too much hassle" and concerned about the potential financial threat, they decided not to sign the monthly reports, which meant promoters were no longer paid. With this decision, the ministry's provisional director of health closed the program without even officially informing those who had worked in it.

A comprehensive external evaluation of the PHC project in Cisne Dos (that went beyond measuring the health impact on children) considered it a failure, stating that "the project failed during the later stages of implementation because of inherent structural problems that prevented it [from] being institutionalized at the Ministry and community levels" (Health and Life Sciences Partnership 1989, section 4.1).

However, this assessment ignored a number of important intangible positive outcomes for Marta and other Frente leaders. The project increased the leaders' organizational skills in guaranteeing and retaining community participation in projects, as well as their technical skills in project administration and management, including the handling of project bank accounts. Unlike the rapid UNICEF project staff turnaround, community commitment was long term, with Marta and six other Frente presidents remaining in charge throughout the program's duration.[7] Similarly, the ten health promoters chosen in 1981 also stayed with the program until it ended. Such commitment increased the credibility of individual community leaders and strengthened community social capital beyond the individual committees, legitimizing the Frente as a cohesive collective network. UNICEF, in turn, showed vision in building on an existing suburbio-level organizational platform—the Frente—to expand the project. This represented a fundamentally different strategy from the divide-and-rule principles of political parties, whose unequal allocation of resources caused constant conflict and schisms among vying committees.

By default rather than design, the role that community leaders played in negotiation procedures during the end-of-project crisis empowered them. In reaching consensus about the nonpayment of the promoters, Marta and other Frente members proved themselves capable of setting the terms for collaboration rather than having them imposed top-down by outsiders. For such leaders, well versed in divisive political patron-client relationships, the PHC project provided a learning experience in nonpolitical community-level service delivery. Above all, this experience equipped them with skills useful in future bargaining with external agencies over the terms and condition of collaboration. Marta summarized the situation after the end of the project as follows: "While the program was related to UNICEF, it was safe. . . . Later, everyone wanted to claim it as theirs and did not wish to recognize it as belonging to the community. Now in my sector, I give the orders, not them. I will implement what the people want, not what they want. They [the international agencies] do not control the sector, they are answerable to me."

Women's Empowerment through the Hogares Comunitarios Program

While the UNICEF PHC project unified the Frente leaders, UNICEF's second program of home-based child care, the Hogares Comunitarios program, gave a number of local women an income-generating opportunity. It also produced an unanticipated outcome: empowerment of these women through increased self-confidence and recognition of an identity beyond that of motherhood. In Indio Guayas alone, for instance, the women from twelve households participated as care providers (*madres cuidanderas*) in the Hogares Comunitaros program, each looking after 15 children ages three months to five years, with a total of around 180 children in the program.

Along with provision of child care, the program was designed to improve the health and educational stimulation of children through supplementary food and pedagogic toys. The program was supervised by twice-weekly visits from nursery school educationalists (*parvularios*). It was highly organized: care providers received some training and necessary home equipment; supervisors inspected their homes to check on toilets, space, and general cleanliness; and providers were required to keep daily records and get their weekly menus and bills verified. Obviously, the care providers varied in their commitment to such back-breaking work (along with a young family assistant or two) for a small stipend, as well as in their ability to implement the educational component of the program. Nevertheless, it was enthusiastically received by all involved.

Unlike the PHC program, this program was incorporated into the Ministry of Social Welfare's portfolio during the Borja government's *Frente Social.*[8] But despite its success, the Ministry of Welfare perceived the program as too costly in labor terms and terminated it in 1992, by which time most of the local women had been gainfully employed for three or four years. While mothers preferred the hogares comunitarios because they offered household-based care with a small number of well-attended children, the Ministry of Social Welfare maintained that community crèches could provide more professional and economically efficient facilities.

This was another example of the failure of an implementing agency to recognize the significance of the program for community women, both care providers and mothers. Mercedes, who lived opposite Marta, and had been a stalwart supporter of the Indio Guayas committee, was lucky enough to get a position. Illiterate herself, she ran it together with her daughter Flor, who had completed high school. She was immensely proud of her appointment, explaining its advantage in the following way:

All the children's mothers work, washing clothes, cooking, or in factories. I only mind the children whose mothers work. If one hasn't been able to get education, you can still help children become better people. I started to work so I could help my children. Sometimes they need to buy a notebook, and now I have something to give them. I'm happier now I have my own job because now I no longer have to tell him [Claudio, her husband] "give me for this, I want it." Now I just get it, it's mine. Now I realize that my husband sometimes gets mad . . . so I think that by being free to work, one is more independent.

The program not only empowered women as care providers but also created opportunities for women with children to enter the labor market and to help other mothers already working, who had to lock up their children at home when they went to work. A survey of thirty mothers who had used the child care program, undertaken six months after the program closed in 1993, revealed its impact on women's lives.[9] Assertions by Ministry of Social Welfare officials that women used the program to give them free time to "sit around chatting" were demonstrably false; in the survey, all the women in the program worked, and as a result of its closure, one in three had had to leave their jobs.

Of those women still working after the program closed, two in five were in unskilled domestic services, and one in five did petty selling, worked at a factory, or engaged in a variety of other income-earning activities. Their husbands were also in low-paid occupations, such as construction work or street selling. Some women managed to keep their jobs while reducing the number of hours they worked; those worst affected once again reverted to locking up their children at home when they went out to work. As a woman shoemaker commented, "It had a very big impact because the hogares comunitarios helped me a great deal with the children. Now the quantity of shoes I make has fallen dramatically. I leave them with their older brother and sister (aged twelve and fourteen) in the house, but in the afternoons I have to look after them so the brother and sister can study."

Some of the women still working reverted to using neighbors or extended family support, one in three went back to live with their mothers, one in four arranged child care with older children, and in one case, a father who worked as a night watchman helped out. But this assistance was not always provided for free. Those with sufficient resources paid family members or neighbors to care for their children.

Women were upset that the Ministry of Welfare closed this service without even consulting them, and they were also concerned about the impact it had on their children, especially the withdrawal of support for early developmental skills that mothers felt they were less able to provide. As one mother commented, "I lack tranquility not knowing where to leave my child—I leave him with my neighbor, but it's not the same as the hogar. He wakes every morning with the idea that he will go to the little school and then starts crying; he lacks a great deal because of the loss of the stimulation that they provided him."

For the care providers participating in the hogares comunitarios, the program's closure was yet another example of having their hopes raised by a community initiative only to have them dashed a year or two later. Mercedes, like some others, became very depressed and never found work again in her own right. Although she continued to support Marta actively in her committee work, the "fire had gone out of her belly." She gradually withdrew into her home, helping her husband Claudio with his dental work. By 2004 she was very depressed, suffered from a range of ailments, and rarely accompanied Marta on her much-reduced committee business. Over the years as other well-intentioned programs came and went, this process consistently repeated itself, leaving local women disillusioned with community initiatives and reluctant to participate in community activities.

Plan International and "Community Participation" to Acquire Social Services in Cisne Dos

In a context of unreliable, unsustainable patterns of external intervention, Plan International was an exception, and over a twenty-five-year period, it undoubtedly did more than any other public or private sector organization to improve the welfare of poor households in Indio Guayas. At the same time, as this section describes, it brought with it a particular model of "community participation" that had long-term implications for community trust and cohesion, the social capital of Indio Guayas.

Plan, one of the largest INGOs today (Sparr and Moser 2007), has its origins in the 1930s' Spanish Civil War.[10] It started working in Guayaquil in 1963, as Plan de Padrinos (Foster Parents Plan), with 95 percent of its funding coming from foster parents in the United States and Europe.[11] At that time it implemented an established social welfare (*asistencialista*) approach based on the quasi-adoption by foster parents of children four to eighteen years old.[12] According to many residents of Indio Guayas in 1978, the program was reputed to pay "gringos" (U.S. citizens) large salaries while exploiting the poor, who received little of the money sent. It was seen as socially divisive, creating jealousy between those families who received funds and those that did not, as well as within families, between the "adopted" child and his or her siblings—even though in many cases the money was used to supplement household expenses.

In the early 1980s, the organization changed fundamentally: its name became Plan International, and it shifted to a "developmental approach," with support for community-level integrated human development. This was to be implemented through raising awareness (*conscientizacion;* see Plan International Ecuador 1985) and self-help (*autogestión*), both of which were intended to empower the community (Burgwal 1995, p. 56).[13] In 1983 Plan developed a strategy to "integrate into the suburbios," with a stated initial ten- to twenty-five-year commitment. To build goodwill, it upgraded the Othón Castillo Primary School and financially supported the building of a three-grade secondary school. In exchange, Plan was given community land on Calle 25, between Calle K and Calle J, to build its central Guayaquil office.[14]

Amarylis Zambrano, the head of the Social Promotion department, described how the Plan's social promoters, as its social workers were now called under the new developmental approach, perceived their task when they first started working in the suburbios: "We reactivated sleeping committees no longer really functioning, without activity and that had lost their strength since infill, water, and light were obtained. Although we work with barrio committees, not political committees, we recognize that if Plan's contract is broken tomorrow, then the only committees with any power will in fact be the political committees."[15]

This comment revealed the limited local institutional knowledge of social promoters, who had not grasped why committees were politicized (chapter 4). At the outset Plan initiated a four-month induction process comprising discussions with those individual leaders "still there," followed by a critically important meeting attended by all leaders, in which they were required to agree to the boundaries of the areas that would be represented by local committees.[16]

In fact, for very good reasons, spatial boundaries for community organizations did not exist; fluidity reflected household preferences, loyalties, and political allegiances. Plan's modus operandi, therefore, represented a serious challenge to the nature of community cohesion. When Plan considered a committee to be "too political," or when leaders chose not to join Plan's program, it simply created new committees in the same spatial areas as existing committees.[17] Marta initially was not approached because she was identified as a "revolutionary" and a "communist" who, because of her close affiliation with the ID, was "into politics up to the dinner (she cooked)."

However, the experience negotiating with UNICEF empowered the Indio Guayas committee to negotiate directly with Plan to ensure that contracts were acceptable, and that the barrio committees had control over the Plan social promoters coming into their sector. Marta mobilized committee members, went down to the Plan office, and declared that they could either work with her or not in her community at all. In 1988 she described the situation:

> If they don't like the leader, they set up an alternative committee in the same area. They break the power of the existing committee, especially if it is political in nature. I control the committee here; Plan does not control my sector. They are answerable to me. The social workers are paid by Plan, but that does not mean that they can control the committee. I will not allow what happened to Contreras to happen to me. He didn't want to join Plan, so they divided the community by setting up another committee.

Table 5-2 is unique; in it I have summarized from field notes the barrio committee structure in 1992, differentiating between those in alliance with the Frente or with Plan. Of particular significance is how Plan overlaid its "nonpolitical" committees onto the same spatial areas as an existing committee; when leaders were identified as "autocratic" (defined as an unwillingness to cooperate with Plan), alternative committees were established. As Marta mentioned, Guillermo Contreras—president of the committee Vencedores de Manglas and at that time also president of a radical political alliance—declined to affiliate with Plan, even though other people in his neighborhood did. In response, Plan set up a new, alternative committee, Fuerzas Vivas, to cover the households in the exact same spatial area. Further complications arose because Contreras also ran a preschool program recognized by the Ministry of Social Welfare and prevented the new committee from meeting in the local schools, so it had to use a private house. It would seem ironic that while the Ministries of Social Welfare and Health, the formal authorities, continued to work with existing committees, Plan, an outside agency, considered the majority too political and nondemocratic and exercised its informal authority to make a profoundly paternalistic and divisive decision to establish another set of committees in the same area.

Table 5-2 also demonstrates the density of community organizations in Cisne Dos. Of the thirteen committees, twelve were spatially overlapping, resulting in considerable fractionalization. Older committees established along with settlement consolidation in the 1970s still had their original presidents, such as Marta and Don Valdez. They were larger in size, had gone through the process of becoming legal entities (*persona jurídica*) necessary to enter into agreements with government, and were Frente members. In contrast, those set up by Plan

Table 5-2. *Barrio Committees in Cisne Dos in Alliance with the Frente, Plan International, or Both, 1992*[a]

Community committee	President	Year est.	No. of blocks	Area, by street (calle)	PJ	Number of facilities			Frente member	PA	Spatial overlap[b]
						CDC	HC	Health center			
1. Indio Guayas	Marta Perez	1976	30	H→Ñ 25→end	√	1	2	1	√	√	No
2. Defensores del Suburbios[c]	Cecilio Valdez	1974	30	A→H 25→29	√	1	2	1	√	√	Yes (13)
3. Vencedores de Manglas	Guillermo Contreras	1971	n.a.	A→H 17→25	√	2	0	0	√	X	Yes (10)
4. Huerfonitos	Olga Mendoza	1978	24	H→L 12→19	√	1	1	1	√	√	Yes (4, 5)
5. 24 de Mayo	Nicolas Ortiz	1979	19	K→M 25→end	√	1	4	0	√	√	Yes (5, 8)
6. 12 de Marzo	Timoteo Morales	1980	4	N→P 21→23	√	1	0	1	√	√	Yes (9)
7. Huanacapa	Diana Espinoza	1984	n.a.	O→end 17→end	√	1	3	0	√	X	Yes (12)
8. Indio Rumiñahui	Laura Petito	1980	n.a.	K→M 25→end	X	0	0	0	X	X	Yes (5)
9. Colmena I	Maria Jose Mendoza	1983	4	O→end 22→end	X	0	0	0	X	√	Yes (6)
10. Fuerzas Vivas	Marilu Alvarez	1989	54	A→H 17→25	X	0	0	0	X	√	Yes (3)
11. 24 de Marzo	Francesca Hurtado	1991	n.a.	H→LL 12→16	X	0	0	0	X	√	Yes (4)
12. Luchadores del Suburbio	Ladislao Guitierrez	1989	4	O→end 17→end	X	0	0	0	X	√	Yes (7)
13. Unidos Venceremos	Maricarla Toldeo	1989	4	C 26→28	X	0	0	0	X	√	Yes (2)
Total					7	8	12	5		10	12

a. Abbreviations: CDC, community development center; HC, *hogar comunitario*; PJ, *persona jurídica* (legal entity); PA, Plan agreement (*convenio*); √ = yes; X = no.
b. With another committee (number indicates which).
c. Later changed name to Committee Central Cisne Dos.

had constantly rotating presidents, were smaller in size, and were not legal entities, which meant that they joined the established committees when negotiating
legal agreements. They were criticized by more established leaders as "not really
working at the community level" and formed simply to get resources from Plan.
Indeed, Plan's policy of signing separate agreements (*convenios*) with individual
community committees diluted the power of the Frente as a collective negotiating institution—a characteristic critical to its earlier successes.

Imposition of Plan International's Model of Community Participation

By the mid-1980s Plan's model entailed assistance to the godchild and her or his
family along with support to the community.[18] Godchild affiliation criteria were
negotiated with committee presidents, and family participation in the community committee (generally by the mother) was an essential prerequisite. In addition, households were means-tested in order to be defined as needy. In Indio
Guayas, 300 new affiliates joined the committee to qualify for benefits and, in
so doing, agreed to attend committee meetings. Plan's rule required mandatory
twice monthly attendance, with nonattendance used as an indicator that a family "did not want to make the sacrifice." This forced presidents, like Marta, to
take on a more contentious monitoring role, with an increased potential for conflict with her neighbors. My diary for August 14, 1988, recorded the following:

> The weekly Indio Guayas meeting was very well attended with 250,
> mainly women, there. Marta and the Plan social worker greeted people,
> with Marta commenting, "There are people we have never seen before
> because we are signing Plan agreements (convenios) today. If you do not
> come again, the agreements will be cancelled." The process took about
> three hours, with handouts for housing improvements, as this is the next
> phase of Plan's housing project and includes infill, bricks, window frames,
> latrines. These [forms] were signed with individual families for different
> housing infrastructure. Depending on necessity and the condition of the
> house (assessed by the social worker assisted by Marta, Mercedes, and
> daughter Adriana), amounts given ranged from 15,000 to 40,000 sucres.
> The order of priority was first infill for patios, then wooden floors, bricks,
> water tanks, and finally latrines.

As laid out in their Family and Community Development Program (Plan
International Ecuador 1985), Plan signed annual work plan agreements and
associated budgets with each community president and committee. Plan saw
itself as fostering community participation by giving out goods on a "community basis." Did this foster participation, or was it simply a mechanism for facili-

tating mass handouts? In reality, it was very difficult to have a "participatory" event with 250 women, and preexisting trust and cohesion were often undermined as they became co-opted by Plan into "top-down participation as a means to get access to resources." Tensions developed between families, who now saw meeting attendance in handout terms, and leaders, for whom such meetings had been the epicenter of community commitment. Thus Marta commented in 1992, "Before, we had to mobilize, we had to show community involvement. Now they just sit there and expect to be given handouts. Many women see Plan as [a] form of assistance."

Finally, there was the thorny issue of Plan's policy of not paying community leaders. Henry Beder, Plan's salaried director in 1988, stated, "We don't pay leaders. There are three sorts of leaders: altruistic; altruist and personally motivated; and those that are solely personally motivated. But to pay any leader is to open up a can of worms. The best leaders are those who have full-time jobs and do community work in their 'free time'—otherwise they could be looking for a way for being paid."[19]

Instead of paying community leaders, Plan created a budget to pay professionals, such as doctors, engineers, nutritionists, and social promoters to provide technical assistance. Yet the work of the committee president, and one or two of his or her closest collaborators, was full time, and this eventually led to the introduction of informal weekly "quota" fees, paid by community members to the committee as operating costs for getting access to the range of works (obras) handed out by Plan.[20]

To ensure that it did not become a permanent substitute for government, Plan began to implement its exit strategy during the 1990s by leveraging ministries to allocate resources to underfunded sectors, such as heath and education.[21] As Plan arranged tripartite convenios with community organizations and the responsible government department, the workload became even more time consuming for a community organization president.

Between 1985 and 2000, under the direction of Marta and with the enthusiastic (and required) participation of family members in local meetings, Indio Guayas benefited considerably from Plan's support, building human capital as well as physical assets such as housing. Educational investments included educational and vocational courses, the construction and repair of schools, support to government adult literacy programs, school equipment, and didactic materials.[22] It also included health sector investments to construct and equip local clinics, and provide informal training in preventative health for social promoters and community members. The links between upgraded physical infrastructure and health were acknowledged by Plan's involvement in sanitation and water projects as well as those for street and patio infill. Finally, Plan provided crisis-level community social protection through an Emergency Fund, while its Family Development Program included various types of individual child support for education (money for schoolbooks and matriculation fees) and health care, as well as targeted household support for housing improvements (1990–92), water tanks, external latrines, and patio infill (1988–89).

In 2002 Plan's assessment concluded that the suburbios of Guayaquil had moved out of abject poverty, and it recommended that Plan shift its program to poorer rural areas, close its suburbio office in Indio Guayas, cease its work program, and withdraw from its institutional role in the community. This undoubtedly left a big gap, particularly in terms of its social protection assistance, which other organizations could not adequately fill. Coincidentally, the Hospice International health center attached to the San Vicente de Paul Church had also moved to a poorer urban area.[23] The only other support came from the evangelical church on Calle K, which only offered assistance to church members and attendees.[24]

With Plan's departure there was a severe reduction in the functions of the Indio Guayas committee and an associated decline in community trust and cohesion. As the original community members got older, and most infrastructure had been successfully acquired, neighbors closed their doors and increasingly relied more on the support of immediate family than others living nearby. With the settlement now well established, it was difficult to rebuild the solidarity that had existed when community members first arrived. Was this decline in community social capital irreversible, as might be thought? In fact, the high level of community trust and collaboration that quickly emerged in 2004, when a crisis occurred around a local gang killing, demonstrated that social capital was dormant rather than dead (see chapter 11). In addition, with the transnational migration linkages of the next generation, new forms of trust and cohesion developed (see chapter 10). Thus, as with other forms of capital, community social capital was not static but reconstituted itself in new and more relevant ways.

Penetration of Private Sector Health and Educational Facilities into Indio Guayas

Over the thirty-year period, what were the outcomes of these government and INGO health and education programs intended to increase human capital in Indio Guayas? Since no baseline data exist, specific impacts cannot be measured. In addition, over the same period, there was a dramatic influx of private,

The suburbios of Guayaquil: In the early 1970s, settlers, such as those who made Indio Guayas their home, built bamboo structures connected by pathways over the tidal mangrove swamplands in order to acquire a dwelling of their own. Thus began their part in Guayaquil's process of incremental consolidation as shown by this aerial photo (photo, Patrick Crooke).

In Indio Guayas: To escape high rents in Guayaquil's city center, households acquired plots and built split bamboo–walled houses. Here, members of an extended family gathered on the front balcony of their new home in 1978.

Catwalks indicated community cohesion and social capital. A communal catwalk required collaboration between neighboring households. Where such collaboration did not exist, parallel catwalks connected individual houses to the road

Hazardous bamboo and wood catwalks were the main means of circulation around communities for local residents and vendors. Young children were more agile in negotiating dangerous walkways, but everyone was vulnerable if they fell into the water—with a few killed by mangrove spikes.

Above:
Despite the lack of basic facilities such as running water, sanitation, or electricity, a mother along with her children was proud of her most important asset—a four-by-four-meter bamboo home. Propped nearby was her husband's bicycle, of little use now they lived on water; the barrel to the left contained the family's water supply.

Right:
To understand how the people in Indio Guayas coped with life in very basic conditions, in 1978 my family accepted the community leader's invitation to build a bamboo house on her plot. Local children soon made friends with our two sons. The community's acceptance of us was greatly assisted by our living there.

As a wife and mother, I made close friendships with the women, who taught me how they survived, lending me water when my supply ran out. Like my next door neighbor, I washed clothes daily in the extreme heat, drying them above the tidal water.

Cooking on a small kerosene stove in such basic conditions was time consuming and exhausting. Without refrigerators, soups, rice, beans, and occasionally meat had to be cooked daily. This neighbor adorned the split-bamboo wall of the kitchen area in her one-room house with a reproduction of da Vinci's *Last Supper*.

Households "pirated" electricity from the main road connections, running cables for kilometers across the swampland. To ensure the system did not overload, a local committee president climbed to the top of a power pole and turned off the main switch at 7 p.m. each night, returning two hours later to turn it back on.

Above:
Water dominated daily life. Forced to purchase from private "cooperatives" that controlled prices and hours of delivery, households were vulnerable to supply constraints, as vendors suspended distribution during the rainy season. Community members quickly filled their barrels before tankers ran dry.

Right:
Households raised pigs as a "rainy day" fund, selling them off to raise quick cash for emergency expenses relating to illness, imprisonment, or an unexpected death.

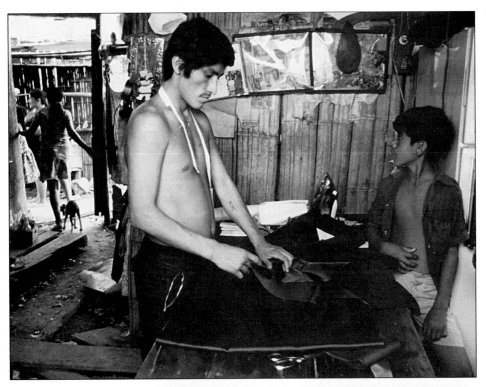

Many local men worked as tailors, making clothes for customers in the community, and as piece-rate outworkers for city center stores. With the family's front room their workshop, and sewing machines an important productive asset, wives and children often helped out.

Washerwomen commonly took in laundry from middle-class households from the other side of the city, leaving their young children locked up while collecting and delivering the laundered goods. Daughters, home from the local primary school, worked alongside their mothers.

Once settled in Indio Guayas, families quickly formed a community committee in order to negotiate the acquisition of neighborhood infrastructure with state, private, and international agencies. With the return of democratically elected government in 1978, the newly formed Izquierda Democrática political party mobilized community members to vote for party candidates with promises to provide basic needs.

Community leaders, both women and men, took active part in any political negotiations that could benefit Indo Guayas, and finally the arrival of in-fill rubble necessary to turn the mangrove swamp into solid land heralded their success. They also remained vigilant to ensure that the community continued to gain what it needed to develop.

As trucks and bulldozers entered Indio Guayas in 1978 to construct the roads, women and children rushed to collect the larger rocks essential for the foundations of the cement houses that would eventually replace bamboo structures

Before we left in 1978, our neighbors wanted a group photo. Their close friendships have continued over the past thirty years during which I have undertaken research in Indio Guayas on ten different occasions

Despite infrastructure improvements, the majority of households continued to live in very basic conditions during the 1970s and 1980s.

Above:
By the 1980s the community committee increasingly focused on social programs such as health care, schooling, and safety net support, negotiating directly with international nongovernmental organizations and United Nations agencies.

Right:
An early success in 1980 was UNICEF's Urban Basic Services program, which included a home-based child care program run by local women caring for up to fifteen children in their houses and courtyards. When the program was handed over to the government ministry in 1986, however, it soon closed because of a lack of resources.

Beginning in 1982 and for twenty-five years the community committee implemented a wide range of programs with financial support from Plan International, including improvements to the community center and the provision of a comprehensive pre-school program. This increased the nutritional and learning capabilities of young children and released mothers from child care responsibilities, giving them the opportunity for paid employment.

Right:
By 2004 Plan International had ceased to provide support to Indio Guayas, and the pre-school program closed, due to lack of government financial support. The community center was emptied and vandalized.

As bamboo walls rapidly deteriorated and houses became an easier target for local thieves, families rebuilt their abodes with cement block and protective window grids. By 1992 the increasing number of second generation households still living with their parents meant building a second floor (see above) or a separate house at the back of the plot (see below).

In 2004 Indio Guayas was no longer a peripheral settlement but well integrated into Guayaquil proper. Increasing differentiation in the housing stock reflected growing inequality. While some households had sufficient income to build upward on the original structure, some neighbors lived in cramped single-story houses.

Local women, many by now grandmothers, continued to buy daily from street vendors selling fresh fruit and vegetables. Such vendors had always ventured into the Indio Guayas community, even when relying on catwalks.

In 2004 five second generation sisters, and their children, still lived either on their mother's plot or nearby with in-laws, or as renters. Their trust supported complex reciprocities around the organization of child care, cooking responsibilities, and local employment.

A proud daughter, owner of a modern kitchen, has running water, a modern stove, and a refrigerator—a world away from the cooking conditions experienced by her mother when she first arrived in Indio Guayas in 1978.

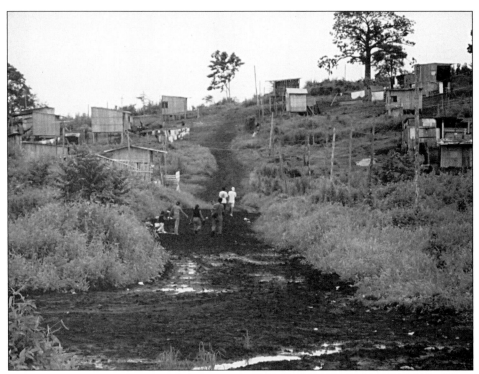

By 2004, with insufficient room for all second generation households to remain with their parents, some children acquired their own plots on Guayaquil's new periphery, its northern hills. There, mud roads, rather than mangrove swamps, presented different challenges relating to settlement consolidation.

Repeating their parents' experience, sons and daughters and their young families built and lived in small split bamboo–walled houses in very basic conditions without running water, electricity, or sanitation.

for-profit health and education services that accompanied settlement consolidation and growing demand. In fact, public sector services, such as the principal local hospital, had never been entirely free, as I documented in my diary the fateful night of the 1977 fire:

> [December 23, 1977] When Lidia's house caught fire and three children were burnt, we rushed to the Hospital de Suburbio. After ten minutes a nurse took the crying, shivering girls, in a state of shock, to be showered. When the doctor finally appeared, he said Danilo must be taken to the fifth floor operating theater. The lifts were not working so could we carry him up? Mercedes, Marta, and I plus about four other men carried him on a stretcher up staircase after dusty, dirty staircase. The doctor instructed Lidia to buy two pairs of gloves at the all-night pharmacy. On her return the surgeon demanded she pay him his fee of 300 sucres, commenting, "We also have to live." Then Mercedes and I rushed off to buy tetanus injections so the nurse could give them to the girls.

The presence of private health sector services began with small over-the-counter pharmacies. However, with the arrival of infill came an influx of doctors, followed by dentists. By 1992, within a seventeen-block area, there were five doctors, five dental practices, one medical laboratory, nine pharmacies giving diagnosis over the counter, and two nurses giving injections and administering rehydration fluids.[25] The numbers of service providers remained the same through the 1990s, reflecting saturation in demand. In addition, there were a range of traditional medicine providers, including traditional birth attendants that catered to women who preferred home births to hospital deliveries (despite Ministry of Health disapproval). There were also women curers (*curanderas*), who filled the demand for traditional remedies, which arose in part as a response to the poor quality of state services and the increasing cost of medicines. Technically illegal, curanderas worked in great secrecy and often combined this practice with traditional midwifery.[26]

Over the three decades, the quantity and quality of educational facilities in Cisne Dos also increased considerably, but as with health services, this expansion occurred in the private education sector. The 1992 community survey showed that households used thirty-nine different preschool, primary, and secondary schools; most were within Indio Guayas, but a number were elsewhere. These schools differed in terms of ownership, fee structure, number of shifts, average class sizes, and availability of services and programs, but they were split more or less evenly between state and private schools.[27] While preschools and primary schools had one shift per day, secondary schools had up to three shifts.

Multigrade teaching was common, especially in the state primary schools. Data from the panel survey show an overall shift from state to private schooling, reflecting changes in parents' educational choices for their children. In 1978 all children attended state-run schools, a figure that had fallen to 75 percent in 1992 and declined further to 66 percent by 2004.

Disaggregating by schooling level, in 1992 almost 78 percent of primary school children attended state schools; by 2004 that proportion had dropped to 67.7 percent. However, this trend reversed at the secondary level, where the proportion of children attending state schools rose from 59.1 percent in 1992 to 91.7 percent in 2004. This pattern reflected both parental recognition of the critical importance of early childhood educational development as well as parental inability to pay the increased fees and transport costs associated with secondary schools located in other parts of the city. Over the 1978–2004 period, there was also a major increase in morning shift attendance and a corresponding decline in the uptake of afternoon and evening school shifts. In 1992 just under half of schoolchildren attended the morning shift, whereas by 2004 this had risen to nearly four out of five children. Even in 1992 the 15 percent of students attending the evening shift were more likely to be boys than girls, and by 2004, because of increased insecurity associated with traveling at night as well as an assessment that evening classes were of limited educational value, evening school attendance had declined to only 3.6 percent.

Accumulation of Human Capital in Indio Guayas

Both direct and indirect measurements show a deep concern with investment in human capital. To what extent did the community's commitment to gaining health and educational services succeed in improving these assets in this consolidating population?

Longitudinal Health Status

In the absence of longitudinal health status panel data, health-related environmental indicators provide some idea of the changes experienced. Of greatest importance was the installation of toilets: in 1978 more than half of households (58.8 percent) used a hole (*hueco*) in the floor over the water while the rest (41.2 percent) used a very basic latrine. By 1992 over a third of households (37 percent) had progressed to using a toilet connected to a septic tank while the remainder were evenly divided between using a hueco or an outdoor latrine (31.5 percent in each case). By 2004 the vast majority (80.5 percent) had septic tanks, many as a result of the Plan project. At the extremes, 2 percent were still using a hueco while 4 percent were hooked up to the city's sewage system and the rest (14.5 percent) relied on latrines.

Garbage collection also can be used as a health indicator. In 1978, when living in Indio Guayas, we incinerated rubbish nightly in a tin can, to our neighbors' amusement. Laughingly they would say, "All rubbish makes good infill," as they chucked all their garbage into their cesspit water-filled patios. However, by 1992, as a direct result of a cholera outbreak, organized rubbish collection was initiated. Municipal authorities first took responsibility but later transferred it to a national-level agency through an agreement between the Ministry of Social Welfare, the Commission of Transport, and the army. In 1992 approximately one-quarter of households had their rubbish collected at no cost; most others either still dumped it or burned it at night in front of their houses. But by 2004 rubbish collection was outsourced to a private contractor, collecting from designated locations on Calle 25, with payment collected through a charge on electricity bills.[28]

A second set of indicators relates to the demand for health services. Panel data from 1992 and 2004 recorded whether treatment from any type of provider had been sought the last time an adult or a child had been sick. These data showed an increase in the percentage of children being taken for treatment, from 63 percent in 1992 to 75 percent in 2004. In contrast, the number of adults seeking treatment declined, from 84 percent in 1992 to 73 percent in 2004.

Where did households get their treatment? Health provider data showed that in 1992 the private sector supplied roughly half of the health care, with 60 percent of adults and half of children consulting private doctors either inside or outside the community. A preference for private sector health care resulted from perceived differences in service quality. Provider choice did not entirely depend on income since free or subsidized health care still entailed indirect costs, such as transportation and wages sacrificed while waiting in line.[29] The choice of private health care practices related not only to the more diverse services offered but also to the availability of credit, short waiting times, and flexible hours. Although public hospitals were free, they were characterized by declining resources and infrastructure, long waiting times, and limited night access.[30]

However, by 2004 two-thirds of children and over half of adults used public health services. By this time, many older adults had serious medical problems such as diabetes, poor circulation requiring amputation, tumors, and prostate problems. Such serious conditions required public hospitals since local private doctors could not treat them, or if they could, it was too expensive.[31] Even so, since state health services had become semiprivatized by 2004, costs for health care in the public sector, such as medications and surgery, had become a big drain on household resources. Thus, while in 1992 child health care (both private and public) cost an average of $8.16 per consultation (including medication), by 2004 it cost $45.40. For adults the amount increased even more steeply, from an average of $11.76 in 1992 to $107.16 in 2004; the latter figure was heavily weighted by the increasing number of serious operations costing over $1,000. There was a direct correlation between poverty levels and the decision to use public rather than private care; very poor households used public health care services more heavily than the poor and nonpoor, and were less likely to seek any treatment due to their lack of resources.[32]

Comparative Intergenerational Educational Attainment and Its Links to Poverty Reduction

Few of the first generation continued their education once they had moved to Indio Guayas. The educational attainment of household heads was one of the factors that influenced household poverty levels. For instance, the 1992 survey data showed that the lower the educational level of the household head, the greater the likelihood that the household was living in poverty. Indeed, over 90 percent of heads with incomplete primary education were associated with poor or very poor households, whereas 63 percent of heads with completed secondary education were associated with nonpoor households. Female heads of household were more likely to have incomplete primary education while male heads tended to have some secondary education.

At the same time, the longitudinal panel data show that one of the most important investments households made was in the education of their children. Did this translate into increased human capital? The comparative educational levels of parents and children as of 2004 suggest that it did: second-generation children achieved much higher average educational levels than did their parents (table 5-3). While only two out of three (66 percent) fathers and just over half (51 percent) of mothers completed at least primary school, 94 percent of their children did; and while only 3.3 percent of fathers and 7 percent of mothers completed at least secondary school, over 46 percent of their children reached this level. In fact, one in ten children acquired at least some post–secondary school education. Gender-differentiated data show that sisters outachieved their brothers at both the secondary and graduate level.

To achieve such extraordinary educational outcomes, households made considerable sacrifices to get their children the best education possible. The 1992 data again are illustrative, since more parents had school-age children at that time than they did in 2004. Education was the single largest category of service

Table 5-3. *Highest Education Completed by Adult Children and Their Parents, Indio Guayas, 2004*[a]

Level of education	Father		Mother		Son		Daughter		All children	
	N	*Percent*	N	*Percent*	N	*Percent*	N	*Percent*	N	*Percent*
Illiterate	3	10.0	9	20.9	0	0	0	0	0	0
Some primary	5	16.7	8	18.6	9	10.0	1	1.5	10	6.4
Completed primary	20	66.7	22	51.2	35	38.9	22	32.8	57	36.3
Completed high school or technical degree	1	3.3	3	7.0	39	43.3	34	50.8	73	46.5
Postsecondary	1	3.3	1	2.3	7	7.8	10	14.9	17	10.8
Total	30	100	43	100	90	100	67	100	157	100

a. "Adult children" are age sixteen and older.

expenditures; over one-quarter of service expenditures was on books, followed by almost one-fifth on uniforms and transportation. Female-headed households relied less on public education than male-headed ones (70 percent versus 81 percent, respectively). Although expenditure on education was similar across poverty groups, it was a heavier burden on poor and very poor households because they usually had more dependents.[33] Poor households compensated by paying less per student for fees, books, uniforms, and other expenses.

The Econometrics of Human Capital as an Asset

Human capital assets are individual investments in education, health, and nutrition that determine a person's ability to work and maximize the returns from his or her labor. As mentioned above, since education is the only category in the human capital asset index, it only provides a partial picture.[34] In measurement terms, it presents a particular challenge, as elaborated in appendix C. The results shown in appendix table C-4 indicate that there was very little difference in the value of being illiterate, having some primary education, or having completed primary school in 1978, with these educational groups accounting for almost 90 percent of the young Indio Guayas population. Over time, however, illiteracy or failure to complete primary schooling became a significant economic drag because these people earned lower wages. Meanwhile, the macroeconomic shock

Figure 5-1. *Trade-off between Household Consumption in 1992 and Market Value of Children's Education in 2004*[a]

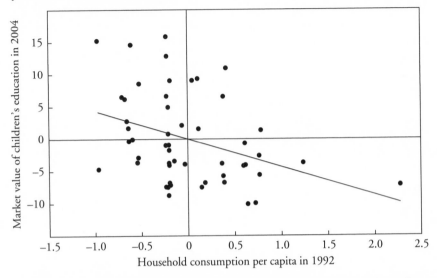

a. The regression of 2004 education on 1992 household consumption is statistically significant at the 95 percent confidence level. Household per capita ownership of consumption goods is measured using the household consumption asset index, adjusted for income by regressing the consumption index on household real income and using the residuals. The market value of the children's education is measured as the residuals from a regression of educational attainment on household real income.

of 1992 was such that wages decreased across every educational group, which explains the across-the-board decline in value for that year (see table C-4).

Finally, the education data show that individual households made portfolio choices between investing in consumer durables or education for their children. A regression of the amount of education that a household's children had completed by 2004 against the level of consumer durables acquired in 1992 revealed a negative, statistically significant relationship (see figure 5-1).[35] In other words, households that invested more in their children's education purchased fewer consumer durables. This negative relationship is even stronger when the income level of the household is factored in because poorer households had less ability to invest in both simultaneously and therefore had to make more difficult choices.[36]

On Calle K it was not just the wealthier households that invested in human capital. Alicia, for instance, went to considerable lengths to give her nine children some education, despite her single parent status, meager earnings as a washerwoman, and the fact that, in income and overall asset terms, she was always very poor. While two of her nine children completed high school, a further two completed fifth grade, one of whom went on to do a nursing course, qualifying her to work in the local clinic.

But did this education help them get better jobs? Were expectations about investing in education in order to get ahead realized? These are critical questions underpinning prevailing development thinking. To address these questions the following chapter examines the changing employment and income-generating opportunities over the twenty-six-year period.

6

Earning a Living or Getting By: Labor as an Asset

"To be honest, I can make enough for food by making trousers . . . but one wasn't born to do just one job. One has to change and do different types of work. I don't enjoy sitting here all day. I get tired of it. I finish this, iron it, go to the center; I pick up the rest of the work, come back and sew again. It's a living but I decided to try another job. I took up dentistry; I have only done it for a few months. In the country you can find more clients because the doctors don't go there.[1] But, I am illegal. I do it because I want to do it well. That's why I have clients. But no law covers me. Before I had absolutely nothing, but now I am rising out of poverty. If God helps me, I want to go to school to see if I have it in me to study. I work 'empirically,' of course, since dental mechanics is an art, but one is competent to go on studying. My aspiration is to make teeth and to go on studying, and in ten or twelve years, to put a sign on my door that says 'Dr. So-and-So,' and to be able to work on my own, so that no authority can say, 'You are not authorized to put that up.'"

—Claudio

Claudio, a tailor, lived with his wife, Mercedes, and two young children directly across the walkway from Marta. As an "artisan producer" Claudio made trousers for local community members while augmenting his income as a "subcontracted outworker" for a city center shop. However, as he described above, in 1978 he decided to diversify his income-earning activities. His confidence about the future was typical of many young men who in 1978 had settled in the suburbios to seek a better life.

To rectify his illegal situation, and improve both income and status, Claudio entered night school in 1980, and by 1984 he had completed high school and gained his dental mechanics diploma. Not content with this, in 1987 he entered the University of Guayaquil to study for a dentistry degree. Since a night school program did not exist, he changed jobs, and with Marta's help worked as a community promoter in the UNICEF preschool program. But financial problems soon developed due to the low stipend paid and the increased competition from young qualified dentists all vying for business in Cisne Dos in the early 1990s. Despite the contribution from Mercedes' stipend running a home crèche (*hogar comunitario*) at the time (described in chapter 5), after two years he was forced to drop out of the university. To earn sufficient income to pay his children's escalating high school expenses, he took a full-time job as a ticket collector at the city's bus terminal. By 2004 he was back working as a dental mechanic, commuting between Indio Guayas and a downriver island, two hours by boat from Guayaquil, where he had built up a regular clientele and had a small clinic.

Abandoning his aspirations to get a dental degree, Claudio transferred his ambitions to his son, Frank. In 1992 Frank completed high school and, as his father before him, enrolled at the University of Guayaquil. Despite free tuition, the costs of equipment and other necessities were astronomical, with a quarter of household income allocated to educational expenses. Frank graduated after his rural service in 2002; there he met his future wife, and together they migrated to Spain. But Frank soon returned to Ecuador and by 2004 was working as a qualified dentist in a rural area in Manabí; he did not have the necessary capital assets—both financial and social—to build up a practice in Guayaquil. The extraordinary, poignant story of Claudio's employment history illustrates many of the issues that men and women confronted over thirty years in Cisne Dos, not only in struggling to get a good job but also in trying to improve their social status. Claudio came from rural Guayas, where his father was an agricultural worker, and by any measure he has "done well." Yet by 2004 he was a disappointed man; his ingenuity, ambition, and incredibly hard work had got the family a long way, but in his words this had not been sufficient to "make it."

This chapter describes the changing employment situation in Indio Guayas between 1978 and 2004, during which both internal life cycle factors, such as increased female and second-generation labor force participation, as well as external factors relating to the casualization of labor and the growing importance of remittances influenced financial-productive capital assets in households.[2] Chapter 9 further explores the implications of changing intergenerational opportunities and aspirations, including the upward mobility of sons, such as Frank, while chapter 10 continues the story of the next generation through the experiences of Frank's peers who, unlike him, remained as migrants in Spain, particularly in Barcelona.

Financial-productive capital derived primarily from work, whether formal sector wage employment, casual work, or informal sector activities (both waged and self-employed), is at the heart of household well-being, with labor often identified as the poor's most valuable asset (Moser 1998).[3] Yet at the macrolevel, rigorous analysis of the linkage between employment, economic growth, and poverty reduction appears to be missing (Islam 2004). As de Haan (2006) has aptly commented, the Millennium Development Goals include no meaningful reference to labor or employment, and when compared to the attention that has been paid to poverty data, employment data and the role of economic productivity in urban growth has been largely neglected. This may not be surprising given the problems with generating robust labor market trend data at the city level, as well as the methodological and definitional problems associated with the issue of employment.

In this complex context, one of the biggest challenges in this longitudinal study was, in fact, to include labor as an asset, something omitted thus far in research on asset indexes. To go beyond income data used in the poverty studies and measure the monetary resources available to households required the identification of index components for financial-productive capital. As described in appendix C, based on the panel data available, the asset index identified three components as composite labor asset indicators: employment security, transfer-rental income as nonearned monetary resources, and productive durables, which were goods with an income-generating capability. Each of these is discussed in this chapter.

Equally limited in terms of robustness is background empirical data on the changing labor market in Ecuador, let alone at the city level of Guayaquil. Such limitations, along with a sample that is representative at the Indio Guayas level rather than citywide, suggest that the comparative advantage of this study lies in a better microlevel understanding of male and female employment choices, and the associated socioeconomic mobility over the thirty-year period. Therefore, by way of background, this chapter describes quantitative panel data changes in the economically active population in Indio Guayas. Since panel data dates broadly coincide with changes in the wider economic context, each section focuses on economic activities that were of particular importance at that point in time, contextualized within the broader employment situation. While in 1978 informal sector differentiation was the dominant trend in Indio Guayas, by 1992 it was labor market intensification and casualization; finally, in 2004 income diversification and the consequences of privatization predominated. The labor market gender segmentation plays a role throughout.

Overall Trends of the Economically Active Population

The economically active population in Indio Guayas comprised all adults sixteen years of age and older who were working or actively seeking work.[4] The economically inactive group comprised all adults who were not actively seeking work, including housewives, the elderly, students, and the sick.[5] Overall employment rates in Indio Guayas were consistently higher for men than women, with three quarters or more always involved in an income-generating activity. However, rates declined steadily over the 1978–2004 period, from 84.9 percent in 1978 to 75.9 percent in 1992 and 74.8 percent in 2004. For women the overall employment rate was significantly lower than that for men, at just over a third, taking into account all female household members. However, the trend differs from that for men; the percentage of women working increased by about 27 percent between 1978 and 1992 (from 34.6 percent to 43.8 percent economically active, respectively) but then dropped back to roughly the 1978 level by 2004 (36.5 percent).

These trends were broadly reflected in Ecuador at both the national and urban level over a thirty-year period (see appendix B). The economic liberalization of the 1980s included greater labor flexibility, resulting in long-term increases in unemployment and underemployment.[6] The urban labor market was also affected by the 1998–99 economic crisis and the ensuing economic and labor reforms (Sánchez-Paramo 2005; World Bank 2004). After 2000 the country's economic recovery related mainly to increased oil exports and improved prices as well as migrant remittances. However, the type of economic growth experienced recently did not mitigate the high rates of unemployment and informal employment in the three main cities of Cuenca, Quito, and Guayaquil, with Guayaquil persistently reporting the highest unemployment rates.[7]

In addition, Guayaquil was more vulnerable to external shocks than were the other two cities; these included the El Niño floods of 1998, a decline in the construction sector, the banking crisis of 1999, and low industrial competitiveness with exports.[8] Guayaquil also had lower rates of migration abroad and associated remittance flows than cities such as Cuenca. Above all, there were serious structural problems in the Guayaquil labor market; six out of ten workers were underemployed in 2005 (Cadena and López 2005).

At the national level over the past two decades, the proportion of women in the economically active population grew, partly because of cultural changes and improvements in female education levels, but also as a family strategy to improve living standards. However, women were affected differently by rising rates of unemployment and underemployment. Despite their lower levels of participation in the labor market, they were a majority of the unemployed and disproportionally represented in informal employment.[9]

The decline in real incomes also affected women more than men. Real wages experienced positive growth from 1994 and peaked in 1996. A sharp decline followed the 1999 crisis (because of rising prices), with a subsequent recovery and another peak in 2005.[10] This trend was reflected locally in Indio Guayas where female participation rates were also affected by internal factors such as gender relationships, the presence or absence of a spouse, the earning power of other household workers, and the extent to which a woman's economic participation was necessary to provide a "family wage."[11] (Factors such as the family life cycle and changes in household composition are further elaborated in chapters 7 and 8).

The average age of the first-generation Indio Guayas labor force changed between 1978 and 2004, along with the life cycle: the mean age of first-generation male workers increased from thirty-three to fifty-seven years, while among first-generation female workers, the mean age increased from thirty-two to fifty-five years. However, the large number of second-generation workers still remaining on the family plot meant that the age of the entire working population increased less than might have been anticipated. Between 1978 and 2004, the mean age of the total Indio Guayas male labor force increased from thirty to thirty-six years, while for female workers the increase was from thirty to forty-one years over the same period.

Table 6-1, which presents the overall employment trends in terms of the Standard Industrial Classification, shows the shifts in economic activities between 1978 and 2004 for males and females in the panel data.[12] (The second generation living off the family plot in 2004 is discussed in chapter 9). The trends reflect changing employment opportunities relating to external economic transformations as traditional sectors declined and new ones opened up. For men the construction sector remained the most stable, employing one in five throughout the twenty-six years between 1978 and 2004. Male employment in transportation dipped slightly in 1992, but in 2004 it had rebounded above the 1978 level. Retail trade and public administration experienced the greatest decline. Finally, the service sector saw a steady growth, almost doubling in the twelve years between 1992 and 2004.

Table 6-1. *Male and Female Employment in Indio Guayas, by Standard Industrial Classification, 1978–2004*[a]

Percent

Classification	1978			1992			2004		
	Male	Female	All	Male	Female	All	Male	Female	All
Agriculture, forestry, fishing	4.4	0	3.2	0	0	0	0	0	0
Mining	0	0	0	2.4	0	1.6	0	0	0
Construction	20.0	0	14.3	20.7	0	13.5	22.8	0	15.7
Manufacturing	31.1	27.8	30.2	29.3	10.9	22.7	23.8	10.8	19.7
Transportation, communications	13.3	0	9.5	12.2	0	7.8	13.9	0	9.5
Retail trade	20.0	44.4	27.0	19.5	32.6	24.4	13.9	37.0	21.1
Services	4.5	27.8	11.1	13.4	56.5	28.9	24.6	47.8	32.0
Public administration	6.7	0	4.7	2.5	0	1.6	1.0	4.4	2.0
Total	100	100	100	100	100	100	100	100	100
Sample size	45	18	63	82	46	128	101	46	147

a. For information on the Standard Industrial Classification, see U.S. Census Bureau, "North American Industry Classification System (NAICS)" (www.census.gov/eos/www/naics).

For women the most important changes occurred between 1978 and 1992, after which the employment sectors remained more or less stable. Most dramatic was the decline in manufacturing jobs for women between 1978 and 1992. Employment in retailing also declined between 1978 and 1992, then stabilized with a little over one in three women finding employment in this sector in 2004. In contrast, the service sector increasingly employed women; the ratio grew from a little over one in four women in 1978, to about one in two in 1992, and remained at roughly the same level in 2004.

Complementing the employment data are data for average monthly wage and nonwage income data, shown in table 6-2. Again these data are specific to Indio Guayas and not representative of either the Guayaquil or Ecuadorian labor markets. The overall trend for both male and female monthly earnings shows a decline between 1978 and 1992, a microlevel situation very much reflecting the economic crisis experienced at the time (see appendix B). Although by 2004 earnings had picked up again, they had still not returned to 1978 levels. Labor income halved between 1997 and 1999, and then recovered by about 40 percent during 2000–02 due to price stabilization (World Bank 2004).

Table 6-2. *Average Monthly Wage or Nonwage Income, by Sector and Gender,*
Indio Guayas, 1978–2004
1992 adjusted U.S. dollars

	1978			1992			2004		
Classification	Male	Female	All	Male	Female	All	Male	Female	All
Agriculture, forestry, fishing	65.5	0	65.5	0	0	0	0	0	0
Mining	0	0	0	107.9	0	107.9	0	0	0
Construction	145.1	0	145.1	93.1	0	93.1	117.3	0	117.3
Manufacturing	121.8	29.1	115.6	79.5	54.0	75.7	113.0	163.0	115.8
Transportation, communications	187.3	0	187.3	96.0	0.0	96.0	141.9	0.0	141.9
Retail trade	131.3	73.9	108.4	83.7	75.1	80.2	95.2	68.6	81.0
Services	108.4	49.5	66.3	79.5	75.1	50.9	91.8	80.6	86.5
Public administration	100.6	0.0	100.6	54.0	0.0	54.0	174.7	174.7	174.7
All sectors	132.6	60.0	117.3	85.3	50.0	73.6	110.2	82.6	101.6
Sample size (number)	45	12	57	81	40	121	86	39	125

Gender disaggregation shows that throughout the 1978–2004 period, women's earnings were lower than those of men; in general, they did not fall as dramatically between 1978 and 1992, nor did they recover as much as those of men. In contrast to the overall trends, women's earnings in three of the four labor classifications increased throughout the period, and in the case of the retail trade sector, they increased (though not very significantly) between 1978 and 1992, and then dipped slightly by 2004.

Changing Opportunities in Wage Work and Income-Generating Activities in Indio Guayas, 1978–2004

Behind this brief descriptive trend analysis is a far more intricate picture. The rest of this chapter seeks to capture this complexity through the narratives of men and women in Indio Guayas, describing the constraints and opportunities they confronted at different time periods in diverse sectors of the local labor market.

1978: Work Optimism in a Buoyant Macroeconomic Context

Although the 1970s produced a period of national economic growth linked to the first oil boom and rapid urbanization linked to increasing rural-urban migration, Ecuador's level of industrial activity was nevertheless relatively low by Latin

American standards. The manufacturing sector was driven largely by domestic demand rather than by exports, and was based on capital-intensive production with little employment creation capacity, such that the national manufacturing sector provided only around 11 percent of employment during this period. It was the service sector, therefore, that absorbed the largest proportion of the labor force, employing almost one-quarter of the total labor force by the mid-1980s (Floro and Acosta 1993). The informal economy was a particularly important part of the growth in services, characterized as "picking up the slack" (Milkman 1976), especially in urban areas where annual population growth rates were around 7 percent for three decades from the 1970s to 1990s. More than half the workers within the informal sector were self-employed, mainly in trade, artisan production, and construction activities (Floro and Acosta 1993, pp. 11–12).[13]

In 1978 Indio Guayas's young working population reflected the lower end of unskilled labor and excluded the professional and managerial classes as well as the white- and blue-collar workers. These microlevel characteristics were similar to those at the national urban level, as Bromley (1977) noted: "The blue-collar proletariat makes up under 5 percent of the urban economically-active population in Ecuador. Much more important is the sub-proletariat that make up over 75 percent of the urban economically active population . . . a diverse group of small scale artisans, traders, transporters and repairers, and of workers in personal and domestic service" (p. 421).

PREDOMINANCE OF THE INFORMAL SECTOR: GENDER-BASED COMPETITION AND PROTECTION. In Indio Guayas the economic outcome of moving to the suburbios for this young, largely unskilled workforce was its impact on informal sector activities. Indeed, the debate about the informal sector that dominated the labor market literature in the 1970s highlighted two issues relevant to Indio Guayas: first, whether a dualist formal-informal division between two separate sectors was useful, or whether it was more appropriate to consider them as part of a continuum of economic activities; second, the extent to which the informal sector generated growth in its own right or was dependent on the formal sector, with structural inequalities in terms of access to raw materials and markets impeding its growth (Bromley and Gerry 1979; Moser 1978; Scott 1979). Results from Indio Guayas during the 1970s contributed to this debate by demonstrating that it was more accurate to identify a continuum of income-generating activities rather than two separate sectors. In addition, the data showed that while for a few the informal sector provided a more profitable source of income than formal sector wage employment, for the majority it was a highly competitive sector characterized by small-scale enterprises producing petty commodities, and underpaid and irregular casual residual work (Moser 1981, 1984).

Recognition of the importance of the informal sector as the primary income source for most of the active labor force also raised questions about gender-based competition within the sector. Here feminist perspectives on labor market research highlighted the way asymmetrical gender relations, which tended to be masked ideologically, meant that in some sectors there was unequal competitive pressure between men and women, as well as the "masculinization" of tradition-ally female work areas. However, in other sectors where existing gender divisions of labor were rigid, this created inflexibility in the labor market, with so-called "women's work" protected (Himmelweit and Mohun 1977; Molyneux 1978). As part of another important labor market debate, this was reflected in my analysis. In 1978, as in later periods, when only a small percentage of the active labor force was absorbed into the stable wage sector, the majority of all workers were involved in a wide range of informal sector activities, including productive work such as tailoring or dressmaking, service sector work in domestic service, and distributive sector marketing activities. The level of competition between men and women varied depending on the activity, as the following section illustrates.

DOMESTIC SERVICE LIFE CYCLE. In Indio Guayas domestic service was "women's work," which meant this was a protected area where men did not sub-stitute for women, a characteristic that still applies in Guayaquil, though not in Barcelona (see chapter 10). Different stages of domestic service were associated with a woman's life cycle, making it useful to identify a continuum of activities rather than a clear-cut division between wage employment and self-employment. Young women without dependents might aspire to factory or shop work but mainly found work as waged domestic servants, conforming to Smith's seminal Latin American domestic service model (Smith 1973).[14] They were uniform clad, lived in during the week, and received a weekly wage. The surplus of unem-ployed, unskilled women meant many middle-class families could afford up to three or four domestic servants, with a strict division of labor and related wage differentials between nannies, cooks, and general housemaids, with the least skilled laundry work at the bottom of the pay scale.[15]

Women with dependents found their options more limited. With nonresi-dential work difficult to accommodate, the numbers who worked at this stage in their life cycle were small. While childbearing and -rearing responsibilities were the reason for their initial withdrawal from the labor force, this decision was often reinforced by the dominant male ideology emphasizing women's domestic role. Those who reentered the labor force did so for economic reasons, with their marital status a crucial determinant. Women within a stable, committed relationship (*compromiso*) worked either to supplement their spouse's inadequate earnings or as the primary breadwinner when spouses were out of work. Since so much male work was contract based or cyclical, women frequently "dovetailed" their work, for example, picking up and dropping laundering jobs, in direct relation to their husband's state of unemployment and employment.[16]

Married women, such as Jessica, constantly remarked, "My husband doesn't like me working, but he has to tolerate it until something comes up." In general, men did not undertake domestic tasks, even when not working, with women assuming the double burden of productive and domestic work (Elson 1991). Their ability to do so depended on female kin, friends, or children old enough to take on related child care responsibilities, as well as on access to adequate infrastructure, particularly domestic water supply. Commenting on the situation when she first arrived in Indio Guayas in 1978, Aida remarked, "Of course, in the Center I used to work doing laundry. But I do not do that now here on account of the water. I have an electric iron, but now I cannot use it because of the light. I have worked all my life. I worked in Urdesa with U.S. foreigners [gringos]. Now I am more dependent on my husband, who hawks toilet rolls around the middle-class areas."

When men were earning well, their spouses tended not to enter domestic work; it was often those women whose relationships had partially or totally broken down that were forced to look for paid work. Claudio, while commenting on the change in his neighbor Carmen's situation, generically remarked, "When a woman goes into laundry, you know there is something wrong."

Carmen's husband, Alonso, was a construction worker, and at the time the couple had three daughters. Local gossip maintained that Alonso's disappointment at having only daughters had led him to set up with a second partner, who bore him three sons and lived in a house located a few streets away. For Carmen this was distressing; not only was she determined to keep bearing children until she gave Alonso a son, but she had to endure stigma and gossip. Above all, she was not able to survive economically because Alonso made very little financial contribution to the household. With no other option, Carmen took up laundering, the most desperately exploitative work, which involved locking up her children, traveling across town to collect laundry from a middle-class household, bringing it home to wash, and then repeating the journey to return the laundered goods. As a washerwoman she was paid a piece rate rather than a fixed income. Washing in her house, with water delivered by the local tankers, she used her own charcoal-filled iron to complete the work. The unreliability of tanker water delivery had a crucial impact on her reputation for dependability.[17]

Over time, in such a hot sticky climate as Indio Guayas, where washing was a very onerous activity, those with sufficient income began to pay neighbors meager piece rates for washing their clothes. This was a conscious strategy,

Table 6-3. *Retail Selling Activities in Indio Guayas, 1978*
Number

Location of seller	Type	Women	Men
Mobile	Cooked food	1	10
	Uncooked food	1	4
	Other	1	8
Shop in home	Cooked food	6	1
	Uncooked food	17	2
	Other	1	2
Shop outside home	Cooked food	4	3
	Uncooked food	2	5
	Other	1	2
Total		34	37

particularly to help young or single mothers avoid work across town, or to support older relatives, which created hierarchical social relations both within the community and indeed families.

RETAIL SELLING ACTIVITIES. Retail selling was another important livelihood activity, varying not only in terms of what was sold (cooked food, uncooked food, and other durables) but also where it was sold (front room shop, a fixed location outside the home, or mobile selling). Both men and women were involved, and as shown in table 6-3, this was a highly competitive sector. Women predominated in running front room shops, since the enterprise's location meant they could engage in retail while minding their children and doing housework. Start-up capital varied depending on the scale of the enterprise and came from savings, spouses, or other kin. But competition was ruthless, with such enterprises opening and closing with great rapidity, and women without particular skills frequently became insolvent.

Larger in scale were the "corner" shops, selling both durable staples and fruit and vegetables, with higher turnover and income because of their reliability and more standardized prices. These required more start-up capital, tended to be owned by men, survived over the longer term, and were operated mainly as household enterprises. On the corner of Calle K and Calle 26, for instance, was Don Nicanor's shop, where I shopped daily when living in Indio Guayas. While he bought wholesale at the city center, his wife Haydee ran the shop, assisted in peak periods by her children. Corner shops were not seen as "men's work," and indeed Haydee took over the shop when her husband went off with another woman in 2000. By contrast, bar ownership was largely a male domain because of its association with drinking and prostitution. A few older women, such as Lola, one of the few Afro-Ecuadorians in the community, ran dubious bars reputedly providing alcohol and marijuana, and did so with widespread neighborhood disapproval.

The third group of retailers consisted of "mobile" vendors (*ambulantes*), selling clothing, kitchen goods, and fresh food such as fish, as well as cooked foods. Because it was difficult for women to combine child care with such activities, mobile sellers were mainly men. However, this gender bias was also legitimized in ideological terms; the fact that "going in the street" was associated with prostitution allowed men, operating in a competitive situation, to restrict if not effectively exclude women by defining space in gendered terms. Consigned to operating fixed-location enterprises, women were exposed to the uncontrollable competition of neighbors, whereas male mobile sellers had the advantage of alternative selling locations.

The competitive relationship between men and women was most acute in cooked food sales, traditionally a female occupation that had become "masculinized" when it became an important source of income. Widespread demand was related to the lack of reliable electricity, which meant that cooking was very time consuming, as well as to the numbers of bachelors who invariably did not cook. When food was sold freshly cooked, such as fried fish or bananas, the fixed stall was usually operated by a woman. In contrast, when cooked food was prepared in advance, the woman cooked it at home, and the man sold it at his stall or on the street corner. In such cases, the woman's unwaged labor was generally not perceived by her as work. Sellers of marinated fish (*ceviche*), such as the Martinez family living on Calle L, successfully operated such an enterprise with the highly structured household division of labor this onerous profession required. At 1 a.m. each day, Nestor and his son Hernan went to the city center wholesale market to buy the fish; upon their return, Nestor woke his wife Eliana, and she cooked and marinated the fish between 2 a.m. and 5 a.m. while the men returned to sleep. Later the men awoke and sold the ceviche on street corners to workers en route into the city, while Eliana started her daily domestic duties. The whole process was repeated in the afternoon to sell to a second daily market, those workers returning home.

DRESSMAKERS AND TAILORS. Women were dressmakers, artisans who sewed dresses, skirts, and blouses on demand for local women and children, with the customer providing the material. They worked independently, relying only occasionally on the assistance of children. Tailors were all men and, like Claudio, were primarily "outworkers" (home-based piece rate workers) for large-scale workshops in the city center, sewing cut fabric into trousers and occasionally jackets. They also worked locally making articles to specific order, although for most this was a secondary income source. Initially, many tailors were anxious about moving out to the city's edge, as Marta described in the case of her husband, Jesus:

> It was terrible for him; he had been born in that house and he had his shop there. He asked, "Who am I going to sew for now?" And I said, "For the little sea crab!" Jesus had a stable job: He worked for a man in a city shop who ordered four or five pairs of pants every day; you know how Jesus sews. So he had steady work; he had been doing it for twenty or thirty years, all his life.

Tailoring was a household enterprise; wives of tailors, such as Marta and Eloisa, Walter's wife (who lived a little further down Calle K), did the women's work of hand sewing hems, buttons, and zippers, and ironing. When Walter's brother Alvaro was a bachelor, he relied on his mother living a few streets away to do these tasks, while he ate his daily cooked meal. But he quickly trained his partner, Yasmin, when they set up home together in 1981. While dressmakers, such as Marta, did this in addition to their own work, they did not expect any reciprocal exchange on the part of their husbands because dressmaking was strictly women's work.

1992: Sending More Household Members out to Work during an Economic Crisis

Mirroring the data from Indio Guayas, national-level urban data indicated that the economically active population increased from 2.3 million in 1974 to 3.3 million in 1990 and 6.1 million in 2004, reflecting both population growth and an increase in the numbers of working women.[18] Along with the extensive urbanization process that started in the 1970s, Ecuador's economy became increasingly service based; by the 1990s it made up more than 47 percent of the economy (Moser 1997, pp. 21–22). Among the urban poor, both women and men were employed in service activities, with the latter also employed in construction (World Bank 1995a, p. 25).[19]

In 1992 more than half of Indio Guayas's employed population was in the informal sector, although there were gender-based disparities. The 1992 survey showed that informal sector activities were more important for women, with almost three-quarters working in this sector, while men were more evenly distributed between the informal and formal sectors (Moser 1997). The increasing importance of this residual sector reflected the dramatic changes experienced by

Table 6-4. *Average Number of Employed Household Members, by Poverty Level,*
1978–2004 Panel Data
Number

Poverty level	1978		1992		2004	
	Avg.	Sample size	Avg.	Sample size	Avg.	Sample size
Very poor	1.58	26	2.52	29	3.38	16
Poor	1.88	17	3.81	16	4.00	15
Not poor	1.00	8	2.50	6	3.30	20
All levels	1.59	51	2.92	51	3.53	51

the Ecuadorian economy in the 1980s and early 1990s. As described in appendix B, along with higher inflation and declining per capita incomes, the economic recession was accompanied by a decline in manufacturing. The service sector also contracted (World Bank 1995a, p. 164) but continued to employ almost one in four workers, remaining the economy's most important sector (Floro and Acosta 1993, p. 11).[20] During this period two trends in income generation stood out: the first was labor intensification as more women went out to work; the second was increasing casualization of the male labor force, particularly in the construction sector. Each of these trends is discussed below.

INCREASING NUMBERS OF WOMEN WORKING. Reflecting national trends at the urban level, by 1992 increasing numbers of household members in Indio Guayas, especially women, were involved in income-earning activities. Supporting evidence is provided by trend data. First, as mentioned above, the number of women in the economically active population increased from 34.6 percent in 1978 to 43.8 percent in 1992, representing a 27 percent increase in the number working. Second, the average number of income earners per household increased, from an average of 1.59 members working in 1978 to 2.92 in 1992; poor households had higher participation rates than did those that were not poor or very poor. This suggests that for those living below the poverty line, an insufficient number of family members in the labor market could push it into the very poor category (table 6-4). Finally, the poorer the household, the more dependent it was on a woman's earnings.[21] The data shown here do not capture the contribution of child labor since information on this issue was not systematically collected. However, chapter 9 compares the economic contribution of sons to the domestic labor of daughters, who frequently assumed child care responsibilities to enable their mothers to enter the labor market.

Table 6-5. *Labor Security, by Job Status, Indio Guayas, 1978–2004*
Percent unless otherwise indicated

Job status (security)	1978			1992			2004		
	Male	*Female*	*Total*	*Male*	*Female*	*Total*	*Male*	*Female*	*Total*
Regular (permanent)	24.5	23.5	24.0	35.5	35.5	35.5	19.5	33.5	24.0
Self-employed	44.0	53.0	46.0	23.5	37.5	28.5	31.0	35.5	32.5
Casual (temporary)	31.5	23.5	30.0	41.0	27.0	36.0	49.5	31.0	43.5
Sample size (number)	57	17	74	90	48	138	103	48	151

CASUALIZATION OF THE MALE LABOR FORCE, PARTICULARLY IN THE CONSTRUCTION SECTOR. For men intensification strategies were less important; indeed the panel data show that the economically active male population dropped between 1978 and 1992. Far more important was the trend toward temporary day labor within existing work categories (table 6-5). This had important implications for employment security, which is one of the components of financial-productive capital assets. Employment security measures how much security individuals have in the use of their labor potential as an asset, and focuses on the way in which employment vulnerability is linked to stability in job status. This category was a composite of two employment survey categories: job status (table 6-5) and employer type (table 6-6). Here components were compositely ranked in terms of vulnerability, from the most secure permanent employment in government, or private enterprises, to self-employed to the least secure temporary or casual worker, most frequently working for private enterprises or individuals.

This trend toward casual, daily labor, which resulted in the greatest vulnerability, was most pronounced in the construction sector. During the 1970s construction boom, workers on long-term secure contracts, such as Lidia's husband, Salvador, were sufficiently confident in their jobs to become militant about their rights as workers. Thus, discussing his work situation in 1980, Salvador complained, "The foreman is an idiot. He didn't even want me to go outside and eat. The engineer was just as bad tempered. I had to go on working until 4 o'clock. But I wouldn't stand for that. I'd say, 'I am going to eat; you can sack me today.' That's the way it is; a foreman gives orders and a worker works like a mule."

However, the buoyant economy did not last. Between 1988 and 1992, waged employment dropped by half and self-employment by almost one-fifth

Table 6-6. *Type of Employer, Indio Guayas Working Population, 1978–2004*[a]
Percent unless otherwise indicated

Employer	1978			1992			2004		
	Male	*Female*	*Total*	*Male*	*Female*	*Total*	*Male*	*Female*	*Total*
Government	6.7	0	4.8	7.3	8.7	7.8	4.0	17.4	8.2
Private enterprise	48.9	11.1	38.1	19.5	15.2	18.0	39.6	19.6	33.3
Private individual	0	27.8	7.9	30.5	43.5	35.2	4.0	13.0	6.8
Self-employed	44.4	61.1	49.2	42.7	32.6	39.1	52.5	50.0	51.7
Total	100.0	100.0	100.0	100.0	100.0	100.1	100.1	100.0	100.0
Sample size (number)	45	18	63	82	46	128	101	46	147

a. This categorization does not specify the nature of the contractual relationship, which for the first four categories could range from waged to temporary worker.

as casual, daily labor increased sharply, encompassing 37 percent of male construction workers by 1992 (Moser 1997). These labor market changes had important implications for households, many of which had become reliant on the relatively high wages earned by construction workers during the 1980s construction boom in Guayaquil. The changing work situation of Alonso, Carmen's wayward husband, was common to many of the construction workers in Indio Guayas. Alonso had always worked as a skilled construction worker (*albanil*), starting in the 1970s as a daily laborer (*oficial*) who queued up outside building sites for casual work. By the mid-1970s, however, he had regular three- to six-month contracts from a subcontractor building the new city center banks and office buildings. Although the rainy season was slack, for the rest of the year, he had a regular weekly salary and paid into a pension fund. After the arrival of infill in Cisne Dos in 1978, he also became a weekend master builder (*maestro*) in his own right in the community. Working in construction gangs with two or three fellow builders, he built both the wooden and split-cane houses used by newly arriving settlers as well as cement-and-block houses for consolidating homeowners.[22]

However, by the mid-1980s the bottom had dropped out of the city center building boom, and despite his considerable skills, Alonso once again had to return to casual day laboring. In addition, local demand within Cisne Dos was reduced as younger men also competed in that labor market, thereby further reducing Alonso's income-earning ability.

2004: Making Ends Meet by Diversifying Income Sources

By 2004 Ecuador had experienced another economic crisis, this time associated with the failure of the banking system, which precipitated the collapse of a number of local banks and led to the associated dollarization of the economy (see appendix B). In Indio Guayas its impact on the local labor market was mediated by life cycle factors, with three main trends identified: declining dependency ratios, diversification into new opportunities, and increasing reliance on other forms of income.

EMPLOYMENT AND DEPENDENCY RATIOS. By 2004 households were less poor than they were in either 1978 or 1992, but they also had more members working, and nonpoor households had a lower dependency ratio (that is, the number of household members supported by each income earner). As the size of households increased, and as original community members' children reached adulthood, so too the number of income earners per household (including those sending remittances from overseas) rose. In each survey period, the number of income earners per household did not vary substantially by poverty category, resulting in much less favorable dependency ratios for larger, poorer households. The average household dependency ratio for all households fell from 4.2 in 1978 to 2.6 in 2004—a substantial improvement—such that by 2004 each income earner supported 2.0 residents in nonpoor households, and 3.3 residents in very poor households

DIVERSIFICATION STRATEGIES. One important type of diversification reflecting the city's changing labor market related to increased demand for white-collar jobs in both government and private sectors. In both sectors long-term trends showed a decline in male employment with an accompanying increase in openings for women in jobs such as school teachers, secretaries, and clerks. In Indio Guayas these opportunities also reflected the higher educational attainment of better educated daughters with secondary and tertiary level schooling. Moving into the labor market between 1992 and 2004, they acquired jobs with greater earning capacity than what was possible in the informal retailing and services sector, where the majority of older or less educated women still worked. Such white-collar opportunities only opened up to young, educated, unmarried women; the long working hours and commuting time made it difficult to combine these jobs with reproductive responsibilities (see chapter 8).

The associated upward mobility of this type of work is illustrated by the story of Virginia, one of Marta's sisters who had lived with her since very young. In 1980, as a seventeen-year-old schoolgirl, she had a son, whom Marta and Jesus was quickly welcomed into their home as another of their children. Determined to be both successful and financially independent, Virginia coordinated child care and cooking on a shift system with Marta and Adriana, her niece, while she completed her high school certificate. After a long struggle, she found her first job as a shop assistant in a large city center supermarket, a position with rolling three-month contracts, low pay, and no social security. After two years Virginia became a sales agent for an office supply company, earning on commission. In 1989, leaving her son with Marta, she moved to another city to live with her new partner. Because he did not want her to work, Virginia studied accounting at night school. By 1991, with the relationship over, Virginia returned to her sister's house, bringing with her a second son. She lived independently with her two children in a room at the back of the plot. With both children in school and dovetailed child care support from Marta and Adriana (see chapter 7), she worked as a secretary at a law office, leaving early each morning with her briefcase and not coming home before 7:30 p.m., to earn a salary double that of a shop girl. In the mid-1990s she moved once again, this time to Quito, where she became a successful traveling saleswoman selling clothing and cosmetics to office workers. By 2004 she had married a European engineer she met in Quito and left the country.

DECLINING CRAFT PROFESSIONS AND THE NEED FOR NEW TECHNOLOGY SKILLS. As described above, in the 1970s men were concentrated in craft jobs in such skilled trades as tailors, shoemakers, plumbers, and electricians. However, over the nearly thirty-year period, more traditional occupations such as tailoring and shoemaking declined, with older artisans finding it difficult to make ends meet. In parallel, new technologies and increased consumer demand from a consolidating, aspiring community opened up other opportunities. Younger, technically trained men took advantage of shifts in consumer preferences to establish more profitable repair workshops for electric domestic items such as the refrigerators, radios, televisions, and cassette recorders that were all flooding the market and increasingly available, either through contraband or credit purchase.

The comparative experience of two brothers, Walter and Alvaro, both neighbors of Marta's on Calle K, demonstrates the consequence of the decline in traditional occupations in terms of financial-productive assets and household well-being. As self-employed tailors in 1978, both lived in poor households. Elder brother Walter had a range of local clients as well as an outwork contract with a city center workshop. With his wife assisting him, they were putting two children through primary school, which represented a considerable outlay. His younger brother Alvaro, then aged twenty-two, had recently begun working on his own after apprenticing with his brother and had acquired a plot next door, bought a sewing machine on credit, and was doing subcontracting work in the center.

By 1992 both brothers were still tailors, but their income levels had changed. Walter, as the more skilled tailor, was making jackets and trousers and had moved out of income poverty. His household had improved by diversifying; Eloisa ran a small home-based enterprise while their elder son, who had trained as a refrigerator repair mechanic while in military service, was now the primary income earner. By contrast, the younger brother Alvaro, who still only made trousers, was severely affected by the arrival of cheap mass-produced trousers into the local Guayaquil market and had moved further into poverty. Although he and his wife both worked seven days a week on piece rate work, with three children to support, they were in a desperate situation. The house lacked side and back walls and part of the roof; the children received free meals three days a week from the evangelical church feeding program, as well as assistance with school matriculation fees from Plan International.

Yet twelve years later, even Walter's best-made plans had failed; his skills had not proved an adequate buffer, and he had fallen back into poverty. Alvaro, on the other hand, was no longer poor. While both households had been affected by the further declining demand for hand tailoring, Walter's productivity was further reduced by ill health associated with diabetes. Two sons still living in Walter's house also worked, but one now had a wife to support, and the minimum wages they earned as temporary contract workers in local factories did not provide sufficient security to keep the family out of poverty. In contrast, Alvaro had benefited from the fact that one of his sons had migrated to Palma, Majorca, and remitted $700 every two months from his wages as a beach attendant. His son also had bought him a new sewing machine, paid for in Spain and delivered to his father in Guayaquil.

INCREASING RELIANCE ON OTHER FORMS OF INCOME.   In 1992 all households, irrespective of their poverty category, received the majority (95 percent) of their monthly incomes from individuals' wages or other individual income-generating activities. However, by 2004 wages and other individual income-generating activities were substantially less important sources of income for all household categories. For all households the figure had fallen to 81 percent; for very poor households the figure was 79.6 percent, and for poor households it was 73 percent.

Over time, increases in unearned income came from remittances, government transfers, and rent. While the first two were transfers of income within society, the third was a return on capital. All these financial flows were identified as the components of transfer-rental income, one of the categories of financial-

Table 6-7. *Process for Obtaining the Solidarity Bond*

Steps	Issuing institution	Actual price
1. Register at a church. Documents required: —Mother's identity certificate —Mother's certificate of voting —Birth certificate of all children under 12 years of age —Information on family address	Catholic or evangelical church Dept. of Civil Registration	$15–$20 for each document
2. Collect the bond (*bono*) from chosen bank in Guayaquil —Day to collect bond identified by the last number on identity certificate —If do not go on specified day, forfeit bond —Bank is located in the city center, so it requires a day to collect bond	Guayaquil bank	$15 per month

productive capital. Transfer-rental income also included government cash transfers (*bono solidario,* or solidarity bond) given to mothers of small children.

While nonwage income made up a relatively small share (2 percent) of total household income in 1992, it increasingly played an important role such that by 2004, it constituted a much larger share of total income. The solidarity bond, for instance, was introduced by the Ecuadorian government in the 1990s as part of its structural adjustment social safety net to protect the poorest households most severely affected by the withdrawal of the cooking gas subsidy. In Indio Guayas the bond was not income linked and was available to all households with children under the age of five (World Bank 1995a). In comparison with land tenure rights (see chapter 3), the application procedure for bonds was relatively straightforward (see table 6-7), resulting in a high level of uptake. While poor households received 4 percent of their total income from the solidarity bond, this and other miscellaneous sources made up 7 percent of the total incomes of nonpoor households.

Remittance income rose most dramatically as a result of the explosion in Ecuadorian emigration of the late 1990s (see chapter 10). The fact that remittances accounted for more than 50 percent of nonwage income in 2004 demonstrated that sending one or more children abroad to work increasingly became a strategy for improving a household's financial situation and a significant household asset. Only 9.8 percent of all households surveyed received remittance income in 1992; by 2004 this proportion had increased to over 35 percent. The distribution also shifted over time: in 1992, 10.3 percent of very poor households and 12.5 percent of poor households received remittances; but by 2004, 25 percent of very poor and over 53 percent of poor households were receiving some kind of remittances—and 30 percent of nonpoor households as well. The percentage of total household income coming from remittances likewise rose, from 2 percent in 1992 to 11 percent in 2004, with the poor and very poor households gaining greater benefit from this increasingly important income source.[23] Thus remittances may have helped a substantial number of households, not just Alvaro's, out of poverty.

It was not only children abroad who supported their parents and families still living in Indio Guayas. Two out of five sons and daughters still living in Guayaquil reported that they provided material support. This varied from regular weekly payments to irregular monetary gifts, as well as nonmonetary support mainly as food. Commonly such exchanges were in cash or kind and did not involve bank transactions, meaning there was widespread underreporting of this income in the parents' panel data.

Finally, rental income was a much smaller and more recent source of income, with most households just starting in 2004 to build extra rooms to accommodate renters, either at the back of their plots or on additional floors to their houses.

Measuring Financial-Productive Capital

Different categories and components of financial-productive capital have been discussed throughout this chapter. In putting this description together, it was also important to consider three durable goods with an income-generating capability in the specific context of Indio Guayas: sewing machines, refrigerators, and cars, with each predominating during different time periods. Numerous families acquired sewing machines in the 1970s. Men such as Claudio, Jesus, Walter, and Alvaro needed them for their work as tailors. While fewer women, such as Marta, used them to generate income as dressmakers, other women had them for family use. Refrigerators, until recently a costly consumer item, were mainly used in small enterprises (such as selling ice, frozen lollipops, and cold drinks). In the 1970s, the lack of reliable electricity meant few took on the costs and risks associated with refrigerator ownership. Even in 2004, the cost and unreliability of electricity made refrigerator ownership viable only for small enterprises. Car ownership, also a more recent phenomenon, required far more capital (usually based on credit). Most local men who owned cars used them as taxis to generate income. While for some this was a full-time occupation, for

Table 6-8. *Use of House for Remunerative Work, by Poverty Level, Indio Guayas, 1978–2004*[a]

Percent of households

Survey year	All	Nonpoor	Poor	Very poor
1978	31.0	25.0	44.0	24.0
1992	36.0	33.0	44.0	32.0
2004				
Panel data	37.0	30.0	40.0	44.0
Off-plot children	21.7	16.7	18.8	33.3

a. Panel data and 2004 survey of off-plot children.

others it supplemented other jobs, particularly on weekends when there was a high demand for such services. Empirical evidence showed that these assets differed from those used purely for consumption

Although the use of housing for a productive enterprise was not employed as an indicator to measure financial-productive capital, its importance related to its function in generating income. Roughly one-third of all families used their houses for remunerative work, with the percentage rising consistently from 31 percent in 1978 to 37 percent in 2004. By 2004 the very poor were much more likely to run a business out of their homes than were the nonpoor (table 6-8). Even within each poverty category, however, those who used their houses for remunerative work had lower per capita incomes, on average, than those who did not. These findings also need to be related to factors such as life cycle, type of enterprise, and changes in employment opportunities in both the formal and informal sectors. For instance, the very large number of households with ambulantes (street sellers) experienced a very serious economic shock when the mayor's flagship inner-city regeneration project obtained a municipal statute banning all street sellers from this area, which had been a prime sales location.

Financial-productive capital increased between both 1978 and 1992, and 1992 and 2004. In 1992, when Ecuador was undergoing major macroeconomic turmoil, financial-productive capital remained low for households below the poverty line but increased dramatically (by more than one standard deviation) on average for nonpoor households. This reflected increasing inequality in the community. In contrast to poorer households, nonpoor households diversified their sources of income and employment opportunities. By 2004 poor households had obtained financial-productive capital at a level essentially equal with nonpoor households, although very poor households remained far behind.

Much of this growth was attributed to increased income from renters and remittances, with households across the income spectrum also having steadily accumulated productive durables

Capital assets were not accumulated in isolation. Throughout this chapter the importance of households, their changing structures and composition, and the trust and cohesion within them, has been a critical variable in determining the success of livelihood strategies. The following chapter returns to the intangible asset of social capital, this time at the household level, to elaborate further on the contribution that family relationships made to longitudinal asset accumulation and poverty reduction among the residents of Indio Guayas.

7

Families and Household Social Capital: Reducing Vulnerability and Accumulating Assets

"My brothers and sisters were used to being with me. I used to sleep in the same room with them. I was the one to bathe them, to feed them, to take them to school. I was like their mother. So that's why I got those plots of land for all of us. When I moved here, they just started appearing. Jesus said nothing. After all, he knew them. And our home wasn't small. Now each one is independent, because I got them each a place of their own. Each is apart, but they still live with me. I have helped them all. I go on helping them because they are my family, and I believe that the principal thing in life is family. The first society in the world was the family, and for me the most important thing is my family. It is through my family that I can do things, that I feel I am useful."

—Marta, 1992

As Marta commented, at the heart of all coping, survival, or indeed accumulation strategies in Indio Guayas over the past twenty-six years was the social institution of the *family*—those joined by consanguinity—that closely overlapped with the *household*—those joined by sharing a common space, cooking pot, and financial resources.[1] Earlier chapters that focused on the importance of community social relationships, trust, and collaboration that constitute community social capital viewed households in somewhat homogeneous terms. The preceding chapter, which described workers in terms of their accumulation of financial capital, tended to view them as individual "atomistic decision-makers." In reality, they are members of social groups, living in households; and the extent to which they collectively participated in community-level contestation and negotiation for infrastructure, or singly mobilized their labor to transform it into income, depended not only on the external context but also on the internal life cycle characteristics of the household in which they were located. This household social capital is the "glue" that holds it all together.

Development debates challenging the "joint utility function" of the household identified it as a site of conflict rather than collaboration, focused attention on the importance of getting inside households rather than just looking at them, and explored intrahousehold dynamics and their embedded unequal gender relations (Evans 1989; Folbre 1986; Sen 1990).[2] Yet the household as an entity and its internal dynamics are interrelated, and both are essential for understanding changing well-being in Indio Guayas. Therefore, this chapter looks at household characteristics and the extent to which headship, size, composition, and associated labor endowments were key factors associated with poverty levels or asset accumulation. Chapter 8 then turns to the internal dynamics within households and examines whether households were asset-holding and cooperative work units whose physical, economic, and social organization successfully allowed for overlapping circles of individual and collective responsibilities, or whether internal conflict increased vulnerability and reduced asset accumulation (Harriss 2007a, p. 15).

This chapter argues that the household itself is an intangible asset insofar as its trust and cohesion—measured in terms of household social capital—fundamentally contribute over time to household well-being (Moser 1998). Households, however, are not static; they are involved in constant, dynamic restructuring processes. It is these processes, rather than the household as an institution per se, that shed light on the significance of households in reducing vulnerability or accumulating assets, and the data from the Indio Guayas households provide a longitudinal perspective unique in such an analysis.

Household restructuring in headship, composition, and size is a response both to internal life cycle factors as well as to the external environment, particularly wider economic circumstances that affect such issues as employment opportunities and changing costs of living. Equally, there are different motivations underlying restructuring. It is well known that household restructuring often acts as a short-term (or long-term) shock absorber, reducing asset vulnerability for individuals joining the household during periods of economic adversity. Thus households provide important safety net protection from shocks (Carter and Barrett 2006). Another aspect less explored is the way in which changes in headship, structure, size, and composition—components for the household social capital asset index—also create opportunities for asset accumulation. Here a very different set of reasons for restructuring relates to strategic longer-term, asset accumulation choices, with success dependent on such factors as the financial and labor contributions of additional intergenerational household members.

Previous chapters have drawn on anthropological narratives about individual family experiences to illustrate particular issues, which were then analyzed by using the asset index econometric data. This chapter brings together the contrasting, increasingly complex life histories of the five principal families but also adds the narratives of other local families in order to enrich the discussion. Understanding differences in life cycles, and the determinants of diversity as they are played out within wide contexts, is not straightforward. The successfulness of various household restructuring strategies depends not only on the beneficiaries but also on whether such changes are short-term responses to shocks to reduce vulnerability, or long-term efforts to increase or sustain household assets.

Over the twenty-six-year period, two dominant trends in household restructuring stand out. The first was the increase in extended households, and second was the growth of female headship. Embedded within these were two additional, critical forms of restructuring: hidden household heads and nesting. In a complex story such as this, describing each trend in turn cannot capture the intricacies. The advantage of a longitudinal study is that it permits a temporal perspective. However messy, it reinforces the simultaneous importance of the interrelated contributions of different characteristics within households to reducing vulnerability and accumulating assets. In the following section, a slightly amended version of de la Rocha's domestic cycle model (1994) provides a broad framework for the three stages of expansion, consolidation, and contraction in the evolution of households over the twenty-six-year period.[3]

Longitudinal Trends in Household Restructuring

The Indio Guayas longitudinal study highlights the tremendous fluidity and constant restructuring of households. For instance, random survey subsample data on all changes taking place within households during a ten-year period, from 1982 to 1992, showed that more than three out of four households (83 percent) had restructured, not just once but on average 3.2 times per household (Moser 1997). Most were long-term changes from nuclear to extended households, or reconfigurations of extended units, rather than temporary, short-term crisis arrangements. Various factors caused restructuring: internal factors included life cycle events, such as birth, marriage, and death, as well as causal issues, such as marital conflict, child care, and care of the elderly; external factors related to access to adequate housing, employment (either loss of a job or working elsewhere), lack of income, and access to adequate education and health care. Although internal and external factors were inevitably interrelated, internal circumstances predominated, accounting for more than half (56 percent) of restructuring, with external pressures precipitating slightly less (44 percent). Lack of access to adequate shelter was the single most frequently cited external cause of household restructuring; marital conflict was the most often mentioned internal reason, contributing directly to the formation of female-headed households.[4] At different stages of life over the twenty-six-year period, different restructuring characteristics dominated, as described below.

1978: Early Expansion Phase in Household Structure

In this first phase, when most young families had recently formed, two types of household structures were particularly important.

Predominance of Small Nuclear Households

In 1978, shortly after households had moved to Indio Guayas and constructed their first very basic houses, three of the five neighborhood families on Calle K were small nuclear households.[5] Mercedes and Claudio and their two very young children lived opposite Marta. On each side lived two other nuclear families: on the right were Lidia and Salvador and their four children, and on the left were Carmen and Alonso and their three young daughters. At the same time, two families did not conform to the dominant structure. Alicia, living three doors down from Marta, was one of the few female household heads, a single woman with seven children. Although her husband had deserted her after the birth of their sixth child to set up a second household, he continued to claim visiting rights and made very occasional, unreliable financial contributions. The other was Marta's family.

Extended Households in 1978: Marta

The fifth family, headed by Jesus and Marta, was an extended household that comprised not only the couple and their daughters Adriana and Ana Maria but also Marta's two single sisters, Lourdes and Virginia, and her youngest brother, Arturo. All shared space in the small two-room house. For Marta this was a vast improvement; as described in chapter 3, she previously had lived with four households in one house. Although she acquired five plots that were intended

Table 7-1. *Household Structure of the 1978–2004 Panel Data*
Percent

Survey year	Male headed		Female headed, single or married	Male headed, single	Single or multiple adults only
	Nuclear	Extended			
1978	62.8	19.6	9.8	0	7.8
1992	33.3	39.2	25.5	2.0	0
2004	11.8	41.2	35.3	9.8	2.0

for herself, sister Lourdes, brothers Roberto and Arturo, and her mother (who only intermittently lived on her plot and then sold it), in 1978, with their houses yet to be constructed, three out of four siblings lived with her.

The Indio Guayas panel data set of fifty-one households confirms the findings for the households on Calle K: in 1978 approximately two-thirds were small nuclear households, predominantly self-defined as headed by male partners but containing a male-female couple. Only five households were headed by women. Two were widows and atypically older, and the other three had never been in a stable relationship (see table 7-1).

1992: Expansion and Consolidation of Households

In 1992, fourteen years after the first survey, households had undergone multiple changes, with new household types reflecting the impact of the economic crisis (see appendix B), which coincided with the peak of the family life cycle expansion stage.

Dramatic Growth in Extended Households: Carmen and Pancho

Foremost was the increase in the number of extended households, doubling from 1978 (see table 7-1), primarily because children have grown up and brought their partners and children into the family. Correspondingly, there also was a decline in the proportion of nuclear households. As multiple families developed with complex sharing arrangements around cooking and related domestic tasks, child care, and use of communal space on the plot, it became more difficult to untangle where one household ended and the next began. While children tended to assume that all space was communal, adults tried to observe boundaries, such as around sleeping space, in an attempt to ensure some semblance of privacy.

Table 7-2. *Average Number of People on the Plot, by Poverty Level,*
1978–2004 Panel Data

Survey dates	All households	Nonpoor	Poor	Very poor
1978	6.0	3.6	4.9	7.4
1992	7.3	5.0	7.8	7.5
2004	8.0	6.4	9.5	8.6

The changes in Carmen and Alonso's household illustrate this well. By 1992 their nuclear household had expanded into a nine-member extended household. During this period Carmen had had two more children—the sons her husband so badly wanted. In addition, her youngest daughter Julia, now eighteen, had just had a baby and her partner, Ignacio, had moved in. As in 1978, the house still had one room, with only the front wall built in brick. Both side walls were those of the neighbors' houses, while the back wall was the original, by now aging, bamboo wall. The entire household slept in three large beds, with hanging curtains to define separate space. By 1992 Julia was looking after the younger children, freeing up Carmen, who had moved on from being a washerwoman to the more lucrative work of a domestic servant. The family shared all space except the stove since Julia cooked separately for her husband, even though she had few financial resources other than the money that Ignacio irregularly gave her. Thus Julia illustrated the first stage of being "independent" (*independiente*) by cooking separately (*aparte*), as well as by moving toward independent financial arrangements.

While the processes of modernization that accompany urbanization are often associated with a decline in household size, this was not the case in Indio Guayas, where the shift was more toward extended households. The panel data showed an average increase in size from around 6 members in 1978 to more than 7 per household in 1992 (see table 7-2). As in Carmen's case, the increase in household size was closely related to poverty level; the poorer the household the larger the household size. Thus household extension primarily was intended to reduce vulnerability by providing an important safety net at a time of deteriorating external economic conditions.

Hidden Female Heads in Extended Households: Alicia

Increasingly, extended households contained subunits headed by younger women, "hidden" from headship statistics.[6] Alicia's household in 1992 illustrates this well. Still a female household head, in the interim since 1978, she had borne two more children by her nonresident "husband." Her eldest daughter Dorotea (by a first relationship)—absent in 1978 while being cared for by her grandmother living in rural Santa Helena—had returned by the early 1980s to live with her mother. When Dorotea became pregnant in 1983, Alicia gave her domestic responsibility for the younger children; Alicia then changed her job from local piece-rate laundering to better-paid, full-time laundry work in the city center. By 1992 Dorotea had three children of her own, but no male partner, and lived in her mother's house as a "hidden household head."[7] Alicia came home three nights a week only, preferring the tranquility of her part-time live-in job, commenting, "There's too much noise at home."[8] With three of her daughters now married, the eleven-member, three-generation extended household was now managed by Dorotea, assisted by her younger sisters. Although Alicia provided financial support to this household, they were still very poor; the evangelical church program fed lunch to two of Dorotea's children, and another child attended a home crèche until it was closed down.

Alicia's household was just one of a growing number of extended households with unmarried daughters, sisters, or other female relatives who chose to raise their children within a larger household, and to share resources and responsibilities with others. Such hidden female heads were the outcome of various circumstances. Some had lived independently but returned to their parents' or other relatives' homes upon the departure of their spouse. Others already resided with their husbands and children in extended households and remained after separated partners left. Finally, there were those like Dorotea, who never had permanent partners but lived in their parental home with children born from different casual, short-term relationships.

The panel data demonstrate the growing importance of hidden female household heads. Extended households with hidden heads doubled from 8 percent in 1978 to 16 percent in 1992, and then nearly doubled again to 28 percent in 2004—by which time one in four extended households had hidden female heads. Three factors influenced this phenomenon. First was financial necessity; for young single mothers with little access to housing or other assets, residence in extended units cushioned the impact of declining incomes and increased child care costs. The poverty data support this finding since hidden female heads were more likely to be located in poorer households. As of 2004 one in five nonpoor households had at least one hidden female head but that proportion increased to approximately one in three among poor and very poor households.

Second was the necessity of establishing child care arrangements so that women could either keep jobs they already had or enter into the labor market.

Even when additional contributions only partially covered expenses, household resource pooling meant that the remainder was picked up by other household members.

Third was the provision of emotional support from family members. Coming out of conflictive conjugal relationships, young women often needed a secure domestic environment to cope with the pressures of raising children alone and to shield them from the social stigma associated with single parenthood. Indeed, young mothers often perceived residence in extended households as improving their chances of finding another partner, often leaving their children with grandparents or other kin if they moved into a new relationship.

Thus hidden headship was a strategy mainly undertaken in adverse economic circumstances in order to reduce asset vulnerability—through the financial and emotional support provided in extended households—rather than to improve the assets of single mothers. Younger second-generation daughters now had a fallback safety net provided by their parental family, which had not been available to their mothers, the pioneer generation invading Indio Guayas. Consequently daughters were more likely to leave their partners or to throw them out of existing households than their older counterparts were. Marital conflict, the most important internal reason for restructuring, was closely associated with economic problems and men's failure to contribute sufficiently to the household. Whereas older women often remained in emotionally and economically vulnerable positions with conflictive partners, the opportunity provided by hidden female headship allowed younger women to free themselves from unhappy relationships even when their economic situation remained tenuous.

Dramatic Growth in Female-Headed Households: Lidia

Another important change between 1978 and 1992 was in the type of headship, with the trend one of increasing female headship. This was accompanied by important differences in the composition and characteristics of male- and female-headed households that had begun to occur. In particular female-headed households were smaller and had a lower dependency ratio than those headed by men. At the same time, there were fewer workers within female-headed households.

The experience of Lidia was typical of many women her age. By 1992 her husband, Salvador, had abandoned her for another, younger woman living ten doors away on the same street. Visiting her at the time I noted in my diary:

Lidia is devastated by the breakdown of her relationship, and that her husband has walked out on her. When I arrived, three of the children were

Table 7-3. *Household Headship in Indio Guayas, 1978–2004*
Units as indicated

Headship type	1978		1992		2004	
	Number	*Percent*	*Number*	*Percent*	*Number*	*Percent*
Male	46	90	38	75	33	65
Female	5	10	13	25	18	35
Total	51	100	51	100	51	100

sitting on the floor eating noodles out of a cooking pan, fighting for the food. The floor has not been swept for weeks, and the red plastic chairs are the same as fifteen years ago but now badly broken from multiple wear and tear. The house is larger, with an upstairs gallery, but without some of the walls. She told me that both her elder sons have changed to night school so that they can work during the day to support the family. Lidia earns very little in the canteen and is drinking a lot. She just doesn't seem to care.

Panel trend data confirm that the most dramatic change was the increase in the proportion of households headed by women, primarily single female heads but with a few married women primary income earners also identifying themselves as heads. Female-headed households grew steadily from only 10 percent in 1978 to 25 percent by 1992 and 35 percent in 2004 (table 7-3). In 1992 this was primarily the result of de jure female headship, and the outcome of separation or divorce, reflecting a second stage in adult male life cycle patterns that was common in Indio Guayas. Frequently young men formed their first relationship with an older, more mature woman by whom they had their first children. By middle age, however, such men abandoned same-age or older wives for younger second wives. This is what happened to Lidia, while in Marta's case she was the second, younger wife of Jesus, marrying him when she was just fifteen years old while he was twenty-eight.

Nesting with More than One Household on the Plot: Marta and Jesus

Regardless of headship and household structure, a final important trend, again first apparent in 1992 but more marked by 2004, was what I have termed "nesting" (Moser 1998), defined as more than one family living separately (aparte) on the same plot. In this case the sharing of space was an intergenerational family extension strategy rather than a household extension strategy, as was the case with extended households. The majority of nesters were adult children and their families, residing independently on their parents' plots. Although they sometimes shared the same living space while running independent households, cooking and eating separately, more often nesters lived in a separate space, either on another floor of the house or in a separate structure at the back or side of the plot.

Marta's household exemplified this phenomenon, changing from a single extended household in 1978 to three independent families on the same plot in both 1992 and 2004, though the constituent families changed over this period. The original plot size of twelve by thirty meters meant that there was room for the next generation to stay on it, particularly as the original house was extended upwards with two additional floors for separate apartments. By 1992 Marta, her husband, Jesus, and daughter Ana Maria were still in the original house; living apart in a separate house on the same plot was elder daughter Adriana, with her husband, Hector, and daughter Laura. Finally, at the back of the plot, Marta had built two rooms with their own toilets. One was occupied by her sister Virginia, and the other was a storeroom where I lived when visiting in the community from 1992 onwards. By 2004 Virginia had moved on, leaving behind her son Emilio, but Ana Maria had built a separate first floor apartment for herself, her husband, Edgar, and their two children.

Nesting was an important support system for family members, usually children, who could not afford to buy their own plots or construct their own homes. This was an intermediate strategy between household extension, where assistance was provided on a daily basis, and the formation of totally independent households. Nesting primarily benefited children in their accumulation of assets such as human and financial capital. However, it also provided advantages for the host households, mainly in the form of time efficiencies through sharing reproductive and household tasks such as child care and cooking. Finally it enabled sons and daughters to care for elderly parents while living independently.

Again, Marta's household illustrated this well. Despite the separate space and management of financial budgets, in 1992, while doing fieldwork, I observed Marta masterminding a complex cooking and child care system along with her work as the community's president. Table 7-4 illustrates how she prepared two meals daily that were eaten by fifteen people—some eating at both meals—for a total of nineteen portions. In so doing she released her daughter Adriana as well as her sisters, Lourdes (who lived next door) and Virginia (who lived at the back), and her sister-in-law, Guadalupe (living across the road), from cooking and washing, the two nonnegotiable types of women's work within households.

Table 7-4. *Marta's Weekday Provision of Lunch and Supper for Family Members (Six Households), 1992*

Relationship to Marta	Lunch	Supper
Self: wife and cook	Marta	Marta
Husband: working	Jesus	Jesus
Sisters: working	Lourdes	Virginia
Nieces: in school	Cecilia (Lourdes' daughter), Guadalupe's daughter	
Daughters: working		Adriana and Ana Maria
Granddaughters: in school	Laura (Adriana's daughter)	Laura
Nephews	Ivan and Emilio (Virginia's sons)	Ivan and Emilio
Sister- and son-in-law: working	Guadalupe	Hector (Adriana's husband)
Nonfamily	Milagros (washerwoman) plus two children	

Helping with the washing was the paid labor of a local woman Milagros, who came three times a week, and also picked up lunch for herself and her two children. Marta balanced cooking with caring for Virginia's two sons, as well as her granddaughter Laura (Adriana's daughter). As described in chapter 6, Virginia's employment strategy was underpinned by extended household support.

2004: Winners and Losers in the Household Contraction Phase

As already described, by 2004 Indio Guayas was a stable urban settlement, no longer on the periphery but integrated into the city as one of its lower-income suburbs. As it consolidated, its population aged: the average age of household members had increased from sixteen years in 1978 to twenty-six years in 2004, with the average age of all daughters and sons increasing from seven to thirty years over that time period. Technically, this was what can be called the family life cycle "contraction" stage, when the children of the original settlers had reached adulthood and started families of their own, either in the same community or elsewhere. At the same time, as the members of the first generation reached the end of their natural working lives and found it more difficult to continue earning an income, support from their children became an increasingly critical determinant of their poverty level as well as the sustainability of their accumulated assets. Further restructuring had also occurred by 2004, some of it conforming to the contraction model, but there were other counterintuitive strategies that did not follow these patterns, as exemplified in the narratives of the five families.

Survival of the Extended Households

By 2004 all five families on Calle K were living in extended households on plots that incorporated both nesting and hidden female heads; however, these arrangements resulted from different structural change processes. In Alicia's case she had given up her work in the center and was back managing the household. Dorotea, her eldest daughter, had finally moved out, settling around the corner with Leonel, Don Ortega's younger son, and her five children by different relationships. Two other daughters had replicated their mother's marital cycle and were raising children as single parents. In Sylvia's case she had lived with her children's father for a while, having four sons, but soon moved home again; Joanna, the youngest, had three children by different fathers while still living at home. At one point Alicia had fifteen people living in her house, although by 2004 it was down to ten, with Sylvia nesting and Joanna as the remaining hidden household head. Although still poor, the household now benefited from extensive financial and nonfinancial support from the nine children (see chapter 9).

Despite the decline in the size of Alicia's household in later years, the panel data showed that most households were not contracting. Half of the second-generation sons and daughters still lived on the family plot, either independently or as hidden household heads. Of these, 78 percent lived within their parents' structure, with a further 12 percent living apart on the same plot. Thus the number of households living on a plot increased, from an average of one household per plot in 1978 to 1.6 households per plot in 2004. While in 1992 the increase had occurred primarily among nonpoor households (1.3 per plot versus 1 for the poor and very poor), by 2004 it was the poor and very poor who had incorporated more households on the plot (2.0 and 1.6, respectively, versus 1.4 for the nonpoor).

Household extension had always been a strategy to reduce asset vulnerability by incorporating kin members at risk; however, as older children themselves became income earners, it also became a strategy to accumulate and consolidate assets. This was not foolproof as it depended on intrahousehold collaboration rather than conflict (see chapter 8). In addition, as members of the next generation started their own families, the success of this strategy depended on the extent to which elderly household heads could still mobilize second-generation kin support. The fact that it was consistently poorer households that had more people (in 2004 nonpoor households averaged 6.4 residents, poor ones 9.5, and very poor 8.6; see table 7-2) suggested that overall this was an asset vulnerability rather than asset accumulation strategy.

Other Restructuring: Adopted Children, Split Households,
Returned Spouses, and Widowhood

Within extended households there were a variety of additional internal changes. For instance, Mercedes and Claudio had adopted a young nephew whom his mother had been unable to maintain. This additional male member arrived around the same time their son Frank left home (see chapter 9), while daughter Flor, who had helped her mother run a home crèche in the 1990s (described in chapter 5), now had her own two children to look after and was nesting in the back of the plot with her husband, a casually employed construction laborer. By 2004 Claudio spent three out of four weeks living on an island in River Guayas where he had set up a dental technician practice. Thus this had become a split household, with Mercedes as de facto household head—though she certainly did not identify herself as such, and therefore the household was not recorded in this category.

Carmen and Alonso's household had long been a split household as he moved between his two families (see chapter 6). But by 2004 Carmen herself had gone to Barcelona, leaving Alonso on his own with his Calle K family. He continued to live there, cared for by his daughters, spending time sitting in his hammock bemoaning his fate, with Carmen no longer there to look after him (see chapter 10).

By 2004 life cycle changes meant that widowhood also was increasing. In many cases the widows were younger second wives, such as Marta, who was widowed in 2001 after Jesus died from gangrene-related complications associated with diabetes. By 2004 one in ten heads or spouses had died. Finally, economic circumstances meant some women were forced to take back errant husbands. This was Lidia's situation in 2004 when Salvador, thrown out by his second partner and having nowhere to live, returned to his original home.

Measurement of Household Trust and Cohesion: Household Social Capital

While changes in household structure have implications for income poverty, they also have important consequences for asset vulnerability and accumulation. Embedded in the complexities of household structures are levels of trust and cohesion, identified as household social capital. As with community social capital, the components of household social capital are basic due to the limitations of the panel data set.[9] Nevertheless, their econometric measurement contributes to the anthropological narrative. Household social capital as an asset is complex because it is both positive and negative in terms of accumulation strategies. It is defined here as the sum of three indicator variables: whether the household is headed by a couple (as opposed to a single female or male), whether multiple households are living on the plot, and whether the main household contains hidden household heads.

The first component, jointly headed households, indicates trust and cohesion between partners and therefore within the family, and applies to both nuclear and couple-headed extended households. In 1978, when the community comprised young families, nearly two-thirds were nuclear in structure. By 1992 this proportion had dropped to a third, and in 2004 only one in ten households was nuclear in structure. By contrast, the reverse was true for couple-headed extended households, which grew from one-fifth of those surveyed in 1978 to two-fifths by 1992, and was slightly more by 2004.

The second component, the presence of hidden female household heads within extended households again points to trust and collaboration. The number increased from less than one in ten households in 1978 to more than one in four in 2004. The third component, other households on the plot, refers to the second-generation children who, with families of their own, remained on their parents' plot. As discussed in the following chapter, this required considerable collaboration, particularly between intergenerational in-laws.

Based on these three variables, the overall asset index results show that household social capital remained at the same level from 1978 to 1992 but increased by 2004.[10] This econometric finding, contrasts with trends in community social capital, which declined over the same time period, and points to the increasing importance that extended larger household structures played in balancing income generation with child care and other domestic tasks. Households best able to achieve this were also those most likely to be both income and asset rich.

Household Headship, Poverty, and Asset Accumulation

Was headship a critical factor in the accumulation of assets, as well as in levels of poverty? The complex changes in headship over the twenty-six-year period raise the question as to whether female-headed households were income or asset poorer than male-headed households.[11] The correlation between poverty and headship has been a contentious debate among development feminists since Buvinic and Youssef (1978) first maintained that female-headed households, a particularly urban phenomenon, were poorer than those headed by males. Since the 1990s this has been further conceptualized and popularized as the "feminization of poverty" by UNICEF, the World Bank, and various bilateral agencies

Table 7-5. *Household Headship and Poverty Level, Indio Guayas, 1978–2004*
Percent of households

| Poverty level | Headship type | | All |
	Male	Female	
1978			
Very poor	48	80	51
Poor	35	20	33
Not poor	17	0	16
1992			
Very poor	53	69	57
Poor	36	15	31
Not poor	11	15	12
2004			
Very poor	33	28	31
Poor	36	17	29
Not poor	31	56	39

(Jackson 1998). Despite widespread evidence of the diversity among female-headed households, and the fact that this concept tends to present women as victims (Chant 1997; Razavi 1999), it is still used—particularly to mobilize donor support—even if it is not necessarily empirically accurate (Chant 2008). Most studies either confirming or refuting this position are based on measurements of income or consumption poverty. The Indio Guayas study contributes to the debate on the differentiation between male- and female-headed households, not only in terms of income but also in terms of the asset accumulation.[12] In addition, its longitudinal perspective allows for the changing circumstances associated with age.

In Indio Guayas in 1978, most households were below the poverty line, but the small number of female-headed households in that year makes it difficult to draw strong conclusions. As table 7-5 shows, the vast majority of households, regardless of headship, were still below the poverty line in 1992, reflecting the overarching economic problems. Female-headed households were slightly less likely to fall below the poverty line than male-headed households, but those that were poor tended to be very poor (defined as having total household earnings fall under 50 percent of the poverty line). The same trend persisted so that by 2004, despite having lower dependency ratios, male-headed households were more likely to fall below the poverty line than female-headed ones (table 7-5). While less than one-third of the male-headed households were not poor, more

Table 7-6. *Asset Accumulation in Indio Guayas, by Headship, 1992–2004*[a]
Standard deviations above average

Headship type		Capital assets				
	Housing	Consumer durables	Human capital	Financial capital	Community social capital	Household social capital
1992						
Male	1.226	0.856	1.124	0.923	1.317	1.132
Female	1.086	0.737	0.906	1.062	0.751	0.082
2004						
Male	1.346	1.590	1.146	1.573	0.877	1.373
Female	1.379	1.784	1.089	1.567	0.681	0.797

a. A traditional test of statistical significance has not been performed on these data because the sample size is so small that most of the data are not statistically significant. Rather, the quantitative data complement the qualitative analysis. For example, anthropological narrative produced the insight that community social capital declined over time; the numbers point in the same direction, and the fact that both methods agree gives us greater confidence in the conclusion.

than half the female-headed households had successfully moved out of poverty. Although a few such households were headed by widows, most women were separated, generally because their male partner had gone off with a younger woman, reflecting a longitudinal pattern of serial monogamy practiced by some men, as discussed earlier.

Thus in Indio Guayas female headship was not necessarily associated with poverty. While the very small number of female-headed households in 1978 were among the poorest in the community (80 percent were very poor), female-headed households were much better off than male-headed households in 2004 (56 percent were nonpoor). This was mediated by age and education. Older, better educated women were more likely to head an extended household with numerous workers, particularly their adult children. By contrast, some aging widowers from nuclear families, unable to any longer generate an income for themselves and lacking an extended family support structure, ended up living in poverty.

Asset Accumulation and Headship

Turning to the accumulation of assets, table 7-6 shows the different types of assets acquired by female- and male-headed households. While most had significantly negative scores in 1978, between 1992 and 2004 most households had positive scores for acquisition of every asset type.[13] The exception was community social capital, which declined. At the same time, there were similarities as well as differences between male- and female-headed households in terms of asset ownership.

Such patterns were influenced by the wider process of development in Guayaquil. Between 1992 and 2004, globalization led to a flood of cheap electrical and household durable goods in the city. Many households naturally aspired to acquire such symbols of modernity. Interestingly, in 2004 female-headed households had higher levels of consumer durables than male-headed households. Among the former, which had higher income levels and larger household size (adult income-earning children that had chosen to remain in the extended family), there was greater demand for consumer goods, especially entertainment and communications equipment like televisions and mobile phones.

The fact that female-headed households scored lower on levels of household social capital was in large part because male-headed households, with an adult couple or partners, counted positively as one of the index components. This obviously weighted against women-headed households that by definition, in most cases, were headed by a single individual. It is important to note this as a limitation of the index. At the same time, the fact that male-headed households had higher levels of community social capital reflected a number of different issues. In 1992 female participation in community organizations was higher among the spouses of male-headed households than women household heads, who were frequently so overstretched managing both productive and reproductive tasks that they simply did not have time for community managing work (Moser 1987). By 2004, when most community based physical and social infrastructure had been acquired and UNICEF and Plan had terminated their programs (see chapter 5), community participation (along with church membership) declined. The higher levels of community social capital in male-headed households in 2004 were associated with male participation in street football leagues, which itself was the outcome of the important municipal improvement to upgrade the streets of the area.

Analysis of the financial capital variable helps with understanding why female-headed households tended to be above the poverty line in 2004. While women were more likely to be unemployed than men in each survey year, female-headed households had more people employed in good jobs in private industry or the government. Men were much more likely to be self-employed or working at temporary jobs. However, male-headed households did as well or better on the other aspects of financial capital, including taking in lodgers and remittance income sent from families abroad. More remittances were sent by

Figure 7-1. *Asset Accumulation in Male- and Female-Headed Households, 1992 versus 2004*

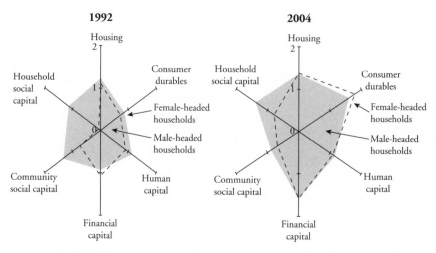

Source: Moser and Felton (forthcoming).

daughters than sons (although there is no disaggregation by gender for amounts remitted). Although high dependency ratios were often associated with poverty, in female-headed households a high level of dependents also meant that households were often better able to balance work and domestic responsibilities. Their size better allowed them to adopt complex intrahousehold divisions of labor that released adult females into the labor market while others undertook cooking, child care, and other household chores.

The different asset portfolios managed by male- and female-headed households are graphically demonstrated in figures 7-1 and 7-2. Figure 7-1 focuses on the different mixes of assets in each year while figure 7-2 presents the longitudinal trends. Since some households moved between being male and female headed, the figures do not show the same households in each year; rather the points shown are the average of each household group for the specific year when data were collected.

Figure 7-2 shows overall differences in the processes of asset accumulation and highlights the limitations of time-specific snapshots. Male-headed households had more assets to start with and these grew more rapidly than among female-headed households, which were slower to acquire most assets. In the long

Figure 7-2. *Asset Accumulation over Time in Male- and Female-Headed Households, 1978–2004*

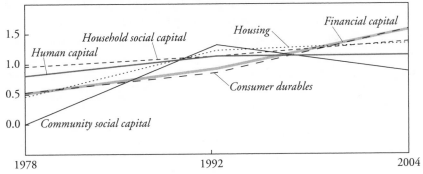

Male-headed households

Standard deviations (0 = mean across time periods)

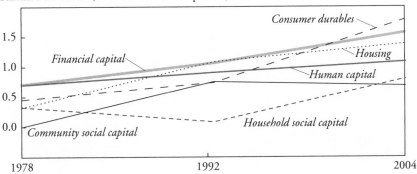

Female-headed households

Standard deviations (0 = mean across time periods)

Source: Moser and Felton (forthcoming).

run female-headed household were less likely to be poor because of their larger number of income earners, but on balance they still tended to have somewhat fewer assets than male-headed households.

This chapter has sought to highlight how household restructuring, although not often considered as such, was an asset in Indio Guayas. Analysis of longitudinal changes shows that renegotiating domestic living arrangements allowed households to adjust to wider economic stresses, thus reducing vulnerability and associated poverty, as well as providing opportunities for asset accumulation. Underlying such adjustments were external economic processes and internal life cycle changes relating to birth, marriage, and death. But were such adjustments also highly dependent on the internal dynamics within a given household, in which men and women, sons and daughters, not only often assumed differential levels of responsibility for household well-being but also received different benefits? The next chapter focuses specifically on the intrahousehold level to identify additional determinants of the capacity of households to both reduce asset vulnerability and accumulate additional assets.

8

The Impact of Intrahousehold Dynamics on Asset Vulnerability and Accumulation

*"If there is no money, you ignore a birthday; if there is, it calls for a great celebration at enormous expense. It's a complex combination of a break in the humdrum existence and a status symbol in the community. This year it's Emilio's birthday party, and it takes place in his Aunt Adriana's house next door. The front room is cleared of furniture except for twenty-five chairs brought from all over to line the walls. The cake is very important—mixed by his mother, Virginia, and Aunts Adriana and Ana Maria, sitting on the floor. With no sign of Adriana's husband, Hector, baby Laura is asleep on cushions. Endless preparation of the numerous delicacies ensues, while Marta and Virginia are in the back of the plot killing and then cooking the chicken for the famous rice with chicken (*arroz con pollo*) dish. The excitement of preparation is very important; it replaces the problems and crises that dominate their lives. The disk jockey arrives and the music plays as loud as possible. 'Hotel California' is still a big favorite along with Julio Jaramillo, and endless yelling Spanish songs. The men start the serious business of drinking sometime after midday.*

Marta has a committee meeting to go to. With the Plan Loan Scheme in limbo, there is no question of not having a meeting. In between, she alters the shirt bought for Alex. The party is scheduled from five to eleven, but there is no real action before seven p.m. Everything of any value is locked up or put out of sight. The women guests come into the sitting room, the majority of men stay outside. All the family's children have new clothes. Birthday boy Emilio has a new shirt (too big), shoes (too big), and trousers. It's all spend, spend, spend. I had forgotten how at parties boys and girls behave like little adults; dressed to kill, behaving formally like their parents, yet dancing with all the physical energy of youth. The food, on formal display on the table while the women sit on chairs around the room, finally gets served; the older men remain outside drinking while the 'young braves' come inside to dance. Marta's brother Roberto, paralytically drunk, somewhat abusively dances with women while his wife, Guadalupe, painfully watches. Everyone rolls home by twelve, and we leave the tidying up for the next day."

—Caroline Moser, diary, July 1992

B irthday parties break the monotony and hardship of daily life, and are times of happiness and celebration. They also provide "apt illustration" (Mitchell 1968) of the pooling and sharing around a family life cycle ritual. This description of a barrio fiesta is timeless; the social construction of gender relationships in the domestic arena played out at such an event has not changed in thirty years. Within the household it is women who are responsible for the preparation and running of the event; as with daily provisioning and household consumption, Latin American cultural norms attribute such female tasks as "natural" women's work, part of daily reproductive responsibilities closely linked to fertility and childbearing. Men socialize and drink separately, spatially apart—except for the "young braves" who enter the women's domain to dance. Since all cooking and child care are considered normal, expected female activities, men are far less involved in the routines of daily life.

But are households harmonious, and if not, how do these internal dynamics affect asset vulnerability or accumulation over time? While chapter 7 discussed the implications of changing household structure and headship for vulnerability and well-being—measured not only as income poverty but also in terms of the reduction or accumulation of assets—this chapter turns to the social construction of intrahousehold gender and generation relationships (with the dynamics of second-generation households examined further in the next chapter). Two recent gender debates raise questions pertinent to this discussion concerning the long-term impacts of intrahousehold dynamics.

First, as already mentioned in chapter 7, the extensive gendered critique of the unitary household model highlights the fact that the household is not a harmonious unified unit; in reality, it is a highly contradictory social structure that embodies both separate and shared individual and collective interests. Its members engage in cooperation, coexistence, and conflict in variable and changing ways over the life course, with these "intersections critical to the working of gender" (Jackson 2007, p. 119). Households are social settings in which daily confrontations and negotiations are often developed in a context of internal inequality and differential distribution of burdens and rewards. Consequently, as de la Rocha (2007, p. 64) maintains, poverty affects women, men, children, and adults in different ways.

Second, do intrahousehold dynamics influence asset vulnerability and accumulation? While the household has been identified as a source of gender and age inequality in terms of access to, use of, and control over resources (Agarwal 1994; Sen 1990), is it also important to recognize the role of individual agency? Are conjugal relations between men and women important in mediating individual preferences and actions so that they are never simply oppositional but are also motivated by varying degrees of solidarity (Jackson 2007, p. 113)?[1]

In examining the responsibilities and obligations that women bear "in the frontline dealing with poverty" (Chant 2008, p. 176), a gender-based disaggregation of asset ownership may assist in measuring to what degree asset accumulation changes intrahousehold power dynamics and the extent to which this empowers women (Parpart, Rai, and Staudt 2002). Furthermore, there may be important differences between mothers and their daughters (discussed in the following chapter). Research surveys of the ownership of land, housing, livestock, and other productive assets tend to collect data at the household rather than the individual level, producing data that are biased and severely limited. Deere, Doss, and Grown (2007) argue that what information exists (focusing primarily on rural land ownership) shows that women are far less likely than men to enjoy ownership or control of assets, and also may not benefit from those held by men in the same household, putting them at a greater risk for poverty and economic vulnerability.[2]

In identifying changing arenas of collaboration and conflict within Indio Guayas households over the past decades, this chapter examines how control over resources and decisions is contingent on equalities in kin social relationships, with implications for the levels of assets accumulated. In addition, the gendered nature of my personal narrative over the past thirty years has influenced my own reflections on marriage as a social institution in Indio Guayas, and this perspective has been incorporated into the discussion.

The Importance of the Institution of Marriage

While conjugal relationships in Indio Guayas could be the locus of conflict as well as cooperation, marriage (church or legal) or consensual unions (*compromisos*) have remained the preferred household institutional structure over the past thirty years, not only for parents but also for the vast majority of second-

and third-generation men and women. Thus any discussion of intrahousehold dynamics needs to be contextualized within the stereotypical Latin American normative framework of a dualist gendered division between machismo and *marianismo.*[3] Here the dominant, aggressive, and fearless role of men contrasts dramatically with the submissive, dependent, mothering female role, a dualism that has been reinforced repeatedly at the popular level, initially over the radio and then by daily television soap operas (*telenovelas*) imported from Mexico, Brazil, Spain, and Colombia. The effect of this could be seen in Lidia's neighbor Jessica. Married with three children, she described her attempt to "better" herself in 1978 as follows:

> I listen to the radio because they give advice about the home, about how to behave with the husband, how the husband should behave with the wife; that he mustn't be bad, mustn't keep her alone at home. It's nice to hear that. When he's here on Saturdays, he listens in and he laughs. Last week it said he should take the wife out to the parks so she is not bored and fed up at home alone, looking after children, cooking and washing. My husband does not like me spending hours talking. A little while, that's alright, like anyone else, but to stay out all day and forget the housework, no. He gets furious if he finds the beds unmade, everything untidy. "Where were you?" he asks. Isn't Don Brian like that?

My own attempts to reconcile my position as a feminist with my own marital relationships have had a particular resonance in Indio Guayas, where my changing status has been variously supported or disapproved. When marriages collapse in Indio Guayas, it is not considered advantageous for women. So when my first marriage ended, there was open criticism by both women and men. Why did I leave Don Brian? He had a job, did not drink, or go with other women, so what was the problem?

For my part, I have been particularly struck by the long-term endurance of most of the conjugal partnerships in the barrio, and the visible grief and suffering of surviving spouses as life cycle changes relating to death and abandonment became more widespread. Therefore, this chapter explores from a longitudinal perspective why marriage is as strong an institution today as it was in the 1970s, despite the daily reality of domestic abuse, abandonment, and neglect. Equally, it identifies transformations and modifications in the value of marriage and domestic cooperation under conditions of broader social change.

In Latin America the institution of marriage presents a contradictory story. On the one hand, as Fusell and Palloni (2004, p. 1201) argue, there has been "the persistence, and universality of marriage" during the past fifty years. For women it occurs early in life and is nearly universal in spite of the social and economic changes and instability in the region. Marriage is central to social life because families serve as an important cultural institution for countering the vicissitudes of the economy. Despite women's easier access to divorce, it is still unacceptable in some social circles, with high associated costs also reducing its occurrence (Craske 2003). On the other hand, the family has changed profoundly since 1970, especially since the 1990s, with greater gender equality in marriage legislation, a decline in the level of marriages, and an increase in nonmarital unions, the age at first marriage, and divorce rates (Jelin 2007).[4] So although the value attached to marriage and maternity is still strong for both men and women, it is no longer the only legitimate role for women, and this change has been accompanied by an increase in women-headed households (a consequence of male abandonment among poor households), a decline in men's role as the main or only breadwinner in the family, and greater flexibility in intrafamily authority systems. Nevertheless, the predominance of the nuclear family, low participation of men in reproductive work, and higher subordination of women within low-resource families all persist (Ariza and de Oliveira 2001). The option of "possible or even probable return to the family" demonstrates how family is a key institution that provides security in times of labor precariousness and dwindling welfare protection (Robichaux 2007, p. 13). How relevant were these descriptions to married life in Indio Guayas?

Women that first went to Indio Guayas came from a generation where the norms of female spatial (courtship) and physical (virginity) protection, as well as the passive acceptance of wifehood, were instilled by parents and other kin. Here is how Jessica described her marital history:

> I was twenty when I got married. A girlfriend introduced me, but I was brought up very strictly. My friends would come over to talk, but I never went out. My mother would beat me if I did. "Don't walk in the parks; don't be out after dark, it looks bad," she would say. When he [her husband] asked for me, I went for little walks for an hour only, with my little cousin to look after me. My father said, "If you want to marry my daughter, you will have to wait four years, so you get to know each other. She is bad tempered. So if you want her like that, alright; otherwise, go and look for another." We were sweethearts for four years.

In 1981 Claudio's wife, Mercedes, related a similar story about how she protected herself from the "downfall" of losing her virginity long enough to ensure that she had Claudio's love.

In all those years with my aunt, I did not have a downfall. And then I fell in love with Claudio. But I did not go with him right away; we were sweethearts for two years, and then I came with him here. The first downfall I have had was with my husband. He is the only one that I have had. I have a cousin who fell in love with a boy at the age of seventeen and had a baby, and then he left her. Seeing those things, and not wanting to get myself into that sort of trouble, I made Claudio wait two years.

Recent reexamination of the institution of patriarchal marriage and its identification as a source of security and entitlement as well as of subordination (Jackson 2007, p. 118) has added to the Latin American literature and provided a basis for understanding the specific situation in Indio Guayas. Ever since Whitehead's insight that "the conjugal contract" is biased in men's favor in most contexts, the focus on gender-based intrahousehold inequality has crowded out the idea that marriage can also be a form of gender cooperation that can be beneficial or favorable for women.[5] In support of this proposition, Jackson states:

> Marriage can also be seen as a set of (variably conditional) entitlements of value to women, and not only as a relationship of power and inequality which disadvantages them. While conventional forms of household organization, kinship and marriage are anything but gender equitable . . . [they] are forms of social cooperation which women participate in because they have real perceived attractions. . . . Marriage is a shifting terrain in which ambiguity, particular (re)interpretations of norms, expectations and special circumstances, changing positions with aging and external conditions, and ever-present gap between stated and actual practice, offer fertile ground for "creative conjugality" (2007, pp. 118–26).

Such a position therefore makes it useful to identify women's agency as directed less at a separatist agenda—aimed at individual autonomy and the rejection of marriage—and more toward reforming the terms of cooperation so that they are more favorable to women. This requires further examination of the two main protagonists, women and men.

Women as "Passive" Wives?

Implicit in a cooperative conceptualization of marriage is the assumption that the woman is "deserving," performs her gender roles with socially acknowledged success, and is also prepared to suffer if necessary to ensure that the marriage lasts. Jessica, reflecting on her mother's advice in 1981, commented:

My mother went with my father when she was fourteen, and they made a deal between them: if she died, he would never take another one; and if he died, she wouldn't either. Of course, my father had another woman, but he never brought her home, he had her outside in the street. He never gave us a stepmother. My mother told me whatever happens, if you are hungry, if you are needy, still stay with your husband, however much you may suffer, because God will provide somehow. It's nasty to go with another and yet another; and the children will grow up, and then who is your father, which one? Don't you see, the next one will be worse and the one after that even worse? When I had my little girl, my husband fell in love with another woman. So I told him, "You clear out." There was an awful fight, and I packed his case and told him to go. He sent money and came to see the children. My father told him, "If you want to go with my daughter, alright, but otherwise stay away, because I can support her." I was going to sue him at the tribunal [court], but after three months he came back. He said, "That woman is nothing to me; I knew you long before."

In contrast to Jessica's traditional marriage, there was Lola's more pragmatic approach to the advantages of staying married. A *morena* (black) woman who ran a bar and food kiosk specializing in cooked offal (much rumored also to be a location for drug sales), Lola was thirty-nine in 1981 when she provided the following description of how she met and remained with her husband:

When I was fifteen, I went off with two girlfriends to Esmeraldas, and we found work as maids in private houses. I met Gregorio (El Negro) by a ditch. They were digging near the house where I was working and he asked for some water. I went off straight away to live with him. We have been in a compromiso for sixteen years. I had twelve children. They all died except for two. They would die when they were a year, nine months, thirteen months. I pay for everything in the house out of my little business. I am fed up, but I stay together so that people will not talk. Here everyone gossips, and if a woman leaves a husband, they don't say it's because she suffers but because she is stupid. I would not be better off separating from my husband and getting another man because there is no man that is not someone else's, so I might as well stick with my own. At present there is no man who will take one with all one's children. At the most he will say leave the children, and if one loves one's children, one is not going to leave them for another man.

While Jackson maintains that "discourses of love are generally promoted by the gender which feels disadvantaged by the power balances within conjugality" (Jackson, 2007, p. 120), in Indio Guayas such discourses tended to disappear fast and be replaced by a pragmatic tolerance of relationships. Even when the emotional exchanges and support had disappeared, it was considered better to remain within a relationship. Single mothers living independently, though they might benefit from the support of female kin, also bore the brunt of relentless criticism. Such was the life of Lourdes, Marta's sister and next-door neighbor, a qualified secondary school teacher earning a regular wage. As a single woman who had had a number of relationships, her morality and behavior were constantly questioned, with her brothers openly calling her a whore (*puta*). In May 2004 I summarized her life in my diary:

> Lourdes' first husband was Denis, the older man who courted her [when she was] a plump fifteen-year-old high school girl in her white school uniform, when we first lived here. He drank too much and was a womanizer, so that ended a few years after the birth of her daughter. Husband number two, Felix, was a construction truck driver [who] moved in and became jealous ("celoso") after daughter Eugenia was born. He started beating Lourdes up, but she was clued up [to] women's rights—having been a community researcher on a women's domestic violence project. So she went to the Women's Commission (*Comisaría de Mujeres*) and took out an order against him. He tore it up, but when the second arrived he packed his bags and left.

Men as Jealous (Celoso) Husbands

Just as women stereotypically are subservient and obedient, so the dominant quality of male machismo is identified as jealousy. In reality this is an ambiguous term. On the one hand, it represents ownership and possession linked to the protection and care that women are perceived to want, making women proud of jealous husbands (hence the common saying that "a man who hits his wife loves her"). On the other hand, it represents control and ownership and possession in a negative sense. This is most frequently manifest through the control over spatial movements, financial independence, denial of resources for the children of a woman's previous relationship, and a perceived control over children, marked by men's constant admission, "I am responsible for the children." Jealous men are also most likely to be womanizers, as though their right to control their wives also gave them greater legitimacy to be unfaithful.

In Indio Guayas the most common way that most women coped with male jealousy was to avoid confrontation and, where possible, to identify subtle ways to address the issue (other than gender-based violence—see below). The following example, illustrates the astuteness with which women dealt with such problems. Roberto, Marta's brother, refused to let his wife, Guadalupe, work, so she did so secretly without his knowing. In 1992 she assisted Marta as one of the cooks in the preschool meal program, crossing the road to work with her each morning after her husband had left for work and bringing her little son along. When Roberto finally discovered this subterfuge, he threatened to beat her, locked her up, and would not let her out. Guadalupe wept and did not confront him. She did not come for a day and then consulted Marta who said her work could be legitimized as "work for the community." In fact, she desperately needed the money to pay transport and school fees for her eldest daughter by a previous relationship.

Like many men, Roberto did not want his wife to bring a child from a previous relationship into the new one. Faced with this situation, women frequently left them with mothers or other relatives; as mentioned, Virginia left her elder son Emilio with Marta, while Alicia left her eldest daughter with her mother for some years. It seemed ironic that jealous Roberto was the brother of Marta, one of the most independent women on Calle K and who essentially raised him. In fact, his behavior may well have had more to do with a rejection of his mother as a role model (see below) than of his sister's independence.

Longitudinal research made it possible to assess how much the stereotypical man was a powerful oppressor as opposed to simply being "useless" in fulfilling his provisioning responsibilities and conjugal obligations (Cornwall 2007). In Indio Guayas men often became less powerful over time, such that when women years into their marriages talked about their husbands, their sentiment was less that these men were oppressing them but rather that the men were vaguely useless and not really giving them much of anything—be it love or money (Cornwall 2002, 2003). Nevertheless, this opinion was not life cycle specific, as my June 2004 field notes on the "uselessness" of Hector, Adriana's husband, indicated:

Hector drifts around all day. He washes his car, which really is not roadworthy. Marta says he always has car problems because he doesn't know about mechanics but is too lazy to do a course. Yet Adriana and he prioritize educating their two daughters in a private city center nun's school. He's a devoted father to "the babies" (*las bebes*), as he calls them. "The baby is ill" was his plaintive cry when eighteen-year-old Jennifer had a slight chill. So Hector spends his day chatting to friends and eating the meals Marta puts in front of him. In between, he drifts in and out of a world of women—his daughters—and he attentively cossets and cuddles Ana Maria's six-month-old baby, while the women sitting around after lunch chatting away ignore him. His only real task twice daily is to attach the pump so as to get water from the tank into the house. Friday and Saturday nights he launches out into the world of real work to drive his illegal taxi, picking up late-night passengers. When he earns and still contributes nothing to the household, Marta threatens to stop cooking for him, but it is only a threat.

Women were also sometimes perceived as "useless," in this case irresponsible in terms of their household tasks. There was much sympathy for husbands who took on the responsibility to hold things together. Alvaro the tailor, Walter's brother, for instance, was left to care for three young children and single-handedly run his tailoring business after his wife, Yasmin, left him. Such household enterprises depended on the contribution of wives (see chapter 6), so Alvaro's mother helped out. In 1992 Alvaro was desperately poor and heavily reliant on local welfare support; the evangelical church next door gave the two younger children lunch, while Plan provided financial help for schoolbooks and uniforms. Because Yasmin did not attend the Saturday community meeting, the family missed out on a septic tank, land titles, and other benefits being negotiated with Plan during that period. In desperation, Alvaro started to attend the meetings. When Yasmin ultimately returned, household well-being improved.

Collaboration and Conflict in Intrahousehold Gender Relations

Over the past thirty years, the dynamics of marriage or consensual unions and their implications for asset accumulation have been influenced by a combination of factors, including changes in the wider economic context and the relentless impacts of the life cycle, as well as individual changes in women's and men's personal agency relating to conjugality. This assessment of marriage "as a more open and dynamic terrain of change" (Jackson 2007, p. 126) recognizes a broader framework of social relations that includes siblings, other generations, and other women. It challenges idealized representations of women's solidarity and autonomy and means it is no longer politically necessary to "[airbrush] away conflicts and contradictions in women's relationships with each other" (Cornwall 2007, p. 152).[6] Identification of the nature of women's relationships with other women, the group with which they primarily interact, makes it possible to distinguish among associations with different relational identities. These issues are incorporated into the following description of diverse arenas of conflict and collaboration within Indio Guayas households.

Multiple Responsibilities and Gender Relationships

When I first lived in Indio Guayas in 1978 together with my family, the strict rigidities in gender divisions of labor and associated male and female responsibilities within households and the community made a profound impression. Without running water for washing and bathing, electricity or gas for cooking, or appropriate sanitation, it was an enormous challenge to fulfill the multiple, daily reproductive responsibilities. Indeed, we learned very early on the perils of breaking strict taboos when Brian did the washing up after the exhaustion of cooking on kerosene in oppressive 95-degree heat reduced me to a state of collapse. Our neighbors quickly spread the gossip that "Don Brian was washing up," which relayed a double message in terms of gender relations: while Brian was emasculated for performing a female task, I was shown to be inadequate both in allowing him to do it and in failing to perform it myself.

Not at that time or any other did my women neighbors question their responsibility for the domestic arena, which they saw as "natural," though their conversations were full of woeful stories of endless misery, with consolation gained from the recognition that this was the fate of all women.

I was shocked by the seemingly unequal burden borne by women. In 1978 the majority of households were small nuclear families with young children, and more than half of the women were not involved in income-earning activities while those that did worked in or near their homes (chapter 6). But women's responsibilities soon extended beyond the household to community mobilization to access social and physical infrastructure (chapters 4 and 5). The delegation of this onerous, long-term task to women was legitimized by men "because women have free time." The weight of this commitment was also invisibilized by external agencies such as UNICEF and Plan, which relied heavily on women's unpaid labor to implement community projects (see Moser 1989b). As such, women's involvement in mobilization was rarely a source of intrahousehold conflict since all were mindful of the advantages that improved physical and social infrastructure would bring.

However, community work relied on women's collaboration. Marta's neighbor Mercedes, a long-term invaluable supporter, commented "As my *comadre*, she is a member of the family, so I cannot say no."[7] However, over time jealousy and conflict often developed between women leaders and rank-and-file women members. My assumptions about female solidarity were challenged by a reality in which relations between women were often dominated by petty envy and distrust, particularly when women leaders moved beyond the community into the wider political arena; as they became more powerful, so too they became increasingly distanced from their female neighbors. Political leaders rushing in and out of the area visiting their homes caused jealousy from women "trapped" at home. Gossiping about their role as mothers was a powerful weapon used to besmirch their reputation. The following accusation about Marta, made by a close neighbor, was typical: "She neglects her children. The girls know how to cook, but they just don't want to. The trouble is that there is no one to make them do it. The children are badly brought up, they just run around the street."

Marta found it difficult to retain friendships with her female neighbors once the local struggle for collective consumption was over and her political work involved lobbying for communities outside Indio Guayas. By the 1990s she preferred to work with men leaders rather than women leaders, commenting that she particularly disliked the way some put on lots of makeup, flirted with men leaders, and wore sexually provocative clothes, saying, "This type of woman is a real problem." So gradually she also lost her friendships with women political leaders, summarizing her opinion as follows: "Women cannot be trusted; they agree with you, they confide in you, and then they turn against you. You know where you are with men leaders."

In Marta's case marital conflict also became problematic. While men initially were proud of their wives' political status, the relationship soon experienced severe pressure due to the time-consuming nature of the work (particularly with national political activity), the rampant accusation that women working with men must be prostituting themselves, and the fact that as women became public figures, they achieved greater importance than their spouses, both inside and outside the barrio. I well recall an incident when we lived in Indio Guayas in 1978. Marta was suddenly summoned to an important evening meeting at Izquierda Democrática headquarters and asked me to accompany her. I was delighted as this was an important breakthrough in my fieldwork. While I was preparing to depart, through the split bamboo wall I could hear her husband, Jesus, complaining, while Brian was equally put out at being left to cope with the children's meal. We finally emerged through our front doors, walked down the unpaved dusty street—Marta elegant in her tight trousers and high-heeled shoes, I in my denim skirt and sandals—and turned to each other, and in unison said, "Men!"

In 1982 Marta described some of her feelings and how she had coped:

I have had problems since I first went on the committee. But I don't go around telling everyone about it. Jesus says it's all right if I am fighting for our street only, but not for all those others. I tell him that's selfish. If I am a leader and people have trust in me, I cannot let them down; I must go on until I get the works for them. Maybe he doesn't like it because most of my work is with men. But if I don't want to do anything, nothing will happen to me, because that depends on oneself. I have been with him for twelve years, and I have never failed him. One week we are all right, and the following week, nothing but fights. But I don't suffer; I eat. If I stopped to think, I would be miserable. I am not going to let him dominate me. He would like me to do nothing and let him do whatever he likes. Once he sees that I don't obey him, he'll have to decide whether he wants to go on, or go to the devil. What does marriage do for us? I have always worked since I was a young girl. So I'll just have to work a little harder if he goes, to support myself and the children. Is that such a problem?

Despite such conflict the relationship survived her lengthy career as a political leader, and by 2004, when Marta was a widowed grandmother, she was deeply lonely living without her husband. Adriana, her elder daughter, had become her political confidante, accompanied her to the range of political activities in which she was still involved, and had informally taken over many of her mother's responsibilities (see chapter 10).

Arenas of Intrahousehold Decisionmaking

Intrahousehold decisionmaking was the primary arena for the daily ebb and flow of collaboration and conflicts associated with household inequalities, and had important implications for asset accumulation.[8] This included both short-term decisionmaking over income flows for consumption expenditures and education, as well as longer-term responsibilities over fertility and family size. Underlying such negotiations were the constant interrelated threats of gender-based violence, abandonment, and male ownership of children.

Income and Budget Decisionmaking

Since the accumulation of assets related not only to the level of household income but also to who controlled income flows (Dwyer and Bruce 1988; Haddad and Kanbur 1989), this was a critical area for intrahousehold discourse. Generally women managed the household budget, controlling expenditures for food and clothing, whereas the men made the decisions about expenditures for personal luxury items, such as cigarettes and alcohol.[9] Data from a 1992 subsample showed that most other fiscal decisions were shared; these included expenditures on furniture and electrical goods, and borrowing money. Although women were consumption decisionmakers, they relied primarily on their husbands' money to purchase food.

Subsample data from 1992 illustrate the budget-making situation at that time; half of the women were entirely dependent on their husband's earnings, with another 38 percent, including household heads, also dependent on further contributions from sons and daughters. Only in 12 percent of households did women contribute most of the household income for such expenditures. Some 40 percent received money for household expenditures on a daily basis, exacerbating the difficult task of budgeting (sometimes husbands working in the informal sector were paid daily), while in other instances men's day-by-day allocations reflected gendered negotiation over resources and an unwillingness to hand over larger amounts of money. Only a quarter of the women received contributions on a biweekly or monthly basis. Such piecemeal resource allocation hindered long-term budgeting and bulk food buying, and the latter had major impact because food was more expensive when bought in small amounts daily, sometimes even by the meal. This not only increased the economic costs of daily survival, reducing resources for other assets, but it also had intangible costs in terms of increased pressure on women's time.

In contrast, education was an area where there was greater joint decision-making. Nevertheless, when this was conflictive, there were implications for investments in educational human capital, as in Lidia's case: "Their father didn't want them to study, and so I told him, 'You are a donkey. I don't want them to be donkeys, too.' That's why we faced all sorts of obstacles, even to pay for their school materials."

Control over Female Sexuality and Associated Fertility

In Indio Guayas women's subordination manifested itself most concretely in male control over female sexuality. Sonia was a close friend of Marta's in the early days of political contestation until she left the area in the late 1980s. Here is her poignant description of her first sexual encounter, her first marriage, and the extreme measures she had to go to in order to get out of an abusive relationship:

> People in the old days were so reserved they never explained to us how to defend ourselves from a man, or how one started to have menstruation. It was all totally obscure. Because I was already fourteen and plump and straight, the father of my children started to make up to me. I had seven children with him, my first baby when I was less than fifteen, and every two years I had a baby. He was super-jealous and wouldn't let me out any-

where. He would go off to work and lock me up. I couldn't even go to look out of the window. In all those fifteen years I was with him, I never went shopping, to the market or store. He would bring everything so that I wouldn't go anywhere, only bring children into the world and raise them, and in all that time, I never had any recreation, a dance, or an outing.

I stopped loving him after I had two children. I was doing it out of a feeling of duty. . . . My separation was dramatic. My mother died, and he opposed my going to her funeral. He said, "No, you can't go, she is dead now, and there is no reason for you to be there." In view of all the love I felt for my mother, my heart went hard all of a sudden and I didn't give a damn. So I said, "I have to do right by her." "Well," he said, "you leave me my children." So he took them away from me; it was a deceit. Obviously had I known then what I know now, I would have made him return the children to me, through the Tribunal [of Minors]. One day in the center, he cornered me against a wall, with a knife to kill me. I became a rural market seller because he had made my life impossible in Guayaquil. I met Dionisio four years later, and I liked him because he was a reserved person, always really respectful, he never grabbed me. He told me how he had suffered, I told him my problems, and after a while we became sweethearts.

Control over women was linked to control over their children, often used as a very real threat to prevent them from leaving. In Sonia's case she was forced to abandon all her children to get away from her husband. Male control was also linked to fertility, and the use of birth control. Although Alicia's husband walked out on her in 1975, and she became a female household head, she had two further children by him, essentially trading sex for money. Discussing her actions in 1981, she said:

I didn't have those other two children through my will; it was against my will. He threatened to beat me up. He said that if I didn't want to be with him, that meant I had another man. I had those two other babies because I needed the money. Without money one is nobody. Every week I have to beg him. Last week it was 100 pesos, 150 the week before. Sometimes I make 50 pesos a week, so I live on 300–400 per month. I tried the Tribunal [of Minors]. But once one brings an action, one cannot have any more children. And there it says there are only six. But once I had another child, I lost the right to claim.

Simultaneously, her husband was having children with another woman. Although by law she should have been able to claim an allowance from her husband through the minors' tribunal, once she had an additional child, she could no longer do so. Needless to say, local women who frequently helped her out were critical of Alicia's continuing relationship with her ex-husband.

For many couples fertility and birth control were an important area of joint decisionmaking. One of the first questions women constantly asked me when I lived in the community in 1978 concerned the type of birth control I was using. The 1992 subsample data confirm, for instance, that four out of five women made their current contraceptive choices together with their partners.[10] For Claudio and Mercedes, and Marta and Jesus, the decision to have fewer children was a conscious strategy to provide the next generation with greater opportunities. As the economic situation worsened and the pressure to earn an income increased, effective fertility control became more of a priority for women. Nevertheless, many families were still large, with unplanned pregnancies widespread. Subsample data from 1992 show a mean of 6.4 pregnancies per women (total pregnancies, 270), ranging from 2 to 13 per woman.[11]

By the 1980s birth control pills were readily available at pharmacies, and intrauterine devices (IUDs) could be fitted at the local Atahualpa Policlinic. However, women increasingly chose tubal ligation as the preferred method of birth control, undertaken immediately after the birth of the last desired child. By 1992 nearly half (45 percent of women) used this form of birth control, with only 12 percent using an IUD. At this time, one in five women was still making birth control decisions without her partner's consent and sometimes against his wishes. However, tubal ligation required a husband's written permission and therefore remained an area of male control.[12] In addition, birth control information was not provided for teenage girls; indeed many women believed it would encourage promiscuity. In commenting about how she inadvertently became pregnant at age seventeen, Virginia said:

> Well, I knew the pill existed, but I did not know how to buy them. You may think it's silly, but that's the way it was, because I didn't want to have a child, and I didn't know about it. It's taboo to talk about sex. Women are ashamed to talk about such things. They may say they were with a boyfriend, and that we did it in this or that position, but they won't say, "I am taking care. I am doing it like this so you can do the same."

By the 1990s, as a result of HIV/AIDS propaganda in Guayaquil, women increasingly articulated the right that marriage gives them to control their own sexuality. In a culture in which men's extramarital liaisons with other women, particularly prostitutes, were implicitly if not explicitly tolerated, women's concern about the dangers of HIV/AIDS related to the potential for transmission without their knowledge. This also led some women to be more vocal in challenging their husband's right to extramarital sexual liaisons. The majority of women considered the concern over HIV/AIDS a problem to be shared by husband and wife. As Marta commented, "It's a problem for both husband and wife; husbands cannot have relationships outside their home. Nobody is free from this danger; it's the responsibility of the pair." Yet, as the HIV/AIDs problem became one mainly associated with gay men, the opportunity for open discussions about sexuality disappeared.

The Impacts of Economic Hardship on Intrahousehold Dynamics

While in 1978 households in Indio Guayas comprised young, upwardly aspiring families, by 1992 changes in the macroeconomic context as well as in family size and associated living expenses had an impact on intrahousehold dynamics. When household economic situations became difficult, the range of responses included women extending their working day or reducing reproductive tasks, children taking on additional responsibilities, and men coping with declines in real income and job security. Not all family members coped equally well since responses were determined not only by known cultural practices but also by individual agency. Increased child neglect, female depression, male substance abuse, and especially gender-based violence exacerbated intrahousehold and intergenerational dynamics.

The most dramatic consequence of the 1980s economic crisis was an increase in the number of women going out to work. Generally, men accepted the family's need for additional income and, with few exceptions (such as Roberto, described above), this was not an area of conflict. Women managed this extra demand not by allocating tasks to male partners but by distributing tasks to other household members, particularly daughters. To manage their multiple responsibilities, women spent longer hours working than did men; the 1992 subsample time allocation data, for instance, showed that men spent an average of forty-seven hours a week on productive income-generating work, while women spent thirty-nine hours. However, women averaged sixteen hours a week on household tasks (excluding child care) versus an average of five hours for men.[13] Less time was devoted to community-managing tasks, but again it was women who spent more time on such activities than did men.[14] While the overall difference between female and male work hours was only three hours, for women it was the complexity of balancing of different tasks over short periods of time that was particularly challenging.[15]

This empirical evidence from Indio Guayas led me to conceptualize women's triple role in performing reproductive, productive, and community-managing work as one of the methodological tools of gender planning (Moser 1989b, 1993).[16] The purpose of this concept was to make visible to policymakers and planners women's multiple, mainly nonvalorized responsibilities within their households and their communities. This evidence contributed to the 1990's feminist debates concerning the unequal burden placed on women by macroeconomic policies associated with structural adjustment, such as forcing them to extend their working day by taking on income-generating work in addition to their reproductive and community responsibilities (see Moser 1992; Elson 1991).[17]

Daughters, Education, and Conflict

When female heads and spouses had little option but to go out to work, there were human capital costs for young children, who frequently suffered neglect, particularly nutritional problems, when not being fed by their mothers. Elder daughters often had to assume responsibility for domestic tasks and dovetail this with their education, first caring for younger siblings and then, by the age of ten or eleven, adding cooking to their tasks. Households with two or more daughters frequently made maximum use of the half-day school shift system by having the girls attend different shifts, thereby freeing up their mother's time for full-time work (see chapter 9).

The 1992 data revealed that two out of three daughters in school provided child care on a daily basis. In many female-headed extended households, mothers effectively handed over all child care responsibilities to their daughters, devoting themselves totally to productive work. Forced to take this on at a young age, elder daughters themselves suffered from reduced parental care and guidance. Although socialized to assist their mothers with domestic tasks, they did not automatically accept the responsibilities thrust upon them and resented missing school. This frequently resulted in intergenerational conflict, neglect of siblings, early promiscuity, and even prostitution. In the 1992 subsample, two out of five women identified conflict with children as the main cause of discord in their homes. Some conflicts were related to economic factors, such as the lack of resources to respond to children's requests; others arose over child care, children not studying, girls not helping in the home, and sons spending too much time in the "street," usually drinking.

Male Drinking, Drug Use, and Depression

In 1992 some 15 percent of women cited conflicts with their husbands relating to jealousy, infidelity, and particularly drinking as a cause of intrahousehold conflict. Indeed, difficult circumstances had a direct impact on men's level of alcohol consumption. In Indio Guayas weekend male drinking had always been an accepted part of suburbio life. It frequently started on Friday evening, at the end of the working week, with men sitting outside their houses with a few male neighbors and a crate of beer. Some men continued to drink through the weekend until Sunday afternoon when their wives dragged them home before they collapsed senseless. The men needed to eat something if they were to be ready for the next working week. Among the neighbors on Calle K, almost all the men drank on a regular basis, with some, such as Marta's brother Roberto (see above), identified as alcoholics.[18] For women, coping with male drinking was a recognized part of marriage; most were not averse to male drinking unless it resulted in violence. As Eloisa, Walter the tailor's wife, commented: "He has always drunk, but it does not bother me because he has never thrown me out of the house; it does not affect me because he quietly goes to sleep."

However, it became a source of conflict when too much money needed for household expenditure was spent on alcohol. Since women had no control over their husbands' drinking expenditures, male drinking frequently was the biggest drain on household resources. A shift from weekend "social" drinking to daily drinking was an important indication of not coping. By the 1990s Carmen's husband, Alonso, was verging on alcoholism; if he got a job, he drank all week as well as weekends while Carmen raised the whole family on her own. During this period Hospice International (see chapter 5) used male drinking as a working indicator (unpublished) to identify families with special needs for subsidized health care. By 2004, however, the same men were drinking far less, if at all. Ill health and age were major factors; diabetes had affected three out of five husbands on Calle K (Jesus, Claudio, and Walter). Finally, there were some men, such as Don Ortega, who gave up drink when he joined the evangelical church.

If drink was a problem with husbands, drugs were identified as a problem with sons. In 1978 a small number of younger "irresponsible" men in their twenties smoked marijuana; identified as deviant outsiders, they were often perpetrators of local burglaries. By 1992 the problem had become more severe, with marijuana widely available. Local distributors included not only men but also women bar owners. The arrival of cheap cocaine paste (*pasta*) exacerbated the situation. The first suicide known to the community occurred in 1988, when a young male cocaine addict hanged himself after his wife confronted him about spending his earnings on his addiction while his three young children were without food. The community perceived a direct causal connection between the growth in drugs and an increase in the number of street gangs and street robberies (see chapter 11).

Female Depression

What did women do when life got to be too much? Female responsibility to keep households going on a daily basis meant that generally they did not drink and never took drugs. But despite assistance from female kin, women did not always manage successfully and became despondent and depressed, most visibly manifested in apathy, exhaustion, and extensive sleeping, as well as constant weeping and feelings of fatalism.[19] Women constantly discussed "depression" (*depresión*), and its severity was illustrated in the 1992 subsample where three quarters of the women acknowledged that at some point they had suffered from this condition. The majority cited as the primary reason an inability to provide adequately for their children, usually expressed specifically in terms of lack of resources or food and worry about the children's behavior.

As described in chapter 7, by 1992 women such as Alicia had "burnt out"; her eldest daughter, Dorotea, had assumed the household domestic tasks with the help of younger daughter Sofia, who attended the community meetings on behalf of the family. Alicia was not unique; her neighbor Lidia's neglectful behavior was the topic of much gossip, with one particularly critical woman commenting:

> Lidia is a pig, she is dirty. Why? Because she does nothing. She is lazy. And she is a gossip. She goes from one house to another, asking, finding out, and then she tells it to the next house, and so on. She is out all day, and her house is so untidy because she is never at home. A shoe falls and there it stays. They have no order.

For her part, Lidia described the tension between retaining her children's affection and commitment, and finding another partner once Salvador had left her, as follows:

> I sometimes feel depressed. I have cried a lot. I have begged, I have told him to come back for the kids. I don't know why this happens, why men leave. Am I better off by myself? My children are already threatening me that if I get engaged to someone else, I won't be able to live here; I'd have to go somewhere else because if I live with another man, my children will go their own way. I don't want to lose my children's affection over a man. Because they have told me if I get engaged, I can forget I have children.

Intrahousehold Gender-Based Violence

Resonating through the histories of intrahousehold marital relationships was gender-based, or intimate, violence. In 1978 male physical abuse of wives and female partners was common in Indio Guayas, with women citing jealousy and alcohol as the two most important reasons for wife beating. While most women tolerated this, they did not condone it. Some women, such as Marta's mother, left an abusive man. In 1982 Marta's sister Virginia, then age fifteen, recalled how it occurred:

> Shortly after I was born, my sister was carrying me and let me fall, and my father got angry and was going to hit her. So my mother said that if he hit her, she would leave him because he had no right to hit her, to let a baby fall could happen to anyone. So my father got furious and they had a fight and he hit my mother. About two months later, at dawn, my mother left him, and we all went away on the boat to Guayaquil.

During the 1990s the deteriorating macroeconomic context and the demands of the expansion phase of the family life cycle exacerbated physical violence and verbal conflict. In the 1992 subsample, half of the women noted an increase in violence in the home, frequently occurring when the lack of sufficient cash for the household budget forced them to ask their spouses for more money. Women distinguished between male anger from frustration at not earning enough and anger when challenged about retaining earnings for personal expenditures, such as on other women and alcohol. In both instances the consequence was the same: men beat their wives. In contrast, a smaller number of women, now earning a reliable income, felt they received greater respect from male partners because of their economic independence, with an associated increase in their personal assertiveness.

Thus women considered that any decline in domestic violence was related to changes in themselves rather than to changes in men. In 1992 Carmen, who used to be beaten by her drunk husband, Alonso, proudly told me how finally she had the confidence to lock him out of the house, commenting that "women now defend themselves; I stopped letting myself be beaten." In fact, by that period many women condemned men that beat their wives. As Marta commented, "The man who beats his wife is not much of a man; they behave like animals."

Carmen's eighteen-year-old daughter was clear from her mother's experience that male inadequacy outside the home resulted in violence within it: "Because he does not feel like a man in the street, he vents his anger in the home."

Leaving, or kicking out an abusive partner, while it reduced the level of conflict, also reduced the number of income earners. By 2004 Marta's sister Lourdes had taken out two actions against her second partner in the Tribunal de Menores (Tribunal of Minors), the first to force him to leave her house, and the second to

Table 8-1. *Legal Procedure to Force Abusive Husband to Leave Marital Home*
Unit as indicated

Process	Institutional actor	Payment in U.S. dollars
1. Consultation with lawyer about the problem and to file complaint	Women's Commission, Ministry of Government	200–300
2. Secretary writes the accusation and makes a declaration of assault	Secretary of the Women's Commission	. . .
3. A first Order of Immediate Presence issued instructing the man to present himself at the Women's Commission[a]	Secretary of the Women's Commission	10–20
4. A second order issued that the man leaves the house and for habeas corpus protection	Secretary of the Women's Commission	10–20
5. An agreement reached with husband with the couple meeting with a court psychologist	Psychologist in the Tribunal of Minors	. . .
6. A third order issued to arrest and detain the man	Police and prison service	10–20, plus an additional 20–40 to the police

Source: Interview with Lourdes, Marta's sister, Indio Guayas, 2004.
a. Duration between each order is eight days.

claim an allowance of $22 per month for her daughter. Both were complex procedures that required time, financial resources, and, above all, sheer determination to undertake—factors that deterred many women in a similar position from doing likewise (see tables 8-1 and 8-2).

Commenting in 2004 on her experiences, Lourdes concluded:

There are enormous changes in where you can go and protest about domestic violence. Mothers used to be more passive before. They endured violence from their husbands. Now they think differently, they're more educated and have the possibility to overcome these limitations. You have to look after yourself and feel worthy. Not think you're worthy because someone comes and says he loves you. The punches they give you don't do any good. You start falling into a depressive mode and lack self-esteem. We don't have justice here, rather injustice. The judges try to get money if they see you have a little bit of money. Here the winner is who-

Table 8-2. *Legal Process to Obtain Maintenance Allowance for a Child*
Units as indicated

Procedure	Institutional actor	Cost in U.S. dollars	
		Nominal	*Actual*
1. Place a complaint	Lawyer	200–300	200–300
Documentation needed			
—Birth certificate of sons and daughters of less than 18 years		6	15–20
—Identity card		6	15–20
—Voting certificate		6	15–20
2. Discussion and agreement: Identification of agreement of quantity	Lawyer	200–300	200–300
3. If not in agreement, issuance of a nutrition judgment	Nutrition judge	0	30–50
4. Agreement of sentence (three to six months)	Judge	20–50 minimum plus overtime	Depends what child's father provides

Source: Interview with Lourdes, Marta's sister, Indio Guayas, 2004.

ever pays the highest price, whoever has more connections. They win any trial or legal dispute.

Intrahousehold Assets and Women's Empowerment

By 2004 the young "pioneering" women such as Marta, Alicia, Lidia, Mercedes, and Carmen—whose commitment, energy, and support had achieved so much for their community and their families—were grandmothers, some widowed or abandoned, many struggling. Their lives had improved remarkably in terms of housing and living conditions since they first arrived in 1978, but it had not been a smooth process in terms of intrahousehold dynamics. They had experienced enormous time pressures as they sought to make ends meet: some of their children had been neglected, resulting in nutritional or behavioral problems; some daughters lost educational opportunities and some sons turned to gangs or drugs; and some husbands had turned to alcohol. Many women had experienced varying levels of physical and mental abuse, though this declined as they had aged and male control of their sexuality had become a less important issue.

How can one measure the empowerment of the women in Indio Guayas? Again a longitudinal perspective puts a very different light on this issue than does a time-bound analysis. This chapter has shown that for many women in Indio Guayas, marriage or a partnership was not simply an unequal contract but also an attractive form of cooperation with evident potential advantages. This meant that conjugal separation was not necessarily seen as a measure of women's power within a relationship. By 2004 older women were enjoying their children's good fortune and caring for grandchildren, and had come to terms with the reality of unfulfilled expectations relating to wayward partners or disappointments over their children's careers. Widowhood had been a terrible blow for Marta, her grief at Jesus's death still so bad that her sister Lourdes commented, "She needs to stop walking around with all this sadness and grief and start living again."

By 2004 Lidia's husband had returned home again and was drinking heavily, while Mercedes was concerned that along with his dental practice down river, her husband, Claudio, was living with a younger woman. While men were still considered "hopeless shits" (*pendejos*), overall it was still considered better to have any man than no man at all. Alicia, with her nine children and twenty-seven grandchildren, stood apart in terms of her sense of well-being; still poor, she was contented and well-protected by her children. Finally, Carmen had left her two-timing husband and gone off to Barcelona where she devoted herself to saving as much as she could to fulfill her ambition of a decent house for her children (see chapter 10).

For women in Indio Guayas, the goal of being "independent" (*independiente*), understood as gaining more control over their lives, was achieved through work and accumulating associated economic resources. But independent income by itself did not necessarily empower them, as has been assumed in many empowerment discourses (Cornwall, Harrison, and Whitehead 2007, p. 15). Another important concrete measure of empowerment was related to ownership of a land title. Thanks to the mobilization by the Indio Guayas committee, by 2004 both Marta, a widow, and Alicia, a single household head, were single title holders, while Mercedes, Lidia, and Carmen, still in nominal or actual marriages, were joint holders with their male partners. By 2004, in a context in which people did not make wills, households were beginning to confront the problem of the gendered nature of inheritance. As Marta's sister Lourdes, who was well aware of legal matters, commented, "I don't have a will which states what belongs to each one. It's not a habit in our culture. Those inside the plot think it's going to be left to them when their parents die and that's how it will be."

To what extent were the tangible and intangible assets accumulated by first-generation women transferred to the next generation, including to daughters and granddaughters? This question not only covers the transfer of physical assets, with or without wills, but also, and more important, the intangible "assets" of "independence" and empowerment. In Indio Guayas empowerment was not necessarily associated with individualization and was often achieved within joint conjugal projects—and that "jointness" did not always mean male domination (Kabeer 1994, p. 14). Chapter 9 continues to explore these issues, focusing next on intergenerational power dynamics.

9

Daughters and Sons:
Intergenerational Asset Accumulation

"Leonel and Mateo, the two sons of Diego and Andrea Ortega who chose career paths in different cities, illustrate the diverse opportunities and associated income levels in Guayaquil and Barcelona. The family settled in Indio Guayas in 1973 with three children, living two doors down from Alicia on Calle K. Don Ortega, with three years of primary education, was a shop assistant, and Andrea, with no formal schooling, a domestic worker. Their son Mateo completed four years of secondary education and worked as a shop delivery driver for ten years before immigrating to Europe. He worked in Italy as a domestic worker before going to Barcelona, where by 2005 he had a permanent job as an industrial night cleaner, earning nearly $1,200 per month. Over the years his wife and four children joined him. His younger brother, Leonel, completed high school and became an oil tank driver. When he lost his job after ten years, he became a chauffeur taking local children to school. In 2004 he earned approximately $120 a month and lived with Dorotea, Alicia's eldest daughter, and five of their children. In 2004 Mateo loaned him $2,000 when he ran into problems, while still remitting $150 monthly to his father."
—Caroline Moser, field notes, July 2005

A thirty-year study makes it possible to track how well parents' aspirations for their children were met, as well as the extent to which children's lives played out in comparison to their own expectations. Such long-term observation relates not only to the sons and daughters of the first generation that settled in Indio Guayas in the 1970s but also to the third generation—their grandchildren. For instance, the five mothers from the five families on Calle K had raised a total of twenty-five children, and by 2004 they had fifty grandchildren.

The similar socioeconomic characteristics and economic circumstances of these and other households in Indio Guayas in 1978 allowed them to be considered as a "natural experiment." Based on the data from this "experiment," what had changed between then and 2004, not only with regard to the first generation but also subsequent generations? To what extent did the first generation's asset accumulation choices affect the second generation and, in turn, the third generation?

In examining life cycles intergenerationally, it is necessary to identify the extent to which differences in the broader socioeconomic and political contexts influenced pathways to adulthood when the parents in 1978 are compared with their children twenty-six years later. Recent research on "emerging adulthood," for instance, argues against the concept of a standardized transition to adulthood and maintains that there is variability and individualization in reaching adult status (Shanahan 2000, p. 671). In industrialized countries the transition from the late teens through to the mid-twenties has been identified as a new period in the life course, one with distinct developmental characteristics (Arnett 2007, p. 68).[1] These characteristics include longer and more widespread participation in postsecondary education and training, greater tolerance of premarital sex and cohabitation, and later ages for marriage and parenthood (Arnett 2007, p. 70). This chapter examines second- and third-generation aspirations and life choices in Indio Guayas in the light of the broader environment as well as in terms of factors relating to individual agency.

Were the Children Richer or Poorer than Their Parents?

The intergenerational data make it possible to evaluate whether households were locked into an intergenerational "culture" of poverty (Lewis 1961) or whether upward mobility occurred from one generation to the next. Although identifying intergenerational outcomes is complicated by diversity among the children—above all in terms of where they lived—this problem is partially addressed by the fact that the most important cross-generational data come from the survey of adult sons and daughters that had moved off the family plot but were still in Guayaquil in 2004 (see appendix A for a detailed account of the research methodology).

The panel data showed that the sons and daughters who had left the household plot and moved to one of four other main locations—other plots in Indio Guayas, other areas in the city, other cities in Ecuador, or Europe, as migrants—had done so near the end of the study period. In 1992 very few children had left (4 percent), whereas by 2004 nearly half had moved out. This trend reflects the expansion phase in second-generation households, with those coming from larger families more likely to move out and set up a new home. Like their parents in 1978, two-thirds of the off-plot children were in nuclear families, and only a fourth were in extended households. Only 2.25 percent of these off-plot households were headed by women, an even smaller proportion than in their parents' generation in 1978 (9.8 percent). When members of the second generation did set up on their own, they constituted a single household, just as their parents had been when invading Indio Guayas.

Similar patterns emerged for households with a family member living abroad. In 1978 there were none, in 1992 the figure was 2 percent, and by 2004 that proportion had jumped to more than 35.3 percent.

Older children were more likely to live away from their parents' plot. Thus the mean age for daughters on the parental plot was twenty-seven years, whereas for those living elsewhere in Guayaquil, the mean age was thirty-two years, and for daughters in the Barcelona sample, it was thirty-one years. The sons followed a similar pattern, with an average age of twenty-eight for those on the parental plot, thirty-four for those living elsewhere in Guayaquil, and thirty-six for sons in Barcelona.

Another small but emerging trend was the number of households with family members in prison. These were not male household heads but rather male children, grandchildren, and nephews. Although the number of household members in jail was not as yet significant as of the last survey year, the proportion increased from 0.6 percent in 1992 to over 4 percent in 2004.

Intergenerational household income poverty comparisons show that the children's households had higher levels of well-being than the parental households. Two-fifths of the children's households were nonpoor, and a slightly larger proportion was poor as opposed to very poor. This means that generally the next generation was better off than their parents were at a similar stage in their lives. Both the external factors and transferred assets enabled the next generation to start with more. In addition, children that settled on the periphery of the city did not have to mobilize through their local community committee to get electricity and basic services, as did their parents. In the later years of the survey period, public and private sector institutions provided services much earlier in the settlement consolidation process than was the case in the 1970s, in part driven by opportunities for profit.

When a poverty ladder (Krishna 2007) was used in a 2004 focus group of second- and third-generation young women to help them convey their perceptions of poverty, the participants identified 10 percent of the community as "rich," 30 percent as "middle class," and 60 percent as "poor." The rich were those who owned properties, businesses, consumer durables, and cars. The middle classes were those who lived in cement houses, had limited consumer durables, and did contract work. Finally, the poor were those who lived in split-bamboo houses or rented rooms, and had no work. This was not a realistic self-identification exercise since the girls all categorized themselves as middle class; regardless of their actual circumstances, they were unable, or unwilling, to identify themselves as poor. Laura, Adriana's daughter and Marta's granddaughter, was the one exception. She argued that if one needed a good education to be in the middle class, she could not be in that category because she had just finished high school. Lack of education was identified as the most important barrier that limited upward mobility and prevented people from moving from poor to middle class, while contacts and access to cash and resources were considered crucial to move from middle class to rich.

To improve their well-being, the second generation had pursued distinct strategies with varying degrees of success. While some had found it safest to remain in their home plots, others had ventured off them, with the most ambitious joining a growing migration out of country, primarily to Barcelona, Spain. When the incomes of all three sets of children—those living on the plot, living off the plot in Ecuador, and living abroad—were compared, those living at home earned the least while those emigrating were the most financially successful. Barcelona appeared to provide much more opportunity than Ecuador: the average income for those who migrated abroad was $820.66 a month, compared with $67.97 for those that moved out of the plot but remained in Ecuador and $60.24 for those that remained with their parents. Parents made less than the children ($58.48) on average in 2004, but their incomes were more stable, with significantly lower standard deviations.

Thus, based on income alone, the children who had taken the most risk and initiative by moving abroad were the most successful, as illustrated by the comparative experience of the two sons of Don Ortega, Leonel and Mateo, described at the beginning of the chapter. In fact, Leonel was better educated than Mateo, and while both started in the transport sector in Guayaquil, Mateo broke out when he moved abroad, where his job as an industrial night cleaner

Figure 9-1. *Accumulation of Assets, Parents 1978 versus Off-Plot Children 2004*

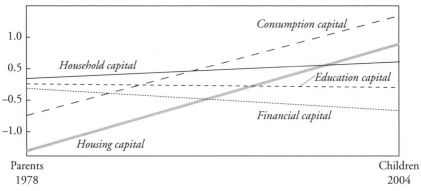

Standard deviation

Parents
1978

Children
2004

Source: Author's calculations.

earned him far more than his brother's work. Indeed, it was Mateo who assisted Leonel financially when a sudden "shock" occurred: Leonel was charged with reputedly raping a female passenger in his taxi and had to bribe his way out of a prison sentence.

The Role of Asset Accumulation in Intergenerational Changes

As with the first generation in the 1970s, it was important when I studied second-generation households to move beyond income poverty measurement and identify the accumulation of different assets. In fact, members of the second generation benefited greatly from the investments of their parents. Figures 9-1 and 9-2 summarize the differences between parents and those children who moved off the plot but remained in Guayaquil. The figures show that the children accumulated different types of capital than did their parents. In particular, they had much higher levels of consumption goods relative to their housing stock and other assets, representing greater lifestyle expectations. Growing up in a more media-saturated world than their parents and therefore exposed to more advertising and lifestyle imagery, the children reversed the asset accumulation pattern of the earlier generation, first acquiring consumer goods and then improving their housing. With credit more readily available, they were also willing to borrow to finance their consumption. Some 68 percent of the children were engaged in borrowing, compared with 58 percent of the parents; indeed,

Figure 9-2. *Accumulation of Assets, Parents versus Off-Plot Children, 2004*

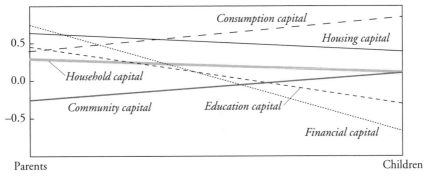

Source: Author's calculations.

the financial capital of the children in 2004 was less than that of their parents in 1978. Since few could afford to buy such consumer goods, local community members attributed the rise in street gangs, theft, and violence in the community (see chapter 11) to the desire for easy money.

In describing intergenerational changes in asset accumulation, it is useful to distinguish between assets that the second generation acquired from their parents, those they themselves acquired, and those that they gave back to their parents. Two issues were particularly pertinent. The first, at the individual level, concerned the gender breakdown for specific capital assets: did daughters do better than sons? Second, at the household level, was the transfer or accumulation of assets between the second and third generation accompanied by significant levels of conflict, both between generations as well as within them?

As with their parents before them, for the next generations, the interrelationship between human, physical, and productive assets was critical in determining their well-being and upward mobility, as described in the following section.

Human Capital

Human capital represented the most dramatic intergenerational change in asset accumulation. As described in detail in chapter 5, overall, children were better educated than their parents. Only 5 percent of parents completed high school compared to nearly half (47 percent) of children, while 3 percent of parents had

Table 9-1. *Comparative Education Levels between Parents and Their Children, 2004*

Percent

Education level	Parents	Children
Illiterate	15.5	0
Some primary school	17.5	6
Completed primary school	59	36
Completed secondary school or technical education	5	47
Tertiary (university) education	3	11
Total	100	100

some college education compared with 11 percent of children (table 9-1). Children living off the plot tended to have better education than those still living on it, while those migrating to Barcelona represented the most educated group.

Within these overall trends were important differences, illustrated by the five families on Calle K. First, the data showed that smaller families were more likely to have better educated children. In 1978 Claudio, as a recently married man, saw this issue very clearly:

> I want just two children because life is hard, and if one is going to be full of kids, one cannot do anything more. What would my efforts [have] been worth? Nothing. Just a kid's illusion. Mercedes agrees. Those two are sufficient so we can give them schooling. We can give them a finer life. I want to send Frank along that [career] line because I think it is the best profession that there is, and as he is little, he has the sense to get ahead. What I was not able to do before, let him learn, don't you think?

And by 2005 Claudio was rightfully very proud of his son Frank's academic achievement: he had a degree in dentistry and was practicing as a dentist while studying to become an orthodontist.

Table 9-2 illustrates the human capital variable, disaggregated by gender, with the values reflecting differences in the absolute level of education achieved. The second generation had more human capital than the first, and fathers had more human capital than mothers, but daughters outpaced sons. This pattern is exemplified by Marta's household. Marta, who heroically bucked the trend for her generation and gained her high school diploma by attending night school during the 1980s, had higher aspirations for her daughters: "For my daughters I want something better. I want them to go to school, to go to university, to be something in this life. Because of this, I only have two girls. When one has

Table 9-2. *Intergenerational Educational Comparisons between Fathers and Sons,
and Mothers and Daughters, 2004*
Units as indicated

Human capital[a]	Males		Females	
	Fathers	*Sons*	*Mothers*	*Daughters*
Mean	17.4	23.7	15.7	27.0
Median	16	24	16	25
Sample size	30	90	43	67

a. The level of human capital was determined by estimating the effect of increasing levels of education on wages and salaries. The values are intended to reflect the market value of the education achieved.

many, it is impossible to give them education; but when one only has few, one can manage."

Both her daughters completed high school and went to university, although only the younger one, Ana Maria, completed her degree in industrial psychology. However, her employment as school secretary at the local secondary school, while providing a stable if very modest income, was not the career envisaged by either her or her mother.

The counterintuitive finding that girls were better educated than boys was reinforced by parents' priorities in terms of their schooling investment. Consistently they were more likely to send daughters rather than sons to private schools. The growth of private sector schooling was a direct outcome of the declining quality of state schools, linked to the cutbacks in social sector expenditure associated with the 1980s macroeconomic reform measures (see appendix B). This pattern continued among those in the second generation who lived off plot in peripheral areas; they also sent their children to private schools. What had changed was the educational level at which parents sent their children to a private school. In the 1990s secondary-level education was prioritized; by 2004 more second-generation parents were paying for private primary schooling for their children (see table 9-3).

Constraints on Sons' and Daughters' Completing Education

Not all members of the second generation did equally well educationally. Larger, poorer families were not only unable to pay for private schooling, but they also sometimes could not provide sufficient supervision. These two factors increased the likelihood that children would have to repeat a grade, which in turn often reduced the probability of their completing school. Alicia reflected on this

Table 9-3. *Type of School Attended by Children of Second Generation,*
by Education Level, Year, and Location

| Type of school | 1992 | | 2004 | | | |
| | | | On plot | | Off plot | |
	Primary	Secondary	Primary	Secondary	Primary	Secondary
State (public)	78.1	59	67.7	91.7	71.4	66.7
Church	3.1	4.6	0.0	0.0	2.9	0.0
Private	18.8	36.4	32.3	8.3	25.7	33.3
Total	100	100	100	100	100	100
Sample size	64	22	31	12	35	9

problem in 1978: "They left the house and said they were going to school. But
they went somewhere else and watched television. I was sure they had been at
school, but from their reports it turns out all three failed in their exams."

Despite her children's waywardness in school, Alicia was still committed to
their education, particularly in the case of her daughters. Discussing the situation in 1981, she commented:

> I talk to my daughters so that they should see how I have suffered. Just as
> they help me to do things, I work for them. They also realize that their
> father doesn't work for them. I tell them to study, to take advantage, to
> make sure their lives are different, to be able to do better work, to think of
> nothing but studying. Mirtha will go for fifth grade. Then I will put her
> to study some trade, a shorter career. Maybe dressmaking, hairdressing, or
> something like that.

By 2004 her three sons had a mean overall educational level of three years of
secondary schooling whereas her six daughters had a mean of four and one-half
years of secondary education. Another factor that influenced school attendance,
with consequences for failure and dropout rates, and implications for accumulation of human capital, was the external economic context in the 1980s, which
had forced more women to go out to work (see chapter 6) and necessitated that
children contribute economically to the household. Sons and daughters adopted
different strategies to balance education and earning an income. Girls were
more likely to take on domestic reproductive activities to release their mother to
work, but they still struggled to stay in school.

One strategy was to alternate school shifts. This occurred in the Garcia family, neighbors of Aida further out from Calle K, whose household included six

children. When the income of the father, Lukas, a carpenter, declined in 1990, the mother, Ida, was forced to go back to work as a domestic servant in order to pay for the costs of three children then in secondary school. Ida left for work at 6:30 each morning, while the two daughters—Veronica, aged sixteen, and Janina, aged thirteen—coped with all the domestic tasks by attending school in alternating shifts—Veronica in the morning and Janina in the afternoon. The eldest son, Cristian, aged fifteen, assisted his father in the afternoon when the order book warranted it. The daughters complained that homework time suffered as they cooked and cleaned for their parents and four brothers. They all recognized that the situation was not ideal, but the family was committed to getting the children through high school.

In the Jaramillo household, also living near Aida, the three eldest of five daughters—Regina, Cristy, and Maritza—had complete responsibility for all household tasks, including attending community meetings on Saturday. Their father, an informal sector fruit juice seller, had virtually abandoned the family; thus their mother, the only income earner, was forced to work a six-day week washing clothes at three city center households. The girls had so many conflicts over divisions of labor that they ended up with a rotation system in which each girl stayed home one week in three, missing school. Regina, the eldest, commented, "I am always behind at school, but there is no alternative if the family wants to eat."

While daughters looked after their younger siblings, sons were more likely to be involved in child labor. The 1992 sample survey data showed that more than two-thirds of working boys aged fourteen years and younger managed to continue their schooling. But for boys involved in earning an income, the tendency was to shift to night school, where the quality of education was lower and failure rates were higher. The case of Lidia's family has already been mentioned; when Salvador abandoned his family, Lidia could not go out to work because she needed to care for the younger children. So her two sons, Danilo and Winston, became construction sector casual laborers to support the family. Although they registered for the 7–9 p.m. night shift at the local school, they were often too tired to go. None of Lidia's children finished high school, but the boys did worse than the girls, averaging just three years of secondary education.

Not only did these strategies reduce the likelihood that children would complete high school, they also resulted in intrahousehold conflict between sons and daughters who wanted to attend school. The girls resented the fact that their brothers did not carry the same level of domestic responsibility; for boys the reduction in parental control was often detrimental. One of the greatest concerns of working women was their reduced capacity to control teenage sons, who were then more tempted to drop out of school, become involved in street gangs, and use drugs (chapter 11).

Pregnancy, Early Marriage, and Education

Daughters often cut short their educational ambitions due to unanticipated pregnancies. Although they placed greater importance on education than did their parents, daughters also shared their parents' high valuation of marriage or a stable partnership. In 1982 Marta's youngest sister, Virginia, then fifteen years old, commented on the dilemma this posed for her:

> Every woman wants to get married, to have a home and children. If you get engaged and you don't get married, then your husband can walk out any time and leave you. But if you are married, he must come back. You are married to him by law and by God. I want to get married civilly, not in church, because once we know each other, if there is any discordance, we can get divorced. If we marry in church, we cannot because the priest says "only death can part you," so that we cannot separate until death. . . . I think that by studying and working, one acquires more education. I will be able to have more important jobs. That's why I want to study. To be someone. I wouldn't want to go on living here; I want to live in the center, to have a house built of cement.

In fact, Virginia was atypical; unlike her peers, when she became pregnant she neither married nor stayed home for long. Her son Emilio was absorbed into her extended family, with her sister Marta and her brother-in-law, Jesus, taking on the parental role. Virginia completed high school and proceeded to have a very checkered career as a traveling saleswoman. As described in chapter 6, she lived in Riobamba for a while with her then husband. After divorcing him, she ended up marrying a European and moving to Europe, thus fulfilling her ambition to get beyond the slums of Guayaquil.

A much more common pattern was to give up education on the birth of the first child and, despite very good intentions, not return to school. This is illustrated by Sylvia's story. Of Alicia's six daughters, Sylvia was the only one who completed high school, a source of much pride. She talked of going on to university but was soon engaged to Milton, who did not want her to work, and Sylvia had four sons in very quick succession. The family lived with his mother, and Sylvia had tremendous conflicts with her over money: Milton would always ask his mother's permission before giving Sylvia any financial resources. In disgust, she insisted they return to her mother's plot, but this did not work as Milton could not get accustomed to life in Indio Guayas. So they split up, and Sylvia was reduced to doing washing work like her mother as well as working at a local restaurant. Thus, despite her education, she repeated her mother's cycle of single parenthood, numerous children, and unskilled employment.

The marriage of Marta's daughter Adriana to Hector illustrates the intergenerational transfer of societal norms around female subordination and marriage, and exemplifies the pressures under which women lived. Soon after she met Hector, her father put considerable pressure on her to marry him. By 2004 Adriana considered that, in retrospect, she had married as much to get away from her father as to set up her own home. She had two children and felt that it was family pressure more than the relationship itself that kept her and Hector together.

Table 9-4 summarizes comparative levels of education, marriage age, family planning, and male attitudes toward wife working in Marta's family over three generations. It shows how little the options for young women in Indio Guayas had changed. By 2004 Adriana's daughter Laura was caught in the same situation her mother had experienced a generation earlier. Even though Laura, as a member of the third generation, was more educated and had better knowledge about contraception, she was still expected to stay at home until she married, and thus go from the control of her father to the control of her husband. She was not expected to live on her own, since this implied loose living and promiscuity, and though she might not have perceived it as such, was subject to the same pressure to marry as soon as possible as her mother experienced.

Financial-Productive Capital: Did the Second Generation Have Better Jobs than Their Parents?

Chapter 6 described the relationship between educational levels and job opportunities for the first generation. This chapter asks whether better education translated into greater income-earning potential, better jobs, and increased financial capital for the second generation. Intergenerational comparisons identify the extent to which improved education was linked to upward mobility for the second generation, in the context of the more recent Guayaquil labor market. Another question addressed here is whether there were gender differences, that is, did daughters do better than sons?

By 2004 the mean age of the economically active second generation, both those still living on their parents' plot as well as those living off it, was thirty-seven years, so the second generation was reaching middle age. The vast majority

Table 9-4. *Three-Generation Comparison of Education, Marriage Age, Family Planning, and Male Attitudes toward Wife Working*

Relationship	Level of education	Age at marriage	Family planning	Male partner's attitude toward wife working
Marta: mother, grandmother	Primary education (completed secondary school as adult)	Fourteen	No sex education or family planning for first child, though used coil after birth of second daughter	Husband allowed Marta to work as dressmaker at home, but conflict arose when she became a community political leader.
Adriana: daughter, mother	Secondary education	Eighteen	Limited sex education (from aunt) and no family planning for first child	Husband was passive; Adriana earned most of the family income and also relied on in-laws.
Laura: granddaughter	Some tertiary education	Nineteen and not married or engaged	Using contraception to allow sexual experimentation	. . .

Table 9-5. *Second-Generation Male and Female Employment in Indio Guayas,*
by Standard Industrial Classification and Earnings, 2004[a]
Units as indicated

Standard Industrial Classification	Percent employed			Earnings in U.S. dollars		
	Male	Female	All	Male	Female	All
Agriculture, forestry, fishing	0	0	0	0	0	0
Mining	0	0	0	0	0	0
Construction	20.0	0	14.7	183.2	0	183.2
Manufacturing	14.6	10.0	13.3	97.5	81.5	94.3
Transportation, communications	29.1	0.0	21.3	143.0	0	143.0
Retail trade	12.7	25.0	16.0	170.4	212.4	185
Services	20.0	65.0	32.0	132.9	95.4	112.6
Public administration	3.6	0	2.7	174.7	0	174.7
Total	100	100	100	100	100	100
Sample size	55	20	75	54	20	74

a. For information on the Standard Industrial Classification, see chapter 6, footnote 12.

were involved in income-generating activities, with slightly higher rates for sons
than daughters, and for those living off the family plot than those still on their
parents' plot (100 percent versus 90 percent, respectively, for sons; and 93 percent versus 83 percent, respectively, for daughters).

With better education than their parents, the second generation aspired to
better jobs than did their parents and were more selective about the work they
would and would not do. Although the majority of them had completed high
school, this was not sufficient education to move them out of the largely semi-
and unskilled jobs at which their parents worked (see table 9-5). Within this
sector, however, there was a shift out of traditional artisan skills (such as tailors
and shoemakers) into modern manual skills such as automotive mechanics and
refrigerator and video repairs.

The construction sector consistently employed a fifth of all men, fathers and
sons alike, from 1978–2004, though, as noted in chapter 6, with decreasing job
security over time. Equally, real wage levels in this sector remained fairly stable,
increasing from $145 to $183 a month over the twenty-six year period. The
biggest decline in employment was in the manufacturing sector, which provided
work for one in three first-generation men in 1978 but less than one in six second-
generation men in 2004. Associated with this occupational change was a decline

in real wages in the manufacturing sector from $121 a month in 1978 for fathers to $98 in 2004 for sons.[2]

Walter, the tailor, was proud that both his sons completed high school. Hard working and motivated like their father, both Dillan and Joaquin, aged twenty-four and twenty-six in 2004, had factory jobs in the Guayaquil Coca-Cola bottling plant and the Pica (plastics) factory, respectively, for which they earned the state-defined basic salary. But this income was not sufficient for either of them to consider moving out of their parents' house and finding their own homes; so the small family house was now crowded with two additional households, complete with a daughter-in-law and grandchildren.

In contrast to manufacturing, the transport sector expanded as a source of employment in which nearly a third of second-generation men worked, though real wages had declined over the 1978–2004 period, from $187 a month to $143. Indeed, this was the sector in which both Mateo and Leonel Ortega worked upon completing their high school education. Service, the third largest sector of employment for second-generation men, was closely linked to transport through the range of associated repair jobs.

Turning to the second-generation women, we see a dramatic increase in work in the service sector, from 25 percent of mothers in 1978 to 65 percent of daughters in 2004, with real income doubling from approximately $50 a month to $100. In the case of women, it was employment in the retail trade sector that steadily declined; from providing nearly half of mothers with employment in 1978, it only absorbed a quarter of daughters by 2004. This trend was linked to the decreasing number of small front room shops as a result of the infrastructure upgrades in Indio Guayas: with the introduction of better transportation and the availability of electricity for refrigerators, the need for daily, small-scale, local shopping decreased. Younger women working in the retail sector were more likely to be in larger-scale enterprises, earning salaries in secure jobs, a change that was reflected in a dramatic increase in earnings; while mothers earned $73 a month in 1978, daughters brought home $212 a month in 2004. However, this did not mean greater independence since the majority of those working in this sector still lived on their parents' plot.

While second-generation daughters still earned less than their brothers, the intergenerational earnings increased far more dramatically for women than for men. While the average earnings for men grew from $132 a month in 1978 to $153 in 2004, women's earning had more than doubled, increasing from $60 a month in 1978 to $131 in 2004. In addition, data from 2004 indicated that second-generation women consistently found more stable employment than did their male partners and kin or their mothers (table 9-6).[3]

Table 9-6. *Security of Employment, by Working Parents and Children, 2004*
Percent

Category of work	Fathers	Mothers	Sons	Daughters
Permanent-regular	4	30	30	47
Temporary	44	30	46	28
Self-employed	52	39	24	25
Sample size	23	23	76	32

Additional data on the type of employer revealed a dramatic increase in the number of women working at government jobs, from nil in 1978 for the mothers to just over one in five of daughters (21.9 percent) in 2004. In contrast, few sons (6.6 percent) were employed by the government; instead, more than two in five (43.4 percent) were self-employed.

As for the characteristics of the second generation who were living off their parents' plots in 2004, the average number of household members working was less than was the case in their parents' households, particularly for those living in the new peripheral settlements. This difference reflected a larger number of wives unable to find any work in these remote neighborhoods (table 9-7). But since their households were smaller than those of their parents when they first set up in Indio Guayas, their dependency ratios were slightly lower: 3.66 dependents per worker for the second generation living off the plot in 2004 versus 4.13 for their parents in 1978. A few second-generation households, particularly those living in peripheral areas, also relied on "other income sources," such as the government solidarity bond (3.3 percent) as well as remittance income sent by siblings (6.5 percent).[4] Only one in five off-plot households used its home for remunerative purposes, such as front room shops, but as residents consolidated their housing on their plots, they increasingly used it for rental purposes.

Even in Guayaquil's stagnant economy, opportunities existed for a small number of the second generation who had completed their tertiary education. Susana, the eldest daughter of Carmen and Alonso, not only had completed university education with a graduate degree in public relations, but as of 2004 she was earning a considerable income of $700 a month as a sales supervisor in one of Guayaquil's banks. She, her husband (who earned $400 a month as a bank loan officer), and one young son lived across the river in Duran, in a modern two-story house that her father, Alonso, had been contracted to upgrade for them. The couple owned a car and paid for child care while they were at work.

Table 9-7. *Number of Household Members Working, by Location, 2004*
Average

Location	Household members working
On parents' plot	2.0
Renting in same barrio	1.9
Own plot in same barrio	1.5
Own plot elsewhere	1.3
Overall average	1.6

In short, Susana's household was one of the few from Indio Guayas that had broken through the glass ceiling to acquire professional jobs and attain a middle-class lifestyle.

Third-Generation Aspirations: Jobs, Education, and Marriage

By 2004 it was the third generation in many households that was completing its education and even beginning to look for jobs. This provided an additional generational perspective on aspirations. Young women in a mixed second- and third-generation focus group identified their primary problem as unemployment and their inability to get a job. Using a problem tree, they attributed this situation to lack of labor market experience, contacts, and university education.[5] They identified that the jobs available did not interest them. These included dressmaker, seller, washerwoman, domestic worker, cook, and child minder—all jobs of their mothers and grandmothers. But their aspirations were for professional jobs, not those of the women in the community. Where would they like to be in ten years? None of the young women identified a good relationship with a man as a priority, with almost all expressing career-related aspirations. Their preferred "professions" were as secretaries, engineers, personnel in the navy, or, as in the case of two Afro-Ecuadorian women, to own their business. The one exception was Flor, the twenty-eight-year-old daughter of Claudio and Mercedes, who was already married with two children and lived in a bamboo-walled house at the back of her parents' plot. Her more immediate concern was to upgrade her home into a cement house.

At one level these young people were doing better than their parents. They had more education and better jobs. But they relied immensely on family resources, including access to the networks required to get jobs and to advance in terms of both education and careers. A focus group of young men revealed deep cynicism about the opportunities for upward socioeconomic mobility.[6]

Thus in their poverty ladder mapping they identified themselves as poor. In contrast, the rich were identified as those who bought their degrees, did not have to work for them, and gave jobs to each other. To move up the poverty ladder to middle class, they identified the importance of well-connected godparents to give them self-confidence and assist them in finding jobs.

Physical Capital and Land Titles

As mentioned above, Flor identified the importance of house acquisition for second-generation children. Half those in the focus group had been directly assisted by the fact they still lived on the family plot. This enabled them to live in better housing than was the case when their parents or grandparents first built their homes.[7] By contrast, those second-generation households that had set up their own homes were not as fortunate, since by the 1990s free "invasion" land was no longer available. By then, the only housing opportunities for those not able to acquire a plot in Indio Guayas were the hills and agricultural land on the city's periphery, sold off by land entrepreneurs. Some 12 percent of the second generation repeated their parents' experience to acquire their own plot by moving out to this new urban frontier, with many moving in 1998. However, the valorization of land over the past twenty-six years meant that the second generation could only afford smaller plots, on average half the size of those acquired by their parents when they invaded in 1978 (137 square meters).

There were other significant intergenerational differences. In 2004 those who owned their plots placed much more importance on legal documentation than did their peers living with parents or the previous generation. Despite their relatively recent acquisition of plots, over half of them already had titles, while others had acquired informal agreements identified as "document from seller" or "permission to occupy," none of which had any legal validity. These sons and daughters were repeating some of the struggles of their parents—but by living in muddy streets rather than over water. However, in comparison, their infrastructure services arrived more quickly; by 2004 half of their households had water main connections, while wider recognition of the health-related impacts of modern sanitation facilities meant that the majority of households had septic tanks (94 percent). At the same time, 75 percent of households were tapping into electricity illegally, despite the large fines imposed on those who were caught by the electricity company.

The fact that these second-generation households did not have to mobilize to acquire infrastructure had significant implications for community social capital.

Table 9-8. *Housing Choices of the Second Generation from the Five Families on Calle K, 2004*

Options	Parent(s)	Children
1. Live in parents' home	Alicia	Joanna, Juanchito
	Lidia	Oscar
	Alonso and Carmen	Bertha, Daniel, Ruben
2. Construct house on parents' plot[a]	Marta	Adriana, Ana Maria
	Alicia	Sylvia
	Claudio and Mercedes	Flor
	Lidia	Dora
	Alonso and Carmen	Julia
3. Live with in-laws nearby	Alicia	Mirtha, Edwin, Martin
	Lidia	Gerardo, Gabby
4. Rent in Indio Guayas	Alicia	Dorotea, Sofia
5. Live with person who already has plot	Alicia	Reina
6. Acquire own plot elsewhere in Guayaquil	Lidia	Winston, Danilo, Fanny
	Alonso and Carmen	Susana
7. Live elsewhere in Ecuador (rural) or abroad	Claudio and Mercedes	Frank
	Lidia	Magali (Spain)

a. May or may not include cooking separately.

Only 14 percent of children living outside Indio Guayas were involved in community groups. However, membership in sports clubs grew among the next generation, with approximately a quarter of young men involved in some type of sporting activity.

For the majority of second-generation households, housing strategies were far more complex than those of their parents. Table 9-8 illustrates the seven options chosen by different members of the five families on Calle K. While all the families had some second-generation family members living on the parental plot, including younger hidden household heads, the rest of the children had been forced to look for other housing options. The most common strategies were to move in with nearby in-laws, rent, or move to the city's periphery.

The advantages and disadvantages associated with remaining on the parental plot were widely recognized. While establishing one's own home provided much sought-after "independence," remaining on the family plot made it possible to draw on household social capital to pool resources and share child care.

Financial resources were essential for achieving independence, as illustrated by the differences between daughters in Carmen's and Marta's houses in 1992.

Carmen's daughter Julia was unable to live on her own, despite her desire for independence. She and her partner, Ignacio, did not earn enough to live elsewhere, and she depended on the family for child care support. In addition, the family plot was too small to build a house in the back. So the best Julia could do was to make her bed into a separate space, curtaining it off to create an illusion of privacy. In contrast, Marta's daughter Adriana was able to live separately in an adjoining house on the same plot as her parents, so she had some privacy yet still benefited from joint child care and other family support. The young women in the 2004 focus group agreed that the ideal housing solution was to live apart but on the same plot. This allowed for maximum help with cooking and child care while providing sufficient privacy for a personal life.

Housing strategies were also influenced by the number of children and the related availability of physical space. Thus, in the larger families of both Lidia and Alicia, some children were forced to find alternative housing because there was simply no room. In both cases, some of their children were able to live with in-laws, an option that generally allowed them to stay closer to home and to continue to benefit from the reciprocities embedded in household social capital. Other of Lidia's children chose to move to the periphery of the city, where they acquired their own plot and built a very basic bamboo-walled house. This obviously reduced contact, and Lidia complained that it meant she had to go a lengthy distance on the bus to see her grandchildren.

Who lived with whom when couples got together? While the majority of sons preferred to remain in their parents' home (with their mothers), their wives often had tremendous problems living with their mothers-in-law, making this a cause of both domestic conflict and marital breakdown. An interesting example that highlights this issue is provided by the Martinez family, who lived one street away on Calle L. As described in chapter 6, the parents ran a successful marinated cooked fish enterprise, with Eliana's skills at cooking and marinating the fish complementing Nestor's stoic persistence in selling on the street corner each morning at 6 a.m. During the 1980s their eldest of six children left home to buy his own plot nearby, one daughter built her house at the back of the plot for her husband and growing family, and a second son, Hernan, brought his bride, Natasha, to live in his parents' house. Next to join the household in 1986 was Isias, husband of daughter Yudit. In 1989 conflicts between Natasha and mother-in-law Eliana forced Hernan and Natasha to become "independent," building their own living quarters on the first floor. By 1992, with two children from an earlier relationship, two children of their own, and two of Natasha's sisters, the upstairs household comprised eight members. While Natasha wanted her own plot, husband Hernan was clear: "I have never left my mother, and I never will." In 2004 Eliana, by then widowed, still lived in the original part of the house with Isias, two grandchildren, and daughter Yudit, who said, "We will not move: mother must not be left on her own." Thus, while in 1978 the Martinez family was a nuclear household of eight members, by 1992 the same plot contained two extended and one nuclear household, two in nesting arrangements, for a total of nineteen people. By 2004 the number was down to thirteen due to the lack of any further room for independent households with more grandchildren.

It is important not to generalize about the gendered nature of second-generation residence. For instance, in 2004, of the five families on Calle K, Marta had two sons-in-law living on her plot but in their own separate homes; in the case of Claudio and Mercedes, their son-in-law lived separately on the plot with their daughter, while their son lived in a separate house in the daughter-in-law's village in rural Manabi. The majority of Alicia's sons and daughters lived with their in-laws, which began to raise the important issue of intergenerational transfer of land titles.

Intergenerational Transfer of Land Titles and Gender Empowerment

Ultimately, the plot acquired by parents in the 1970s will be transferred to the next generation. However, in a context where the legal issues affecting the transfer of assets are as yet neither understood nor recognized, this is likely to pose problems, especially in large families. For daughters this is particularly important since land ownership can be an influential factor in empowering women (see Moser 1987; Moser and Felton, forthcoming).

Alicia's family housing history illustrated this situation well. The history of her plot ownership was linked to the stage of urbanization when she came to Indio Guayas. As one of the early residents, she owned her plot and acquired her title. With nine children the choice as to which of them received space to live on the plot, let alone who would inherit it, was a difficult one, reflected in the range of different housing strategies adopted by her children (see table 9-8). Since all but one of her sons had moved out to live in the homes of their in-laws, it was her daughters who were most likely to contest ownership of the plot. Daughter number three, Sylvia, was adamant that as a single mother herself she had primary rights; she had refused to live with her mother-in-law as her ex-husband had expected, wanting the independence of her own home. So she returned to Alicia's plot and set about building her own basic, bamboo-walled home at the back of the plot, repeating her mother's experience a quarter of a century ago. Even when the house burned down, she adamantly persisted with her requirement for separate space, partially rebuilding it with cement blocks, with assistance from the evangelical church and relying on her father and brothers to do the construction work.[8]

For the rest of Alicia's children, the lack of their own house was their biggest problem. In 2004 Joanna, a single mother with a third child on the way, still lived in her mother's house, while Mirtha, aged thirty-eight, lived in her in-laws' house. That year Mirtha suffered the extreme indignity of dealing with the fallout from her husband's involvement with another woman. He was employed at a workshop making windows and often claimed to have no money, so the family was highly dependent on the $6 a day she earned as a clinic nurse. While she was clear that her husband's action was not the result of insufficient attention in cooking, cleaning, and washing for him, she had increasingly realized that living in her in-laws' house meant that she lacked her own land title and was therefore forced to continue living with her husband's family.

Alicia's second youngest daughter, Sofia, was living with her husband and young child in local rental accommodation; with rent at $40 a month, this strategy was only viable because of her husband's permanent job and associated benefits. As a result of their experiences, all of Alicia's daughters recognized how important it is for women to have their own land titles or, at the very least, have one jointly in the names of both partners.[9]

Problems of Intergenerational Lack of Communication

While the sons and daughters of the households that settled in Indio Guayas benefited from the transfer of assets, they also identified constraints in intergenerational relationships, particularly between fathers and sons. These were more specifically articulated by third-generation youth, through focus group discussions with both girls and boys in 2004.[10] The most important problem was their relationship with their parents, including a lack of support and communication, and, to a lesser extent, physical abuse. Three quarters of the male focus group participants said this was a problem with their fathers, and to a lesser extent with both parents or their mothers. A lack of confidence was among the consequences identified. Young men argued that parents favored daughters, giving them far more attention and support, while the sons were supposed to be independent and therefore left to make their way on their own. Nevertheless, sons still emulated fathers, particularly in aspiring to become womanizers. Young males also indicated that the breakdown in family structure and the rupture in parents' relationships had an adverse impact on their lives, including pressure to leave school in order to earn for the family.

What Assets Did the Second Generation Transfer Back to Their Parents?

Parents transferred assets to their children, whether it was the "sacrifices" made to pay for their education or the provision of shelter on their plot for the next generation and their dependents. One indicator of increasing intergenerational well-being related to the second generation's capacity or willingness to reciprocate by supporting their parents, especially once they were no longer able to generate an income. In a context where almost none of the households received state social security or pension support, this was particularly important given the number of elderly households that slipped back into poverty when the income earners were no longer able to work. The story of Claudio and Mercedes was particularly poignant in reflecting how aspirations for intergenerational reciprocity were not necessarily fulfilled.

As described in chapter 6, Claudio always wanted to be a dentist and went to enormous lengths to better himself, completing his high school diploma and starting to study dentistry at the university. When he was forced to quit in 1987 due to financial constraints, he transferred his aspirations to his son, Frank, who successfully graduated from Guayaquil University as a dentist. While doing his rural dental service, he married a local woman, and both migrated to Madrid, Spain. Frank soon returned to Ecuador "to work in his chosen profession" since the only work he found in Spain was in agriculture and the postal services. He moved back to his wife's rural area and established his own practice. In 2004 he was giving his parents $30 a month, which was all he could afford while undertaking further part-time graduate training in orthodontics. While very proud of their son, the now poor parents would have welcomed a greater return on their human capital investment.

Despite his parents' disappointment, Frank's contribution of $30 a month was much higher than the average support provided by the second generation living in Guayaquil. The importance of this support is demonstrated by the fact that as of 2004 remittances had become the single most effective mechanism for keeping a family out of poverty. Those living in Barcelona were most likely to support their families back in Guayaquil, with average remittances of $143.46 a month in 2005 (with more than three out of four remitting), compared to an average of $9.31 for children living on their parent's plot and $7.75 for those living elsewhere in Guayaquil or Ecuador as of 2004. Among the second generation, therefore, those remitting from abroad were more successful than those staying in Ecuador by an extremely large margin. On average, a single individual remitting from Spain single-handedly brought nearly three relatives above the poverty line in Ecuador, and still kept a substantial amount to live on. Furthermore, nearly everyone who migrated to Spain remitted.

Remittance data obtained from Guayaquil, whether from the 2004 panel survey or the 2005 survey of children off the plot, left a large number of unanswered questions. Were such remittances often context specific and time bound? Were women more reliable remitters than men because they were more likely to have left children behind in Guayaquil? Over time were men more likely to pay for their families to join them in Barcelona, and once they had obtained legal residence, to settle there? To answer questions such as these, and to better understand the ways in which second-generation migration contributed to the sustainability of those assets accumulated by the first generation, it was necessary to also undertake fieldwork in Barcelona. The next chapter, therefore, goes beyond Indio Guayas to explore the experiences of international migrants from the community.

10

Migration to Barcelona and
Transnational Asset Accumulation

*"I have a nice life here (in Barcelona). I've been honest, sincere, and hard working,
and I've achieved everything by myself. This doesn't mean that what my family or
friends have given me doesn't count. But I like to earn my own living and owe no
one anything. In Guayaquil it isn't possible. You don't have a stable life, the kind of
stability you get when you have a good job, and they don't employ you in the areas
you studied. The labor market is very small; all the jobs are tied to industries, so
whoever gets in stays there forever, and those who remain outside have to work in
whatever they can, tough jobs or at the bottom of the scale. I'm not good at studying,
and I decided not to go to university because I didn't see much of a future for me in
my country. My parents said I should stay. But when I looked for work, I saw long
lines of people with long CVs; they had university titles. I realized I'd rather leave
than be another one in the long line and struggle all my life for a job. I thought that
here, if you seek and you work hard, then you'll find something. That's my mentality,
and so far it's worked."*

—Douglas, son of neighbors living further down Calle K,
aged twenty-five in 2005

*"My house is here; I haven't got one over there. The difference is how you break from
poverty. I think it's the same here and there, because if you want to waste your life,
you can also do it here. But if you really want to progress and come here with the*

206

goal of doing better, you actually achieve it. If you stick to your old habits, then that's the end for you. When I went back to Ecuador for vacation, I couldn't get used to it. Here they tell you at what time they expect you to arrive at some place, and you get there on time. In Ecuador you shop for groceries every day, but here you do it on a weekly basis. You don't have time otherwise. It's easier here, you have more comforts. Over there you hand wash everything, but here you just throw everything in the wash. In Ecuador you can't afford to buy things, everything has to be by credit; so you end up paying twice the amount that you would have paid if you had been able to pay in cash. Here you can even buy by credit without interest, and twice a year they have huge sales, and you take advantage of them and buy at very good prices."

—Mateo, son of Marta's neighbors, the Ortegas,
and brother of Leonel, 2005

"I came here because I kicked my husband out of the house when I found out he was having an affair. I think I felt more ashamed than he did, knowing people were talking about this. When I was walking around the area, people would say things to me, so I told my daughters I wanted to leave. I borrowed money; I pawned some things and paid $900 for the ticket and $2,000 to take with me. About two days before I left, my husband came to ask for forgiveness. Same old story. But we made a deal. I told him I was leaving; he could stay in the house, and I was going to work and save money so he could build the house for me. If I had stayed there, I couldn't build my own house. Salaries in Ecuador are too low, you can't do anything. I've been sending 600 euros each month over four years. In one year I'll send enough to finish my house. I am more independent here. No one tells me what to do or what not to do, or that I can't go somewhere and have to stay home. My daughters tell me that my husband's getting old. They ask me if I'm going to go back to him when I return to Ecuador. I tell them I will, because he is their father and I don't have much of an option—even though he has never appreciated me and always flirted with women right in front of me, pretending he didn't care for me."

—Carmen, wife of Alonso and Marta's neighbor,
aged fifty-four in 2005

The three individuals whose stories introduce this chapter have all migrated from Calle K to Barcelona. This chapter turns to household members, particularly second-generation sons, daughters, and friends of the families in Indio Guayas—and a few first-generation exceptions such as Carmen—who have migrated to this Spanish city. They exemplify the comparative levels of well-being of migrants who have moved abroad versus those who have remained in Guayaquil. As in previous chapters, the macro- and city-level economies and their associated job opportunities provide the broader context within which their lives are positioned. In the case of Ecuadorian emigration, the national financial and banking collapse that led to the dollarization policy at the end of the 1990s played a critical role in driving millions of Ecuadorians to leave their homes and migrate, not only to increase their income but also to try to ensure that their aspirations for upward mobility were met.

International migration adds another factor that affects the capacity of Indio Guayas households to escape poverty, namely, remittance flows. In the past decade, the dramatically escalating phenomenon of remittances has been identified by the Inter-American Development Bank and the World Bank as a critical new development "entry point," playing an instrumental role not only in the economic growth of remittance-receiving countries but also in the reduction of their poverty levels (Maimbo and Ratha 2005; Adams and Page 2005; Orozco 2005; de Vasconcelos 2004). According to the Central Bank of Ecuador, remittances went up from $643 million in 1997 to $1.41 billion in 2001 (Jokisch and Pribilsky 2002).[1] In macroeconomic terms these flows have supported consumption and construction, contributing both to the survival of families and to the expansion of business and employment (Acosta, López, and Villamar 2004). At the microlevel in Indio Guayas, the role that remittances have played in helping some families either stay out of poverty or escape it between 1992 and 2004 has already been described in chapters 3 and 8.

While a distinction is commonly made between the use of financial remittances for consumption as against investment (see Ballard 2002; Chimhowu, Piese, and Pinder 2003), this chapter broadens the focus beyond financial transactions to include the transnational accumulation of a range of assets. These include assets that migrants transfer with them when they migrate, those accumulated while in Barcelona, and finally those consolidated assets that directly or indirectly are taken back to Guayaquil.[2]

The migratory experience is complex, and migrants' experiences vary according to their gender, class, ethnicity, and immigration status (Pedone 2002; Actis 2005; Ruíz 2002). This chapter looks at the issues of identity and individual agency from a transnational asset accumulation perspective and examines the distinction between migration as a family versus individual accumulation strategy.

Another issue explored concerns relative perceptions of migration as either a negative experience that erodes assets, or a positive one in which assets are accumulated. Considerable Ecuadorian research has represented migration as a painful, tragic process, one entailing emotional costs relating to the separation and destruction of families, and precipitating changes in gender and generational relations (Camacho and Hernández 2005; Instituto Latinoamericano de Investigaciones Sociales [ILDIS/FES] and others 2003; Pedone 2002). A contrasting view emphasizes the way in which migration increases self-esteem and empowers women as a result of greater independence, income gains, and changes in gender roles (Herrera 2005; ILDIS/FES and others 2002; Ruíz 2002; Portes 2009).

The Indio Guayas study, which incorporated a migration circuit from a specific barrio to a specific city abroad, provides a particular comparative perspective with which to examine whether this negative emphasis was borne out in reality, or whether there were overall gains. Given the contentiousness of this debate, this chapter incorporates many of the narratives of the migrants themselves. Finally, while migration studies have tended to view people in one place, either before or after migrating, fundamental technological change such as declining telephone rates, e-mail, and Skype, as well as cheaper air travel, means that increasingly people can have multilocational status. This, in turn, raises questions concerning the multiple identities of migrants.

Why Did People Migrate from Indio Guayas to Barcelona?

The exodus of second-generation sons and daughters from Indio Guayas to Barcelona was in part the microlevel response to the macrolevel economic and political crises at the end of the 1990s (CEPLAES 2005).[3] Appendix A explains why fieldwork was undertaken in Barcelona and describes the research methodology and sample size. These Indio Guayas residents migrated in the 1990s when employment opportunities were opening up in Europe, particularly Spain. Here economic growth and an aging population led to a labor demand for young workers, preferably Spanish speakers. Simple visa requirements also eased the move as workers from Guayaquil poured into Barcelona, a port city home away from home. Such were the numbers leaving that by 2004 some 2 million Ecuadorians were working overseas (15 percent of the total population). Around 550,000 left the country after 1999, one-fifth of the labor force. Emigration peaked in 2000 and subsequently dropped due to controls introduced by the European Union, especially Spain, after the September 11, 2001, attack in New York (Hall 2008). Appendix B elaborates on Ecuadorian migration patterns and associated Spanish migrant policy.

As so succinctly expressed by Douglas, above, young single men like him, aged seventeen to twenty-five, came to Barcelona to find better work and a better life.

These included his brother Eddie, along with Gonzalo, Marta's nephew, and a close neighbor, Rene, all from Calle K. Patterns of male migration varied by age and marital status. Married men, such as Mateo and Marlon, a cousin of Douglas's, came first, and, at a later stage, brought over their wives and children. A smaller group of married men came alone, formed relationships with women in Barcelona, and abandoned their wives and children in Guayaquil. While most men came for economic reasons, a few came to escape the law or drug-related death threats. One Indio Guayas migrant had been imprisoned for selling drugs in Guayaquil. His sister-in-law paid off the police to get him out of prison and got him a ticket to Barcelona; she was afraid that once out of prison he would be killed by other drug distributors for unequal distribution of drug money.

In the case of men, migration tended to be a family decision. Douglas's brother Eddie explained why he came and how he got into Spain:

> My parents, as any parents, want the best for their children. They told me I would be better off here. I'm grateful to them because they pushed me to come here, and it was the right decision. I've done well and I wouldn't be any better off had I stayed in Ecuador. They gave me $400, and my brother helped me out with the rest. Back then it cost about U.S.$800. I brought my passport and U.S.$2,500 to get in. The way it worked was that you got into Europe through Amsterdam as a tourist. You went through immigration there, and the police asked you what you intended to do in Spain. When you answered you were going as a tourist, they asked you how much money you had on you, you showed them the money, and they let you go through. The money was only to show to the police.

However, as the stories of Alonso's wife, Carmen, and Nadia (Eddie's partner in Barcelona) showed, for women this was more likely to be an individual decision, varying according to age and life cycle stage. The majority of women emigrated while in their twenties, often for social reasons associated with escaping difficult marriages and partnerships.[4] Nuria, a friend of Carmen's who left two children in Guayaquil, commented, "It's worse to leave your husband and go off with another man in Guayaquil than it is to leave him and the kids and go off to Barcelona. Then they say you are doing it to improve everyone's lives."

Barcelona provided women with the economic justification to get away from abusive male partners or those not providing for their families. It offered these women opportunities to look for a new husband or partner while also improving their economic situation. As Nadia, now living with Eddie, explained:

I had a troublesome relationship with my husband. He didn't have a stable job; whenever he had a job, he'd quit. This brought lots of problems, and so I made up my mind about coming. My mother didn't want me to come; she pointed out how the kids were so young. I only told my husband I was coming the night before I left. He replied that he would throw a party the day I left. I arranged all the documents without telling anyone. Another man would have done something about it, but not him. The children stayed with him, but three months later he left them at my mother's place.

Like Nadia, the majority of women came alone, leaving behind children and spouses in Guayaquil. Pilar (Gonzalo's partner in Barcelona), Nuria, Violeta, and Belen (the latter two old school friends of Adriana's back in Indio Guayas) quickly formed new relationships (compromisos) in Barcelona. Another category of female migrant included young, single women, such as Douglas' wife, Eva, who came to Barcelona on her own and formed her first relationship there. A third, far smaller group was made up of older married women, such as Carmen, who did not seek to form another relationship in Barcelona but migrated as "target workers" to accumulate as much money as possible. Finally, there were wives, such as Mateo's wife, Malena, who came to Barcelona after her husband had established himself, finding a job and place to live. Some partnerships survived the relocation, but others did not. The relationships their husbands formed with other women prior to their arrival often remained more important, with Guayaquil wives left on their own with their children in Barcelona. A final group was composed of married women who came first and then brought their husbands; here again not all relationships survived the move.

Assets that Migrants Transferred from Guayaquil

Migrants from Indio Guayas to Barcelona did not arrive empty handed as is often thought to be the case. Even if they lacked financial capital, over and above the statutory $2,000 required to enter the country, they brought two critical assets with them. First was the human capital relating to education and health status enabling them to rapidly enter the labor market. In addition they transferred with them intangible social capital at both the household and community level. While the latter was absolutely critical for their integration into Barcelona, the former, namely a strong culture of household social capital, influenced the decisions they made as they rapidly adapted to a new culture and lifestyle.

Indio Guayas Community Social Capital

Douglas, whose family lived virtually opposite Marta, was the first person from Calle K to arrive in Barcelona. Known as "the father of everyone here," his story is remarkable. At age seventeen, he left for Barcelona, just fifteen days after graduating from high school. His mother's sister was there, and initially he stayed with her; however, he soon moved out, rented his own place, and rapidly provided refuge to other younger men from Calle K and nearby streets. As he explained:

> I was first here; I think I've had about 100 people come through in my apartment, almost the entire neighborhood. The first one to arrive was Mateo and then Marc, then Rene, Mateo's cousin, followed by Andrade. Before coming they all already knew where they were going to stay. And they knew they wouldn't have to pay for anything. I haven't had any problems with them; I've helped them. Whenever they run out of money, they come to me, and I've lent them money without any interest. They pay me back when they can.

The transfer of community social capital from Indio Guayas explained why such a large number of people from Calle K came to Barcelona. In a classic chain migration pattern, it provided the crucial start-up support structures for food, housing, and job contacts—with almost everyone assisted by a friend or family member upon arrival. While some came directly from Guayaquil, others went first to other countries, particularly Italy. Ariel, for instance, was lured to Italy by his uncle, only to find there was no work at all; he then went to Barcelona and was begging and sleeping in doorways until he got Douglas's address. Douglas took him in and gave him a bed until he gradually got himself going.

For many the arrival in Barcelona was a real shock, thus contributing to the view of migration as a miserable and exploitive experience.[5] Douglas's interpretation, with the benefit of hindsight six years after he migrated, provided a somewhat different perspective:

> At the beginning, when they first arrive, they think things here are the same as in Ecuador. Things are very different; there are norms that you have to respect, and you have to be responsible. You have to look after yourself. Everyone cooks here. When they arrive, they think that someone is going to wait on them and do things for them. But then they realize that things don't work like that here, and they change. You have to do everything yourself. You can help them, but you tell them right away that they have to cooperate, everyone has to help.

Again, Carmen, who left behind her five children and extended family, made an important differentiation between suffering and loneliness:

> You don't suffer here. More than suffering, loneliness gives you the blues. You remember everything you left behind, you feel lonely, and you really are on your own. I don't suffer about food or clothing. I suffered very, very, very much then when my husband took his lover back in Guayaquil, and if I had stayed there, my house would be exactly the same as it was when I left.

The "Culture" of Household Social Capital

On arrival in Barcelona, both men and women did not stay on their own long but very quickly found partners from Indio Guayas itself or nearby. The extreme loneliness they experienced related to the fact that they were not socialized to live on their own. As described in chapters 7 and 8, in Indio Guayas it was customary to live in large, often extended households. Therefore, regardless of their marital status in Guayaquil, almost all migrants soon established a relationship with a partner in Barcelona. As Mateo, Don Ortega's son, explained:

> I never went away from home before I came to Europe. I did not go into the army or get a job in another city. My wife moved into my parents' house, and our children were born there. It was a terrible shock when I came to Europe. I went to Italy first and was so lonely I would cry for days. And then I came to Barcelona, and Douglas helped me. I slept on the floor in his flat—there were nineteen of us when I first came—can you imagine the queues for the bathroom?

In a similar vein, Gonzalo, Marta's nephew, commented:

> Because of the tradition in Guayaquil, we are not accustomed to live on our own, and we feel very unhappy. The first Christmas I spent here was terrible, despite the fact that my aunt and uncle [Mateo and Malena] were living here. I felt very lonely; I was used to saying farewell to the year with my family. I spent the whole night crying. Even now, when the end of the year gets near, you feel homesick. I hate saying happy New Year on the phone instead of saying it in person. I find it very hard to speak to my father because he starts crying and that makes me cry.

Most migrant men from Calle K had live-in partners or wives rather than girlfriends. Almost all were from Indio Guayas or nearby suburbio areas in Guayaquil, rather than from other cities or countries. Partners met through parties organized by relatives or friends from home, at the innumerable Latino discothèques where many went on Saturday nights, or at the Parque Centenario where Ecuadorians gathered on Sundays. Pilar, for instance was selling cold drinks next to Adam when Gonzalo met her. In Mateo's case, he quickly formed a relationship with another woman, also on her own there, before bringing his wife, Malena, and four children over from Guayaquil.

The second reason for quickly forming a partnership in Barcelona was economic, relating to the necessity to share expenses. A partnership meant sharing the costs of food, basic services, and, above all, accommodation. As Pilar, who lived with Gonzalo, explained, "One joins together more for economic necessity than for love; a single person cannot cover all the costs, so we have to share all the expenses. We have an advantage because we rent two bedrooms, and the one that Gonzalo and I share, we go halves; he pays for the board, but I contribute to the rent."

Not all women were as financially pragmatic as Pilar; some saw establishing relationships as a way to address emotional as well as economic needs. While living with another was cheaper, it also reduced loneliness. In Nadia's words, "It's a mixture of friendship and business." But such quickly formed relationships could also be fragile, particularly if the family was not known. As Eva, married to Douglas, commented, "Couples here are less stable than in Ecuador because we don't know each other well. You can't get to know each other in one night, and a few weeks later you are living with that person. Later on each one's faults begin to surface, and you don't like each other so much; your tastes differ, and the spell that brought the couple together breaks sooner or later."

Human Capital

Migrants to Barcelona also brought with them human capital assets associated with their educational achievements. They were not illiterate or primary-school-level workers. As discussed in chapter 9, while sons who remained in Guayaquil were better educated than their fathers, the fact that half of male migrants had completed secondary school meant that on average they, in turn, were also better educated than their peers in Guayaquil. However, these migrants had not completed tertiary education. Indeed, many considered that the type of work opportunities available in Guayaquil were not commensurate with one's level of education. Douglas exemplified this attitude; he chose to migrate immediately after he had completed high school, having observed that young men with university-level education were unable to find suitable employment.

Daughters in Guayaquil were better educated than both their mothers and their brothers, and those migrating to Barcelona were better educated than men in general and their contemporaries in Guayaquil. All had completed high school while an additional small proportion had acquired some postsecondary education. Because the motive behind migration was to earn an income, almost none of the migrants from Calle K used the opportunity of being in Barcelona to seek further education. Two women were the exception; both had working partners and took courses to gain the child care qualifications (*licencia por maternidad*) necessary to acquire work in state child care facilities.

Assets Accumulated in Barcelona

While assets transferred from Guayaquil were important, those accumulated while in Barcelona undoubtedly made a critical difference, not only economically but also in terms of associated mobility, as this section illustrates.

Financial-Productive Assets: Work Opportunities in Barcelona

Ironically, the fact that Guayaquil migrants had not completed tertiary education meant that the jobs they found were those that other migrant groups were unwilling to do. Although these were similar to those of their parents and peers in Guayaquil, they were better paid, offering the possibility of accumulating financial capital. Migration was not an answer to unemployment but rather a response to low salaries, economic precariousness, and limited social mobility (CEPLAES 2005; ILDIS/FES and others 2003). As mentioned in chapter 9, the average income for the second generation from Calle K varied considerably, from $820.66 a month for those who migrated to Barcelona to $67.97 for those that moved out of the plot but remained in Ecuador and $60.24 for those that remained living with their parents.

In Barcelona job options changed over time. On arrival, without work papers and "street sense," both men and women had real problems finding jobs, and when they did, they were often exploited. Some employers underpaid while others did not pay at all, situations that produced unhappiness as well as insecurity. Adriana's second cousin Marlon commented:

> When I didn't have resident status, I worked in a company for four months, and they only paid me for two months. Some of the workers, who were residents, hired lawyers and were able to demand their pay. But

those of us who weren't residents couldn't do anything but get ripped off. I couldn't get the other two months' worth of salary. That's the discrimination you're victim of at work if you do not have a work permit. But not all companies behave like that; some observe the law.

Migrants from Indio Guayas agreed that women found work more easily than men, while the location of men's work also made it more risky for them. Douglas's wife, Eva, for instance, indicated that there was less work for men than for women. Men often had to work in construction and so were visible on the street, whereas women found work in domestic service inside houses where they could not be spotted by the police. In this way women could hide their illegal employment from the authorities while men were far more exposed.

The importance and potential of getting legal residence documentation meant that both male and female migrants rapidly acquired the requisite knowledge about Spain's complex migration policy. In fact, the massive Ecuadorian migration flows of the late 1990s were initially facilitated by a 1963 Hispano-Ecuadorian agreement that allowed migrants with $2,000 (the tourist "purse," or *bolsa*) to enter Spain for ninety days as tourists without a visa and subsequently to look for a job as a first step toward obtaining a work permit. However, as migrant numbers grew, Spain revised its policy and amended the legal framework and regulations (Jokisch and Pribilsky 2002). Of particular importance were the amnesties that provided opportunities for legalized status (in 1999 and then 2005 when some 130,000 Ecuadorians applied [CEPLAES 2005]); the increased pressure put on employers to normalize their employee situations, which improved the likelihood that migrants could obtain residency (temporary or permanent) through employment; and finally an extension from two to five years in the temporary work permit period required for residence eligibility (see appendix B for elaboration of Spanish migration policy).

Nadia summed up the process as follows:

The hardest thing is the ID (identity card). Once you have it, you're not scared anymore. It's just that and getting a job. My employers sorted out my papers three months ago, and I've had the ID card for the past two months. It's valid for one year. My employers didn't have a problem arranging everything. My boss filled out all the forms, and we both signed them. Given that I had no time to take the documents back and forth, I hired a lawyer to do it for me. I paid €220, including for my passport and my photos. After this card, another one is issued for two years. But you must have a job; otherwise you don't get the card. It is not complicated.

Table 10-1. *Indicative Comparative Employment Sector Data*
Percent

Occupational category	Fathers (1978)	Sons (2004)	Men, Barcelona (2005)	Mothers (1978)	Daughters (2004)	Women, Barcelona (2005)
Construction	22	27	27	0	0	0
Manufacturing	32	19	46	29	20	9
Transportation	16	18	0	0	0	0
Retail trade	20	6	0	47	36	9
Services	3	28	27	24	41	73
Public administration	7	2	0	0	3	9
Total	100	100	100	100	100	100

This particular group of migrants also benefited from the 2005 amnesty, and most had legalized their residency, while some were applying for citizenship. Romeo, one of Adriana's old school friends, indicated that he was applying for dual citizenship to reduce the annual problems of getting all the paperwork together to renew work permits.

Both men and women filled niche labor markets for which there was a specific demand for foreign labor. Like their contemporaries in Guayaquil, one in four men worked in the construction sector, but unlike in Guayaquil, many others continued in the same skilled crafts that their fathers did, such as carpentry, soldering, and furniture making. All were jobs requiring craft apprenticeship training rather than formal education qualifications, and many of the men had acquired such skills from their fathers or other male relatives in Guayaquil (table 10-1). The dramatic difference between male employment in Guayaquil as against Barcelona was in the higher proportion employed in better paid factory manufacturing work in Barcelona. Unlike in Guayaquil, however, there were apparently no opportunities for men in the transportation and retail trade sectors in Barcelona, while service sector jobs such as factory cleaners and household workers were better paid and regulated. Gender roles were not as rigid as in Guayaquil: both men and women cleaned and looked after the elderly, sick, and infirm—the latter certainly defined as women's work in Guayaquil. Once they obtained their documents, the majority of men got work that was well paid, and those that wished to could augment their standard eight-hour work day with overtime work or in informal enterprises.[6]

After the long working hours in Guayaquil, the eight-hour workday, along with the wage differential, presented a new and challenging work culture for many young men. Brothers Douglas and Eddie, for instance, complemented their eight-hour day jobs in a tire factory by setting up their own small enterprise specializing in apartment repairs and upgrading. While fixed work hours required changes in work behavior, it also demanded new levels of responsibility, which increased self-esteem. As Douglas noted, "My life has taken a ninety-degree turn. In Barcelona you have to be punctual; you have to get to work on time. If you're an outsider, you have to adapt to the laws and punctuality. It's very important in Europe. There is far greater responsibility to keep time, to work hard, and to change your work ethic."

Eddie's self-esteem increased due to a combination of factors; not only were he and his brother Douglas the only Ecuadorians working in the tire factory; but also he got work quickly; held down more than one job, and did not experience the kind of exploitation that occurred in Guayaquil, with its customary nonobservance of labor laws. As he summarized the situation, "There is more equality and less discrimination between types of work and different nationalities. We feel equal."

Like men, women took up the same or even less skilled jobs than in Guayaquil, but they were better paid, obtained documentation papers, and were recipients of social security. Of the thirteen women interviewed, eight worked in a range of domestic or cleaning jobs inside houses (including multiple cleaning jobs, full-time domestic servants, and live-in care for elderly women), or as cleaners in hotels, while the remainder worked as shop cashiers, seamstresses in small workshops, or as part-time legal auxiliaries. More than one in three augmented their work with a second job, generally as cleaners. Back in Guayaquil, slightly more of those surveyed were factory workers or owned their own shop, but their earnings were much lower. Although some women were better paid than men, they worked longer hours and were not protected to the same extent by labor laws that affected formal sector male employment.

For instance, when Adriana's school friend Violeta arrived to see us at 6:30 p.m. one evening, her handbag was bulging with hotel freebies such as half-used shampoos and conditioners. She had finally got what was considered an excellent job as a bed maker (*camarera*) in an upscale hotel chain. She cleaned fourteen bedrooms a day, and after her shift she collapsed in exhaustion, her body aching from the physical effort, but she was triumphant to have landed the job.

Working as a domestic servant was not as well paid as hotel work but was not as hard physically, and once accepted, these women tended to be better treated. Nadia recounted how her employers ran their fingers across the table to check there was no dust and deliberately left out money to test whether she would steal. Once over these hurdles, good money could be earned. Nadia was one of two maids working for a very rich family that lived in the mountains above Barcelona and owned a retail chain of forty shops. She did the cleaning, cooking, and washing, while the other maid looked after the children. Nadia had earned more in this live-in job, which entailed virtually no overhead, than she now did living out, but she chose the latter when she became fed up without a social life, and she wanted to buy an apartment.

Carmen, the washerwoman who lived with Alonso across the street from Marta, had a full-time live-in job and saved the most amount of money among the migrants surveyed. She worked as a care provider twenty-four hours a day, six days a week, tending to the needs of a ninety-three-year-old woman with Alzheimer's disease, living in her client's apartment in Barceloneta. In just under four years, she had saved $20,000, and unlike her fellow migrants from Calle K, she had no interest in a relationship in Barcelona. She remitted almost all her monthly salary to rebuild her house for her children, not for her ne'er-do-well husband, Alonso. During my visit with her in Barceloneta, Carmen explained what a tough, lonely job it was. When the old lady slept, she "escaped" to get a few moments of fresh air or do the odd bit of shopping, though never for more than ten minutes at a time.

As was true of Ecuadorian women in Spain generally, most of the women from Indio Guayas were working below their qualifications, thus deskilling. Despite their educational level, they were mostly restricted to domestic work. So although women found it easier to get work, men generally earned more. Nevertheless, women still earned more than they would in Guayaquil, and they gained greater independence (Herrera 2005; ILDIS/FES and others 2002; Ruíz 2002).

Physical Capital: Housing as an Asset in Barcelona

In Barcelona migrants not only accumulated financial capital but also had the opportunity to accumulate the physical capital asset of housing. Most male migrants adopted a similar strategy; they rented rooms until they had acquired their documents and then purchased a flat with a mortgage of up to 100 percent (in 2005 the interest rate was 3.2 percent, according to Mateo). The average mortgage payment was €750 a month; the average rent was €566 a month. In order to pay either rent or mortgage, as many rooms as possible were sublet or rented out. So as in Indio Guayas, lots of people lived in a small space, sharing a communal kitchen and sitting-dining room, with the focus of attention the permanently turned-on TV. The difference was that in Barcelona they were buying apartments whereas in Guayaquil their brothers and sisters were still living on the family plot or beginning the self-help housing process on the city's periphery.

To get a mortgage, it was necessary to have legal residence documentation. This not only included a contract of fixed work (*contrato de trabajo fijo*), but also a second residential permit documentation (*la segunda tarjeta de residencia*) to demonstrate permanent residence in Barcelona, along with a copy of a third paycheck to show permanent wage work status (*el tercer rol de pago*). Of the fifteen men interviewed in the survey in 2005, six already owned their own (mortgaged) apartments, and another three were in the process of acquiring the necessary documentation to arrange a mortgage to purchase a flat. Douglas, for instance, lived with his wife, Eva, and son, as well as two younger sisters and a brother-in-law in a rented apartment, meanwhile renting out his own flat that was located further out of the city. Because people from Guayaquil quickly formed relationships, the level of trust between a couple was often not very high. For many the litmus test of commitment was whether the mortgage was put in both their names. Eddie's partner, Nadia, summed up the situation as follows:

> Eddie pays about €600 for the mortgage because it's in his name. If my name had been included, I would help him. Since I didn't have any documents, the apartment is in his and his brother's name. But I want to own a place, and I've told him that now that I have documents, he should add my name. He should take out his brother's name and include mine because I'm the one living with him. But he doesn't say anything to me. I help a little bit with the food, but that's all. Why should I pay for the apartment? If we split up, I'm the one who's going to leave because it's his apartment. So if it's in my name too, I'll help with the mortgage. But otherwise when would he pay me back if I left?

For Eddie's part the issue was one of marriage (complicated as Nadia had left a husband and two children in Guayaquil). He maintained that they were not sure they would stay together, so the apartment would stay in his name until such time as they got married.

Transformation of Household Social Capital in Barcelona

Nadia and Eddie's difference of opinion showed that while the transfer of a "culture" of household social capital meant migrants quickly established relationships in Barcelona, the nature of such capital itself was not only fragile but also could be rapidly transformed. Factors such as the economic necessity for both partners to work, as well as cultural and legal influences, had implications for intrahousehold roles and responsibilities, and the associated empowerment of women.

The economic rationale behind migration to Barcelona meant that both partners wanted to work. With no extended family to pick up domestic tasks, the most important change within many households was the increased domestic responsibility taken on by male partners, even if, as Gonzalo's partner, Pilar, commented, "The change in role is more an economic necessity than a voluntary one." Gonzalo confirmed this when he recounted the way he had been forced to change, even before he found a partner:

> In my personal life, the biggest change I've noticed is that you have to do things for yourself. You can't expect someone else to do them for you. When I was single here, neither Mateo nor Malena did anything for me. Out of the seven days in a week, I had to cook twice, Mateo twice, Malena twice, and the children once or twice. I had to learn how to cook. Doing the laundry is easy because you just throw the clothes in the washer; you don't wash anything by hand. You iron your own clothes; it's not like in Ecuador where you have your mother. I didn't even know how to wash a dish, so I had to learn here. This is the most dramatic personal change I've undergone in my entire life.

Cooking was an important starting point, and changes brought on by living in Catalan society helped make it easier. Meals were simpler than in Ecuador, shopping was done weekly rather than daily, both partners shopped, and households were frequently smaller. Even though the men did it out of necessity, they did not complain. In working out their strategies to balance productive and reproductive work, behavior changes occurred. Eddie, for instance, noted that:

> The typical Ecuadorian male is very macho. When I had a girlfriend there (in Ecuador), I expected her to do everything. I've learned to do things here. Women here liberate themselves. We share the housework; if she cleans, I tidy up the room, clean the sink, or do the groceries. I don't expect her to do all the work. It's a total change, even she notices it. Over there, women get home tired from work and have to cook, but I never did this over there.

Only when there was considerable trust between a couple, such as between Douglas and Eva, did they have joint bank accounts combining both salaries. Generally, men tended to be more transparent than women, who often hid resources because of a lack of trust in long-term relationships. As Eddie commented, the independence of Spanish women was seen as a critical influence. The Ecuadorian men had strong and not necessarily positive opinions about Spanish women; Gonzalo spoke for many when he said that "Spanish women do not look after their husbands. They do not like doing household tasks. They go out to dance, they go to the discothèques when they like; they do not have to say anything to their husbands about their movements. Husbands are expected to assist in household tasks. Here you cannot hit a woman—she calls the police immediately and you are charged."

Equally, not all Ecuadorian women totally agreed with the new "liberating" opportunities that Spain offered to women. Pilar, Gonzalo's partner, reflected on the contradictions felt by Ecuadorian women, particularly older ones, when faced by such a different situation:

Here you adapt to this lifestyle. The Spanish women are amazed that one gets up each morning to make breakfast for one's husband, to make lunch, and to do the washing and ironing. They tell you to wake up and find something to do. In Ecuador you're used to getting up and waiting on your husband. Here there are women who want to be better than men, but it shouldn't be that way. We come from another country, and we know well how we've lived our lives over there, so I don't see why we have to change. Here there is more support for women, so they want to dominate men. Sometimes it's too much.

Despite these doubts about Spanish women, Pilar's lifestyle reflected the changes Ecuadorian women made in Barcelona: she dressed more informally in jeans and t-shirts; wore flat shoes, rather than high heels, when traveling on the metros and buses; and wore less makeup and costume jewelry. Pilar, like many of the women we interviewed, visited Adriana and me in our little flat for long conversations and supper without anxiety or criticism from Gonzalo, her partner. Catalina, Douglas's younger sister who came to Barcelona to study under his supervision, reflected the thinking of younger Ecuadorian women who had migrated while single, commenting:

I have my own expenses, so I work and study for myself. Of course, my brothers pay for my food because I live with them. But I'm independent, I don't depend on them. In Ecuador I used to go home from school and later from university, and that's all I did. My dad didn't want me to work, and so I had to ask him for money, even for the bus ride. I had no independence at all. But here I can look after myself. Here you really have to share, coexist, and be responsible. I'm not going to be like I used to ever again. If I ever go back, I'm not going to change. I have become more mature; I have gained from the migration experience.

Increased control over fertility and an associated decline in the number of children related once again to the lack of extended household members to provide assistance. As Douglas's wife, Eva, coping with the logistics of one small son, said, "Both women and men want fewer children here. In Guayaquil you do not think when you are going to have children because there is someone who can look after them. Here there is no one to look after them. Here you either work or have children."

Acquisition of Civil Capital and the Associated Knowledge to Claim and Contest Rights

Accompanying the changes in household social capital was the acquisition of what can be called "civic" capital. While still in the process of being articulated as an intangible capital asset, this comprises civic understanding and tolerance, and the capability to contest and claim rights as well as to fulfill responsibilities. The recollections of three young Guayaquileño men in Barcelona all reflected this. Douglas, for instance, summed up the differences between Barcelona and Guayaquil as follows: "Laws are stricter here; life is more controlled, less wild. Politics works here better. You can see it in the streets—they're clean—and people are honest and kind. This is what Europe has to offer."

For his brother Eddie, citizen identity was associated with greater opportunities for upward socioeconomic mobility in a more inclusive society. This increased his awareness of class-bound constraints in Guayaquil, an important realization: "The structure of society in Guayaquil is more demarcated. Nobody goes to a good restaurant, as they 'feel bad.' In contrast, here there is more social liberty. I can go into any restaurant and get served."

Associated with the benefits that such a society could offer was also increased awareness of citizen responsibilities. Gonzalo's comments again mirrored those of many of his migrant friends from Guayaquil:

Here you can't hit your child because someone may report you. Not to mention [hitting] your partner. If you try to beat her, the police will take you away. There's more respect here. You get used to the discipline here: I've become used to listening to music at a low volume; I no longer drink in the street because if you get caught, they arrest you. Parties have to be at home or in a bar, but not like in Ecuador, where you can blast the stereo as much as you like. The police officers treat you well. They ask you to show them your documents, and they thank you and even apologize for bothering you. It's very different in Ecuador, where they ask you to show your ID, and they beat you right away.

For women increased knowledge about legal rights and responsibilities was reflected more specifically in their personal lives, with those arriving earlier transferring this information to more recent arrivals. Enhanced understanding about the protection against domestic abuse that a functioning democracy with accountable institutions provided meant that Ecuadorian women became far more assertive about their rights. Nadia, already into her second relationship with Eddie, was well aware of this:

Eddie has a tough temper, but I ignore him. Men here are macho like in Ecuador, but here they can't touch us because we get much support from the police. Eddie can't raise his hand [to] me because I can go straight to the police and press charges. My husband in Guayaquil sometimes insulted me and hit me, but I never went to the police, never said anything. But it's different here; I've told Eddie that if he ever lays a hand on me, he knows what I'll do. I don't put up with that crap over here.

The transnational status of migrants also presented particular challenges concerning rights and responsibilities relating to the breakdown of marriage and the distribution of assets, such as housing. The particular profiles of male and female migrants from Indio Guayas meant that it was the women who were more likely to have such problems. As illustrated in table 10-2, these related to divorce and to the writing of wills, associated with distribution of earnings saved in Barcelona. For instance, when Carmen proudly told the Barceloneta fishermen sons of the elderly woman for whom she cared that the purpose of her hard work and savings was to give her children a better home, they suggested she should make a will and change her house title deed back in Guayaquil. Otherwise, she would have no guarantee that the upgraded house did not go to Alonso's many other children.

Adriana, visiting from Guayaquil, had local knowledge of such issues and very quickly took on a leadership role in providing advice, also offering to follow up once she was back in Guayaquil. Just as Marta had acted as a community leader around issues of physical and social infrastructure, her daughter took on a similar role, but this time around the range of rights women were contesting. For the second generation, it was this type of transnational community social capital, linking Barcelona to Guayaquil, that was now more important (see table 10-2).

Table 10-2. *Types of Assistance Required to Settle "Domestic" Legal Problems in Guayaquil*

Legal problem	Professional assistance	Example	Adriana's role
Will to distribute assets	Notary and lawyer	Carmen	Find lawyer to make a will
House title deed changes	Notary and lawyer	Carmen	Find lawyer in Guayaquil to change house title deeds
Legalization of divorce settlement	With lawyer before a judge, and afterwards a notary	Belen needed to finalize the divorce settlement by implementing the divorce agreement and children's living arrangements	Advise Belen's daughter in Guayaquil what to do
Start divorce proceeding from Barcelona against husband in Guayaquil	Lawyer	Nadia lacked knowledge of divorce process, including her rights to bring children to Barcelona. She was advised that someone, such as a sister, could represent her in Guayaquil and was told what process to follow if her husband refused to divorce.	Provide advice on procedures to present the petition for mutual agreement

Assets Transferred back to Guayaquil

The strong linkages back home in Indio Guayas meant that an important part of most migrants' strategies while abroad was the transference of a range of accumulated assets back to their families and community. These included not only financial remittances but also less tangible assets.

Remittances and Transnational Accumulation

The economic support embedded within household social capital provided the basis for remittances, the most visible transnational asset transferred to family back in Indio Guayas.[7] With more than three out of four migrants remitting, the amount sent home depended on numerous factors. As described in chapter 9, migrants in Barcelona supported their families back in Guayaquil with an average remittance of $143 a month, compared with an average of $7.75 a month support from children living off the plot but still in Guayaquil. Nevertheless, such remittances might ultimately be time bound. While women who had left children behind in Guayaquil were likely to be more reliable remitters, over time, as men with families in Guayaquil brought them to Barcelona, they were less likely to remit to remaining family members, particularly once their parents had died. Whereas support from children still living in Guayaquil tended to be provided at time intervals ranging from daily to annually, four out of five remitters from Barcelona (both male and female) did so on a regular monthly basis. As discussed in previous chapters, it was not only the amounts of remittances but also the reliability that was critical in keeping Indio Guayas families out of poverty.

Remittance financial capital was used for short-term crises as well as longer-term consumption. Thus while Mateo bailed out his brother from prison by sending U.S.$2,000, he was also sending money monthly to enable his father to pay for the expensive medicine required for his Parkinson's disease. Nadia's remittances, sent to her mother, were for maintenance expenses relating to the food, clothing, and education of her two children. Carmen's remittances illustrated how, with older children and less demand to meet daily needs, it was possible to invest in assets such as housing. For men money transfers also were often linked to power and identity back in Indio Guayas—whether it was manifested through building a bigger house, generally for one's mother, or holding fiestas when one came home for a visit.

Remittances, however, were also the financial manifestation of complex familial relationships and acted as a mechanism that redefined or ruptured social relations. For wives left behind in Guayaquil, the failure to send remittances was an indicator of abandonment. When one of the men from Indio Guayas acquired a partner in Barcelona and stopped sending money home, it caused criticism among friends in Barcelona. Concern for children left behind in Guayaquil often resulted in serious stress and depression for their mothers. But this was not straightforward. While women wanted to bring their children to Barcelona, they could not cope with the complexities of child care in the city. In addition, over time they often became accustomed to living freer lives without the encumbrances of children, and to earning decent wages. So they felt guilty and justified separation from their children in terms of the culturally acceptable practice in Guayaquil that children can be raised by other kin, particularly mothers and sisters.

Community and Household Social Capital and Transnational Identity

While the migration literature tends to focus on the monetary aspect of remittances, the experiences of migrants from Indio Guayas to Barcelona showed that increasingly there were additional types of transnational assets. Of considerable importance were the links and reinforcement of trust and social capital back home, at both the household and community level. As Gonzalo commented, "Guayaquil is your home, but you do not want to go back and live there. You know what the situation is there."

Thus when Luis Alberto, the renowned drug baron who lived on Calle 26, was suddenly killed in the community during the time we were doing fieldwork, within twenty-four hours everyone in Barcelona from Indio Guayas knew about it, and over the following week, it was a source of intense discussion in all the households we visited.

Returning to Guayaquil was a critical rite of passage for migrants living in Barcelona. The dates and costs of trips back to Guayaquil were much discussed. When were people going? Who was going when? How much would they have to pay? As August and December were the most expensive months to travel, being linked to the Spanish holiday cycle, social status was attached to the timing of visits. While the successful migrants went at Christmas, those who were poorer went off-season. Thus Mateo said, "I am so poor I asked the travel agency when the cheapest time to go is, and they said April, so I will go in April."

Yet when migrants visited home, it was not always an easy transition. Political, spatial, and environmental issues had a profound impact. One young man, for instance, said that when he went back after seven years, he could not stand the lack of order—the chaos—and the fact that everything was a mess. But for those migrants that were young adults, it was the dynamics of their marital relationship that were particularly affected by the transnational context. Partnerships formed in Barcelona were perceived as Barcelona-specific institutions. Barcelona was seen as "apart"; what happened there had nothing to do with what happened in the barrio. As Pilar, Gonzalo's partner, put it, "The women you have here, are to have here. But not to present to your family. Here you have the liberty to have whomever you want without worrying about what your family thinks."

In these relationships formed without family approval, the tension between two separate worlds surfaced when families returned to visit Guayaquil, with conflicts often occurring even among married couples. Eva, for instance, had a tremendous fight with her mother-in-law when she returned, and so she and

Douglas solved the problem by each staying with their respective families. Men returning as local heroes to their family homes took on a different identity than they had in Barcelona. Thus Eddie's mother reputedly told Nadia (Eddie's Barcelona partner), "When you come to Guayaquil, you go to your family, and Eddie comes to his family."

Those who had left children back in Guayaquil faced added complications. When couples went back, they often went their separate ways, with women going on their own to stay with their children. Pilar highlighted the causes of this particular complication:

> It is harder for a woman. I've spoken with all Gonzalo's family, but he hasn't spoken with mine. I didn't leave their father; he was the one who left. I'm not going to tell them on the phone. I know that if we speak face to face, I'll be able to explain. My mother knows I'm living with someone here and has advised me to start thinking about how I'm going to break the news to my children. Sometimes children oppose, but I think mine won't."

Transnational Identity and the Next Generation

If women who had left children behind in Guayaquil worried about the likelihood of being judged about their new partners, those who brought children with them were beginning to experience the complexities of multiple identities. Parents who had given birth to children in Barcelona accepted, as a matter of fact, that their children would be Spanish. Thus Eva, Douglas' wife, logically stated:

> My son is Spanish. Not so much because of his birthplace but because of his life experience. His habits, his language, his traditions will be from here. Sometime in the future he'll say he's Spanish or Catalan because he was born here and lives here. Of course, he won't be 100 percent Spanish because it's clear he has Ecuadorian blood. Sure he'll travel with us whenever we go back to Ecuador, but we won't tell him he's Ecuadorian because he'll reply he's not because he doesn't live there."

For this generation, Ecuador would become the place to visit to discover roots rather than to maintain social capital. As Mateo reflected, "I'm Ecuadorian and my new granddaughter is Spanish, of Ecuadorian descent. My grandchildren will grow up here and live their lives here. If they go to Ecuador at all, it will be to visit the place where their grandparents and parents were born."

Yet it was unclear whether the original migrants from Indio Guayas would return. With the economic situation not improving, and links weakening over time, these migrants looked more likely, along with millions of others, to assimilate into Barcelona. Thus Pilar poignantly commented:

> The situation in Ecuador gets worse each day; I don't know whether I could go back. It's going to feel like a new place. It's been three years since I last visited. I don't have a house, and it was all very strange. I felt Ecuador was little, the city was little, and there are so many needs. Here you don't see so much poverty in the streets. I felt very sorry for my country."

The experience of migration and living in Barcelona resulted in significant changes, not only in the accumulation of financial and productive capital but also in social capital, associated with identity and empowerment. For men this related more to the wider society in which they lived, and with their increased awareness of their rights came a growing recognition that the persistent inequality in Guayaquil constrained them both as citizens and as workers. For women the migrant experience was about empowerment accompanying their release from the trap of patriarchal gender inequalities. Thus they gave much greater priority than men did to renegotiating gender relations.

The Barcelona research also revealed the extent to which options for young women in Indio Guayas differed from those in Barcelona. As described in chapter 9, Adriana's daughter Laura was still expected to live at her parents' home until she married and passed from the control of her father to the control of her husband. In Barcelona, by contrast, Douglas and Eddie's twenty-three-year-old sister, who had been living in their flat, had announced her intention to live on her own. Although they were thousands of miles from home, Ecuadorian migrants still attempted to retain some of their traditional social and moral codes; therefore her declaration was badly received by all her family, including twenty-nine-year-old Nadia, Eddie's partner. Even in Barcelona the implication of such independent living would be that she was a prostitute. Yet despite such criticism, she had far more control over her life than would have been the case in Indio Guayas.

When Adriana and I completed the fieldwork, she summarized some of the differences between the lifestyles of friends in Barcelona and those of friends and families in Indio Guayas that most impressed her. These included changes in gender roles and responsibilities, that is, how men took on far more of the domestic responsibilities of cooking, cleaning, and shopping, and how women, in turn, were far more independent. The increased self-esteem of people able to find and keep work particularly resonated for her, while the fact that women aged sixty were out socializing in the cafes at night made her reflect on the way that the mobility and activities of older women, such as her mother Marta, had been curtailed. Finally, the independence of women in Barcelona made Adriana resolve to make herself more independent, while challenging her husband, Hector, to take on more domestic tasks when she returned home.

For regardless of the number of second-generation sons and daughters who had gotten out of Guayaquil, the majority had remained in Indio Guayas, facing a situation without the same economic opportunities or chances for upward mobility that Barcelona offered. The next chapter, therefore, returns to Indio Guayas and addresses the serious new challenges the community faced.

11

Youth Crime, Gangs, and Violent Death: Community Responses to Insecurity

"Mario, a healthy (sano) young man who was studying at uni [university] had to kill a criminal in self-defense. Stefan had always been threatening and hitting Mario. Stefan was a criminal who took drugs; he stole from everyone and broke into houses. He was the leader of this criminal gang, rascals from this street, the 26 [street] and K. He called Mario, 'Come here,' he said, 'kneel down and kiss my feet.' Mario just got tired of the same taunting always. Mario and his friends have always gathered around here in the neighborhood, practicing [football] at night. One night they had been drinking all night. Stefan arrived and took out his gun and threatened Mario, "I'm gonna kill you right now." Mario grabbed Stefan's gun and shot him, and Stefan fell down in the street. Alberto, Mario's brother, rushed out to help him, and Mario fled from the neighborhood.

Stefan's gang went to burn Mario and Alberto's house down. When we neighbors saw Alberto was being attacked, we called the police and the gang ran away. The police wanted to take Alberto with them, so Adriana, Ana Maria, and I formed a group to support him. Alberto was a good, innocent guy. All the gangsters, because so many knew us as preschool students, remained silent. The attorney arrived, and they wanted to take Alberto away. But Alberto bribed the police officers with U.S.$150 because the penalty for him would be that the group would kill him in prison. The girls chipped in so they would drop him back at his family house. Then the man next door offered a truck so Alberto's mother could take away their stuff to her *mother's, because those people wanted to burn it all. People have a bit of fear; if it happened with Mario, it may happen with any of us here. I am fearful because I live alone with my daughters, and if they saw me go there to intervene in Mario's favor, and they recognize me, they might do anything."*

—Lourdes, schoolteacher, Marta's sister and neighbor

The previous chapter described how some young men got out of Guayaquil and made new lives as migrants, predominantly in Barcelona, Spain. However, the majority remained in Indio Guayas. As highlighted by Lourdes's account of the tragic January 2005 killing of the gang leader Stefan by Mario, a university student, violent conflicts were occurring within the community, most often among its young men. Lourdes distinguished between gangs of young *sano* (literally, "healthy") men that hung out on street corners playing football and drinking as a recreational activity, and gangs that were involved in criminal thieving and drug-selling activities. In addition, she highlighted the instantaneous response from close neighbors to help a neighbor in need. Finally, she recounted the unquestioning reaction to the police—to bribe them rather than allow an innocent young man go to jail.

A violent incident such as this exemplifies the level of gratuitous, daily violence more recently experienced in communities such as Indio Guayas, and highlights the problems associated with youth crime and gang activity.[1] In a context where drug dealers, criminals, and domestic abusers lived side by side with law-abiding citizens, the killing of Stefan rocked the neighborhood. In earlier decades the Indio Guayas committee had to contest and negotiate with the state for physical and social infrastructure (see chapter 5); by 2005 it not only had to contend increasingly with the ubiquitous gangs and high levels of crime and violence in its midst, it also had to resolve such conflict without relying on the support of formal state institutions. With both the police system and judiciary perceived as corrupt and ineffective and therefore untrustworthy, increasingly power and control were contested informally as local citizens witnessed and confronted violence on a daily basis. This context is not unique; as Koonings and Kruijt (2007) argue, cities throughout Latin America increasingly contain territory where formal or effective governance is either absent or ineffective; in such spaces where the "uncivil logic" of coercion takes over, such zones become synonymous with violence and insecurity.

In describing the second-generation youth gang phenomenon, this final empirical chapter returns to the Indio Guayas community and to the very recent past of 2005. It describes how a crisis, such as the killing of Stefan, served as a catalyst for reaching consensus on informal social norms of legality and illegality relating to violent crime that did not necessarily coincide with those of the state. This highlights a number of issues. First, the poor living in peripheral urban areas are not simply passive recipients of "low-intensity conflict" that they are powerless to confront; rather they are active agents that make decisions and take proactive measures to cope with their "encounters with violence" (Moser and McIlwaine 2004). Second, such responses to justice with regard to illegal and violent activities are not homogeneous; different social actors display a range of judgments, based on their particular interests and associated power to confront or respond to violence on their own terms (Pécaut 1999). These factors militate against simplistic perceptions of exclusion, fear, and passivity, and show how communities confront, collude with, and judge violent crimes (Robben and Nordstrom 1995; McIlwaine and Moser 2007).

Finally, this chapter examines how the growing problem of crime and violence has had serious implications for asset accumulation in Indio Guayas.

Background: Increasing Levels of Violence and Insecurity in Indio Guayas

As discussed in previous chapters, between 1978 and 2004, Indio Guayas overall was a relative success story, both in terms of asset accumulation and income poverty reduction. However, the general increase in prosperity was also accompanied by a growing insecurity. In twenty-six years the neighborhood went from a marginal squatter settlement—lacking services and infrastructure but also lacking youth violence and street gangs—to a consolidated well-serviced neighborhood—one where many second-generation children completed high school but some engaged in crime and violent activity. With better services and education had come increased aspirations but not necessarily jobs, with an associated unfulfilled capacity to earn a decent living and acquire consumer durables. Linked to this was a slow but insidious acceleration in the levels of daily violence, and along with this, increased fears about personal property security and personal safety from assault.

It is important to recognize that violent crime in the barrio was not new; rather it was the nature of its manifestation that had changed, as well as how, over two decades, it had become a pervasive part of daily life. House burglary always occurred in Cisne Dos. During the 1970s, when the majority of houses had easy access through split-bamboo walls, it was very common. Houses built over water were the most vulnerable, easily accessible to burglars, who generally lived outside the community and came at night by canoe, a tactic that rendered them invisible. During the 1980s, investments in reconstructing houses from cement provided greater security and protected physical assets from fire and bad weather. As residents became more preoccupied with crime, they also invested in additional precautions, such as bars on windows and steel doors, making trade-offs between these security measures and investment in other assets.

By 1992 the situation had deteriorated to such an extent that in the 1992 subsample, women identified personal insecurity as the second most pressing community problem after inadequate water supplies.[2] Over a six-month period, nearly one-third of women interviewed had had their home burgled, including Marta, as described in my diary in 1992:

> Over a two-week period, Marta's house was robbed twice. The first time the robbers climbed up ladders being used for construction and stole Emilio's school uniform and shoes. Last night two chickens were stolen from the back yard, just outside the room in which we sleep. The big cock that has plagued our existence, crowing at 1 a.m. every night, is suddenly no longer there, and everyone misses him. The robber apparently came through the hole in the wall between Marta's and Lourdes' houses at 4 a.m. Marta and Jesus heard something, but when they got up, he had gone.

Of greater concern, however, was personal assault in public places, particularly on local buses. During the same survey period, half the respondents reported witnessing a robbery while on a bus, and one-fifth reported being robbed. Almost one-third of women had been accosted on the street, with the most dangerous area identified as the main road, Calle 25, particularly at the corner of Calle K—half a block from community leader Marta's house—where the buses stopped and a large number of street vendors congregated.

The danger in this area was exacerbated by the fact that local gangs repeatedly vandalized the existing street lighting. In 1992 the problem of *pandillas,* as local gangs of male youths were commonly called, was identified as increasingly serious, cited by nearly half of the respondents as the main problem in the community (although only one in five people had personally had bad experiences with them). Working in small groups, young men armed with knives or machetes—and occasionally even handguns—moved through local buses, threatening passengers and robbing them of jewelry, watches, and money.[3] Women began to curb their mobility, fearing transport was not safe, especially at night, thereby reducing their participation in local community activities. In addition, it affected night school attendance, particularly by younger women. In a context where night school was widely utilized by working adults to secure a better job—indeed both Claudio and Marta had completed school in this way—many either dropped out or stopped enrolling. The greatest impact was felt by poorer households, whose children, as described in chapter 8, attended night school since they were busy during the day caring for children or earning an income, or because their families could not pay high school matriculation fees for daytime classes. The inevitable outcome was a reduction in opportunities to accumulate human capital associated with better education.

When local people were brave enough to intervene when gangs attacked on the bus, the outcome could be tragic, as Mercedes, Claudio's wife and an active member of the Indio Guayas committee, described:

> Bruno, president of another local committee, tried to defend some women and girls on the bus. There were also about three men passengers (on the bus) when three men hopped on and wanted to rape them. Bruno remarked how was it possible that so many men didn't do anything to help those girls, and that he was not going to allow it to happen. So they got angry. "You cheeky one . . . we're going to kill you," they said, and they killed him. . . . I didn't see it, but blood spurted everywhere.

By 2004 the situation had deteriorated even further, with daily life dominated by the "banality" and complexities of dealing with everyday violence, particularly as a consequence of the widespread availability of small arms, increased access to cheap drugs, higher levels of drug consumption, and associated crime to pay for the habit. Men in the police and armed forces (such as Ana Maria's husband, Edgar) had always had access to guns, but cheap supplies meant that men working as taxi drivers, credit collectors, and small shop owners also possessed guns. Daily gossip captured in my diary during one week in March 2005 contained constant references to thefts, either witnessed firsthand or heard about:

> Alvaro the tailor, sitting in his mother-in-law's house celebrating mother's day last Sunday, watched two thieves running past the house with a large TV and a DVD system on their shoulders. Half an hour later, the police drove down the road. . . . On Tuesday, across the road, two men with guns jumped out of a car and stole a woman's bag and a man's briefcase while neighbors silently watched it happen. . . . Last Saturday Lourdes and Adriana, coming home along the Calle 25th around 8 p.m., watched two young men rob women, laden with Saturday purchases from town, as they got off the bus. Walking past, the men held their guns ready for the next bus. . . . Last Wednesday, half a block away, in view of the whole street, ten police patrol cars surrounded a truck parked by a house. The

Figure 11-1. *Map of Dangerous Locations, Events, and People, Indio Guayas,*
December 2004–March 2005 [a]

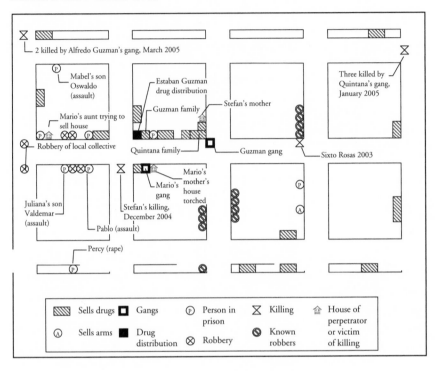

a. Perception map based on input from focus group of four local women.

men who lived there had highjacked a truck with its contents. First gossip from Mercedes opposite was that it was full of cooked chickens. In
fact, it was electrical goods, and the police drove away with some of the
culprits. It was rumored that the police dropped them off after a $200
payoff.

The sheer complexity of crime and violence, where perpetrators and victims lived side by side, as well as in the proliferation of income-generating
activities associated with robbery and drugs are illustrated by figure 11-1, a
perception map created by four local women over a four-month period during
2004–05. While their spatial knowledge of murders extended well beyond
their immediate vicinity, their knowledge of lesser crimes and associated indi-

viduals was most extensive in relation to their street and decreased with distance from home. As the figure shows, in a two-block area of the same street, comprising some 100 households, they identified the following manifestations of crime and violence:
—six gang or drug-related killings;
—fifteen known robberies;
—three young men currently in prison for robbery;
—the residence of one of the biggest drug distribution leaders, a stone's throw from their houses; and
—a minimum of fifteen small shops known for selling drugs—mainly cocaine paste—along with other, legitimate household items.
Describing the situation as the map was drawn, one woman commented:

Where are the thieves? They are all around. One man is in prison; he's only eighteen years old, very young and good looking. The drug boss lives in the corner house. Also there is his brother-in-law. All of them sell drugs, even the old woman, his mother. He is capable of killing a woman; he shot one and killed her. So those people have threatened the old lady in revenge. There were seven who entered the community from the river by canoe and killed three in one go. It happened before February. They did it in a second; we didn't even notice. The police came, and there were dead people. It was horrible because it triggered revenge. It was very scary. It's all calm now, but you feel you have to ask for police presence; but they still don't do their job."

Given the assertions about the widespread nature of violence in Latin American cities, it is important to identify whether the killing of Stefan and the extensive number of people involved in some way or another in violent criminal activities in Indio Guayas were typical for Guayaquil as well as other urban areas in the country. At the national level, Ecuador was rated as an "intermediate" country in terms of violence (Loor, Aldas, and López, n.d.); nevertheless homicide rates in Ecuador had gradually increased from 6.4 per 100,000 citizens annually in 1980 to 10.3 in 1990, and to 15.3 in 2000, as compared with world rates of 5.5, 6.4, and 8.9, respectively (Villavicencio 2004). Although the highest levels were in the Colombian border area, three out of four of the total number of "deaths by external causes" (homicides, suicides, and road accidents) nevertheless occurred in urban centers, mainly Quito and Guayaquil. While the latter had the highest level of homicides caused by firearms, the former had higher levels of general violence (Andrade 2006, pp. 16–17). Although systematic or reliable data on organized armed violence in Guayaquil are lacking, particularly with regard to the involvement of children and young adults, it is clear that over the last two decades, violence in Guayaquil grew, diversified, and mostly affected the poor. Of note was the large increase in organized crime, with most of the victims among the poor (Villavicencio 2001).

The widespread prevalence of youth gangs in Guayaquil has been recognized by researchers, who have developed a typology of three different groups: the aforementioned pandillas, *bandas,* and *naciones* (Loor, Aldas, and López, n.d.). Their presence has been noted in twelve urban marginal areas in Guayaquil, of which three—El Guasmo in the southeast, Isla Trinitaria in the southwest, and Bastión Popular in the north—have been identified as the most dangerous, given their concentration of all three types of organized gangs. These three areas all adjoined Cisne Dos; yet community members in Indio Guayas referred interchangeably to "bandas" and "pandillas" without categorizing them specifically, and made no reference to naciones. For community members the critical characteristic was whether or not gangs were sano (healthy).[4] Although Loor, Aldas, and López (n.d.) have linked the origin of these groups to the 1970 conflicts surrounding land invasions and the emergence of new marginal neighborhoods, this was not the case in Indio Guayas, where gangs played no part in land invasions (see chapter 3). By the mid-1980s youth gangs were recognized as a main contributor to criminality in Guayaquil. In 1987 the police reported that 1,000 groups were operating in the poorest neighborhoods. While gang operations were at first limited to the "red areas" of the port, by 1988 they had extended to middle-class areas and then increasingly into the extensive low-income barrios. Of particular relevance to the Indio Guayas context when one discusses pandillas is Andrade's (2006) concept of the "circularity" of violence, which: "is produced and resolved inside the territories that coincide mostly with popular and marginal neighbourhoods. This is the most common type of violence among these social formations: the elimination or intimidation of the members of other pandillas from popular sectors and/or people from other sectors of the population equally deprived" (p. 23).

Such a description corresponds with the evidence on the killing of Stefan, where structural causes, alcohol, and the easy availability of guns were the risk factors that triggered a fatal encounter.[5]

Causes and Consequences of Youth Gangs and Their Associated Violence

Perceptions of the causes of youth violence in Indio Guayas varied depending on the identity and agency of different social actors. Women such as Marta and her sister Lourdes—who were not only mothers but teachers in the preschool program (see chapter 5)—felt that the problem arose from a lack of care and guidance in the home environment. This raised questions about the importance of household social capital. Thus Lourdes commented:

> Young men [*muchachos*] from a very young age participate in gangs and are part of them for nine, eleven years. They're armed. You can tell because they wear very wide pants. And you can tell if they're doing drugs, which are provided by Luis Alberto, their boss [mentioned in chapter 10 as being killed while we were doing fieldwork in Barcelona]. What happened to all those young boys in preschool we taught who decided to take this other road? Look at Stefan: he was abandoned by his mother when she went out to work and raised by his grandmother. His uncle smoked a lot already, so I think he didn't have a good role model to guide him. Because there were always drugs for sale in the neighborhood, they got trapped in that world of drugs. Those young men didn't have any guidance. Their mothers were illiterate; Stefan's mother couldn't write or read. Sheer lack of direction, guidance, of someone to look after them and make sure they progress.

Marta expressed a very similar view:

> They are violent because there is no authority. Their father let them do as they pleased, and that doesn't work either. You may love your children very much, but you have to put limits on them so they understand that life is not that easy and that they can't do whatever they want but what is good for them. Because they think the way to go is to do drugs, steal, and have women. They know everything from a very young age, and they're there, with lots of beautiful girls, skinny, nice, blonde, blue-eyed, drunk, high on drugs, fighting, getting tattoos on their arms, navels. . . . It's total depravation.

In their broader, Guayaquil-level analysis, Loor, Aldas, and López (n.d.) concurred with the normative view of community women, that a majority of gang members came from single-parent households (mainly headed by mothers) or from extended families. Mothers often had to work long hours to sustain the family, leaving their children unattended; these children and youth often lived with other relatives in very small spaces, leading them to escape to the streets.

While single women on their own could find it more difficult to cope with sons, it is important not to generalize. Within Indio Guayas, for instance, Alicia brought up nine children without any of them ending up in a violent gang. Nevertheless, even within the area of Calle 25 and Calle K, there were tragic cases of child neglect associated with single working mothers. Nancy, living four doors down from Marta, headed one such household. She described how when she and her sister went out to work as domestics, they locked the girls inside the house to prevent them from becoming pregnant, while they locked Elvis, the son, outside the house, leaving him to roam. When he became a gang member, going around with three other knife-carrying friends, Nancy said it became a real problem for her. Waiting for him to come home at night, she could not sleep, which was difficult since she had to go to work in the morning. So she threw him out of the house and stopped communicating with him. In 1992 she said she knew that he had gone to do military service. By 2004 it was known in the community that he had been killed, although people were unclear what had happened.

Young people, particularly men, joined street-based groups, where drugs and weapons were readily available. Many of these youth did so because they were searching for the support, trust, and cohesion—social capital—that they maintained their families did not provide, as well as because of the lack of opportunities in the local context. This theme was identified by a group of "sano" young men in Indio Guayas during a focus group discussion. They saw a lack of communication as well as friendship with their parents as an important cause of the problem (see figure 11-2). However, among a range of reasons for joining gangs, they also identified external structural causes relating to the lack of educational opportunities and the availability of drugs and weapons, as well as aspirations relating to a desire for quick money, and the fact that expectations had changed while the opportunities for fulfilling them had not.

Academic analysis of the causes of violence in Guayaquil generally concurred with that of the young men in Indio Guayas who identified interrelated structural factors that caused some groups to become increasingly violent. These factors included the growth of the drug trade in Guayaquil, increased availability of small arms, and, above all, a sense of growing alienation and exclusion. The gap between aspirations and reality meant that conflict occurred not only between groups but also within them (Tilly 1999). In Guayaquil, now part of the global economy and full of consumer goods (TVs, DVDs, refrigerators, and washing machines), social norms had changed such that crimes against neighbors and within the community occurred in ways that never happened a generation ago. The situation in Indo Guayas illustrates well Woolcock's observation that "inequality can serve to undermine any hope by those at the bottom of the income ladder that 'hard work' and 'playing by the rules,' rather than criminal or subversive activity, can yield them (and/or their children) a life of basic dignity (let alone economic advancement)" (2007, p. 5).

Figure 11-2. *Causes and Effects of Gangs and Drugs in Indio Guayas, 2005*[a]

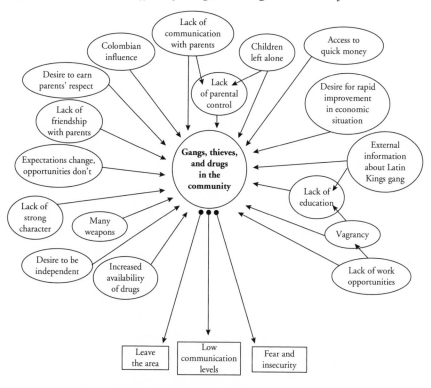

a. Based on input from focus group of eight young men.

As described in chapter 2, while some households escaped poverty, in Indio Guayas, as in the city of Guayaquil more generally, inequality had increased.[6] Such economic exclusion was also accompanied by growing spatial segregation within the city, promoted by urban renovation plans that increasingly separated the "modernized" sectors from the so-called hidden areas—the illegal settlements and marginal neighborhoods. The highly acclaimed rehabilitation of the city center of Guayaquil was hailed as a development miracle that fundamentally changed the city's image internationally. But such an urban renewal and renovation plan also incorporated repressive policies. Of particular significance was the banning of thousands of hawkers (ambulantes) who had walked the city streets selling everything from TV antennas to sweets. In privatizing public spaces, this policy increasingly marginalized many young men living in non-renovated areas (Andrade 2006).

Solutions to Gangs and Violent Crime

In contexts where the state failed to address growing crime and insecurity, local community organizations were often left to deal with the problem themselves, as was the case in Indio Guayas.

State Responses to Drugs and Violence in Guayaquil

The state and local government response to drugs, crime, and the rise of the pandillas focused primarily on repression. The 1990 judicial framework resulted in antidrug policies that further reinforced a "punitive policing" approach by applying such policies to small dealers, and even users, and extending repressive measures to the "popular" or low-income sectors of the city. The institutionalization of such policies resulted in increased human rights violations as well as in the personification of common criminals as "social enemies" and evil people (Villavicencio 2001). It was this repression that reputedly led in the 1990s to the emergence of the more organized gangs such as the naciones (Andrade 1994).

Antidrug policies in Guayaquil often served as an excuse to justify the use of wider repressive measures against the popular sectors, given the association between the pandillas and the consumption of illegal drugs. For instance, the *Más Seguridad* (More Security) plan, based on the policies of Mayor Giuliani in New York, was launched by the municipal authorities in 1990 to control the spread of crime in the city and mainly targeted street vendors and popular sectors (Andrade 1994, p. 142). The repressive apparatus was further strengthened in 2004, under a new plan to increase the number of police officers, improve their equipment, and spread the use of security cameras.

Assessments maintain that the state's response achieved little success. Despite the commitment of considerable financial resources and effort, the results in terms of reducing the volume and types of crime were poor. In part this relates to the inefficiency, inefficacy, and corruption of the police and judicial apparatus, and to the limited legitimacy of the prison system, which served more to corrupt and further harden criminals than rehabilitate them. Overall, this was identified as a sign of the wider crisis within the country (Villavicencio 2001, 2004).

Community Responses to Gangs and Violent Crime: The Aftermath of Stefan's Death

Community assessments of the judiciary and policing system coincided with those of the analysts. Lourdes's description of the community's reaction to the police after Stefan's killing illustrates this well. The immediate response to the arrest of Mario's innocent brother, Alberto, was to bribe the police rather than let him be sent to jail where gang members would likely kill him. However, in the aftermath of the killing, the community still had to face the wrath of Stefan's gang without any police support. Taking up the story, Marta recounted what happened:

> I was cooking lunch when my neighbor came running, "Help, help." All the gangsters returned on bicycles, with sticks, stones, and were taking away things that were left in Mario's parents' house. They broke everything—a door, a window—and threw kerosene to burn them. We felt we had to win over respect for our neighborhood. "Damn you," I told them, "Do you want to have another scare? You are going to have more dead people if you continue to mess around here. Cut the nonsense— where are your parents?" Our neighborhood deserves respect. They have no reason to offend us. After that we were able to gather support from the police, with help from the governor's office, to get a policeman to stay outside Natalia's—Mario's mother's—house and to keep an eye on the neighborhood. But now the roof has been stolen, the door removed, and even the fence has been taken away. Those thieves have destroyed her house.
>
> Stefan's grandmother, Erica, is my comadre. She came and made a scandal, saying he was innocent, he was no thief. So I told her, "Hey, comadre, you have to say the truth, show some respect; you don't have to hide the fact that your grandson has robbed because we all know he's a criminal. I have to defend Mario." The community felt sorry because we knew them both since they were little. They were Emilio's schoolmates, and then all of a sudden this situation. We don't harm anyone, and they come here to cause problems because they get involved in drugs.
>
> Natalia, Mario's mother, is the secretary to the Indio Guayas committee. I have to support her. I don't know where she is now. The gangsters threatened her in the school where she teaches and said they were going to kill her. So she requested a transfer from the school, and she's somewhere else, but I don't know where. When Stefan died, those people began to harass everyone. They felt they owned the sector because no one dared to face them. Thieves used not to be like that. Now they are abusive; they use high-caliber weapons, not like the ones before. Now they use bullets that destroy your body, one bullet—that's all. You don't need more.

Although Marta was not on the scene at the time of the incident, she witnessed its aftermath when gang members tried to torch and destroy Mario's family house in retribution for the killing of Stefan. As the president of the Indio

Guayas committee, Marta commanded wide respect in the neighborhood—the outcome of her successful leadership for more than thirty years to obtain the social and physical infrastructure in the area. She also felt a deep love for and proprietary ownership of the community and considered that it should be respected by younger men.

Her support for the perpetrator, rather than the victim, reflected a widely felt community consensus that the killing was not Mario's fault but a tragic end to a situation in which he had been taunted beyond measure. For Marta, as for her neighbors, the tragedy was that the future career and happiness of a young *sano* university student would be permanently marked by this event, along with the lives of all his family. In addition, his mother, Natalia, was the secretary of the committee, and loyalty to her meant that Marta supported her safe exit from the community. Equally, Marta justified her stance to Stefan's grandmother, Erica, also a community leader and a very close political colleague over the past twenty years (with the friendship formalized as *comadres*), explaining that her grandson was not an innocent bystander but a well-known criminal, particularly a drug dealer.

With this incident, as with other increasingly recurring violent crimes, residents demonstrated little faith in the capacity of officials in state institutions to protect them, let along reduce crime levels or punish culpable offenders. Although a number of policemen lived in the area, the community effectively policed itself. It did not have a police station, and the nearest one was situated three kilometers away in another area of the *suburbios*, the Battalion del Suburbios. As a result local community leaders played a prominent role in law enforcement and solving community disputes. Although a program to provide policing posts was introduced in Guayaquil during the 1990s, with some twenty-five posts established, Marta, as barrio leader of Indio Guayas, declined to accept one in the area. Her refusal was the consequence of the Indio Guayas committee assessment that police posts were a mixed blessing because of the perceived level of corruption in the police force.

Her reaction and those of her neighbors were based not only on mistrust of the police but also of the entire justice system. As she commented:

> Justice is terrible here. We don't have justice, rather injustice. They [the judges] try to get money from you, milking you to the last cent. Here the winner is whoever pays the highest price, whoever has more connections. They win any trial or legal dispute. The man who sells ceviche, he saw everything [Stefan's death] but says nothing in order to protect his business. If he talks, he'll be on death row because the gangsters get rid of

anyone who talks, and the police will do nothing. They always get out of jail with bribes, and it's even more difficult because they come back full of hatred to keep killing with a desire for revenge.

Confronting the Problem at the Individual and Household Level

Households in Indio Guayas took a number of proactive steps to try to address the violence and crime problem. First was the importance of monitoring closely the friends with whom their sons played. As Marta recounted, "Emilio and Milton's sons were also buddies, sometimes playing ball together. I told Emilio that I had heard that Milton's son was stealing. And I also told Juan Carlos [Carmen's son], 'Carlitos, watch out!' "

A second sensitive strategy, and by no means always effective, was to try to talk to the mothers of young male criminals, to make them aware of the issue and to try to get them to take responsibility. Marta described her efforts to raise the issue with one of her women neighbors, also her comadre:

> My comadre's son steals; he's a criminal and mugs people. But every time the police come to capture him and take away the stuff he's stolen, she says it's a lie. What's worse is that these parents accept that their son brings home stolen goods. But he doesn't respect his parents, and used to beat his father because he wanted to keep the house. His father was being asphyxiated, and his son wanted to shoot him in the head. I told her, "Comadre, it's your fault because you always please him. You know how your son is, and you just accept it. You're not seeing the sheer ambition behind all this . . . because he doesn't have the money to do drugs, he wants everything that's here. How can it be possible that he's going to leave you without anything? Where's your authority over your children? This is your prerogative, and even if you're old, you're entitled to break his head." One day I went and told their son, "It isn't fair; you're like the devil; the last thing that can happen in life is that a son beats up his father. . . . Where's the respect?" Imagine that. . . . Taking drugs, smoking; it's a disgrace. But thank God, he's found a woman and left the house and already has a child.

Confronting the Problem at the Community Level

Despite the significant erosion of community social capital, associated with the acquisition of physical and social infrastructure and the withdrawal of community-based services (see chapter 5), Marta and other local barrio community leaders still wielded informal authority in Indio Guayas. Although they felt increasingly disempowered by the new drug dealer elites and the gun-related violence, with both perpetrators and victims in the same communities, they all recognized that the solutions had to come from within the community. Those suggested by them tended to be practical and related particularly to creating incentives to keep young men in school, as well as to ensure that they were directed to appropriate training opportunities. As Marta commented:

> How do we solve the problem? It's all around us. Three more local youths are now in prison for kidnapping a taxi driver. They put him in the trunk of the car and drove him around. They were thieves; we never imagined they would turn out like that. What can be done to bring the community together? We're on our own; we can't face them alone. Everyone has to help because it's going to happen to you one day, and no one is going to give you a hand. Everyone is under threat, but it doesn't mean we're going to die. We have to try and defend ourselves.
>
> Something can be done, but what happens is there are no resources or institutions that provide support. Without resources you can't do anything. When Plan was here, we could try to solve some problems. For example, if children were not going to school, wanted to change schools, or wanted to study technical careers, we put together projects, to get scholarships for technical careers, and the kids went to learn a trade. We tried to get them into the *Filantrópica* [one of the polytechnics]; there were very good kids there and they studied a lot. But now it's very difficult to get in, there are many people, and those who manage to get in do so thanks to connections.

For those second-generation sons in Indio Guayas who joined gangs and became robbers and drug runners connected to drug dealers, drugs or stolen DVDs and other consumer goods may have provided short-term gratification. However, they could also have tragic consequences, as epitomized by Stefan's violent death. For households in Indio Guayas, the all-pervasive crime was the tip of the iceberg. Underneath was far greater anxiety and fear associated with gratuitous murder.

Mario's involvement in Stefan's killing became the epicenter of an ominous dread that overtook the local street. The point was Mario was sano—young and arrogant, but *sano*—and he was driven to kill out of self-defense. He had finished high school and was in the first year of university, and he hung out on one street corner with other sano kids from the same street, such as Marcelo, the son of Alonso and Carmen, and Cristophe, who lived two doors further down. In suburbio terms they were a "gang" and were perceived as turf rivals by another gang lead by Stefan, widely known as a thief and drug seller but also the grandson of Erica, another community leader and Marta's old campaigning colleague.

Ultimately there were different versions of what happened, but essentially Stefan taunted Mario, put a gun to his head, and tried to shoot him—in a game of Russian roulette during which Mario escaped. To protect himself, Mario borrowed a gun from a friend. One Saturday night he and his friends sat drinking throughout the night. As dawn approached, the others went home while Mario waited for the ceviche seller to appear. Drunk, hungry, and angry, he killed Stefan out of self-defense, but he killed in a premeditated fashion, given that he had acquired a gun.

Not all youths in Indio Guayas were victims or perpetrators of violence, since individual agency as well as structural and household factors played a critical role. Yet the onset of intracommunity turf wars increasingly diminished the space for the type of benign gang to which Mario belonged. It was not just the killing that shook the community but also the manifold repercussions. While Mario escaped, Stefan's gang attacked his house where his brother was sleeping. His mother, secretary of the Indio Guayas barrio committee and a teacher at the state primary school on Calle 25, was forced to flee the neighborhood, along with her husband, an itinerant seller, and her son. Community perceptions of justice differed from those of the state or other institutions. In the eyes of local people in Indio Guayas, Mario, as the leader of a sano gang of youth seeking education and better opportunities, was the real victim. He was taunted and harassed to the point where he got a gun and, after a steady night of drinking, shot the perpetrator, Stefan, a known leader of a drug-dealing gang.

Indio Guayas is not yet a Rio-type slum run by drug lords. But the fear and the impotence of local barrio community leaders to deal with the gun-related violence and drugs confronting them suggest that in another ten years it may become just that. It appears to be halfway along the continuum between the peaceful community it was twenty-six years ago and the extremely violent neighborhoods that currently exist, for instance, in large Brazilian cities.

If rising prosperity is accompanied by increased levels of crime and violence, it is important to return to the overall theme of this book and identify some of the long-term implications of this phenomenon for the accumulation of assets, as well as the preservation of those already accumulated. The constraints on accumulating human capital, due to the reduced ability to access educational facilities via public transportation, have already been mentioned. Increasingly apparent is the way that violence has reduced the value of physical assets such as housing, with the associated undermining of the emerging local housing market. Cisne Dos now has the reputation of a dangerous place, and people do not want to move there; thus Natalia's sister was unable to sell her house after her sister left the community. Closely linked to this is the erosion of financial capital associated with the lost earnings of local shopkeepers and bar owners that are constantly robbed.

Finally, another potentially negative dimension concerns the impact of violence on the least visible but most critical intangible asset: social capital. Does violence erode or reconstitute community social capital? Here, the analytical distinction between productive and perverse social capital may be useful (Moser and McIlwaine 2004). While productive social capital generates favorable outcomes for both the members of the group and for the community at large, perverse social capital—frequently based on the use of force, violence, and illegal activities—may produce benefits for group members but generates negative outcomes for the wider community.[7] Thus while Marta and her barrio committee, along with other leaders, have struggled to maintain productive social capital embedded in the trust and cohesion in the community, the gangs themselves have increasingly constituted an alternative form of social capital that is perverse in nature. This may bring short-term benefits to gang members but ultimately is highly likely to increase the extreme fear and sense of impotence among local leaders such as Marta, with multiplier effects in terms of the erosion of a range of assets.

To end on a personal note from my diary, recorded March 2005:

> Fear and violence are a state of being. Once it hits you, once you become aware of it, it's all pervasive; it's everywhere, all the time. It's not dramatic or sensational much of the time, just ordinary, mundane, and persistent. From the renter in the next room who shouts abusively at his wife when he comes home at 12:30 a.m. at night after the night shift has ended (and he has drunk an hour or two at the bar on the corner), to the local debt collector who drops into his wife's lap his cap and collector's cards along with his pistol as he enters the kitchen, to the police cars cruising the neighborhood that indicate that something has been reported, not necessarily that a thief has been caught. They come and they go, rarely out of their vehicles, mostly distrusted and certainly not at all integrated into the community. And so it goes on. Everybody sees it everywhere; people know whose husbands or sons are perpetrators. Nobody reports it; everyone is fearful of reprisals. And slowly one of the greatest qualities of the community—its great trust and cohesion—breaks down. I have never felt Indio Guayas so disempowered.

12

Research and Policy Lessons from Indio Guayas

Although the final chapter of a book is the conclusion, the struggles of the five Indio Guayas families to get out of poverty and accumulate assets, and their efforts to retain a cohesive community really have no definitive conclusion. Rather, they constitute a continuous intergenerational process in which a nearly thirty-year cutoff period is as arbitrary in many ways as any other shorter period would be. Indeed, the global financial crisis of 2009 will undoubtedly have an impact on income-generating activities in Guayaquil as well as on migrant remittance levels from Barcelona, with important implications for the sustainability of accumulated household assets in Indio Guayas. Nevertheless, this final chapter seeks to identify some of the lessons that can be learned from such a longitudinal study, as well the contribution it makes to poverty research methodology and poverty reduction policy.

The Importance of Longitudinal Studies

The study's nearly thirty-year span provided important longitudinal insights on local processes of development rather than a short-term diagnostic of asset portfolios at a specific point in time. This allowed for long-term tracking of asset accumulation processes with an intergenerational perspective and illustrated the ways in which changing external political and economic factors, as much as internal social life cycle processes, influence asset accumulation outcomes. For instance, the greater rigidity of the socioeconomic structure in Guayaquil as opposed to Barcelona had important consequences for employment opportunities available to second-generation youth.

Longitudinal studies, such as this one, point to the limitations of short-term "snapshot" assessments of poverty and associated time-bound poverty reduction strategies, very often based on quick-fix objectives to meet the needs of politicians, celebrities, or donors rather than the poor communities themselves. Such short-term assessments can easily miss long-term trends; for instance, the high volatility of income often obscures the steady asset accumulation identified through longitudinal studies. They can also fail to notice a range of changing perceptions about well-being, both within and between generations. These include changes in aspirations, identities, and gender power relations— all of which there was sufficient time to examine in the Indio Guayas study. In an increasingly results-based development policy context, the Indio Guayas study shows the arbitrariness of single-asset studies and short-term indicators, and it points to the limitations of "measuring" control group–related results when in reality these depend on complex processes rather than simple linear progressions. Even if conclusions such as these fall on deaf ears in the current climate, they are important to document for those who continue to recognize and endorse the importance of broader historical contexts and longer processes.

Narrative Econometrics: The Advantages of Multiple Methodologies

This study combined quantitative econometric measurement of assets with qualitative in-depth narratives gained from anthropological fieldwork undertaken while the researcher lived in the community. This effort to combine multiple methodologies had a number of significant advantages over the single use of one or another of these methodologies. The econometric measurement of assets, using an asset index, was critically important in providing quantitative trend measurements of the accumulation of different assets. For instance, the fact that households invested in housing before other assets might have been apparent from anthropological empirical observation and the narratives of local households. But in itself this was "anecdotal" information. It was the econometric quantification that made this finding significant for policymakers, and as a result, for instance, it has contributed to the justification for including housing as part of an Inter-American Development Bank loan for a low-income settlement program in Guyana.[1] Similarly, the fact that invisible and unrecognized intangible social capital assets were able to be measured econometrically legitimized the role of "soft" and "fuzzy" social relations in the accumulation of tangible assets. This included community social capital, which enabled local communities to contest and negotiate for physical and social infrastructure—adding the value of public services to well-being—and household social capital, with its constituent trust, cohesion, and support acting as an essential determinant for the accumulation of financial and productive capital.

At the same time, such econometric measures could not have been robustly constructed without the detailed, context-specific, and empirical understanding that anthropological methodologies provide. The dependence on such narratives is concretely illustrated by the components of different asset categories. These included the components of intangible assets such as community and household social capital (for example, "hidden" female-headed households). Data derived from anthropological narratives also challenged evaluation of the components of tangible assets, such as financial-productive capital, in relation to both employment security and productive durables. It was local knowledge that identified refrigerators not just (or even) as consumer durables but as investment items. While the asset index identified overall trends, as the detailed descriptions of the complexities of household structure and intrahousehold dynamics showed, it could not explain causality, and therefore was unable to clarify why some households did better than others. A detailed anthropological narrative was necessary to understand the correlation between social relations and the accumulation of physical, human, or financial assets.

The stories of the five families living on Calle K, first introduced in chapter 1 and followed through subsequent chapters, illustrate the advantages of mixed methodologies. The econometric measurement of asset and income poverty trends presents the correlations and highlights the patterns of increasing differentiation and growing inequality, even within a small community such as Indio Guayas, over the nearly thirty-year period. Complementing this is the analysis of changing external structural circumstances as well as the narratives of social relations within households and their associated individual agency. This helps explain the causality underpinning overall trends, why and how some households managed to get out of poverty and accumulate assets while others did not. Not only does anthropological research provide explanations, but its on-the-ground experience can help distinguish between purely spurious correlations (that show up as "statistically significant") and true relationships. When statistical results and anthropological knowledge both lead to the same answer, then there is obviously greater confidence in the answer than if it were derived from either approach alone.

The econometric data show that most households were income and asset poor just after they arrived in Indio Guayas in 1978. The individual narratives highlight the exceptions. In 1978 Carmen and Alonso were nonpoor, benefiting from his buoyant work situation as a local house builder and construction worker, described in chapter 6. By 1992, with a complex household situation and the downturn in construction work associated with the economic crisis, they had slipped into poverty. In 2004 they were income and asset nonpoor, largely due to Carmen's remittances linked to structural employment opportunities in Barcelona, as described in chapter 10. Two of the five households, those of Alicia and Lidia, were very poor in terms of income as well as assets, and remained so throughout the twenty-six-year survey period. In Alicia's case this was the consequence of her domestic situation as a single mother with a large dependent household, as described in chapter 7. For Lidia and Salvador, the situation was not helped by structural shifts in the labor market that left Salvador unemployed, or by the fact that he abandoned her for a decade, leaving Lidia a single mother; nevertheless, they still remained very poor even when he returned home in 2004. Mercedes and Claudio's story shows how the decline in artisan tailoring and limited opportunities for dental mechanical work, together with the enormous resources invested in their son's education, meant that they slipped from being poor in 1978 to being very poor by 1992, and remained at that level in 2004 without ever managing to move out of asset poverty.

Undoubtedly, the most successful household was that of Marta and Jesus. Although still asset poor in 1992, they had moved out of income poverty and maintained this mobility through 2004, by which time Marta, widowed and living with her two second-generation families on the same plot, was both asset rich and nonpoor. The econometric data used to construct table 12-1 highlights the churning (Carter and Barrett 2006) in income and asset poverty that occurred over twenty-six years within this small group of households on Calle K; the anthropological narrative, in turn, deepens understanding of the underlying causality.

The Contribution of an Asset Accumulation Policy

If assets matter to low-income communities grappling with poverty—and this study demonstrates unequivocally that they do—then it is useful to conclude by discussing their role in poverty reduction policy. Just as an asset-based analytical

Table 12-1. *Comparative Levels of Income and Asset Poverty of the Five Families on Calle K, 1978, 1992, and 2004*

| | Level of poverty | | | | | |
| | 1978 | | 1992 | | 2004 | |
Family	Income	Asset	Income	Asset	Income	Asset
Marta and Jesus	Poor	Poor	Not poor	Poor	Not poor	Not poor
Lidia and Salvador	Very poor	Poor	Very poor	Poor	Very poor	Poor
Alicia	Very poor	Poor	Very poor	Poor	Very poor	Poor
Mercedes and Claudio	Poor	Poor	Very poor	Poor	Very poor	Poor
Carmen and Alonso	Not poor	Poor	Poor	Poor	Not poor	Not poor

framework, with its associated asset index (see chapter 2), provided a useful heuristic analytical device to help make sense of the complex struggles of extraordinary families in Indio Guayas, so too the longitudinal findings inductively make the case for the elaboration of a such a policy framework in its own right.

Asset accumulation policy uses an asset-based framework to focus directly on creating opportunities for the poor to accumulate and consolidate their assets in a sustainable way. Its objective is to identify opportunities and constraints, incentives and interventions that can assist poor communities and households, similar to those in Indio Guayas, to accumulate and sustain their assets. The goal is to optimize scarce resources and transform them into assets, thereby short-cutting the heroic but often tragic experiences of increasing numbers of the urban poor as they struggle to get out of poverty.

How does asset accumulation policy relate to other poverty reduction policies and programs? Two antipoverty programs, closely associated with the shifts in the poverty debate toward growth-led poverty reduction (Kanbur 2007), are of particular relevance. In the late 1990s, the sustainable livelihoods approach gained prominence when prioritized by bilateral donors such as the U.K. Department for International Development and international NGOs such as CARE and OXFAM.[2] Yet this quickly dropped off the donor policy agenda when it was superseded by social protection policy.[3] The latter was directly influenced by the 2000 World Development Report on poverty (World Bank 2000) and has been widely adopted by donors, governments, and NGOs alike (Moser 2008; Dani and Moser 2008).[4]

Within its overall focus on poverty and vulnerability, the breadth of the coverage under social protection policy is extensive (Barrientos and Hulme 2008).

Table 12-2. *Recent Poverty-Reduction Frameworks and Their Associated Objectives*

Analytical framework	Primary objectives of operational approach
Sustainable livelihood approach	Sustaining activities required for a *means of living*
Social protection	*Providing protection* for the poor and vulnerable against negative risks and shocks that erode their assets
Asset-based approaches	*Identifying, enabling, and generating opportunities* for sustainable asset accumulation

Associated programs include ex-ante protective cash transfer measures, such as the Ecuadorian bono solidario described in chapter 6, as well as the widely acclaimed Mexican Progresa-Oportunidades program (Levy 2006). In contrast, there are the ex-post safety nets, such as those implemented after such natural disasters as Hurricane Katrina (Liu 2007) and the 2006 tsunami (Fan 2007). Such safety nets seek to go beyond food aid to "productive" safety nets with the goal of ensuring that those experiencing asset-based shocks remain above the poverty threshold and do not fall into a poverty "trap," with the associated longitudinal chronic poverty (Carter 2007).

What can an asset framework offer that the social protection or sustainable livelihood approaches cannot? The apparent overlap among them makes it important to identify the differences and complementarities in objectives between these three poverty reduction frameworks. With closely aligned objectives, interventions associated with one framework can contribute to the objectives of another; nevertheless, each is distinguished by a specific entry point. Table 12-2 summarizes the objectives all three approaches.

One key difference relates to the way in which each approach deals with the issue of risk. As the name implies, asset accumulation policy is concerned specifically with assets and their associated long-term accumulation strategies. Assets are closely linked to growth and risk management. For asset accumulation, risk is a fundamental part of its strategic planning. Managing such risk is about proactively *identifying and investing in opportunities,* so the biggest risk is not taking a risk.

For social protection policy, risk is a danger, with risk management strategies designed defensively to reduce or overcome the associated shocks, stresses, and vulnerabilities. Thus, social protection's priority is to *protect* the poor so that the assets they have are not eroded, or, if they are, to assist the poor in recovering them. When people reach a "poverty threshold" below which it becomes extremely difficult for them to accumulate assets on their own, productive safety nets act as a "cushion" by creating an environment in which they can move forward toward accumulating assets (Carter and Barrett 2006).[5]

The sustainable livelihood approach overlaps with both asset accumulation and social protection, and consists of a loose set of strategies to improve well-being through a combination of investing in assets, creating agency, and providing protection where necessary to deal with existing vulnerabilities. These strategies are primarily concerned with daily *well-being* per se and are particularly associated with rural populations.

Asset accumulation policy can only be useful in its own right if, along with its different objectives, its associated strategies are clearly distinguished from those of livelihoods and social protection. Table 12-3 provides a hypothetical illustration of this distinction in the case of Ecuadorian international migration, constructed from a case study by Hall (2008). It highlights the distinctions among strategies designed to strengthen livelihood, protect those most affected, and accumulate long-term sustainable assets. While all three are important their objectives, their time frames, interventions, and outcomes are different.

Opportunities and Constraints in Asset-Based Policies

Analytical work specifically on asset-based approaches, described in chapter 2, has also resulted in a range of associated operational approaches (see table 12-4). Each has a slightly different focus; some, such as asset-based assessments (BASIS 2004), asset mapping (Fossgard-Moser 2005), and asset-based community development (Mathie and Cunningham 2003), provide operational tools and techniques for the identification of community and household assets. Others, particularly Sherraden (1991), Boshara and Sherraden (2004), and the Ford Foundation (2004) have developed operational interventions.

Components of an Asset Accumulation Policy

Informed by the longitudinal research results from Indio Guayas, the asset accumulation policy proposed here has a number of characteristics that differentiate it from other asset-based approaches. First and foremost, it is important to establish that it is not a set of top-down interventions, such as the transfer of cash or the building of housing per se. Though it may include interventions that focus on strengthening individual assets, it is essentially a framework that provides an enabling environment with clear rules, norms, regulations, and support structures to allow households and communities to identify and take advantage of opportunities to accumulate assets. To facilitate asset accumulation, it is

Table 12-3. *Operational Approaches and Associated Interventions for International Migration from Ecuador*

Operational approach	Primary objectives	Interventions	Agency or institution
Short-term *strengthening of livelihoods* (Carney 1998)	To provide immediate coping strategies	Remittances provide income for basic family needs such as food, clothing, and health care, and act as cushion against lack of domestic employment opportunities	Migrant workers and their families
Provision of welfare support and *social protection* (Barrientos, Hulme, and Shepherd 2005)	To assist those experiencing the costs of migration	Measures to assist with psychological outcomes of changing family structure—particularly children left with extended family relatives Initiatives to better equip migrants to cope in destination country Legal protection of migrants in Spain	Church and NGO organizations of civil society funded by European Union; churches; Spanish government
Longer-term enhancing, diversifying, and consolidating the *asset* base of migrant families (Moser 2007; this book)	To accumulate sustainable assets	Promotion of productive activities through —human capital (education training) —physical capital (water, electricity, land housing) —financial capital (savings, loans) Communications to increase social status and retain homeland links to strengthen social capital	Civil society organizations such as Ecuador-Plan for Migration in high out-migration provinces funded by Spanish aid; small migrant self-help organizations[a] Banco Solidario (Solidarity Bank)

Source: Constructed from Hall (2008).
a. Spanish aid from Agencia Española de Cooperación Internacional (Spanish Agency for International Cooperation).

Table 12-4. *Summary of Associated Asset-Based Operational Approaches*

Operational approach	Authors or institutions	Examples of implementation: tools and techniques
Asset-based assessments	BASIS (2004); Carter and Barrett (2006)	Tools to identify poverty traps and undertake asset assessments
Asset building and community development	Ford Foundation (2004)	Support for building assets in financial holdings, natural resources, social bonds, and human capital
	Mathie and Cunningham (2003)	"Transformative" methodology of asset-based community development to help communities build assets
	Fossgard-Moser (2005)	Community asset mapping to enable members of communities to identify collective and individual asset portfolios
Asset-based welfare policy	Sherraden (1991) Boshara and Sherraden (2004)	Financial support to set up individual financial accounts: Corporation for Enterprise Individual Development Accounts (United States); Child Trust Fund (United Kingdom)
Asset accumulation policy	Moser (2007; this book)	Nexus linking assets-opportunities-institutions; distinction between first- and second-generation policy

necessary to simultaneously address components at three interrelated levels: structural, institutional, and operational (see figure 12-1).

STRUCTURAL LEVEL. The fact that structural factors can have direct and indirect impacts on asset accumulation at the local level demonstrates that development is not just a technocratic process but also a structural one. The process of accumulating assets involves complex political contestation as well as the negotiation of social power relations as much as technical solutions. Thus asset accumulation is rarely achieved simply by mapping poverty, identifying target groups, and introducing top-down poverty reduction interventions.

At the structural level, it is useful to distinguish between two components: external structural factors and internal social processes. The Indio Guayas study showed that the process by which individuals and households are endowed with assets and acquire or transform them *does not occur in a vacuum*. Opportunities to accumulate assets and also to ensure their long-term sustainability are influenced by *complex causal relationships* between both external structural factors and internal social processes.

Figure 12-1. *Asset Accumulation Policy Framework*

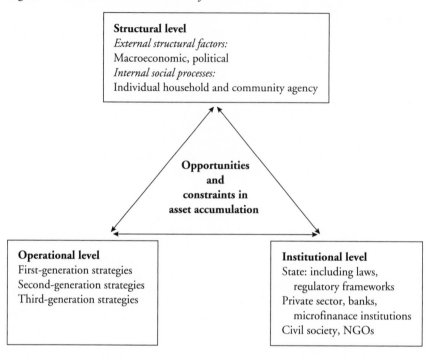

Structural level
External structural factors:
Macroeconomic, political
Internal social processes:
Individual household and community agency

**Opportunities
and
constraints in
asset accumulation**

Operational level
First-generation strategies
Second-generation strategies
Third-generation strategies

Institutional level
State: including laws,
    regulatory frameworks
Private sector, banks,
    microfinanace institutions
Civil society, NGOs

External structural factors include macroeconomic and political conditions. In Indio Guayas, for instance, the 1980s structural adjustment packages and the 1990s financial crisis resulting in dollarization both had important effects by increasing income poverty and eroding assets such as human capital. In contrast, globalization increased the availability of consumer durables, making it easier for some households to increase productive assets, and also made emigrating to work abroad an attractive option.

Equally, the long history in Indio Guayas of contestation with national and local-level politicians and their political parties illustrated how the opportunistic, co-opting, vote seeking by politicians could be used by poor peripheral communities to acquire assets. This history also points to the substantial gaps between political promises and community expectations (chapter 4).

Internal social processes in Indio Guayas included the critically important role that community social capital played in the accumulation of assets. Community-level trust, cohesion, and collaboration were essential in the first decades to challenge external actors, such as the state and private sector, to obtain the basic physical and social infrastructure necessary for asset accumulation. From the late 1990s onward, there was a close relationship between the social capital of second-generation sons and daughters who migrated to Barcelona and their ability to take advantage of the opportunities to accumulate financial and productive capital in a booming urban context.

The study also highlighted the key role played by household social capital—the collaboration within nuclear and extended families—not only as a safety net for vulnerable extended family members but also as a resource for moving out of poverty and achieving upward socioeconomic mobility. Household social capital encompassed the microlevel dynamics of life cycles as well as individual, household, and collective agency. Such elements explain why, among households starting with the same asset endowments in this "natural experiment," some achieved more success than others, particularly at an intergenerational level.

INSTITUTIONAL LEVEL. State institutions at the national and local level, as well as political parties, the private sector, and civil society organizations and NGOs are critical in providing an "enabling environment" for the accumulation of assets. While the state establishes the normative and legal frameworks that can either block initiative or provide incentives, private sector entities, including banks and microfinance institutions, support the opportunities and facilitate access to promote asset accumulation in a variety of ways that include the provision of resources.

The Indio Guayas study highlighted how individuals, households, and communities, when presented with clear sets of rules, norms and procedures, used opportunities for negotiation, responding rationally and with initiative to build assets. For instance, when the municipal decree released suburbio swampland for the poor, households took advantage of this to invade and acquire land. In a similar way, during the 1970s democratization process, a clear relationship existed between political parties, such as the ID, and the electorate around infrastructure provision in return for votes—a situation that the local committee adroitly took advantage of in order to get basic services. At the same time, as described in chapter 4, this complex patronage system generated distrust and conflict in what was not an inherently conflictive community. By the 1980s the procedures had to change in order to negotiate with international agencies. Nevertheless, Marta and the other community leaders adapted their strategies to continue to acquire a range of interventions to improve their community.

Despite such successes, the long-term experience of Indio Guayas showed that the low level of state-delivered services as well as their privatization reduced levels of expectation as well as trust in external institutions. The lack of a strong or accountable institutional state presence forced the local community committee to micromanage the processes of service acquisition, and forced households to rely increasingly on growing numbers of income earners to pay for essential but privatized services, such as education and health care.

More recently, in a globally changing external context, local community institutions have been forced to struggle to retain safety and order in an increasingly violent context where the norms and procedures are far less clear than they were when infrastructure was being contested. The virtual absence of state institutions now imposes very real challenges that threaten to erode many of the capital assets accumulated over the past three decades. This points to the critical importance of the institutional level in an asset accumulation policy.

OPERATIONAL LEVEL. Assets are not static. In a changing global political, socioeconomic, and environmental situation, it is important to recognize their constant revalorization, transformation, and renegotiation. In addition, the accumulation of one asset often results in the accumulation of others, while insecurity in one can also affect other assets.[6] This means that at the operational level, an asset accumulation policy framework recognizes prioritization, sequencing, trade-offs, and negotiation potential, and combines a range of context-specific strategy options. As the evidence from Indio Guayas shows, it is useful to distinguish different stages or "generations" of asset accumulation strategies.

A *first-generation asset accumulation strategy*, as identified in a newly established community such as Indio Guayas, clearly encompasses a sequencing of asset accumulation processes. Physical capital (basic shelter) was the prerequisite for the accumulation of other assets. Local residents used the opportunity presented by invading municipal land to start the process of getting out of poverty. The provision of physical and social infrastructure was then essential for the accumulation of assets such as human and financial capital—with better education translating into better jobs for both men and women.

It has been widely assumed that interventions to strengthen human capital provide the necessary precondition for individuals and households to accumulate assets and to move out of poverty. Thus current pro-poor policies still focus, almost exclusively, on first-generation strategies, as illustrated by the Millennium Development Goals. These include the provision of water, roads, electricity, housing plots, better health care and education, and microfinance. Once provided, it is assumed that individual well-being improves and "development" naturally occurs. However, as important as these are, the conditions necessary for further accumulation do not necessarily bring the expected development returns. For instance, when strategies to increase human capital (enhanced education levels and health conditions) do not result in the expected job opportunities, rising aspirations can lead to a sense of exclusion, accompanied by increasing crime and violence that in turn can erode community social capital along with financial-productive capital.

Second-generation asset accumulation strategies, therefore, are intended to strengthen, sustain, and maintain accumulated assets, to ensure their further consolidation and prevent erosion. Such strategies go beyond issues of welfare and the provision of basic services, to embrace a range of concerns relating to citizen rights and security, governance, and the accountability of institutions. The Indio Guayas study demonstrated the importance of household social capital for asset accumulation; yet there were no widely recognized formal procedures to ensure that assets were successfully transferred from one generation to the next. When inherently conflictive circumstances pervaded the intergenerational distribution of assets, this easily resulted in the erosion of family trust and cohesion.

Necessary interventions include strengthening the judicial system to incorporate a broad range of preventative and punitive interventions. This requires the empowerment of local communities to access information about legal, economic, and social rights so that they can use this knowledge to address second-generation asset concerns. It also includes developing and strengthening appropriate financial institutions to ensure that households that have gotten out of poverty can save and retain their financial capital.

The widespread international migration phenomenon may require specific asset-based strategies. The first-generation migrant asset accumulation strategy is primarily concerned with financial services. This includes the establishment of safe, efficient, and cheap channels for sending remittances as well as the creation of financial institutions for saving, banking, and credit. It also requires welfare and legal protection services, and social protection to mitigate costs of migration. For migrants abroad this includes the establishment of services to protect them from exploitation and to assist them with documentation and job opportunities.

Migrants may require specific second-generation strategies to sustain accumulated assets and ensure that they are not eroded. Of particular importance, as illustrated by the demands of Indio Guayas migrants in Barcelona, is the provision of legal advice on property transfer, divorce, and wills to ensure the proper distribution of financial and physical assets. Equally important is the development of mechanisms to channel knowledge on political capital and

Table 12-5. *Asset Accumulation Operational Matrix*

Intervention stage	Asset accumulation opportunities and constraints at different levels		
	Structural	*Institutional*	*Operational*
Appraisal	_____	_____	_____
Implementation	_____	_____	_____
Evaluation	_____	_____	_____

citizenship—acquired through migrant experience—as resources for building a more equitable, opportunity-based society back in Guayaquil. Finally, another second-generation strategy may be creation of a range of legal, financial, and social services accessible to nonpoor households accumulating assets. Institutions offering business and labor advice would not only provide financial, legal, and business support to returning migrants but also would promote job opportunities by using and developing the skills that migrants have acquired.

Third-generation strategies, specifically employment-related asset accumulation, are still in the process of elaboration. The failure of sons and daughters in Indio Guayas to find jobs commensurate with their education pointed to the importance of city-level employment strategies to ensure that gains in human capital are not eroded. The entry points for opportunities for local development in urban areas may vary; sectoral interventions to build one asset need to be strategically mapped in terms of their implications for the accumulation of other assets. For instance, what could be the impacts of housing loans or microcredit on productive assets that generate employment? Third-generation strategies also require facilitating linkages between different institutions and the strengthening of the crucial role that local government plays in the delivery of a range of financial and institutional and services. In such contexts asset accumulation by institutions based on collective or group agency may become increasingly important.

Since components at these three levels are interrelated and mediated by each other, the identification of each is a prerequisite for interventions that address existing structures and systems associated with sustainable asset accumulation strategies. By way of illustration, table 12-5 concludes this section with an operational matrix that shows the importance of opportunities and constraints at different levels throughout the different stages of an asset accumulation strategy.

Concluding Comments

If we lived in Indio Guayas for the first time now instead of in 1978, what would we find that is different? Certainly the logistics of daily life would be a great deal easier. Women no longer cook on dangerous kerosene stoves and wait daily for the water tanks to arrive, rationing water or borrowing from neighbors. Households eat by electric light rather than by candles, and TVs now dominate the front rooms; consequently it is likely that there would not be the high demand for teaching English classes to local teenagers and adults that we experienced in 1978, when people lived by candle light and without the entertainment of TV. Titus would attend a primary school built of concrete—though the classrooms might still be overcrowded and pedagogic methods still based on rote learning. It would no longer be necessary to learn to walk on rickety bamboo walkways. Transportation times to the center have been halved, and we would not arrive at our destination dusty and hot.

But with life much more centered round the extended household on the plot, it might be more difficult to get to know neighbors and to sit around outside small bamboo houses gossiping. Equally, with the demise of local home-based enterprises, the cooked-food sellers, tailors, carpenters, shoemakers, and other craftsmen employing artisan skills would be disappearing. With traffic passing back and forth, as well as streets now serving as football fields for the gangs of youths that hang around in the late afternoons and weekends, public social space has diminished. There would hardly be any community organization activities within Indio Guayas or mobilizations and contestation with political parties, municipal officials, or international agencies—all of which provided the basis for an extraordinary level of collaboration and collective organization and indeed a means for meeting households living far away from Calle K.

Finally, and perhaps most significantly, we would find daily life far less safe and secure. Titus or Nathaniel could not just wander around the community with friends they had made, without much supervision. I would no longer take the bus into town, fearful of being robbed, but would rely on expensive taxis for round trips. I would get another woman to accompany me if I walked around the community, and if it were necessary to go out at night, I would avoid known drug-dealing areas. Like my neighbors, I would be guarded if questioned by the police roaming the streets in their fast cars. But as on all previous visits, I would support the efforts of Marta and other leaders to maintain security and the visibility of their community organizations. I would participate in small group planning meetings, providing advice, as they discuss the possibilities of raising more external financial support to assist them in addressing these new problems, as well as implementing the second- and third-generation policy solutions described above.

Over the past thirty years, I have been privileged to be welcomed, trusted, and taught by these "ordinary" households about their extraordinary lives. This book can only be a very small gesture in comparison with what I have received. It seems appropriate, nevertheless, to conclude by commenting on what the people of Indio Guayas would want from policymakers.

They would recount how in the early years, when their needs related to first-generation infrastructure policy, they were able to identify a common cause affecting everyone, regardless of income or status. The nature of community response was to mobilize through a series of logical steps with known political and state institutions and to use recognized procedures to leverage for change. They would acknowledge that once this was achieved, community social capital became less important, and the support structure within expanding households became an increasing priority. Thus efforts to accumulate human, financial, and productive capital, as well as other second-generation policy needs, were undertaken at the level of individual households. Finally, turning to the present, they would express their extreme concern about the growing fear and insecurity increasingly dominating their daily lives, linked not only to theft and gangs but also to illicit drug-related enterprises within their community.

Fear and insecurity challenge Indio Guayas to once again organize collectively to make their lives safer. With a mistrusted police presence and a judicial system that is open to corrupt and nontransparent processes, the response of the state is very weak, if not nonexistent. To whom do they turn to deal with such complex issues that include drugs, guns, and brutal deaths? The Indio Guayas community organization, along with their neighboring committees in Cisne Dos, will need to learn different tactics and solutions, while the state, private sector, and civil society and NGOs will have to shift from infrastructure and social protection priorities to address this critical concern.

Though local families in Indio Guayas have never asked for handouts, they are less likely than before to resolve their current problems on their own. Without collaborative support and real concerted action from the range of external institutions, their accumulation of assets may not be sustainable. Their problem is not unique; as fear and insecurity increasingly encompass poor urban neighborhoods in cities across the world, citizen safety and security emerge as a top policy priority. The people of Indio Guayas are not only saying that this is their biggest and most immediate challenge, but they are also telling policymakers that what they need to face this challenge is the collaboration of other social actors and institutions.

A

Research Methodology: Guayaquil Fieldwork

W hen I first went to the *suburbios* of Guayaquil in 1978 as the anthropological adviser to the documentary TV film *People of the Barrio*, I never imagined that I would continue to maintain a professional as well as personal relationship with the people of Indio Guayas for the next thirty years. Therefore, the research methodology used to collect the data used in this book did not follow a preestablished plan but evolved over the course of extended field visits undertaken first in 1978 and then subsequently in 1980, 1982, 1988, 1992, 2004, and most recently in 2005. However, over the course of my research in Indio Guayas, there have been consistent strands in the approach underpinning the evolving research methodology.

One critical strand derives from my formal training as an urban anthropologist. I have always maintained that the range of qualitative techniques developed largely for the study of rural societies (Long 1968; Van Velsen 1967) has a clear application to urban contexts. Participant observation, for instance, was essential in a variety of contexts to better understand household dynamics as well as the political negotiation associated with the acquisition of basic services. I would accompany Marta, the community leader, to meetings with the municipal authorities to discuss the extension of one or another public service and instantly become "invisible" when introduced as her "adviser."

I was able to identify as key informants not only the main actors in the five families that enrich this study but also other members of the community whose insights were important and whom I interviewed each time I was in Indio Guayas. Similarly, I was aware that "apt illustrations" (Mitchell 1968) could often provide a greater understanding of issues and attitudes than data collected through the application of other techniques. The transcripts of interviews collected as background for the TV documentary provided a wealth of information, with the voices of community members enriching the narrative. Equally, conversations informally taped over the years in kitchens and on back patios were invaluable, despite transcription difficulties because of the background noise associated with daily living. Finally, I assiduously kept diaries during my visits in order to record my insights into events, seemingly mundane and parochial, that had an impact on people's lives. Interestingly some of the entries from 1978 have acquired greater significance over time, throwing explanatory light on events that have a bearing on the narrative presented here.

I endeavoured to achieve similar robust standards when collecting data for quantitative analysis through the application of sociological household surveys. The 1978 survey (implemented with Brian Moser), which was a census of the population living in six of the eleven blocks constituting Indio Guayas, was followed in 1988, 1992, and 2004 by the implementation of random household sample surveys applied in the same six blocks.

The mix of qualitative and quantitative research methods has varied over time. In the 1982 research visit, for example, I explored the nature of the relationship between community organization and political processes. This required interviews with the top officials of the Izquierda Democrática party and other political leaders immersed in the democratization processes then preoccupying the country. Interestingly, one key insight was the recognition of women's community leadership responsibilities, which subsequently helped me elaborate the concept of women's triple role, namely, in reproduction, production, and community managing (Moser 1989b; 1993). The insight about women's community managing roles (described in chapters 4 and 5) illustrates an important dimension of the evolving research methodology. This related to the fact that poor people do not compartmentalize their lives into the political, the economic, the social, or the community but are political, social, and economic actors simultaneously, and that an understanding of such multidimensionality necessitates complementary data collection techniques and instruments in order to undertake the required comprehensive analysis.

For the 1988 research visit, I was accompanied by my partner, Peter Sollis, a Latin Americanist with extensive research and community development experience. With a research focus on the social costs of structural adjustment policies, the scope of the research design expanded correspondingly to embrace the execution of an integrated microlevel "qual-quant" methodology. This comprised three interlocking survey instruments: a random survey; a follow-up in-depth interview with selected respondents to drill down on key issues; and a community survey to triangulate the interviews with key local-level developments in the areas of basic infrastructure, community organization, and welfare programs (Sollis and Moser 1991).

The 1988 qual-quant methodology post facto became the pilot research for a much larger project that I subsequently directed at the World Bank. With additional financial and human resources available, the 1992 Indio Guayas research team (myself, Alicia Herbert, and Peter Sollis) executed an enhanced set of qualitative and quantitative instruments. This constituted a random sample survey of 263 households; a subsample survey, using both structured and open-ended questions, to collect qualitative data on such issues as the intrahousehold divisions of labor, domestic violence, and attitudes to child labor (undertaken with around 40 households selected as representative of household types from the random sample survey of 263 households); and a community survey focused on qualitative data, including in-depth analysis on the local development of social service—health, education, and child welfare—provision by public and international agencies and private providers. This threefold methodology, including all the questionnaires, was later published in both English and Spanish and has been widely disseminated to researchers in the last two decades (Moser, Gatehouse, and Garcia 1996).

An important innovation in the 1992 work was the integration of local people into all aspects of data collection. A team of researchers was trained to apply the sample survey questionnaire and to collect community-level development data. Though additional quality control monitoring was warranted initially, the immediate benefit of using locals was soon apparent in terms of enhanced access and level of detail in the information collected. The longer-term return to the investment in creating a local research team became evident in 2004. With a refresher course on the importance of quality and accuracy, I was able to use the same team, bar one member who had left the community, to undertake the third survey constituting a pillar of this longitudinal fieldwork. The local research team comprised Angela Vinueza (1992 only) and Lucy Zavalla, Rosa Vera, and Carmita Naboa (1992 and 2004).

Implementation of the 1992 research within the institutional setting of the World Bank also permitted a second innovation. The 1992 survey results that highlighted the importance of housing as an asset, among other issues, were

Table A-1. *Construction of the Panel Data Set*
Units as indicated

Longitudinal study survey data	Survey date	Panel size	Size and nature of source	Percent attrition rates
Household panel data sets	1978	56	244 (universe)	0
	1992	56	263 (random sample survey)	0
	2004	51	56 (panel data set)	9
Second-generation households living outside family plot but in Guayaquil in 2004	2005	46	61 (universe of sons and daughters)	24
Second-generation households living in Barcelona	2005	3[a]	23 interviews from 4 different data sources	. . .[b]

Source: Based on Moser (2007).
a. Since only three households came from the panel data set, these were augmented by households from three additional data sources.
b. Not appropriate as not a universe or random survey.

used as input into the design of the bank's Living Standards Measurement Study. Embedding microlevel insights into a nationwide survey subsequently enabled the analysis of Indio Guayas's representativeness at the national level (World Bank 1995a).

The 1978, 1992, and 2004 Panel Data Set

The 1978, 1992, and 2004 surveys resulted in a panel data set of 51 households that had lived continuously over twenty-six years on the same family-owned plots (table A-1). The 1978 survey of 244 households covered all households living in six blocks over an eleven-block area that constitutes Indio Guayas. The selection of the blocks reflected the focus of the initial research, namely, the settlement and consolidation process in the suburbios; thus two blocks were located in the longest established area (with occupation of up to ten years), two blocks were from areas settled in the early to mid-1970s (with an average age of about five years), and two blocks were recently settled (some of whose households had been in the area no more than a few weeks when they were first interviewed).

The 1992 random sample survey of 263 households, undertaken in exactly the same spatial area as the 1978 survey, picked up fifty-six households that also

Table A-2. *Causes of Attrition in Original Panel Data, 1992–2004*

Causes	Comments	Number
Sold plot	Returned to countryside or other area in Guayaquil	3
Renting plot	Marriage broke down (wife left him) and now living nearby with another partner	1
"Lent" to extended family members (nephews)	Original owner and her immediate family have all migrated to New York. House now occupied by four nephews and their families, none of whom were part of the original household	1
Total		5

had been in the 1978 universe survey. In 2004 these same fifty-six households were tracked, and fifty-one were revisited and interviewed for a third time with the same questionnaire covering the same issues as in previous surveys. Over the 1992–2004 period, there was a 9 percent attrition rate as five panel data set members had moved out of the community. This indicates a high degree of stability in the overall composition of this particular group of households. The causes of panel data set attrition are presented in table A-2.

The 2005 Second-Generation Survey

The 2004 survey revealed an additional dimension of stability with respect to the panel data set households. Table A-3 shows the location of all the sons and daughters identified from the 2004 panel data set. Half of the number of children of the original respondent households, or 120 sons and daughters (the second generation), still lived on the family plot, either in their parents' home or "apart" on the same plot; a further quarter, some 62 children, lived in almost equal numbers either nearby in Indio Guayas or in another area of Guayaquil. The remaining quarter lived in other cities in Ecuador or abroad.

In 2005 I returned to Indio Guayas to interview the second generation who had moved off the family plot to live locally or in other parts of Guayaquil. Of the sixty-two people in this group, I managed to locate and interview forty-six adult sons and daughters who had left the family plot by 2004 but were still living in their new households as of 2005, either in Guayaquil or its immediate environs. To contact these sons and daughters, it was necessary to seek the assistance of parents, mainly mothers, who identified the barrio where they lived and informed them about the survey. As my field notes indicate, physically locating children living elsewhere in Guayaquil was quite another matter,

Table A-3. *Location of All Sons and Daughters over Sixteen Years Old from 2004 Panel Data Set, as of 2005*

Units as indicated

Category	Location	Number per location	Number per category	Percent of total
Still on family plot	In parents' house on plot	94	120	50.0
	Living "apart" on parents' plot[a] (secondary households)	26		
In Indio Guayas	Same barrio with other family members (in-laws)	20	33	13.5
	Same barrio, rent	8		
	Same barrio, own plot	5		
Other areas, Guayaquil	Another barrio, Guayaquil, own plot	29	29	12.0
Other city, Ecuador	Another city or town in Ecuador	23	23	9.5
Abroad	Spain	9	17	7.0
	Italy	1		
	United States	4		
	Germany	1		
	Venezuela	2		
No information (parents have lost touch)		19	19	8.0
Total		241	241	100.0

Source: Based on Moser (2007).

a. Although, in some respects, these form separate households, the level of collaboration in cooking, food acquisition, and sharing of space means that overall they constitute members of the same household plot.

with the complexity of making the connection accounting for some of the attrition rate:

> We are tracing the sons and daughters outside Indio Guayas by taking the parents to visit them. Since no one knows the precise address, and in most cases most of the sectors do not even have them, this is the only way of doing it. So we hired a small bus from a colleague of Adriana's at the Tribunal. The bus, called a *flujonetta*, seats sixteen, and it's essential to fit us all in to go off on our expeditions, usually on the weekend. It's quite a ritual. Food is bought, cold drinks prepared in an icebox, and everything put in the bus. Today we are off to Fortin, and everyone wants to go—as

Table A-4. *Causes of Attrition in the Guayaquil Second-Generation Survey, 2005*
Units as indicated

Cause	Number	Percent
Parents not in contact with children due to family conflict	7	47
Parents do not know address	2	13
Family unwilling to provide address	3	20
In prison	1	7
Family unwilling to go to area considered unsafe	1	7
Traveling while survey undertaken	1	7
Total	15	101[a]

a. Greater than 100 percent as an artifact of rounding.

many, like us, have never seen these peripheral areas. So Marta, as community leader, has a prize place in the front of the bus along with one of the accompanying parents. They all bring a daughter, son, or grandson along as well, and then there is the team of interviewers, Rosa, Lucy, Carmita, and me. One weekend my husband, Peter, came to visit and joined us.

The journey is long, and it's a leap of faith. The parent guiding us not only goes to sleep and has to be woken to show us the way, but often cannot recognize the neighborhood since previous journeys were undertaken by bus. So we end up following bus routes. Of course, the son or daughter, although forewarned, is not always there when we arrive, so although we can see the house and get a feel for the neighborhood, we may not get the interview. Where we manage to make the connection, we are warmly welcomed by the sons and daughters of our friends in Indio Guayas, proud to show us their homes, however modest. It reminds me of our early days in Guayaquil, except now they are not living on water but deep in muddy streets and on the side of hills on the city's new periphery (see chapter 9). Our return journey is equally eventful, with the bus filled to overflowing with relatives and neighbors whom we drop off at different points en route, or bring back to Indio Guayas for an unplanned family visit.

The 24 percent attrition rate with the second-generation group would have been substantially higher if not for the detective work of the local research team, who doggedly followed up different information leads to locate family members, even estranged offspring. The causes relating to constraints in locating the second generation are presented in table A-4.

In 2004 and 2005, along with the anthropological participant observation instruments used during previous field visits, I added participatory urban appraisal methodologies, reflecting shifts in poverty research generally as well as developments in my own fieldwork methodology (Moser and McIlwaine 1999; 2004). This included participatory tools such as focus group listing and ranking, institutional mapping, and a poverty ladder. Time lines in particular proved important in constructing comparative perception data, allowing community leaders to recall the sequencing of mobilization for infrastructure provision, which could then be triangulated with earlier documentation and participant observation of such events. In addition, to include people's own "voices" in terms of their perceptions on achievements and aspirations, focus groups were conducted in Indio Guayas with men and women from both generations.

Barcelona Fieldwork

It was not possible to follow up with those children who lived outside Guayaquil in other parts of Ecuador. However, to provide a comparative perspective, an additional survey was undertaken in 2005 with second-generation sons, daughters, and partners that had migrated to Barcelona. I went to Barcelona because when we mapped all the houses on Calle K between Calle 25 and Calle 26 in 2004, we found that one in four families had members abroad, the majority of whom were in Barcelona. Adriana Perez, Marta's daughter, accompanied me to Barcelona to undertake fieldwork, living with me in the very small apartment we rented in the city center. Her personal friendships with so many of these second-generation migrants provided a unique entry point, manifest in the warm welcome we received and the trust shown during interviews.

In addition, Adriana also provided important insights and reflections on her perceptions of change among her contemporaries. Our access was also assisted by the fact that some of these second-generation young men and women knew me from back in 1978 when my family and I first lived in the suburbios, and they recalled playing with Titus and Nathaniel. Adam (who lived on the corner of Calles K and 26) and Mateo (whose father, Don Ortega, lived five doors down from Marta) both remembered coming to our house twice weekly in 1978 for English lessons and being taught by candlelight.

The second-generation sample in Barcelona was drawn from four sources:

—the fifty-one-household longitudinal panel sampled in 1978, 1992, and 2004;

—the 2004 survey of all households along Calle K between Calle 25 and Calle 26, undertaken to identify migrant members living abroad;

—the spouses or partners of mainly younger men migrants from Calle K who had formed relationships in Barcelona with women from Indio Guayas or nearby suburbio barrios in Guayaquil; and

—a network of school friends of Adriana's, all of whom attended the Colegio Provincia del Azuay in the nearby barrio of Battalion del Suburbios.

Because of differences in migration experiences, all household members were interviewed, reflecting differences of age and gender. These open-ended questionnaire interviews were conducted jointly by Adriana Perez and me. The level of trust between Adriana and the migrants made it possible to tape the interviews, with additional conversation often elaborating on important issues. The rejection rate was very low; only two individuals, who appeared to be leading somewhat irregular lives in Barcelona, refused to cooperate.

Twenty-one people filled out questionnaires. This group included sons and daughters from Calle K, as well as their partners; in some cases these were new partners they had met in Barcelona; in other cases they were partners who had accompanied or followed spouses to Barcelona. This group of migrants from Indio Guayas and nearby barrios was not dissimilar to their siblings and contemporaries that remained in Guayaquil. They were slightly older than siblings still living on their parents' plots and in other areas of Guayaquil and had all been in Barcelona between four to six years. Therefore, their perceptions and experiences reflected the fact that they had settled into life in their adopted city.

B

Guayaquil's Political and Economic Context

This appendix situates the low-income community of Indio Guayas in the broad historical context of Guayaquil's growth as Ecuador's largest city, main port, and major center of industry and trade. It is by no means an exhaustive treatment of the political, economic, and social processes that have shaped the city but rather is intended to provide contextual background for the local-level issues addressed in the chapters of this book.

As briefly described in chapter 1, the two most important cities of Ecuador are Quito, the highland capital, and Guayaquil, the lowland coastal port, whose growth and prosperity historically have been linked to its optimal location for the transport and export of the tropical produce cultivated in the city's large hinterland. Thus its development has been determined by the boom-bust cycle associated with Ecuador's history as primarily an export-oriented economy (MacIntosh 1972). This began in the late nineteenth century when cacao cultivation and exports flourished. Indeed, by 1920 cacao accounted for more than 70 percent of the country's exports, creating a monocrop economy while generating great wealth for a small group of Guayaquil-based entrepreneurs. The small internal market for basic commodities, created by profits from cacao exports, stimulated investment in basic industries such as starch products, processed dairy foods and grain products, beverages, and clothing. At the start of the 1930s, as cacao production waned, the arrival of the United Fruit

Company initiated Ecuador's banana boom. Facing little competition, Ecuador was soon the primary banana producer worldwide, supplying a fifth of the global market by the 1950s (Gerlach 2003). Economic prosperity driven by banana exports meant that over this decade Guayaquil's population grew at 5.8 percent a year. This was also a period of rapid import-substitution industrialization as existing processed food, textiles, and beverage industries expanded, and new ones were created in chemicals, paper, pharmaceuticals, cement, and durable consumer goods (Hidrobo Estrada 1992). Guayaquil's economic elite made money exporting agricultural products and importing machinery, and diversified their investments into domestic commercial banks and agricultural processing plants (Navarro Jiménez 1976).

Macroeconomic and Political Development

As discussed in chapter 1, this broader contextual history can usefully be divided into three phases, covered in detail below.

The 1970s—The Oil Years: Economic Growth and a Burgeoning Guayaquil

With the end of the banana boom, the discovery of oil in the 1970s marked a definitive turning point for Ecuador, as indicated in the time line presented in figure B-1. Oil exports displaced agricultural products as the main source of government revenues, financing national development. In 1970, for instance, the export of traditional products, such as bananas and cacao, constituted 90 percent of total exports, and oil only accounted for 0.8 percent. By 1981 oil had climbed to two-thirds of export revenues, contributing to foreign exchange reserves that reached $631 million in 1979 (Hidrobo Estrada 1992) and effecting significant changes in the relationship between national politics, economics, and society.

Of fundamental importance, the oil boom shifted economic and political power from Guayaquil to Quito, the seat of national government. As central government gained greater control over economic and social policy, spending also increased on the armed forces, confirming the military as a significant political actor (Gerlach 2003). Indeed, an enhanced military seized power in 1972, taking its cue from the military government in neighboring Peru. Unlike previous occasions when the armed forces seized power from unpopular civilian governments mired in economic crisis, in this case they did so in the belief that they could better manage the new oil wealth than civilian politicians (Corkhill and Cubitt 1988).

The new president, General Guillermo Rodriguez Lara, saw himself as a reformer committed to the "dispossessed classes," promising to "carry out a

Figure B-1. *Economic Time Line of Ecuador 1976–2003: GDP, Inflation, Policies, Presidents, and External Shocks*

Annual inflation rate (percent)

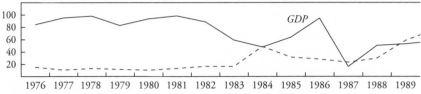

1976–1979	1979–1981	1981–1984	1984–1988
Burbano (mil. Junta)	Roldos (CFP)	Hurtado (DP-UDC), VP assumes office	Febres Cordero (PSC) Term concluded
1970s—Structural dependence on oil exports, debt accumulation	1981—President dies in office	1982—Substantial tariff reductions from avg. 43% to 28%	1984–86—Tight fiscal policies to reduce govt. expenditures
Spectacular economic growth: average annual real GDP growth 1971–80 is 9.1%		1982—Adoption of market-oriented exchange rate, removal of price controls on agricultural output	1984–86—Conclusion of new Standby Agreement with IMF, a rescheduling agreement with Paris Club members, and financing package with commercial banks
1975—El Niño		1983—El Niño	
		1983—Central Bank assumes debt	1986—Oil prices collapse
		External debt grows 74% between 1980–85	1987—Earthquake
			1987—Payments on external debt halted

Sources: World Bank Development Indicators; World Bank (2005); Solimano (2002).

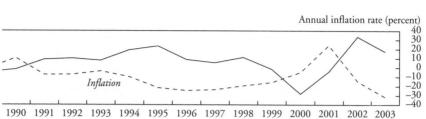

Annual inflation rate (percent)

1988–1992	1992–1997	1998–2000	2000–2003
Borja (ID) Elected, term concluded	Duran-Ballen (PUR) Elected, term concluded in 1996, VP	Mahuad (DP-UDC) Elected, resigned	Noboa (DP-UDC) Installed by military
Continued implementation of financial and trade liberalization, significant structural adjustment	Services begin growing as share of GDP. Foreign private capital flows increase drastically	Reversal in capital flows after 1998 equivalent to 20% of 1998 GDP	Increased privatization of industry, fiscal balance improves
1986–92—Liberalization of agricultural and marketing arrangements	1992—Public Budget Law sets legal basis for modernizing budget creation	1998—Drop in capital flows

1998–99—Oil prices decline | Continued volatility of petroleum revenue

2000—Dollarization

2003—Despite recovery, real education spending per beneficiary was 40% below 1980. Health spending is also still low. |
1989—Inflation reaches 75.8% as a result of policies during Febres Cordero presidency	1993—FISE created (Emergency Social Investment Fund), social safety net	1999—Currency crisis begins after Feb. decision to float exchange rate	
	1993—CONAM: Council to facilitate modernization and privatization	1999—Default on Brady Bonds (beginning of debt crisis)	
	1994—General Law of Financial Institutions	1999—Restoration of income tax	
	1994—Debt and Debt-Service Reduction by IMF/World Bank/ IDB		
	1995—Drought, border dispute with Peru		
	1997–98—El Niño		

revolutionary transformation of profound social changes" by significantly increasing the public sector's role in promoting economic development (Isaacs 1993). The military government therefore immediately nationalized the steel, fishing, air transport, and petroleum industries while investing heavily in roads, irrigation, health infrastructure, and other basic utilities. Industrial output primarily focused on consumer commodities, but capital goods also increased as a share of total production, while public works expenditures also stimulated the construction industry (Hidrobo Estrada 1992). With industrial output increasing sixfold between 1972 and 1977, the economy grew at over 5 percent over the course of the 1970s.

This was a period of great opportunity in Latin American cities as economic growth disproportionately benefited urban communities (Roberts 1978). Guayaquil enjoyed the advantages of public investments in infrastructure and services, experiencing rapid economic and industrial growth as well as a population increase related to brisk in-migration (Santos Alvite 1989). By 1978 the city had a population of around 1 million inhabitants, with 30 percent of its growth fueled by migrants.

With development policies benefiting the urban middle class, inequalities increased both within cities as well as between urban and rural areas. Faced with growing social tensions caused in part by unequal growth and accelerated urbanization, the military increasingly became more repressive, losing its political legitimacy as opposition increased. An attempted internal coup in 1975 undermined military confidence, precipitating the formation of a military triumvirate (led by Admiral Alfredo Poveda Burbano) that over the following three years led the country back to civilian rule (Isaacs 1993).

Though the military government aimed to decrease foreign dependence, new loans along with poor negotiations with foreign oil companies left Ecuador more indebted than before the coup. The new civilian government inherited a national debt that had swelled during the 1970s from approximately U.S.\$209 million in 1970 to over U.S.\$4 billion in 1980. The military's development policy of subsidies and tariff barriers left national industry poorly prepared to confront the challenges of an increasingly globalized economy. For the 65 percent of Ecuadorians who were living below the poverty line in 1980, the first oil decade was a time of lost opportunities and unmet expectations (Floro and Acosta 1993).

1978–92: Economic Stagnation, Structural Adjustment, and Stabilization

The fourteen years between the first and second panel data sets in this study (1978 and 1992) were characterized by weak civilian governments, each in turn unable to address adequately the mounting economic crises dominating the period. Guayaquil's economic activity was fundamentally affected by the 1980 economic downturn resulting from a 15 percent decline in oil prices; this was exacerbated by the 1982 floods that severely damaged banana, coffee, and cacao crops, causing a U.S.$350 million export loss. Indeed, in 1981 President Osvaldo Hurtado Larrea summarized the situation by announcing that the era of oil prosperity had ended and the era of austerity had begun.

The low taxation policy of the 1970s made the end of the first oil boom particularly painful. Though oil revenue had been dwindling, the population remained accustomed to subsidized public services (such as gas and electricity). As foreign currency reserves dried up, domestic demand decreased, and national industry was unable to produce sufficient affordable goods for limited domestic demand. After 1982 industry shrank at an average rate of 0.4 percent a year, which included contraction in the production of basic goods for internal consumption.

Governments during the 1980s responded to economic crisis with a strategy of opening up new oil fields and producing beyond OPEC quotas. While this eventually led to Ecuador's 1992 withdrawal from OPEC, GNP started to grow again over the short term, reaching 4.3 percent in 1985. But economic crisis returned when a 1987 earthquake destroyed the country's primary oil pipeline (Hidrobo Estrada 1992). Despite plummeting revenues, impending elections prompted the government to increase social spending, which was financed largely by printing money, devaluation, and the creation of a debt conversion system to assume private debt in the central bank. The result was a bout of heavy inflation and a severe economic crisis that drove Ecuador to agree to a World Bank–International Monetary Fund structural adjustment program. This conditioned a U.S.$100 million loan on implementation of an austerity package of fiscal and monetary measures that included cutting government spending and freezing public sector pay as well as the minimum wage (Floro and Acosta 1993).

The 1988 Borja government inherited a country in economic crisis, with inflation running over 70 to 75 percent a year and a fiscal deficit exceeding 10 percent of GDP. While Borja succeeded in stabilizing the economy, poverty levels increased as informal sector employment expanded rapidly. The response was the Frente Social, an integrated social program comprising a set of interventions designed to bring primary health care, preschool education, labor training, and a network of crèches for children of working mothers to poor urban populations.

Successive governments failed to make good on economic reforms, in large part because of an underlying instability in the political system that ensured that any policies would be determined by the central government rather than the provinces. Changes in national level political leadership over the 1978–96 period reflected an ongoing coastal-versus-highland rivalry between Guayaquil and Quito. In almost every presidential election, the victor came from an opposition party, not the ruling party, usually winning by a slim margin but without a working majority in the national parliament. The return to democracy in 1978, described in detail in chapter 4, was fronted by a Guayaquil-led government that was replaced by sierra-based Osvaldo Hurtado. He, in turn, was succeeded by Leon Febres Cordero, a U.S.-educated Guayaquil businessman whose unpopular neoliberal policies led to the election of the sierra-based Izquierda Democrática liberal leader, Rodrigo Borja. In a break in this pattern, Borja was succeeded in 1996 by Quito mayor Sixto Duran, largely because two Guayaquil candidates running against each other divided the coastal vote (Schneider 2006).

1993–2004: Dollarization Crisis and Dramatic Out-Migration

From 1993 to 2004, the search for economic stability occurred against a backdrop of ever increasing political instability. Though governments failed to make good on the 1980s economic reforms, they did start to adopt consistent policies to promote economic growth. Subsidies benefiting the rich—for example, on gasoline—were eliminated while those targeting the poor—on electricity and cooking gas—were maintained. Ecuador's political leaders took steps to integrate the country into the global economy—Ecuador joined the World Trade Organization in 1995—with the result that exports and imports rose between 1991 and 2001 from 53 percent to 59 percent of GDP (Fretes Cibils, Giugale, and López-Cálix 2003). However, the government failed to service the public debt, particularly over the 1987–94 period, and arrears accumulated "to be paid at some unspecified later date" (World Bank 2004). When Ecuador entered the Brady Plan on debt restructuring, the country's debt was $13.5 billion, equivalent to 80 percent of GDP, one of the highest debt burdens in Latin America (Fretes Cibils, Giugale, and López-Cálix 2003).

Policymakers once again had to contend with the twin specters of falling oil prices and natural disasters when oil prices weakened in 1997–98 and El Niño–related rains severely damaged crops and harmed agricultural exports. By the end of the 1990s, therefore, Ecuador was again suffering a cycle of severe recession and associated hyperinflation. With GDP shrinking by 7.3 percent in 1999, high inflation rendered the sucre worthless, as average prices increased by nearly 30 percent a month (Solimano 2002). As a consequence, the proportion of Ecuadorians living in poverty increased to 56 percent of the population, a level similar to that of the 1980s (World Bank 2004).

The East Asian, Russian, and Brazilian financial crises also reverberated through the Ecuadorian economy as the International Monetary Fund withheld crucial loans (Solimano 2002). By 1999, under increased macroeconomic pressures, Ecuador became the first country to default on its Brady bonds, a crisis that propelled out-migration between 1997 and 2003 equivalent to 3 percent of the population. The ensuing remittances reached an amount equivalent to 5.4 percent of Ecuador's GDP in 2002 (World Bank 2004).

Although the Ecuadorian authorities introduced a variety of crisis measures, none proved effective until early 2000. Then, in order to reduce skyrocketing debt, defaulted Brady bonds were exchanged for Eurobonds at a 40 percent reduction, and the country dollarized its currency in a move to curb inflation. After dollarization, Ecuador enacted a debt reduction plan to reduce its foreign debt by 40 percent as of 2010 (World Bank 2004). Dollarization gradually ended hyperinflation and, equally important, restored confidence in Ecuador's banking system, resulting in a modest 2 percent growth over the 2000–03 period (World Bank 2005). Though Ecuador still faced formidable challenges with an economy still overly reliant on oil exports, this economic performance was noteworthy given the succession of weak presidents over this period.

The four-year cycle of rotating presidents from Guayaquil and then Quito was replaced between 1996 and 2006 by a more unstable political arrangement. The winner of the 1996 election, Abdalá Bucaram Ortiz, was declared mentally unfit to lead by the National Congress some months later, resulting in a national political crisis. The establishment of a constituent assembly in 1997, followed by another round of presidential voting, culminated with the election of Jamil Mahuad in August 1998. However, his policy to peg the sucre to the dollar led to his overthrow in January 2000 after riots in the capital. Congress also fled to Guayaquil and appointed then vice president Gustavo Noboa, former head of Guayaquil's Catholic University, as president, the sixth in four years (Schneider 2006). In 2003 he was replaced by Lucio Gutiérrez, a populist ex-military officer, who appealed to an impoverished electorate with a promised war on corruption. Yet, in spite of 6.6 percent growth in 2004, Gutiérrez was also thrown out in 2005 amidst popular protests (Schneider 2006).

Crime, Violence, and Youth Gangs in Guayaquil

If instability at the level of presidential politics was a key factor disrupting macroeconomic management, increased crime and violence in Guayaquil was a destabilizing factor locally from the 1980s onwards. While chapter 11 primarily discusses the situation at the local, Indio Guayas level, the brief overview here is intended to provide further macrolevel information.

During the 1980s and 1990s, "social violence" in Guayaquil grew, transformed, and diversified (Villavicencio 2001, 2004). Crime levels rose by 10 percent a year over the mid-1980s, with violent crimes—rapes and homicides—concentrated in Guayaquil (Andrade 1994). Between 1996 and 2000, reported daily crimes in Guayaquil increased 43 percent. In 1990 organized gangs were stealing about four cars daily, and homicide rates ranged from 12 to 19 a year per 100,000 inhabitants throughout the 1990s, reaching 20 per 100,000 in 2001 (Villavicencio 2001).

National prison data also reveal the changing nature of crime in Guayaquil. During the first part of the 1980s, most were "crimes against property" or "crimes against people" (Andrade 1994). By 1990 an increasing portion of the crimes were drug related: 35.3 percent compared with 18.5 percent in 1982. The incidence was even higher for women offenders: 72 percent of the national female prison population had committed drug-related crimes (Andrade 1994). This change in the relative prevalence of crime types may reflect Guayaquil's changing role in the international drug trade.

Sustained increases in insecurity and fear have accompanied the large rise in both organized and common crime (Villavicencio 2001, 2003). Newspapers report that fear of crime now affects seven of every ten people in Guayaquil, while international organizations contend that violence has become a public health problem in Ecuador, in general, and Guayaquil, in particular (Villavicencio 2004).

Most of the victims of urban violence are the poor. Villavicencio (2001, 2004) has differentiated between the following three types:

—organized crime, which includes activities related to narcotrafficking, money laundering, smuggling, bank robberies and assaults on other types of businesses, stolen cars, house robberies, road assaults, "coyoterismo" (illegal trafficking of people), kidnappings, and public and private corruption;

—common or street crime, which involves mainly gangs, small-time drug vendors, neighborhood violence, domestic violence, suicides, assaults on urban public transport, and similar activities; and

—other types of social violence, such as traffic accidents, labor-related accidents, and malnutrition (food insecurity).

In research undertaken in urban areas in Colombia and Guatemala, a slightly different classification distinguished between political, economic, social, and institutional violence (see Moser and McIlwaine 2004, 2006).

At the same time, perceptions of insecurity are likely to be much greater than would be expected based on the reported levels of crime since systematic and reliable data on organized armed violence in Guayaquil are lacking, especially concerning the involvement of children and teenagers in gangs (Loor, Aldas, and Lopez, n.d.). While gender and intergenerational conflict and violence are also recognized as big problems, there are few reliable data about them. Although violence against women achieved some visibility in Ecuador by the end of the 1980s, mainly through the efforts of women's organizations, it is still the case that the problem has been approached by "blaming the victim" and has remained a "silenced" issue (Andrade 1994, pp. 135–37).

An increase in crime and violence has been associated with the emergence of the youth gang phenomenon. Gangs were perceived to become increasingly violent over the 1980s and to use more sophisticated and powerful weapons. The three types of gangs differentiated by researchers (Loor, Aldas, and López, n.d.) are *pandillas, naciones,* and *bandas organizadas* (organized bands). Bandas are armed groups of young people (between the ages of eighteen and thirty) led by adults and organized mainly to commit crimes (mostly drug related). Minors are used as informants and to distract attention, dismantle stolen cars, and sell drugs. Each banda has around thirty to forty members. In contrast, pandillas (gangs) comprise younger boys (ages eleven to eighteen), have an informal hierarchical structure, and are organized in a specific geographical neighborhood around common interests (music, dancing, and sports). Pandillas have no formal leader, although those who are most violent tend to be in charge. There are no rules, and some members have access to weapons and drugs. Recently, they have started identifying themselves by specific hand signs and the use of particular colors. There are an estimated 1,000 pandillas operating in Guayaquil, each with around twenty to forty members. Finally, naciones ("nations") emerged in the 1990s, in reaction to official repression against pandillas. They are better organized along a hierarchical, pyramid-like leadership structure, with a wider geographic base; naciones have branches in different sectors of the city and country. Their objective is to dominate a territory and obtain the recognition of other groupings. There are approximately fifty of them, each with 100 to 1,000 members between the ages of twelve and twenty-four.

A peak year for youth gangs was 1987, when the police reported the existence of more than 1,000 of these groups operating in the poorest neighborhoods. By 1989 some official data suggested there were between 1,200 and 1,500 gangs in the city whereas other official data estimated the number was

75 in 1988 and 150 in 1990 (Andrade 1994). Data on the number of gang members are similarly imprecise, with figures ranging between 40,000 to 65,000 (Loor, Aldas, and López, n.d.; Andrade 2005).

To acquire resources, these groups have opted mainly for illegal activities that generate large sums of money in the short term. Their main criminal activities are the trafficking or selling of drugs outside of schools, mainly in economically marginal urban areas; sale of stolen vehicles and parts; trade in stolen mobile phones; production and sale of false phone cards; sale of other stolen goods (acquired from robbing people, shops, and houses); and the organization of parties and hiring of discos to raise funds. They have connections with other criminal gangs mainly involved in the drug trade at both the national and international level (Loor, Aldas, and López, n.d.), a relationship that involves both the illegal trade in drugs as well as their consumption.

Migration from Ecuador

If gangs and increased levels of violence exemplify critical problems increasingly affecting the daily lives of households in Indio Guayas, international migration represents a safety net and way out of an economically stagnant city lacking the jobs to meet rising expectations. Chapter 10 gives an account of the migration of mainly young, second-generation men and women to Barcelona. The discussion here is intended to provide contextual background data on this important phenomenon.

In reality, migration is not a new phenomenon in Ecuador. Internal migration has played an important role in the country's social and economic history since the nineteenth century, mainly relocation from the *sierra* (mountains) to the *costa* (coast). These population flows intensified and diversified in the second half of the twentieth century, when international migration started to become significant (Centro de Planificación y Estudios Sociales [CEPLAES] 2005). Migrant flows to the United States increased in the 1960s and 1970s. During the 1980s debt crisis, there was second flow of emigrants, still primarily to the United States and led mainly by rural *mestizo* males, with urban and indigenous males, and some women, joining later. However, the third and most important migrant flow started in 1998, coinciding with the worst economic and political crisis in the country. This "new emigration" had different characteristics (Acosta, López, and Villamar 2004; CEPLAES 2005; Hall 2008; Herrera 2005; Jokisch and Pribilsky 2002).

Starting in 1998, there was a dramatic increase in the number of emigrants, which peaked in 2000, with further growth in 2002–03 (just before the introduction of EU visa restrictions). According to some estimates, roughly 1.4 million Ecuadorians left the country between 1990 and 2004, and did not return (not taking into account illegal migration by land or sea; CEPLAES 2005). Other estimates indicate 1.8 million to 2 million Ecuadorians living abroad by 2001, which would be 15 percent to 20 percent of the total population (12.8 million according to the 2001 census; CEPLAES 2005). Other estimates identify 2 million to 2.5 million Ecuadorians in the United States, around 500,000 in Spain, and 60,000 to 120,000 in Italy, with smaller communities in other countries (ILDIS/FES and others 2003; Acosta, López, and Villamar 2004).

As U.S. immigration policy became stricter, and as borders were tightened in Mexico and Central America, routes to the United States became more clandestine, risky, and expensive. Therefore, destination countries diversified, mainly shifting toward the EU. Between 1999 and 2002, an illegal trip to the United States could cost $10,000 to $12,000 and take up to three months, while the cost of going to Europe was $3,500 to $4,000 (CEPLAES 2005, p. 61). The main destination countries of the new migrants from the 1990s onwards were Spain (45 percent), the United States (32 percent), and Italy (9 percent), but there was also migration to other EU countries and within the region (to Venezuela and Chile).

According to CEPLAES (2005), women account for 44 percent of Ecuadorian migrants living in the United States, but in Italy and Spain, the numbers of male and female migrants are roughly equivalent. Women migrate mainly as independent labor, not for family reunification, often leaving their families behind and becoming their main financial support (Herrera 2005). The feminization of immigration to Europe related to the greater ease of migrating to the new destinations (at least until 2003) and the specific labor demand for domestic service. Most women migrants are from the coastal region of Ecuador, of which 55 percent are from the Province of Guayas. According to 2001 census data, 57 percent of male and female migrants were between the ages of eighteen and thirty when they left (CEPLAES 2005, pp. 28–29).

Specifically with regard to Ecuadorian migration to Spain, in 1997 more than 58 percent of migrants were women (Jokisch and Pribilsky 2002). This proportion increased to almost 70 percent in 1998, but later it declined to 56 percent in 2000 and 51 percent by the beginning of 2001 as more men joined the migrant stream (Jokisch and Pribilsky 2002; Pujadas and Massal 2002; Herrera 2005). The estimated total number of Ecuadorians in Spain, including illegal immigrants (which could account for half of the community) increased from 32,000 in 1998 to 470,000 by June 2004 (320,000 of them of working age). In this short period, Ecuadorians became the largest Latin American migrant group in Spain and also the largest migrant group in Madrid (Actis 2005). Earliest references to Ecuadorian migrants in Barcelona were to a small presence of *Otavaleño* (indigenous sierra migrants from the town of Otavalo) street musicians and vendors starting in the late 1980s (Actis 2005; Jokisch and Pribilsky 2002). But by 2000 there were nearly 215,000 legal immigrants in Barcelona (3.4 percent of its total population). According to data from the 2002 *padrón* (the list of people registered in each municipality), Andean migrants (from Ecuador, Colombia, and Perú) in Barcelona accounted for over 31 percent of the total migrant population; the 2001 *padrón* showed there were 8,209 Ecuadorians in Barcelona (see Pujadas and Massal 2002). Ecuadorians have settled throughout the city but mainly reside in the working-class districts of Nou Barris, Sant Andreu, and San Martín.

For many Ecuadorians international migration was not an answer to unemployment (a majority were working before they migrated) but rather a response to low salaries, economic precariousness, and limited social mobility in Ecuador (CEPLAES 2005; ILDIS/FES and others 2003). The 1999 crisis contributed to a widespread negative vision of the country and its future possibilities. Thus international migration became a mechanism for social advancement (Acosta, López, and Villamar 2004, 2006). Despite the recovery in economic growth in 2001, international migration has continued, partly because such improvements have not been experienced by a majority of the population (CEPLAES 2005).

One economic consequence of international migration has been the increase in remittances. According to central bank data, these grew from U.S.$643 million in 1997 to U.S.$1.41 billion in 2001 (Jokisch and Pribilsky 2002). In 1993 remittances represented only 1.3 percent of GNP; by 1999 they constituted 6.5 percent and rose to 8.3 percent by 2000, only to decline thereafter to 6.7 percent and 5.9 percent in 2001 and 2002, respectively (Acosta, López, and Villamar 2004). Apart from contributing to the survival of families, remittances have a beneficial impact on the economy, mainly through consumption and construction. On the downside, migration has fueled a "brain drain": the UN estimated that by mid-2002 some 200,000 professionals had emigrated from Ecuador (Acosta, López, and Villamar 2004).

Over time Spain has repeatedly changed its policy toward immigration. After World War II, Europe initially identified immigration as essential for economic recovery, but by the 1980s, in the wake of the oil crisis, most countries reoriented their policies to reduce immigration. In the late 1990s, however, acknowledgment that zero immigration was impractical resulted in a shift to cooperation with countries of origin, creation of a common EU asylum system, improved treatment of non-EU migrants, and management of migration flows (Cortés Maisonave 2005; CEPLAES 2005). The process of joining affected Spain's immigration policy, with the first *ley de extranjería* (Law on the Rights and Freedoms of Foreigners in Spain) introduced in 1985 just prior to entry into the European Community.[1] In 1993 a system of quotas sought to discourage illegal immigration. After the regularization of 1996 and the introduction of a new labor quota system in 1997, the situation became more complex for irregular migrants. Before 1997 they had been able to regularize their legal status through the *régimen general* (general regime under which illegal immigrants with a job offer could be regularized if they already had a job offer *in* Spain), but this was no longer possible. Nevertheless, the number of illegal immigrants in general who had no residence permit grew massively, from 35 percent of people registered in the padrón who had no residence permit at the beginning of 2000 to 50 percent three years later (Actis 2005; Pujadas and Massal 2002).

A new law passed in January 2000 tightened the borders but gave all migrants already living in Spain (including the undocumented) generous rights, including access to education, health services, and other social benefits, as well as the right to join trade unions and to "associate, meet, demonstrate and strike." In addition, an amnesty was offered for those who had arrived before June 1, 1999. However, the new Aznar government that emerged in March 2000 reversed some of the most progressive aspects of this new law with additional legislation in December 2000. The amnesty was maintained, but the borders were further tightened, pressure on employers of illegal immigrants increased, and legalization procedures were made more complex.

In January 2002 the régimen general was terminated, a reflection of stricter laws not only against illegal but also legal immigration. The latter was to be based on agreed quotas, and although preference was given to Latin American workers, the numbers admitted so far under this system have been much lower than expected. Under the bilateral agreement signed with Ecuador in January 2001, only 1,300 Ecuadorians had arrived in Spain under this system as of July 2004, well below the ceiling of 30,000 initially allowed; and as of August 2003, Ecuadorians wishing to travel to Spain (and the EU in general) needed a visa (Actis 2005; Giménez Romero 2002; Pujada and Massal 2002). Finally, in May 2004 the newly seated Spanish government reoriented migration policy with a new *reglamento* (regulation) for immigration legislation, which maintained the law approved by the previous government in 2003 that contained new components intended to improve the status of the undocumented (Actis 2005).

C

Econometric Methodology

CAROLINE MOSER AND ANDREW FELTON

I n the past decade, development economists have increasingly advocated the use of assets to complement income and consumption-based measures of welfare and wealth in developing countries (Carter and May 2001; Filmer and Pritchett 2001). Income used to be the favored unit of welfare analysis because it is a cardinal variable that is directly comparable among observations, making it straightforward to interpret and use in quantitative analysis. However, by the 1990s this was often superseded by consumption-based measures (Ravallion 1992). The analysis of assets and their accumulation is intended to complement such measures, by extending our understanding of the multidimensional character of poverty and the complexity of the processes underlying poverty reduction (Adato, Carter, and May 2006). Closely linked to the asset-based approach is recent methodological work on the measurement of assets with a range of new techniques developed to capture aggregate ownership of different assets into a single variable. This econometric appendix augments the description of assets in chapter 2, as well as the discussion on research methodology in appendix A, by elaborating further on the econometric methodology developed to construct an asset index based on the longitudinal panel data set from Guayaquil.

Chapter 12 identifies the contribution of mixed methodologies. From an econometric viewpoint, it is clear that since traditional econometrics only incorporates variables that can be measured, it is often vulnerable to misspecification, particularly due to endogeneity. Endogeneity occurs when the independent (explanatory) and dependent (outcome) variables are linked in a way that is not specified in the model. For example, an explanatory or "treatment" variable such as migration may be itself directly caused by unobservable household characteristics (entrepreneurial spirit) that affect the dependent or outcome variable (household income). The model is misspecified because it should include immeasurable variable x but instead contains a measurable variable y.

Because the discipline of anthropology includes the identification and analysis of intangible factors, it can enhance econometric analysis in several ways. One of the most useful is its ability to help explain outliers. When one uses small, detailed data sets (the kinds of data sets for which an anthropological perspective is most effective), outliers (or, more generally, a limited number of observations) can make a big difference to the results. Anthropologists can provide insight into whether these should or should not be included, and why the outliers are dissimilar to the other observations.

Assets and Income

While economists often use income to measure wealth, welfare, and other indicators of well-being, income data have limitations of both accuracy and measurement, particularly in developing country contexts. For instance, in informal labor markets, incomes are often highly variable. Income can be seasonal, such as when earned from farming or the tourist market, or just variable and lumpy for small business owners. Taking a snapshot of income at one point in time may therefore produce a less reliable picture of these types of workers than those who receive regular paychecks. Furthermore, such workers may be engaged in barter and other nonmonetary forms of trade. In all of these cases, there is a high potential for error in data based on the recollection and value of all sources of income. Since income does not necessarily provide a reliable measure of well-being, expenditures and consumption now are also used to measure well-being.

Measuring expenditures solves some of the problems of income, such as seasonality. Households can save their income from flush times as a buffer against bad times. This "consumption smoothing" is both theoretically appealing and has empirical regularity. Households also tend to be more forthcoming about expenditures, which generally are a less sensitive topic than household income. However, a number of the same difficulties with income also apply to expenditure, such as measuring the value of bartered goods. Work done for oneself, such as house improvement, also tends to be missing from expenditures. In addition, although economists have shown that consumption data provide more robust information on well-being than income data (particularly in rural areas), income data are still used in a number of research studies.

In Guayaquil, as mentioned in chapter 2, longitudinal anthropological research revealed that even people's short-term recall of consumption expenditures was often inaccurate or underestimated. People buying many of their basic consumption items on a daily basis simply did not remember what they spent. Data from expenditure diaries, for instance, proved to be widely inconsistent with expenditure data from anthropological participant observation. In contrast, because of the trust that had been established, there was a high level of compatibility across the fifty-one panel data households in terms of income relating to both formal and informal sector earnings. For this reason the study used income measures.

In addition, there is often less likelihood of recall or measurement problems when people are asked what they own from a list of assets. Furthermore, assets may provide a better picture of long-term living standards than an income snapshot because they have been accumulated over time and last longer. However, a list of assets lacks money's advantages of cardinality and fungibility. The following discussion explores the theoretical difficulties of creating a set of "asset" variables.

Suppose that a household's capital portfolio can be measured in terms of a number I of types of capital, C^i, where i runs from 1 to I. Each type of capital C^i is composed of J types of assets $a^{i,1} \ldots a^{i,J}$. Each of these a's may be measured using a binary, ordinal, or cardinal variable. We want to assign a weight w to each item and then sum up the weighted variables to arrive at our estimate of C^i, as follows:

$$C^i_{n,t} = \sum_{j=1}^{J} w^{i,j}_t a^{i,j}_{n,t},$$

where n stands for the household number, i represents the type of capital, j is the type of asset, and t indicates the time period.

There are a number of ways in which to measure the weight w, as described below.

Method 1: Prices

One intuitive way to weight the assets is to use monetary values, so that

$$w^{i,j}_t = p^{i,j}_t,$$

where P_t^{ij} is the price (or some other monetary measure of value) of asset (i,j) at time t. The sum

$$\sum_{j=1}^{J} w_t^{i,j} a_{n,t}^{i,j}$$

would then be the total monetary value of the household's asset wealth. However, this approach is problematic for some of the same reasons that income data are. Price data can be difficult to obtain in some contexts, especially in economies that have high levels of barter. Even more fundamental is the problem that it is difficult or impossible to assign prices to intangible assets, such as human or social capital. Of course, assigning any numbering to those types of capital is tenuous, but the ordinal scale that we developed in this research project seeks to overcome the implied fungibility of prices.

Method 2: Unit Values

Another method is to simply sum up the number of assets owned, which is equivalent to setting $w = 1$ for each w. This method has the virtue of simplicity, but it also has the limitation of assigning equal weight to ownership of each asset. For example, this method would assign equivalent worth to owning a radio and a computer, although in reality their contributions to the capital variable are surely different.

Method 3: Principal Components Analysis

Recently, development economists have followed the recommendation made by Filmer and Pritchett (2001) to use principal components analysis (PCA) to aggregate several binary asset ownership variables into a single dimension. PCA is relatively easy to compute and understand, and provides more accurate weights than simple summation. The intuition underlying this method is that there is a latent (unobservable) variable $\tilde{C}^i$ for each type of capital C^i that manifests itself through ownership of the different assets $a^{i,1} \ldots a^{i,J}$. For example, suppose household n owns asset $a^{i,1}$ if $\tilde{C}^i > w^{i,1}$. It turns out that the maximum likelihood estimators of the w's are the eigenvectors of the covariance matrix, also known as the *principal components* of the data set. Usually only the eigenvector with the highest eigenvalue is used because it is the vector that provides the most "information" about the variables. The first eigenvector is the vector that minimizes the squared distances from the observations to a line going through the various dimensions.

This is an appealing method for combining variables for two reasons. First, it is technically equivalent to a rotation of the dimensional axes, such that the

Figure C-1. *Regression Minimizes Dashed Lines; PCA Minimizes Gray Lines*

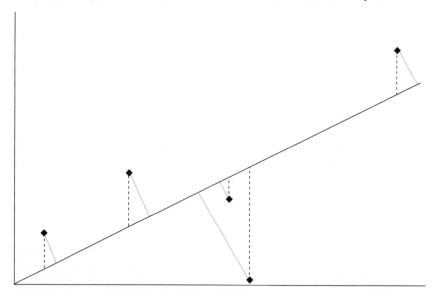

variance from the observations is minimized. This is equivalent to calculating the line from which the orthogonal residuals are minimized. It is similar to a regression in terms of minimizing residuals, but in this case the residuals are measured against all of the variables, not just one "dependent" variable. Figure C-1 demonstrates how regression minimizes the squared residuals from a dependent variable to a line, while PCA minimizes the distances from points in multidimensional space to a line.

The second reason that PCA is a valuable approach is that the coefficients have a fairly intuitive interpretation. The coefficient on any one variable is related to how much information it provides about the other variables. If ownership of one type of asset is highly indicative of ownership of other assets, then it receives a positive coefficient. If ownership of an asset contains almost no information about what other assets the household owns, then it receives a coefficient near zero. And if ownership of an asset indicates that a household is likely to own few other assets, then it receives a negative coefficient. Higher and lower coefficients mean that ownership of that asset conveys more or less information about the other assets.

This makes PCA excellent for modeling a presumed underlying continuous variable, such as wealth. If ownership of a certain asset is highly correlated with owning the other assets that were asked about in the survey, then it is probably correlated with owning other types of assets that were not in the survey as well. To return to the earlier example, wealthy households are more likely than poor ones to own a computer, but radio ownership is spread evenly across the spectrum. Therefore, possession of a computer provides us with more information about that household's wealth than possession of a radio does, and therefore it receives a higher weighting.

Multivariate Analysis

Most research so far has only used PCA and its related techniques to model ownership of a single type of asset, usually a variant of "wealth" (see table C-1). However, social scientists are often interested in examining portfolios that include different asset types in order to better understand the specific root causes of poverty. Hulme and McKay (2005) provide an overview of techniques used for multivariate asset analysis, briefly mentioning index construction methods like PCA before moving on to a variety of other methods used by economists, sociologists, and anthropologists. Most of the examples of multivariate asset analysis they cited do not use PCA or other sophisticated techniques of aggregating assets. For example, Klasen (2000, 2008) identifies fourteen components of well-being and sums up the number that are unsatisfactory for a given household to arrive at a "deprivation index." However, as Hulme and McKay point out, while giving all components the same weight might appear to be "fair," there is a complex set of value judgments built into such an assumption. For example, can nutrition—where a low score could indicate a child's malnutrition and stunting that may reduce his or her capabilities throughout life—be weighted the same as transport mobility—where a low score may simply represent a temporary inconvenience?

In their work on PCA, however, Filmer and Pritchett (2001) fail to adequately address the important methodological issue that the variables must positively correlate with the latent variable and with each other. If all the variables are positively correlated, then the estimates will all be greater than or equal to zero and bounded at the top by the value of the first eigenvalue (which is itself less than or equal to the number of variables in the matrix). If they are not, then the first eigenvector may have negative values, which means that the estimated latent variable would be *reduced* from ownership of an asset. This is only remedied by interpreting ownership of those assets as a sign of lower wealth. If this is plausible, then even negative values of estimated wealth are acceptable because the estimated variable is ordinal and can either be used as is or rescaled so that they are all positive.

Table C-1. Some Asset Indexes and Associated Categories and Components

Source	Focus	Details	Categories	Components
Sahn and Stifel (2003)	Asset index (asset-based poverty indicators)	Factor analysis 2. Comparisons between expenditure and asset poverty with no discount for household size	1. Household durables 2. Household characteristics	Per capita values of radios, stereos, TVs, sewing machines, stoves, refrigerators, bicycles, motorized transportation Source of drinking water Toilet facility Household construction materials Hectares of land and number of livestock
Filmer and Pritchett (1998)	Asset index	List of assets (12–21 variables) PCA to derive weights Sorting by asset index and then cutoffs Bottom 40 percent: poor Middle 40 percent: middle Top 20 percent: rich PCA	3. Human capital 1. Assets 2. Characteristics of housing	Years of education of household head Radio, TV, refrigerator, bicycle, motorcycle, car Electricity used Source of drinking water Type of toilet facility Number of rooms for sleeping Type of materials used for construction
Maluccio, Murphy, and Yount (2005)	Linear socio-economic index		1. Household consumer durable goods 2. Housing characteristics	Own radio, record player, bicycle, sewing machine, refrigerator, television, motorcycle, automobile; own plot of land for house; own their house; number of rooms in house/number of individuals; live in a formal house; high-quality flooring; high-quality roofing; high-quality walls; kitchen separate room in house; formal cooking medium; has electricity; latrine/toilet; drinking water from well

Source	Approach	Method	Components	Details
Adato, Carrer, and May (2006)	Livelihood weighted multi-asset index	Multivariate analysis	1. Human capital 2. Natural and productive capital	Educated and uneducated labor Land, livestock, small business machinery and equipment, unearned or transfer income
Grootaert and others (2004)	Social capital	Multivariate analysis	Integral questionnaire	Groups and networks; trust and solidarity; collective action and solidarity; information and communication; social cohesion and inclusion; empowerment and political action
Whitehead (2004)	Distribution of material, durable assets	Division of households into three categories	Livestock status Asset status	Point value assigned to each kind of livestock on basis of local price Top 10 percent: poor but secure Middle 75 percent: poor and vulnerable Bottom 10 percent: destitute
Siegel (2005)	Asset-based approach	Descriptive relationship between assets, context, behavior, and outcomes	Assets determine the opportunity set of options Context	Productive, social, and locational Political and institutional milieu and the existence or absence of risks
Rakodi (1999)	Capital assets framework	Descriptive relationship between context, livelihood strategies, and three assets	Livelihood strategies Natural capital Physical-produced capital Human capital Social capital	Household's revealed behavior Land, security of tenure Basic infrastructure; financial resources (savings, credit, remittances, pensions) Labor; education; health status

Others have advocated other techniques. Sahn and Stifel (2003) use factor analysis, which is designed more for data exploration than dimensional reduction. Booysen and others (2008) use multiple correspondence analysis, which they promote as better at dealing with categorical variables than PCA. Finally, Kolenikov and Angeles (2005) describe a new technique, polychoric principal components analysis, which improves on regular PCA and was designed specifically for categorical variables. Unlike multiple correspondence analysis, it can also be used for continuous variables and is especially appropriate for discrete data. It supposes that the discrete data are observed values of an underlying continuous variable. Similar in spirit to an ordered probit regression, polychoric PCA uses maximum likelihood to calculate how that continuous variable would have to be split up in order to produce the observed data.

Among those social scientists that have used PCA or similar methods, Sahn and Stifel (2003) come closest to implementing a multidimensional approach. They categorize their index components into three types of capital (household durables, household characteristics, and human capital), but then they combine them all together into a single index. Asselin (2002) also groups his variables into categories (economy and infrastructure, education, health, and agriculture) but then combines them all during his analysis. To the best of our knowledge, no research so far uses PCA on the components of each type of capital before undertaking their analysis.

The main advantage that polychoric PCA has over a regular PCA is that it is optimized for using ordinal data, which most asset data are. Researchers often ask about the quality of construction of a home, for example, which might be recorded on a scale of 1 to 4. While Filmer and Pritchett (2001) advocate splitting this into four binary variables, this introduces a large amount of distortion into the correlation matrix, as the variables are automatically perfectly negatively correlated with each other. Furthermore, the knowledge that the researcher brings—that some values are better than others—is lost, as the PCA treats every variable as the same. Polychoric PCA solves these problems by ensuring that the coefficients of an ordinal variable follow the order of its values (that is, coefficients of "better" assets have a greater magnitude than those of lesser assets). Kolenikov and Angeles (2005) ran a Monte Carlo exercise on simulated data and found that polychoric PCA predicted the "true" coefficients more accurately than regular PCA.

Another advantage of polychoric PCA is that it allows us to compute coefficients for both owning and not owning an asset. This is desirable because sometimes not owning something conveys more information than owning it. If almost everyone owns indoor plumbing except for the very poorest households, then the coefficient on owning indoor plumbing will be around zero (since it does not help to distinguish household wealth among those that own it). However, not owning indoor plumbing will be negatively correlated to ownership of other assets, and the coefficient of not owning it will be highly negative. This further distinguishes among wealth levels.

Empirical Application of Polychoric PCA in the Guayaquil Panel Data Set

This section describes the application of multivariate analysis in the Indio Guayas study. The household asset index is based on the empirical data available from the fifty-one-household panel data as well as local anthropological knowledge of asset vulnerability in the community. While the asset index is grounded in a literature review on livelihoods and asset accumulation, the specific assets chosen were determined by the questions available in the data set. As mentioned in appendix A, constraints relate to the fact that when the research project first started, it was not originally defined as a study of asset accumulation.

The following variables were adapted from the questionnaire data from the 1978–2004 panel data. Two types of physical capital were identified: housing and consumer durables. Financial capital was extended to incorporate productive capital, while human capital was limited to education because of a lack of panel data on health. Finally, social capital was disaggregated in terms of household and community social capital. A fifth type of capital, natural capital, is commonly used in the assets and livelihoods literature. Natural capital includes the stocks of environmentally provided assets such as soil, atmosphere, forests, water, and wetlands. This capital is more generally used in rural research. In urban areas where land is linked to housing, this is more frequently classified as productive capital, as is the case in this study. However, since all households lived on similar-sized plots, this was not tracked in the data set.

Table 2-1 in chapter 2 outlines each type of asset analyzed, the category of capital that it belongs to, and the specific components that make up its index. The following sections detail the construction of the index to measure each of these capital types and discuss the associated challenges. Polychoric PCA was used for many, but not all, of the asset categories; as the subsequent sections demonstrate, its advantages and limitations become clearer when one moves from theory to practice. As with any statistical technique, the devil is in the details, and we lay out below exactly how and why we chose specific variables out of this detailed data set for use with different techniques.

Physical Capital

Physical capital is generally defined as the stock of plant equipment, infrastructure, and other productive resources owned by individuals, businesses, and the public sector (see World Bank 2000). In this study, however, physical capital is more limited in scope. It is subdivided into two categories and includes the range of consumer durables households acquire as well as their housing (identified as the land and the physical structure that stands on it).

As described in chapter 3, housing is the more important component of physical capital. In Indio Guayas households squatting on a mangrove swamp under severe conditions rapidly constructed wooden stilts and a platform, and then incrementally built very basic houses with bamboo walls, wood floors, and corrugated iron roofs. However, such houses were insecure—bamboo walls could easily be split by knives, and the construction materials quickly deteriorated. Consequently, as soon as resources were available, households upgraded their dwellings. This started with infill to provide land, followed by permanent housing materials such as cement blocks and floors. This very gradual incremental upgrading took place over a number of years.

This process is reflected in the econometric findings on housing based on the four indicators: type of toilet, light, floor, and walls. These are ordered in terms of increasing quality (for instance "incomplete" walls are those in the process of being upgraded from bamboo to either wood or to brick or concrete), with the data showing a high degree of interhousehold correlation. The ordinal nature and positive correlation of the variables makes this part of the data highly suitable for using polychoric PCA to construct the weights for housing as a physical asset. (See table C-2.)

The estimated coefficients rise with the increasing quality of each asset, and larger numbers (either positive or negative) mean that the variable provides more "information" on the household's housing stock. For example, the greatest negative coefficient is on having no electric lights. This means that a household that lacks electric lighting is extremely likely to fall into the lowest categories of the other types of assets: toilet, floor, and walls. Similarly, a household with a flush toilet (the highest coefficient within the toilet category) is likely to have scored highly on the other items as well. This is because flush toilets were owned by the fewest people, and it was only in 2004 that almost all households acquired one. In contrast, by 1992 many people had connected to the main electrical grid and upgraded their floors and walls to either brick or concrete.

The consumer durables variable illustrates a new type of difficulty with PCA. Because the data cover multiple time periods, the "values" of many of these assets

Table C-2. *Housing Stock Polychoric PCA Coefficients, 1978–2004*

Asset	Coefficient
Toilet	
Hole	−0.5629
Latrine	−0.0735
Flush toilet	0.4541
Light (electricity)	
None	−0.8869
Illegally tapped electricity	−0.2605
Main electrical grid	0.4063
Floor	
Earth or bamboo	−0.8672
Wood	−0.3052
Brick or concrete	0.3658
Walls	
Earth or bamboo	−0.5687
Incomplete	−0.1847
Wood	−0.1340
Brick or concrete	0.3631

have changed between observations. For example, a black-and-white television was relatively more valuable in 1978 than in 2004. In 1978 it was a sign of wealth to own a black-and-white television, but in 2004 it was a sign of poverty because color televisions had become available. By 2004 a number of electronic items that had become available were simply not on the market during earlier surveys.

This issue can be addressed either by conducting a separate analysis for each year or by aggregating the data across time. The first three columns of table C-3, which calculate values for each item in each year, illustrate the changing values of many of the variables. In 1978 a black-and-white television had a strongly positive coefficient because it was a sign of wealth then. Its coefficient decreased during each time period as it became less indicative of wealth. This demonstrates that in addition to its ability to create a single variable, asset index construction is useful for tracking the relative value of items.

Aggregating the time periods proved to be the most efficacious method of combining the variables since it allows relative comparisons across, as well as within, time periods. Items that were once luxury items can receive a negative

Table C-3. *Consumer Durables Polychoric PCA Coefficients, 1978–2004*

Asset	1978	1992	2004	All years combined
No TV	−0.5358	−0.4168	−0.4687	−0.4616
Black-and-white TV	0.5797	−0.0317	−0.2939	−0.0564
Color TV	a	0.2782	0.0194	0.3093
Both black-and-white and color TV		0.5229	0.3778	0.7321
No radio	−0.8888	−0.6856	−0.2631	−0.1069
Radio	0.1761	0.1358	0.0943	0.0277
No washing machine		−0.0402	−0.0914	−0.0492
Washing machine		1.4188	0.7685	0.7507
No bike		−0.1190	−0.1802	−0.1428
Bike		0.3009	0.1665	0.3973
No motorcycle		−0.0949	−0.0240	−0.0253
Motorcycle		0.7978	0.2020	0.3464
No VCR			−0.0623	−0.0258
VCR			0.6574	0.8706
No DVD player			−0.1477	−0.0580
DVD player			0.6507	0.8844
No record player	−0.1738		−0.1236	−0.0639
Record player	0.4394		0.6239	0.3718
No computer			−0.1100	−0.0519
Computer			0.4843	0.7910

a. Blank cells mean that the asset did not exist in the village sample during that year.

score in later time periods, which means they are, on average, indicative of poverty. However, because we estimate the value of not owning the asset as well as the value of owning it, a household with a black-and-white TV in 1978, although receiving a negative score in aggregate, still ranks much higher in 1978 than a comparable household that does not own a TV at all. In fact, the average household in 1978 had a negative score for its consumer durables capital, but the ordinal rankings remain the same since the coefficients were calculated separately for each year. Therefore, the rankings make sense both within and across time periods.

This method produces a feasible and accessible continuous variable representing ownership of consumer durables. Figure C-2 shows the kernel density distributions for the consumer durables variable in each round of surveys. In 1978 and 1992, the variable is roughly normally distributed (when the households are just beginning to diverge from their equal starting points), but by 2004 it resembles the log-normal distribution commonly found in studies of

Figure C-2. *Consumer Durables Capital Density Estimates, 1978–2004*

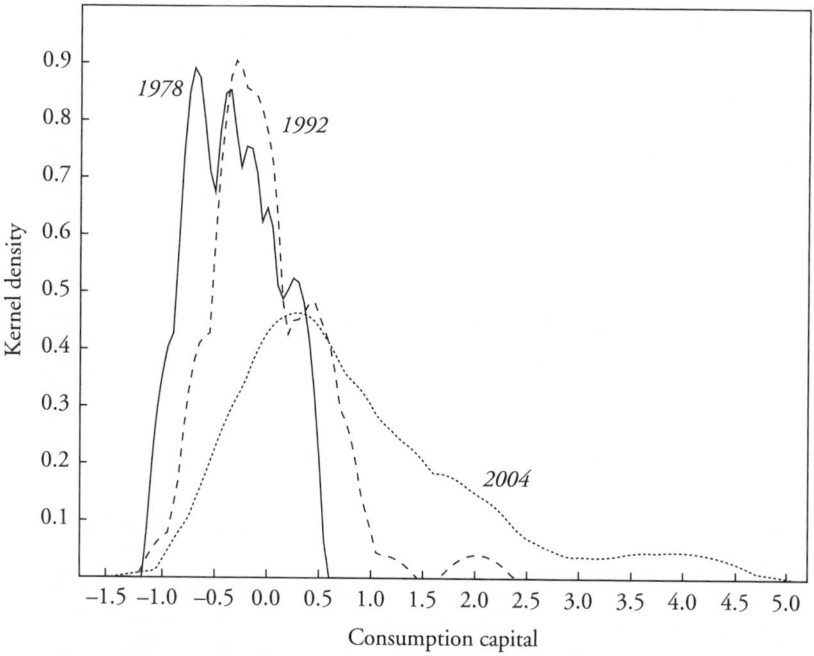

Source: Authors' calculations.

income distribution (which parallels the actual growth of income and asset inequality in Guayaquil).

Human Capital

Human capital assets refer to individual investments in education, health, and nutrition that affect people's ability to use their labor and their returns from that labor. Education is the only component in this index and therefore provides only a partial picture of human capital. As described in chapter 5, the study contains detailed information on health status, particularly in terms of shocks relating to serious illnesses or accidents, as well as the use and cost of health services. However, the lack of an adequate methodology to translate these into a health asset index means that the information remains at the narrative level.

Human capital presents a different challenge from previous categories because it is usually measured at the individual, not household, level. If we want to measure human capital at the household level, we need to develop a method of aggregation. Furthermore, there is only one key measure of human capital at

Table C-4. *Value of Educational Levels*[a]

Educational level	1978	1992	2004
Illiterate	3.52	2.15	3.18
Some primary	3.20	2.47	3.09
Completed primary	3.31	2.51	3.19
Completed high school or technical school	3.09	2.66	3.21
Tertiary education	3.98	3.12	3.37

a. Coefficients for age, age squared, and gender not shown.

the individual level: years of education (or, alternatively, level of completed education). Levels of education are defined as illiterate, some primary school, completed primary school, secondary-technical degree, and some college or more. Since there is only one variable, we cannot use any of the varieties of PCA at the individual level because PCA measures the correlation between two or more variables. Finally, educational human capital is an intermediate asset, rather than an end in itself, that must be applied so that it can help households get out of poverty.

We could assign an equal weight to every year of education and add them up, but this brings us back to the earlier methods described above, with the same attendant problems. Instead, we make use of the fact that the survey contains the income earned by every individual, and so are able to estimate the monetary return to education. The education variable was split into five levels: none, some primary, completed primary, completed secondary or technical, and some tertiary (see table C-4).

This approach contrasts, for instance, with physical assets that in themselves are indicators of whether a household has risen out of poverty. However, because the study also tracked individual income earnings, it is possible to estimate the monetary return to education. In this way, the value of human capital is estimated in income terms, calculated using the labor market value associated with attaining each extra qualification. Income earned from wages is regressed on the level of education, age, and age squared to proxy for experience, and on a gender dummy variable. The regression is estimated separately for each year because the value of each type of degree changes every year as the job market changes. Therefore, the value of the education capital of a household can change even though the composition of the household does not, as described in chapter 5.

Results show that in 1978 there was very little difference in terms of wages in the value of being illiterate, having some primary education, or having completed primary school. These educational levels applied to almost 90 percent of the young settlers of Indio Guayas at the time. Those few that had higher education earned considerably more in the labor market. Over time, however, being illiterate or lacking a primary degree became more disadvantageous because less-educated people earned lower wages. Meanwhile, as table C-4 illustrates, the macroeconomic instability of 1992 decreased wages (and therefore the value of education) for every educational group.

Human capital is usually valued for its use in the labor market, so it is one type of capital that may be measured in monetary terms relatively easily using techniques similar to those described above. Years of education and salaries are frequently available in surveys. On the other hand, endogeneity and other issues are problematic in this methodology. For example, many people with a low level of education are not in the workforce—neither including them as zero income nor excluding them is wholly satisfactory. If those with low levels of education are disproportionately absent from the formal economy, then the estimation of returns from low levels of education might be biased upward because only the most talented of the poorly educated have income. Table C-4 shows that illiterate people often earn more than those with more education, suggesting that this problem may indeed exist in our data.

Furthermore, the use of other variables like age and gender, while important, also leads to complications. Younger generations, on average, had more educational opportunities, and the importance of education changes over the years as the economy develops. By using income as the dependent variable, we are measuring the market value of education rather than some level of inherent human capital specific to the individual. Finally, we may disagree with the values the labor market places on human capital. For example, people with no education at all in 1978 earned more than any other group except those with a college education (only one person). And yet, we want to assign to those people the lowest level of human capital. For these reasons, estimating the level of human capital using other variables may produce worse results than an arbitrary ranking.

Ideally, PCA or a similar technique can be used if there is a variety of data on individuals assumed to correlate with the unmeasurable human capital, such as test scores, grades, and education. In fact, the literature on measuring intelligence often uses PCA to collapse scores along a number of dimensions into one variable (Jensen 2002). However, data of this nature are not usually available, especially in developing countries.

Financial-Productive Capital

Financial-productive capital comprises the monetary resources available to households. In developed countries this usually translates into financial assets—

Table C-5. *Financial-Productive Capital Polychoric PCA Coefficients,*
All Years Combined

Asset	Coefficient
Sewing machine: no	−0.0158
Sewing machine: yes	0.0173
Refrigerator: no	−0.3344
Refrigerator: yes	0.3133
Car: no	−0.1351
Car: yes	0.8356
Home business income: no	−0.1036
Home business income: yes	0.4999
Rental income: no	−0.1152
Rental income: yes	0.9031
Remittances: no	−0.1326
Remittances: yes	0.4779
Job vulnerability	−0.1606

such as bank holdings, stock and bond investments, and house equity—that can
be drawn on in case of need. However, few citizens of developing countries have
any of these. In this case a monetary measure is actually less useful than an asset
index because the assets are likely to be intangible and not easily quantified in
monetary terms.

The financial-productive capital asset index has three components:

—labor security, which measures the extent to which an individual has security in the use of his or her labor potential as an asset;

—transfer-rental income, which covers nonearned monetary resources; and

—productive durables, which are durable goods with an income-generating
capability.

To measure ownership of assets, the marginal extra income from obtaining
one of these items was calculated, and polychoric PCA was used to construct the
weights of financial-productive capital. (See table C-5.)

Labor security is undoubtedly the most challenging component in the index.
However, it represents an effort to include labor as an asset (omitted thus far in
the work on asset indexes) and to include employment vulnerability as linked to
stability of job status. The composite component derives from combining two
work categories on employer type and work status (International Labor Organization). These are ranked in terms of vulnerability in the Guayaquil context
through local anthropological knowledge: the most secure type of job is working
for the state, the second is as a "permanent worker" (with a formal, stable job) in

the private sector, the third is self-employment, and the least secure is contract or temporary work. The ordering of the top two job types should be uncontroversial, but the latter two require some explanation. Entrepreneurs, even on a small scale, build up business knowledge, contacts, and habits that can help sustain them through a downturn. They can continue in their business even during times of reduced demand (Moser 1981). Temporary workers, however, have less to fall back on when they are let go. Consequently, we make the judgment that the self-employed have more job security than contract workers. Unfortunately, we must still arbitrarily assign weights to each type of job: we give temporary work a 4 on the vulnerability scale and move downward to government work, which gets a weight of 1. We then aggregate up to the household level by computing the average vulnerability of each household. Although this method retains some of the arbitrariness that we have been trying to avoid, we at least manage to turn labor security into an ordinal variable that can be used for polychoric PCA.

The main sources of unearned income are remittances, government transfers, and rent. The first two are transfers of income within society and the latter is a return on capital—similar to income from physical goods as analyzed above. Nonwage income has played an increasingly important role in household income. Remittance income has risen most dramatically, linked to the explosion of Ecuadorian immigration in the late 1990s associated with dollarization and the banking crisis. As described in chapters 9 and 10, the fact that this accounted for over 50 percent of nonwage income in 2004 shows that having someone abroad is a real household asset. Remittance income constituted more than half the total income for some households. Rental income is a much smaller and more recent phenomenon as households have specifically built on extra rooms to accommodate renters, either at the back of their plots or in additional floors to their house.

Finally, productive durable goods count as financial-productive capital because they represent a current or potential income stream. In the context of Guayaquil, sewing machines, refrigerators, and cars were popular examples of this type of goods, with each predominating during different time periods. Numerous families acquired sewing machines in the 1970s. Men primarily used them in their work as tailors, either self-employed or as subcontracting outworkers. A lesser number of women had sewing machines for use both within the family and also to generate income through work as dressmakers (Moser 1981). Refrigerators are generally used as the basis of a small enterprise, for selling ice, frozen lollies, and cold soft drinks. Car ownership is a more recent phenomenon and one that requires far more capital (usually based on credit loans). Almost all local men who owned cars used them as taxis to generate an income.

Table C-6. *Community Social Capital Polychoric PCA Coefficients*

Variable	Coefficient
Does not attend church	−0.7449
Attends church	0.2744
Does not participate in community activities	−0.3511
Participates in community activities	0.3650
Does not participate in sports league	−0.4358
Participates in sports league	0.6050

While in some cases this served as a full-time occupation, in other cases it supplemented other jobs, particularly during times of high demand, such as weekend nights.

Social Capital

Social capital, the most commonly cited intangible asset, is generally defined as the rules, norms, obligations, reciprocity, and trust embedded in social relations, social structures, and societies' institutional arrangements that enable its members to achieve their individual and community objectives. The index differentiates between community-level social capital and household social capital. The latter is based on detailed panel data on changing intrahousehold structure and composition (see chapter 7). Social capital is usually considered extremely difficult for social scientists to measure because the assets are nonphysical and hard to translate into monetary terms. In the asset index framework, however, they are measured in terms of binary variables such as household participation in various activities and groups. Again it is important to note that the original study in 1978 was not designed to "measure" social capital; consequently, the groups identified do not represent the universe but are those for which comparative data are available.

This data set uses three variables to determine household social capital, as identified in table C-6, and the index was constructed using polychoric PCA. The three variables are positively correlated with each other. Participation in a sports league was the best indicator of social capital: of the twelve observations in which a household had a member participating in a sports club, only one of those did not also have someone who either went to church or participated in community activities. Not attending church was the best indicator of a lack of social capital, garnering a large negative coefficient.

Household social capital as an asset is complex because it is both positive and negative in terms of accumulation strategies. On the one hand, households act as important safety nets, protecting members during times of vulnerability, and can also create opportunities for greater income generation through effective balancing of daily reproductive and productive tasks (see Moser 1993). On the other hand, the wealth of a household may actually be reduced by having to support less productive members. Over time, households change in size and restructure their composition and headship in order to reduce vulnerabilities relating both to life cycle and wider external factors.

Household social capital was defined as the sum of three indicator variables. The first component, jointly headed households, serves to indicate trust and cohesion within the family between partners, and is applied to both nuclear and couple-headed extended households. Within many extended households there are also "hidden" female heads of household; this second component consists of unmarried female relatives raising their children within the household to share resources and responsibilities with others. The third component is the presence of other family-related households living on the plot—usually the households of sons or daughters.

Unfortunately, none of the varieties of PCA could be used here because the variables are not all positively correlated, but we wanted to give them all a positive value. PCA or a similar technique would have given at least one of the coefficients a negative value. We therefore had to give them all equal weight (or some other arbitrary weight). This is an area where more research is needed.

Asset analysis can be particularly useful when used in conjunction with income data. Figure C-3 shows the level of housing and consumer durables owned by three income groups during each time period. It demonstrates that households of all income levels started out with similar average levels of housing and consumer durables, but by 2004, even though housing levels were similar, levels of consumer durables diverged considerably. This implies that poor households place a much greater emphasis on accumulating housing than consumer durables.

These numbers are not adjusted for household size, although size is obviously a significant issue. Poorer households tend to be larger households, with greater needs for housing space and physical infrastructure. Also, larger households, *ceteris paribus,* tend to have more people working and greater total income than smaller households, although large households also tend to have lower per capita incomes than small households. This means that the larger household may have an advantage in accumulating assets and therefore look wealthier, but those assets have to be shared among a greater number of people. Some assets can be shared without diminishing their utility for any one person. A radio, for example, can be listened to by multiple people at once. Cars can be shared to some extent, but

Figure C-3. *Patterns of Housing and Consumer Durables Investment, by Income Group, 1978–2004*

Standard deviations from average

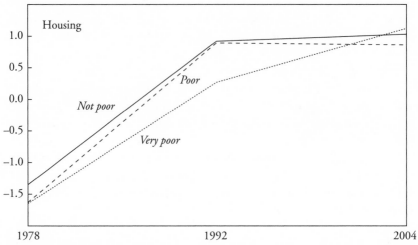

Standard deviations from average

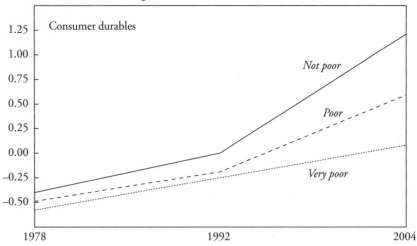

Source: Moser and Felton (2007).

Figure C-4. *Star Graphs of Household Asset Portfolios*

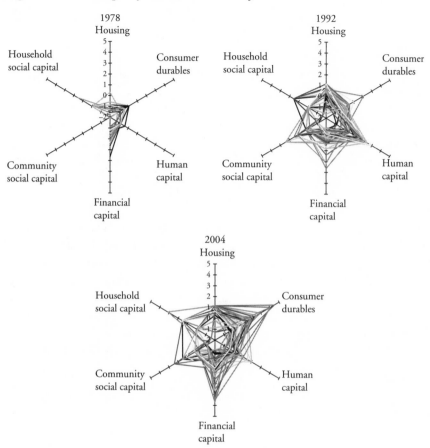

Source: Authors' calculations.

they cannot be driven by more than one person at the same time. Naturally, jobs and education are not shared. Finally, the index is not adjusted for household size because PCA techniques used to calculate the asset indexes do not have units and would therefore be unsuitable for interpreting variables on a per capita basis.

Figure C-4 uses "star graphs" to display the changing composition of household portfolios over time. Because this type of graph cannot display negative numbers, the estimated levels of assets were scaled so that the minimum score was 0 and average score was 1. The graphs display how the average portfolios increased in size and changed in shape. For example, there is a clear outward shift of financial capital and consumer durables by 2004, as well as a noticeable increase in variation.

Conclusion

Although progress has been made over the last five years in the development of asset index methodologies, a number of issues remain. For example, principal components analysis, in all its variations, still depends on whether the observed variables are positively correlated. Another unresolved issue is how best to aggregate assets from the individual level to the household level without involving arbitrary methods like summation or averaging. Similarly, there is no clear way to adjust levels of assets for household size. Finally, this is obviously not a methodology that can be immediately applied to many data sets. It requires considerable knowledge of the different variables in order to select and transform them into appropriate subjects for polychoric PCA.

Despite these constraints, existing PCA techniques contribute to the accuracy and robustness of asset accumulation analysis. The methodology described in this appendix demonstrates how grouping a large number of assets into a smaller number of dimensions facilitates an intermediate level of analysis. Use of an asset index to examine how households allocate their resources permits analysis of specific poverty mechanics without the need to examine an overwhelming quantity of individual variables. Asset indexes are an important complement to pure income data because they paint a clearer picture of the strategies households in various income groups have employed to acquire different types of assets, and as such contribute to our understanding of poverty reduction.

Notes

Prologue

1. While the surveys were undertaken between 1978 and 2004, a twenty-six-year period, my fieldwork started in 1977 and my contact with the community of Indio Guayas continues to this day, hence the disparity between the dates used in the overall study and the more specific references made to comparative survey data.

2. As Chambers argues, "The prescriptions then tend to be economic, buttressing and justifying policies of economic growth. Those who plough this furrow dig themselves into a reductionist rut. Wider and more complex realities disappear out of sight and out of mind" (2007, p. 18). As the anonymous limerick goes: "Economists have come to feel / What can't be counted can't be real / The truth is always an amount / Count numbers, only numbers count / Poverty becomes what has been measured."

3. The importance of human agency lies at the heart of a paradigm that recognizes the role of social actors. As Long clarifies, "The notion of agency attributes to the individual actor the capacity to process social experiences and to devise ways of coping with life, even under extreme forms of coercion" (1992, p. 23). Differences in identity positioning also affect perceptions of poverty. Basic elements in identify formation include gender, ethnicity, age, and race. Identity formation is not only dynamic but also geographically and historically specific (see Moser and McIlwaine 2004, p. 68).

4. For a detailed definition and further elaboration of community social capital, see chapter 2.

5. In 1950 there were 88 cities in the world with a population of more than 1 million; in 2002 there were 400, and by 2015 there will be at least 550 (United Nations Development

Program [UNPD] 2002). However, as Satterthwaite (2006) argues, the degree of urbanization depends on the definition used.

6. It was only in 2001 that the United Nations Settlements Program (UN-HABITAT) became a full-fledged United Nations program, and in 2003 that the "international community agreed on a single definition of 'slums' " (see Perlman and Sheehan 2007, p. 173).

7. See "The Oprah Winfrey Leadership Academy for Girls" (www.oprah.com).

8. See Sen (2006) for an insightful critique of Easterly (2006) as the "man without a plan," and Broad and Cavanagh (2006) for a short critique of Sachs's "misguided focus" in terms of five myths about development.

Chapter 1

1. Molyneux (2002, p. 170) defines networks as recurrent patterns of face-to-face interactions usually involving expectations of reciprocal assistance.

2. A natural experiment is a naturally occurring event or situation that can be exploited by a researcher to help answer a research question. These events or situations constitute quasi-experiments in that the experimenter has little or no control over the situation that is being observed (see Marshall 1998). The use of a natural experiment to document changes in slum communities has also been referred to in a study that measures the impact of land titling on household well-being in a slum community in Buenos Aires, Argentina. In a *Wall Street Journal* article, Matt Moffett comments, "The way San Francisco Solano (the community) was settled makes it a 'natural experiment' for testing titling's effect. 'It's a dream kind of empirical study . . . a treasure,' says Nobel Prize–winning economist Douglass C. North." See Matt Moffett, "Barrio Study Links Land Ownership to a Better Life." *Wall Street Journal,* November 9, 2005, p. A1.

3. Chapter 2 describes the differences between income and consumption poverty and also compares asset accumulation measures of well-being.

4. See chapter 4 for a definition of social capital and a discussion of its associated debates.

5. The rate of decline in industrial production was especially alarming given the 9.7 percent annual growth in industry from 1970 to 1981 (Hidrobo Estrada 1992, p. 50).

6. *People of the Barrio,* a fifty-two-minute documentary, was shown on the ATV network in the United Kingdom. Brian Moser was the producer-director while I was the consultant anthropologist. In its time the film, intended to be part of the *Disappearing World* TV series that Brian and I originated, was unique in two ways. It used subtitles, thus allowing people's voices to be heard, rather than the voices of actors, a more common practice. In the 1970s the TV industry did not think audiences would be prepared to read subtitles, which thus would lower the all-important audience rating figures. In addition, it did not include a "front man"—a popular commentator such as David Attenborough—speaking to the camera and acting as an interlocutor between the slum dwellers and U.K. audiences.

7. For further details on Lewis's concept of the "culture of poverty," see chapter 2.

8. Ena Kendall, "Into the Swamp: How a London Family Set up Home in a South American Slum," *Observer Magazine,* 1981.

9. We stayed much longer than originally anticipated due to a trade union dispute in the United Kingdom over the crew size to shoot the film. Because of this we left the community without a film in 1979. The film was subsequently made in 1980 and broadcast by Central Television in a series called *Frontiers.*

10. As the 1980 *South American Handbook* colorfully states, "Warning: Guayaquil is notorious for thieves and pickpockets, often working in pairs. Guard valuables and luggage closely" (Brooks 1980, p. 529).

11. Peter's contribution ensured the robustness of the survey techniques by assisting with the triangulation of a random sample survey, an in-depth subsample, and a community survey (Sollis and Moser 1991; Moser, Gatehouse, and Garcia 1996). See appendix A for further details on the fieldwork methodology.

12. In 1978, as a wife and mother, my responsibilities included teaching my children, cooking, and shopping, along with the anthropological fieldwork. As described in the *Observer* article, "In the morning I would wash clothes at 7.30, then teach Nathaniel and cook at the same time. By lunchtime I was absolutely flaked from cooking on kerosene and Brian used to do the washing up. But the neighbors used to laugh—'Look, Don Brian is doing the washing up'—so we had to be careful not to overstep the norms. A woman's position is very defined." See Kendall, "Into the Swamp," p. 28. Because of time limitations, I interacted intensively with my closest neighbors, developing trust and reciprocal support that were the basis for long-term friendships. Brian, in contrast, was much more spatially mobile and developed extensive rather than intensive friendships.

13. For overviews of development debates, see Booth (1994); Kothari (2005); Kothari and Minogue (2002).

14. For further elaboration of this issue, see Moser (2003).

15. See appendix A.

16. While a community case study is qualitative in terms of scale, it nevertheless provides quantitative information; this is one of the confusions. In the case of Ecuador, conclusions from the study (such as the importance of housing as an asset) were further tested in a nationwide Living Standards Measurement Survey. This provides an example of the way in which qualitative research can highlight issues whose robustness can then be tested further at a national representative level (World Bank 1995a).

17. The sensitivity surrounding the social impacts of structural adjustment was illustrated by the fact that, before publication of my World Bank study (Moser 1996), a World Bank vice president reviewed the final version. With his red pen he eliminated all mention of the word "adjustment," replacing it with the word "crisis," which was deemed more appropriate.

18. The cross-disciplinary combined methodologies research initiated by Ravi Kanbur at Cornell University is now a research program at the Center for International Studies at the University of Toronto. See "Q-Squared: Combining Qualitative and Quantitative Approaches in Poverty Analysis" (www.q-squared.ca [November 2006]).

Chapter 2

1. While some academics argue against the presentation of "yet more conceptual frameworks" (see Woolcock 2007, p. 14; Nederveen Pieterse 2000), practitioners frequently find that for operational purposes, it is useful to systematize concepts and data into a logically coherent framework.

2. This chapter draws on previously published documentation on both asset vulnerability and asset accumulation frameworks (see Moser 1998, 2007).

3. This term has evolved over time, adapted for different purposes. Thus, according to the *Shorter Oxford English Dictionary* (Oxford: Clarendon Press, 1973), assets were originally

defined as "sufficient estate or effects" (1531) and extended to "all the property a person has that may be liable for his or their debt" (1675).

4. For a review of the sustainable livelihood approach, see Moser (2008) as well as earlier work by Chambers and Conway (1992), Scoones (1998), and Carney (1998).

5. Appadurai (2004) discusses "the capacity to aspire," but the concept is reworded here to better "fit" with the other types of assets mentioned.

6. The reaffirmed commitment to poverty reduction as the World Bank's overarching operational objective was reinforced by a policy paper (World Bank 1991a), an operational directive (World Bank 1991b), and a poverty reduction handbook (1992).

7. In the field of food security and famine, a well-accepted definition of vulnerability is "an aggregate measure, for a given population or region, of the risk of exposure to food insecurity and the ability of the population to cope with the consequences of the insecurity" (Downing 1991).

8. For a detailed review of definitions of vulnerability, see Longhurst (1994, p. 17–19). In a Peruvian panel data set study, vulnerability was defined as "a dynamic concept, generally involving a sequence of events after a macro-economic shock" (Glewwe and Hall 1995, p. 3).

9. Drèze and Sen define entitlements as "the set of alternative bundles of commodities over which one person can establish . . . command." A wage laborer's entitlement is given by "what he can buy with his wages, if he does in fact manage to find employment" (1989, pp. 9–10).

10. Swift (1989, p. 13) argues that assets create a buffer between production, exchange, and consumption. Production and exchange activities create assets, and in case of need, assets can be transformed into production inputs or directly into consumption. Reducing assets increases vulnerability although this may not be visible.

11. Productive capital is defined as land, machinery, tools, animals, farm buildings, trees, wells, and the like; nonproductive capital, as jewelry, dwellings, granaries, some animals, cash, and savings; human capital, as labor power, education, and health; income, as crops, livestock, and nonfarm and nonagricultural activity; and claims, as loans, gifts, social contracts, and social security (Maxwell and Smith 1992, p. 16).

12. In urban areas, where risks and uncertainty are the consequence of lower real incomes, higher prices, and declining quantity or quality of economic and social infrastructure, two tools from the food security literature were relevant: first, the distinction between "income-raising strategies" (to acquire food) and "consumption-modifying strategies" (to restrain the depletion of food and nonfood resources [Devereux 1993, p. 57]); second, the importance of "strategy sequencing" (the sequential uptake of coping strategies), highlighted by empirical evidence demonstrating that the preservation of assets often took priority over meeting immediate food needs (De Waal 1989). This showed that households selected from a range of nutritional, economic, and social responses available to them, with sequencing being "the product of a number of complex (though largely intuitive) calculations concerning the feasibility, relative costs and expected return of each option, both immediately and for the future" (Corbett 1988). It was useful to explore, in an urban study, whether a linear sequence or "discrete stages" could be isolated, or as some rural studies show, the "the simultaneous adoption of several responses confounds this" (Devereux 1993, p. 59).

13. Thus Operational Directive 4.15 states, "The WDR 1990 showed that sustainable poverty reduction could be achieved by (a) broadly based economic growth to generate effi-

cient income-generating opportunities for the poor, and (b) improved access to education, nutrition, health care, and other social services—to improve welfare directly and to enhance the ability of the poor to take advantage of the opportunities described in (a). The approach also includes a social safety net for the poorest and most vulnerable segments of society" (World Bank 1991b, p. 1). Although originally identified as a twofold strategy with the third component, the safety net, identified as an "important complement to the basic two-part strategy" (World Bank 1990, p. 3; 1991a, p. 18), more recent references cite the approach as threefold in nature (Toye and Jackson 1996).

14. The distinction between idiosyncratic and covariant risk is between selective losses in a location (say, a household that suffers idiosyncratic shocks like noncommunicable ill-ness or frictional unemployment) and cases where all are hit at the same time (through covariant shocks like drought, flood, inflation, or financial crisis). More mechanisms are available for coping with idiosyncratic than covariant shocks. The latter can be particularly devastating, leaving households with nowhere to turn for relief. It should be remembered, however, that for poor and isolated households, even idiosyncratic shocks are difficult to cope with (Holzmann and Jorgensen 1999).

15. An earlier approach of the international development community to alleviate both rural and urban poverty was the basic needs strategy associated with redistribution with growth (see Streeten and others 1981). Promoted by Robert McNamara, it was the first World Bank policy to directly address poverty as a development concern. Despite its extensive limitations in not addressing structural causes of poverty (see Wisner 1988; Sandbrook 1982), almost fifteen years passed before James Wolfensohn, as president, refocused the World Bank on poverty reduction as the institution's priority mandate.

16. See Green (2006) for an extensive elaboration of this position.

17. Harriss (2007a, p. 17) argues that such studies have tended to highlight many of the same broad set of factors: features of households (high dependency ratio, female headship, ill health of members); assets (holding few productive assets); education (illiteracy); and nature of occupation (lack of regular waged employment among household members, whether resi-dent or working elsewhere).

18. Although consumption data are more commonly used to measure poverty, this study used income data when it became apparent from conducting longitudinal anthropological research that people's short-term recall of consumption expenditures was often inaccurate or underestimated. For instance, women buying many of their basic consumption items on a daily basis simply did not remember what they spent. Data from expenditure diaries were widely inconsistent with the expenditure data obtained from anthropological participant observation. In contrast, due to the trust established by living in the community, income panel data about formal and informal sector earnings showed a high level of compatibility across the fifty-one households and over time.

19. International Monetary Fund, "World Economic Outlook Database, September 2004" (www.imf.org/external/pubs/ft/weo/2004/02/data/index.htm).

20. Chapter 7 provides a detailed description of the ensuing changes in household structure.

21. Because income in developing countries is particularly volatile, consumer durables may in fact provide a better measure of the household's long-term income potential than any one year's income. According to the permanent income hypothesis, households make pur-chases based on expected future income as opposed to income during any one year.

22. To implement a simple version of the Carter and May approach, Andrew Felton and I estimated the probability that a household is below the poverty line using a logistic regression of the four assets—physical, financial-productive, human, and social—that have been measured in the three panel data sets. (See appendix C.)

Chapter 3

1. Housing is defined as an asset that comprises both the land and the physical structure built on it (see Rakodi 1991).

2. Although physical capital is commonly defined as comprising the stock of plant equipment, infrastructure, and other productive resources owned by individuals, businesses, and public sectors, as elaborated in chapter 2, this study uses a narrower definition that consists of housing and the range of consumer durables acquired by households.

3. This contextual background draws on Moser (1982).

4. Because of the limited area of non-swampland, Guayaquil was very compact, with its city center net density over 600 hundred people per hectare.

5. As elaborated in appendix A, the 1978 panel data of 51 household is complemented by statistical information from the 1978 universe survey of 244 households. The fact that the two data sets are highly compatible means that 1978 universe survey data provide additional information, particularly on housing. The 1978 universe survey identified that four out of five (80 percent) women and three out of four (75 percent) men were born outside Guayaquil. However, a considerable proportion had migrated with their families to the cities as children; 58 percent of women had come to Guayaquil when less than twenty years old, as had 30 percent of the men.

6. Even in Indio Guayas houses were frequently very overcrowded, with as many as six to eight adults living and sleeping in an area of less than forty square meters.

7. In cities such as Lima, which was surrounded by state-owned desert land, or Valencia (Venezuela), with large areas of low-lying municipal land, wide-scale squatting occurred. However, where the private sector or state was highly resistant to the threat of invasion, as in Mexico City, São Paulo, and Bogotá, illegal subdivisions were the only alternative strategy for the poor (Collier 1976; Gilbert and Gugler 1982).

8. In 1905 part of this land was appropriated by a Peruvian (Miguel Terencio Gutierrez) but was returned to the municipality by a 1928 supreme court decree.

9. The use of land as a source of political patronage was a well-known, widely identified phenomenon, particularly in the case of publicly owned land. Comparable experience has been documented in Lima (Collier 1976), Chile in the last years of the Frei government (Cleaves 1974), and Valencia (Gilbert 1981).

10. The extent to which these "urbanizers" exploited the poor and made large profits in a process that could not be controlled by politicians or planning authorities is widely contested (Gilbert 1981). Moore (1978, p. 201) mentions land speculators in Guayaquil "who make from 50,000 to 100,000 sucres 'selling' lots to participants," but the evidence from Indio Guayas does not bear this out.

11. See Estrada Ycaza (1977, p. 234), Acción International Técnica (1976), Junta Nacional de Planificación y Coordinación Económica (1973), Lutz (1970), and Plan Integrado para la Rehabilitación de las Areas (PREDAM) (1976).

12. National Assembly Decree 151 of July 14, 1967, stated that the contract of sale dated June 30, 1950, was between the national government (represented by the governor of the Province of Guayas) and Jose Santiago Castillo, Raid Maruri, Manuel Maria Cevallos, and Carlos Ronaldo Repeto. The amount of land sold was 13.02 hectares, at a price of 10 sucres per hectare (Saavedra and Loqui 1976, pp. 147–48).

13. Both Estrada Ycaza (1973, 1977) and Saavedra and Loqui (1976), in their analyses of decree 151, emphasize the double-edged nature of the legislation; while it required "illegally" owned land to be returned to the municipality, the municipality was then required either to sell it or give it to the moradores, with the sale dependent on whether or not it was in a shore zone (*zona de playa*).

14. In fact, the politically motivated use of the term *zona de playa* for much of the suburbio area forced the municipality to hand over much of the land without payment (Estrada Ycaza 1973, p. 24).

15. The 1978 universe survey showed that 85 percent of plots were occupied by the owner, with a further 10 percent owned by another member of the family; there was very little renting or subletting.

16. Plots laid out in this manner in Guayaquil's suburbios wasted considerable land. As MacIntosh (1972, p. 58) commented, "All the suburbio roads are at least twice as wide as is necessary and take up 40 per cent of the land." This increases the cost of infrastructure, particularly infill.

17. The panel data showed the same general trends, with 40 percent buying their plots, 55 percent invading or squatting, and the remainder acquiring plots through their family.

18. Since invasions occurred at night, one method to prevent an unoccupied house from being invaded was for a family member (generally a son) to actually sleep there, but without participating in any community activities. The large number of conflicts over ownership that arose with "house minding" arrangements meant that this method was less common.

19. See Moser (2005) for a discussion of this issue in terms of poverty and the rights of the poor

20. There was considerable variation in the extent to which households in streets lacking infill were willing to provide the necessary capital and labor time to collectively build a catwalk system. This depended a great deal upon the level of trust between neighbors, illustrated by the fact that while some streets had a communal catwalk running down the center of the street, in other streets a series of parallel catwalks ran to each house. Figure 1-1 shows how Calle K was spatially divided according to different levels of collective responsibility along the street.

21. In 1978 the small four-by-eight-meter house in which we lived on part of Marta's plot was constructed in five days by Carmen's husband Alonso and his crew, with Marta managing the process.

22. See chapter 4 for a description of the associated dispute negotiation process.

23. It is important to note that by 2004 some of the wealthier households were expanding the size of their buildings to accommodate second-generation family members or to rent out rooms. For methodological and other reasons, it has not been possible to code such data as indicators of physical capital. However, these changes are reflected in indicators of financial capital (rental income) and household social capital (numbers of families still living on the plot).

Chapter 4

1. The empirical data in this chapter draw partially on Moser (1987, 1997). See appendix B for a detailed description of the changing political and economic context in Ecuador and Guayaquil.

2. For instance, Paul (1987) identified a fivefold continuum of the objectives of community participation, ranging from empowerment to building beneficiary capacity, increasing project effectiveness, improving project efficiency, and, finally, cost sharing.

3. The fact that residential-level struggles were seen as inherently weaker than those associated with production was said to relate to the fact that issues of collective consumption did not necessarily coincide with class interests or antagonisms. Saunders (1981, p. 275) argues that urban politics have their own specificity, with no requisite relationship to class politics.

4. Bebbington and Bebbington (2001) propose that a minimum distinction should be made between formal civil society organizations, such as NGOs, and informal ones, such as social movements and community and grassroots organizations (see also McIlwaine 1998). By the 1990s other more political forms of mobilization in Latin America had developed, linked to identity agendas associated with indigenous, Afro-Latin American, and women's rights (Eckstein 2001).

5. For histories and varying uses of the concept, see Woolcock (1998); for descriptions of its adoption by the World Bank, see Bebbington and others (2006) and McNeill (2004); and for fundamental critiques, see Fine (1999, 2001) and Harriss (2007b).

6. Recognition of the negative dimensions or "dark side" of social capital (Putzel 1997; Portes 1998) contrasts with the work of Putnam (1993) and Fukuyama (1995), both of whom have tended to assume that social capital is not just a "public good" (that is, a by-product of social and economic activity) but "for the public good" (Putzel 1997, p. 941). Not only do some individuals have a greater endowment of social capital than others, but they may also have more access to instrumental sources (reciprocity exchanges). This can imply the "exclusion of outsiders, excess claims on group's members, restriction on individual freedoms, and downward leveling of norms" (Portes 1998, p. 15).

7. See chapter 11.

8. See Moser and Peake (1996) for a literature review of women's urban struggles and community management. See also Alvarez (1990), Jelin (1990), and Massolo (1992) for accounts of women and Latin American social movements.

9. It is important to note that the original study in 1978 was not designed to "measure" social capital; consequently, the groups identified only represent those for which comparative data are available.

10. Female consciousness could be considered a politicized version of *marianismo*, or feminine spiritual superiority, though it is more useful to see such consciousness as something learned through political mobilization around issues associated with nurturing (Craske 1999). Kaplan (1982, p. 545) has described historically this connection between motherhood and political action through the networks of everyday life. See chapter 8 for a fuller discussion of gender roles.

11. The committee was finally registered as a legal entity (known as *vida juridica*) with the municipal authorities on August 31, 1979.

12. By the mid-1980s, as a result of the reputation of women presidents such as Marta, younger women were founding their own committees, many under Marta's guidance.

13. For instance, Don Valdez, president of the neighboring committee, was an official in the local fire service union, while Umberto, a local shopkeeper and member of the Indio Guayas committee, had previously been active in union work in a banana-packing company at the Guayaquil docks.

14. Personal communication, December 1978, Guayaquil.

15. In the 1970s this was a widespread phenomenon in Latin American cities, described by researchers such as Cornelius (1973), Portes and Walton (1976), and Nelson (1979).

16. In 1977 the Frente de Lucha Suburbana split in two; while the Frente was co-opted by the ID, the other entity, the Organizaciones Barriales Asociadas del Ecuador (Organization of Ecuadorian Neighborhoods), also supported a newly formed left-wing party.

17. *El Universo* (Guayaquil), December 6, 1977.

18. The politicoeconomic interests associated with infill were illustrated by an earlier decision not to implement the recommendations of a USAID-financed technical study of the flooding problem undertaken in 1966–67 (Junta Nacional de Planificación 1967). The study conclusively showed that building dikes was a better method of flood control than infill, and proposed that levees be constructed around the land to the south and southwest of the city. Estimates showed that filling in the land would cost nine times as much as the levee scheme. The decision not to implement this scheme apparently was made for political reasons. As MacIntosh (1972, p. 57) has argued, "Firstly, it required a long-term outlook by the implementing agency, which the general political instability of Ecuador does not engender. The average national president is in office for only 28 months and the average mayor of Guayaquil for only 6 months (1950–65). Secondly, dyking would be impartially beneficial to all squatters whereas the method of fill allows each political regime to aid only those neighborhoods that support it."

19. Table 5-1 in chapter 5 itemizes the principal social and physical infrastructure obtained between 1978 and 2004.

20. See Swyngedouw (2004) for an extensive analysis of the politics of water in Guayaquil.

21. Each tanker held fifty-five cubic meters of water and sold it at 5 sucres per barrel. "The water in Guayaquil costs 2 sucres per cubic meter for the rich, while its price in the suburbios is 16 sucres per cubic meter." *Diario el Expreso* (Guayaquil), March 14, 1976, p. 5 (see PREDAM 1976, p. 56).

22. Indeed, wealthier households often returned to purchasing drinking water from street vendors (perceived as being purer in quality). In addition, such households were able to invest in water pumps to deal with supply interruptions caused by low water pressure during certain times of day and seasons.

23. Linking social capital has the potential to cause discord, although to date this has been observed mainly on ethnic grounds (Portes and Landolt, 2000; Kyle 1999). In this typology, a third type of social capital, "bonding social capital," is defined as "strong ties among relatives, neighbors and close friends" (World Bank 2000, p. 128), which is very similar to household social capital (see chapter 7).

Chapter 5

1. Three miles from Indio Guayas was the Hospital de Guayaquil, a 240-bed facility built incrementally between 1960 and 1978 with USAID grant support. Its maintenance and

operations budgets were inadequate; incubators lay unutilized for lack of spare parts, and elevators did not work. Although it owned its own electricity generator until 1992, it did not have running water, depending on tank-delivered supplies. A ten-minute bus ride from Indio Guayas was the Mariana de Jesus Maternity Hospital and health center, established in 1967, which targeted pregnant and lactating women and children under five. It lacked electricity but had running water. Finally, the Atahualpa Clinic, built in 1979 on infilled land on the other side of Calle 25, provided mother-child services but was underutilized as the area was considered very dangerous by those living outside the immediate locality. See Peter Sollis (1992). As of 1985, in the sixteen areas that constituted the city's entire suburbios, there were only ten health subcenters, one health post, one health center, and one hospital–health center with a combined capacity to attend to only 76,500 people. This meant that 500,000 people— nearly half the population of Guayaquil—were "not covered by the formal health system" (UNICEF 1985a, p. 5).

2. Insecticide spraying could not eradicate disease-carrying mosquitoes. Although, as advised, people covered their water barrels, they had not completed the infill of their patios (some were still totally under water while others were inundated during the rainy season), which defeated the purpose.

3. Descriptive information on the UNICEF PHC project draws on Moser and Sollis (1991).

4. UNICEF saw urban basic services as the best delivery mechanism to the most vulnerable groups in marginal urban areas, namely, pregnant and lactating women and young children. Its objective was "to support the initiation and development of social programs benefiting children and women to the point where there is a national approach and broad-based capacity to expand delivery of community-based services in low-income areas" (UNICEF 1984, p. 2).

5. The technical and financial agreement to set up a PHC program in the suburbios was signed between UNICEF and the Ministry of Public Health in 1980, and was renewed in 1983 until 1985.

6. The frequent use of *negociar* (to negotiate) in project documents rather than *consultar* (to consult) or *discutir* (to discuss) suggests that a negotiation process was considered necessary to persuade skeptical communities of the program's importance (UNICEF 1985b).

7. During the first year of implementation, the UNICEF PHC project director was replaced four times (Luzuriaga and Valentine 1988).

8. In the late 1980s, Rodrigo Borja's government, in response to the public sector health care cutbacks, pioneered a new national-level social policy, the Frente Social, designed to implement cross-sector collaboration between the Ministries of Education, Health, and Social Welfare. One component to provide local primary health care was the targeted Salud Familiar Integral Comunitaria (SAFIC) community health program established in 1989. At the local level, through a Community Network (Red Comunitaria), it established two health care centers in a targeted forty-block area and used the Indio Guayas community center facilities, as well as those in Don Valdez's community, for doctors, dentists, and obstetricians to hold afternoon clinics. But again, this was a short-lived initiative, terminated for lack of resources after the change in government in 1994.

9. The thirty women surveyed had a mean of 1.35 children in a hogar comunitario; nine of the thirty had placed two or three children in child care.

10. Two journalists, concerned about the plight of abandoned orphaned children, devised a war orphan program, Plan de Padrinos (godfathers), in which orphans were to be "adopted" by their friends as "godsons" (*ahijados*). By the Second World War, the Foster Parents Plan, as it was called by then, broadened its scope to include orphans in war-torn Europe and later Korea. By the 1960s, it had expanded its mission to include children in marginalized poor communities in Latin America, Asia, and Africa (Plan International Ecuador 1985).

11. In the 1990s, for instance, 38 percent of funding came from Holland (Burgwal 1995, p. 56).

12. The children, identified as godsons or goddaughters, wrote letters to godparents abroad in return for cash payments made to their mothers by supervising social workers. At the time it was widely rumored that the program was linked to fertility control; children on the program were dropped if their mothers then had more children.

13. The information on Plan International was obtained from interviews with a number of its staff, including Henry Beder, director; Amarylis Zambrano, head of social promotion; and the social promoters, as well as from community members and participant observation.

14. A staff of 114 worked there, with suboffices working in other low-income areas. By 1988 it was supporting sixty-eight committees in Cisne Uno and Cisne Dos, including Indio Guayas.

15. Amarylis Zambrano, interview, Guayaquil, 1988.

16. To accompany this process, the Ministry of Education organized a "Concourse of Local Histories," in which barrio communities were encouraged to produce written histories. Marta, her daughter Adriana, and other committee members wrote the document on Indio Guayas (Committee Indio Guayas 1986).

17. Interestingly, Plan, like the community leaders, saw the evangelical church as divisive to community participation. As a Plan official commented, "They have an ideology of elitism and are only interested in their own members, and consequently collaborative projects with them have been disastrous for this reason."

18. In changing focus, Plan got rid of the "army of social workers" and gave voluntary "collaborating mothers" (*madres colaboradores*) the responsibility for collecting godchildren's letters for godparents in the United States or Europe. This was a less reliable method, with Marta as president often organizing the biannual process, at Plan's insistence.

19. Interview with author, Guayaquil, August 1988.

20. While the quota in Indio Guayas was 20 sucres a week, in Valdez's committee it was 50 sucres. Women working or otherwise unable to attend would try to get friends to pay for them; this was not a permanent solution as their nonattendance was soon noted by community leaders, and so it was only allowed in emergencies.

21. By the late 1980s, Plan was not the only institution with programs in Cisne Dos. One of the initiatives introduced by Rodrigo Borja's Frente Social between 1988 and 1992, under the Ministry of Social Welfare and Health, was the Asociación de Organizaciones Populares Pro Defensa de los Programas no Convencionales, which covered six areas in Guayaquil. It aimed to implement community-level education and health improvement projects. This short-lived initiative once again called on the Frente to provide the committee, and because of their expertise, Guillermo Contreras was elected as vice president and Marta Perez as *prosecretaria*. While a detailed description of the program is beyond the scope of this chapter, it is noteworthy that this initiative added more "voluntary" work for overstretched local community leaders.

22. During the 1990s Plan, along with government agencies and NGOs, introduced a range of adult education and vocational courses. In 1992, for instance, there were nineteen courses provided, ranging from dressmaking to accounting, twelve of which were managed by Plan. Despite this inundation of courses, problems abounded; useful courses were generally far too short (usually only three months) to produce any real proficiency, and those targeted at women focused on increasing nutritional or homemaking skills rather than improving their income-earning capacity.

23. The Hospice International health center was established in 1978 and run by a Mill Hill missionary, Father Frank Smith, a Catholic priest from Manchester, U.K. Located a fifteen-minute walk from Calle K, it was used by Lidia, Mercedes, Carmen, and Sofia for minor health problems. It charged nominal consultation fees, ran health talks, and also helped families in emergencies. By the mid-1990s it assessed that the area was adequately serviced by the public sector and moved to Isla Trinitaria, a more recently invaded marginal area with less access to public services, where it continues its mission to this day.

24. The Iglesia Evangélica Huerto de Olivos, located on Calle K ten houses from Marta's home, was established in 1977 with support from U.S. parishioners and provided a modest range of welfare services. Their policy of only helping members and not supporting the Indio Guayas committee meant it was considered a divisive institution by most in the community.

25. Sollis (1992).

26. A well-known midwife in Indio Guayas was also renowned throughout Guayaquil for her hemorrhoids treatment; women from the elite side of town visited her secretly in the barrio.

27. In 1992, of the nine preschools (two located outside the community), five were community schools and four were private; of the nineteen primary schools (three located outside), ten were state schools and nine were private; and of the eleven secondary schools (five located outside), five were state schools and six were private.

28. To fund this investment, the municipality added a 15 percent surcharge on electricity bills paid to the local electricity company. Thus households with legal electricity connections subsidized garbage collection, both for those free riding with illegal connections as well as those without electricity.

29. In 1992 public health care facilities were free or at very low charge, but consultation at a public hospital was estimated to have an indirect cost between 2,600 and 3,100 sucres. In contrast, private practitioner costs were significantly higher, at 5,560 sucres for children and 9,680 sucres for adults. See Sollis (1992).

30. Ibid.

31. For instance, Marta's husband, Jesus, fought an eight-year battle against diabetes, enduring gangrene and amputated limbs before finally succumbing to the disease.

32. In 1992, 56 percent of very poor households used public health facilities, compared with 43 percent of poor households, and 27 percent of nonpoor households.

33. There were 1.03 students per nonpoor household compared to 1.86 and 2.42 for the poor and very poor, respectively. In 1992, for instance, 58 percent of nonpoor households used public education, compared with 81 percent and 86 percent of poor and very poor households, respectively.

34. Although the study contains detailed information on health status, particularly in terms of shocks arising from serious illnesses or accidents, as well as the use and cost of health

services, the lack of methodology to translate these into a health asset index means that the information remains at the narrative level.

35. By 1992 the original generation of settlers had reached middle age and most had school-age children. By 2004 many of the second-generation children had finished school and moved out on their own.

36. The data are adjusted for household income because wealthier households may be able to afford more consumer durables *and* educate their children better. The amount spent on children's education is not calculated on a per capita basis but rather represents the total investment that households made in their children's human capital; this parallels the treatment of consumer durables ownership, which is also not evaluated on a per capita basis.

Chapter 6

1. Claudio chose to look for clients in Manabí, not just because trained dentists did not go to this remote rural area but also because Mercedes' social network of relatives there provided him with the entry point for steady work, both from tooth extractions and making false teeth.

2. As its name implies, the casualization of labor refers to the shift from permanent jobs, associated with job security, wages, benefits, and often trade union membership, to nonpermanent, more casual labor arrangements that lack the characteristics of permanent jobs (see Moser 1987; Elson 1991).

3. Following the International Labor Organization definition, the "informal sector" refers to the self-employed and enterprises of five or fewer workers. In a dualist definition, the "formal sector" refers to enterprises of six or more workers (Moser 1997).

4. Because sixteen is the legal minimum age for wage employment in Ecuador, adults were defined as those aged sixteen years and over.

5. The unemployed category also included some housewives who were looking for work. Economically inactive housewives were those who devoted all their time to reproductive work and who were not looking for paid employment.

6. See Victor Aguiar, "El mercado laboral ecuatoriano: Propuesta de una reforma," electronic edition, 2007 (www.eumed.net/libros/2007a/240/). According to the Instituto Latinoamericano de Investigaciones Sociales (ILDIS), unemployment went up from an average of 4 percent throughout the 1970s (3.2 percent for the three main cities [Cuenca, Quito, and Guayaquil] in 1978) to between 8 percent and 15 percent in the 1980s and 1990s (8.4 percent in 1994 for the three main cities), while underemployment rose from an average of 26 percent in the 1970s (29.8 percent for the three main cities in 1978) to 54 percent by 1991. ILDIS–Fundación Friedrich Ebert, "Economía ecuatoriana en cifras, 1970–2006" (www.ildis.org.ec/old/estadisticas/estadisticas.htm). The World Bank data calculated unemployment at 11.5 percent in 1998 and 14.4 percent in 1999 (World Bank 2004).

7. Urban unemployment rates fell from 14.1 percent in 2000 to 8.6 percent in 2002, thus recovering to precrisis levels, while migration abroad also helped to ease the pressures on the rigid labor market. See Aguiar, "El mercado laboral ecuatoriano." Between 1996 and 2001, the equivalent of 8.3 percent of the economically active population emigrated (Acosta 2006). By 2003 the urban unemployment rate increased again to 9.8 percent, and to 11.1 percent in 2004, while underemployment stood at around 56.4 percent (World Bank 2004).

The formal unemployment rate in Guayaquil was around 7 percent in the first half of the 1990s, reached 17.1 percent in 1999 at the height of the crisis, and had fallen to 9.5 percent in 2005, still above precrisis levels. Sistema Integrado de Indicadores Sociales del Ecuador (SIISE), "Desempleo en el Ecuador," Boletín 8 (www.siise.gov.ec/Publicaciones/INDICE8. pdf).

8. SIISE, "Desempleo en el Ecuador."

9. In 1997 the female labor force participation rate was only 43.3 percent (versus 71.1 percent for males), but their unemployment rate was 12.4 percent (versus 6.6 percent for males; World Bank 2004). While women's participation rates increased to 46.2 percent in 1998 and 48 percent in 1999, their unemployment rates rose to 15.5 percent and 19.2 percent, respectively (versus 7.8 percent and 10.2 percent for men, respectively). Even in 2004 after economic recovery, unemployment rates for women were still double that for men (10.8 percent for women versus 5.8 percent for men [World Bank 2004]). Unemployment among women has affected the young, those with medium education levels, and those from poor areas. See SIISE, "Desempleo en el Ecuador."

In 1997, before the crisis, the informal employment rate (informality) for females was 58.8 percent (for males, 49.7 percent), while the female underemployment rate was 13.5 percent (for males, 7.2 percent). Female informal employment rose to 63.2 percent in 1998 (52.6 percent for males), and the underemployment rate rose to 21.3 percent in 1999 (12.2 percent for males). By 2002 the rate for female informality had only declined to 62.1 percent (52.5 percent for males) while the underemployment rate had dropped to 19.6 percent (11.3 percent for males). See World Bank (2004).

10. Aguiar, "El mercado laboral ecuatoriano."

11. The historical subsistence "family wage" is defined as a single wage sufficient to maintain a working-class family at a certain standard of living (see Himmelweit and Mohun 1977).

12. The Standard Industrial Classification (SIC) is a U.S. government system for classifying industries by a four-digit code. See U.S. Census Bureau, "North American Industry Classification System (NAICS)" (www.census.gov/eos/www/naics/).

13. Growth in the manufacturing sector declined from 10.5 percent during the period 1970–80 to 0.2 percent during the 1980–92 period. While average annual growth in the service sector also declined, from 9.4 percent during the period 1970–80 to 2.3 percent during 1980–92 (World Bank 1995a, p. 164), it nevertheless contributed most to GDP, accounting for more than 47 percent in 1990 (Floro and Acosta 1993, p. 2).

14. In Latin America the popular conception of the domestic servant was of a young, rurally born migrant, "integrating" into the city, dressed in uniform, living in a middle-class household, and utilizing this as an opportunity for upward mobility within the wide spectrum of the working class. In her research on Lima, Peru, Smith (1973) defined domestic service as a "bridging occupation," a transitory rather than lifetime career; a young girl worked seven years on average before dropping out of the labor market to run her own household and raise her children (p. 203). While Smith's evidence showed that after a certain stage women devoted themselves to their children, it failed to identify the later stages in the life cycles of ex-domestic servants.

15. However, these are by no means all rural migrants using the work experience in domestic service to "integrate" into the city. In the barrio-level sample, 50 percent of domestic servants were urban born.

16. In the construction sector, regardless of the contractual nature of the work, such jobs only occurred during the dry season, with a slack period occurring during the wet season.

17. The fact that upper-income households with washing machines still employed washerwomen for all laundry except bed linens—maintaining that a washing machine ruined personal clothing—indicated the state of the labor market and the concentration of income in the city.

18. ILDIS, "Economía ecuatoriana en cifras, 1970–2006."

19. From the late 1970s to the early 1990s, urban unemployment levels remained fairly constant, with a slight decline between 1987 and 1990; unemployment was concentrated in the three largest centers of Quito, Guayaquil, and Cuenca (Floro and Acosta 1993, p. 13).

20. The 1992 Indio Guayas survey sample also showed that more than 40 percent of men (42.2 percent) and women (45.9 percent) were self-employed (Moser 1997, p. 34).

21. The Indio Guayas sample survey data showed that in 1992, women in poor households contributed more than half of the total monthly income, while in nonpoor households, they provided only one-third (Moser 1997, p. 29).

22. In 1978 Alonso's construction gang built the four- by eight-meter bamboo-walled house for my family on part of Marta's plot.

23. The fact that in 2004, 37.3 percent of households had at least once member abroad suggests that a small number of the emigrants were not sending remittances.

Chapter 7

1. While the family is a social unit based on kinship, marriage, and parenthood, the household is a residential unit based on coresidence for such purposes as production, reproduction, consumption, and socialization. It is easy to conflate the two since many assumptions about the nature of intrahousehold relations are based on marital and parental relationships. In this chapter I have attempted to avoid this, referring to familial relationships in terms of the family, while using the household, now the preferred unit of analysis for census and statistical purposes, as the spatial unit for survey data (see Moser 1993, pp. 19–20).

2. Becker (1965) combined arguments about the economic rationality of household behavior with neoclassical theory of the firm to develop what was termed new household economics, in which a complex array of relationships and exchanges within households was collapsed into a function similar to that of an individual decisionmaker. Models based on new household economics identified the household rather than the individual as the most relevant unit of "utility maximization" (Evans 1989; Moser 1993).

3. In her work in urban Mexico, de la Rocha defines the household as a domestic unit subject to changes influenced by the domestic cycle, with the three-stage analytical constructions derived from observation of repetitive, measureable aspects of domestic life. She defines these as expansion, when the domestic unit increases its number through the birth of new members; consolidation, when the unit has the capability of being more economically balanced; and dispersion, when members of the household separate, with associated economic implications (de la Rocha 1994, pp. 24–25). The model, as such, does not include external structural changes; equally, given the complexity of the final stage, contraction, rather than dispersion, is a more applicable term.

4. Marital conflict illustrates the overlap between internal and external factors in that most incidents of discord between partners arose in connection with male unemployment or the pressures of trying to make ends meet within households (Beneria 1991, pp. 177–78; Chant 1991, p. 216).

5. A nuclear household comprises a couple living with their children. An extended household comprises a single adult or couple living with their own children and other related adults or children. A female-headed household comprises a single-parent nuclear or extended household headed by a woman; if married, the woman identifies herself as the head usually because her husband is not the main income earner.

6. The phenomenon has also been termed elsewhere as submerged, embedded, or disguised heads or as subfamilies in Latin America and elsewhere. See Bradshaw (1995) on Honduras; Buvinic and others (1992) on Chile; Chant and McIlwaine (1995) on the Philippines; and Varley (1993) on Mexico.

7. A woman is counted as a hidden head of household if she lives on the family plot, is unmarried, and has at least one child.

8. In an earlier analysis, I referred to women who reached the point when they simply opted out of domestic responsibilities as "burnt out" (Moser 1992).

9. It is necessary to recall that in the panel survey data there was no a priori definition of household social capital as such. The construction of components at the data analysis stage was influenced by the availability of comparable data from all three surveys.

10. The difference between 1978 and 1992 is not statistically significant; however, the 1992–2004 difference is statistically significant at the 1 percent level.

11. This section draws on Moser and Felton (2009).

12. Male-headed households can also be called couple- or jointly headed households. However, in this analysis, I follow local perceptions of headship in which any household with an adult male partner or husband was considered to have a male head of household. There were one or two exceptions, such as when women were the primary income earners and considered the head. Otherwise, in all households deemed to be headed by women, there was no male partner.

13. A positive or negative score does not mean anything in itself; it is simply relative to the average for the entire data set.

Chapter 8

1. Jackson (2007) argues that the intersections between the separate and shared well-being and interests of members, which include both conflict and cooperation, are critical to the workings of gender. These gender relations have become muted partly because of the "domination of these research organizations by economists for whom gender disaggregation and comparison is methodologically more tractable than researching the relational significance of gender. Analyzing behaviors in ways that take account of social relations is a complex matter" (Jackson, 2007, p. 109).

2. Deere, Doss, and Grown (2007) identify five reasons for the importance of gender-disaggregated asset data. First, household data may not be equivalent to the welfare of the individuals within it (Sen 1990). Second, men and women use income in different ways (Haddad, Hoddinott, and Alderman 1997) and may also use wealth in different ways, with associated impacts on well-being. Third, individual asset ownership also relates to empower-

ment arising from land ownership (Agarwal 1994). Fourth, household dissolution, whether due to divorce, separation, abandonment, migration, or death, is increasingly common and in many countries is associated with female poverty. Finally, in modern legal systems, property rights are often granted to individuals, not to households. Consequently, analysis of "household wealth" ignores fundamental issues governing individual property rights.

3. One of the best definitions from Stevens (1973, p. 90) states, "If the chief characteristics of machismo, the cult of virility, are exaggerated aggressiveness and intransigence in male-to-male interpersonal relationships, and arrogance and sexual aggression in male-to-female relationships, then marianismo is the cult of feminine spiritual superiority, which teaches that women are morally superior and spiritually stronger than men."

4. Linked to this are lower fertility levels, higher numbers of female-headed households, and increased participation of women in the labor force. Brígida García and Olga Rojas, "Las uniones conyugales en América Latina: Transformaciones en un marco de desigualdad social y de género" (www.eclac.org/publicaciones/xml/9/22069/lcg2229-p3.pdf). Divorce presents a major conundrum for Latin American women: on the one hand, it is deemed crucial for women's autonomy; on the other, women are generally left worse off after divorce, particularly in more conservative social groupings where the status of divorcée is perceived as problematic (Ariza and de Oliveira 2001, p. 33).

5. Whitehead defined the conjugal contract as "the terms on which husbands and wives exchange goods, income, and services including labor, within the household" (1984, p. 83). Her work also focused on the complex dependencies and interdependencies in marriage, women's incentives from household consumption, and the support and affinity of shared interests that confound analysis of women's interests as only separate and individual (Whitehead 1984).

6. As Cornwall reflects, "Get women into groups, the development mantra goes, and they will be transformed into social, economic and political actors. Get women into parliament and they will represent women's interests. Give women access to independent incomes, and they will be freed from dependency on men. . . . These representations might be usefully characterized as myths, as much for the work they do as their actual narrative content" (2007, pp. 150–51). In reality there is an instrumentality about many women's groups that relates to transactions rather than solidarity, best epitomized when men are brought in to administer the financial resources.

7. "Comadre" is a Spanish term identifying the co-mother relationship between two women (or men as compadre) when one is godmother to the child of the other. This culturally institutionalized relationship is taken very seriously.

8. The role of perception is critical in determining intrahousehold inequalities, particularly in relation to control of different aspects of income flows or spending patterns (Sen 1990).

9. Data from a 1992 subsample confirmed this, showing that 80 percent and 64 percent of women had control over food and clothing purchases, respectively.

10. Data on women's fertility histories show that earlier decisions to use the pill or an IUD frequently had been made without the consent of the husbands, who were unaware that their wives were using any birth control.

11. Subsample data showed that 84 percent of pregnancies resulted in live births. Another 5 percent of pregnancies resulted in babies who died at birth or within the first year. The remainder ended in spontaneous (8 percent) or induced (3 percent) abortions.

12. In 1988 one resourceful woman whose husband would not give permission persuaded the hospital to accept instead the written permission of her mother and brother, arguing that the two together were equal to her husband (Moser 1992, p. 115).

13. The twelve intrahousehold activities given numerical weightings were cooking breakfast, cleaning the house, washing clothes, buying food, cooking the midday meal, cooking the evening meal, looking after domestic animals, taking children to school, fetching water, fetching fuel, house maintenance, and disposing of garbage. Child care was calculated separately.

14. The ten community activities identified were participation in the Catholic church, evangelical church, women's group, community group, parent teacher association, trade union, political party, youth group, sports club, and Plan International.

15. Subsample data showed that in a typical week, female heads and spouses were awake and active longer than their male counterparts. In the thirty-two households with both male and female partners present, women slept on average 6.6 hours a night while men slept 7.9 hours. More than two in five women got up earlier than their husbands and went to bed later. Rest patterns also varied by gender; most men (96 percent) acknowledged taking rest time after work, while just over half of women (54 percent) who stayed home took a rest period after lunch, when they watched television while simultaneously caring for children, ironing, sewing, or preparing food. Women rarely rested in the evening because they were busy with household chores, especially if involved in paid work during the day. The data also showed functional and spatial dimensions; females were primarily responsible for tasks inside the house (laundry, cooking, and cleaning) while males did a limited number of tasks outside the house (shopping and fetching water). See Moser (1997).

16. The triple role was defined as follows: The reproductive role was defined as the childbearing and child-rearing responsibilities and domestic tasks carried out mainly by women to guarantee the maintenance and reproduction of the labor force. The productive role was defined as work done by both men and women for cash or kind, including both market and home or subsistence production. The community-managing role related to work undertaken primarily by women at the community level to ensure the provision and maintenance of such collective goods as water, health care, and education. In contrast, a community politics role involved formal political organizing undertaken primarily by men at the community level. See Moser (1989b, 1993).

17. The concept of "gender planning" was developed in the 1980s to make policymakers aware of gender as a new and important development issue. It has since been critiqued as "technifying" and "depoliticizing" the complex politics of gender relations. Despite the significant limitations of this concept, no widespread new operational gender planning framework has since been developed, and it has been superseded by a more complex analysis that identifies gender in terms of social relations rather than as a focus on women and men as separate categories (Jackson 2007; Kabeer 1994; Cornwall 2003).

18. The excessive drinking habits of some men were defined as alcoholism by family and friends rather than by medical practitioners.

19. Depression was self-defined by the women rather than by medical practitioners.

Chapter 9

1. Elder (1998) identifies life course theory as a framework for relating social pathways to history and development trajectories. He argues that this goes beyond life cycle to encom-

pass a sequence of social roles associated with stages of parenthood, from the birth of children to their departure from the household and then their eventual transition to the role of parent, setting in motion another pathway. Life course theory provides a way to study the myriad changes that affect children in today's world; it connects changing environments with changing behavior. Its focus is the real world where people work out their paths of development as best they can, and it illuminates how lives are lived within biological and historical contexts.

2. This was calculated in constant terms based on year 2000 U.S. dollars.

3. Employment sector data were complemented by employment security data. These, in turn, were linked to income stability, one of the asset index categories.

4. When disaggregated by poverty level, 16.7 percent of very poor households relied on remittance support versus 5.6 percent of nonpoor households.

5. The focus group participants all lived locally and in some cases were related. All but one younger girl had completed high school. The group constituted a broad ethnic mix, including mestizos (from Guayaquil), serranos (family from the highlands), and Afro-Ecuadorians.

6. There were ten participants in the male youth focus group, ranging in age from fourteen to twenty-three years (average age, seventeen and a half). Three were studying at the university or polytechnic institute; the average education of the rest was just under four years of secondary school.

7. Half of the second-generation panel data households still lived on their parents' plots, with one in five (21 percent) living "apart" in a separate physical structure on the plot. Another 14 percent of the second generation lived off the family plot but still in the same area of Indio Guayas, mainly living on their in-laws' plot.

8. Sylvia's house burned down when she had left her four young sons locked inside on their own—a common last-resort child care strategy of single mothers. One of the children purportedly was playing with matches, and because the walls of the house were made of split cane, the whole house and all its possessions quickly caught fire. Neighbors who noticed the fire were unable to enter the house because the front door was locked. They climbed over the wall to rescue her children. Her seven-year-old son was so badly traumatized that he was unable to do schoolwork, and Sylvia had to consult the school psychologist to try to help him cope.

9. It was difficult for Alicia's daughters to analyze why their parents split up. They did not automatically blame their father but commented that their mother was "strong" and "very angry," and that the breakdown of the relationship was essentially the result of their both having a strong character.

10. Of the six participants in the girls' focus group, only three actually lived with their parents. All the others lived with grandparents, with the middle generation missing.

Chapter 10

1. Whereas in 1993 remittances represented only 1.3 percent of GNP, by 1999 they constituted 6.5 percent, and by 2000, 8.3 percent. They then declined to 6.7 percent and 5.9 percent of GNP in 2001 and 2002, respectively (Acosta, López, and Villamar 2004).

2. According to Orozco (2007, p. 227), a migrant's economic linkages to the home country include four practices: family remittance transfers; demands for services such as telecommunication, consumer goods, or travel; capital investments; and charitable dona-

tions to philanthropic organizations raising funds for the migrant's home community. Orozco includes "intangible" transfers, such as the transfer of knowledge, support to communities, and other exchanges under the general heading of social capital within the category of goods and services.

3. See, for instance, Jokisch and Pribilsky (2002); Acosta, López, and Villamar (2004); ILDIS/FES and others (2003).

4. A few young, unmarried women came for economic or educational reasons, as was the case with Douglas's two younger sisters. Yet behind this was personal trauma resulting from violence. Douglas's younger sister had been attacked at a party, and her mother's motive was to get her out of Guayaquil as fast as possible. Her older sister was required to accompany her.

5. See Camacho and Hernández (2005) for the United Nations Development Fund for Women study of families left behind in Ecuador and their perceptions of their migrant relatives.

6. The average gross earnings for the fifteen men interviewed in Barcelona were $1,226 a month.

7. The migrants from Indio Guayas, Ecuador, did not use the term *remesa* (remittance) but rather referred to *envio* (something sent) or *ayuda* (help).

Chapter 11

1. In using a specific incidence as the basis for discussing broader structural issues, this chapter adapts the anthropological methodology of "situational analysis." This type of case study approach is intended to show how "actual observed behaviour fits into the structural frame" (van Velsen 1967, p. xxv) and through the exposition and analysis of a series of concrete social situations, it aims to highlight the variability and flexibility inherent in any social situation (Long 1968, p. 8).

2. The data in this section come from the 1992 random sample survey subsample (see Moser 1997).

3. I personally witnessed such an attack while traveling on a microbus between two local neighborhoods one Sunday afternoon in 1992. Fortunately Virginia, Marta's sister, had cautioned me to remove my modest earrings, and hiding low in my seat, I escaped notice as three young men with machetes rapidly stole watches, wallets, handbags, and jewelry from accessible passengers. Probably the most disturbing aspect, aside from the fear, was the sense of total disempowerment experienced by men taking their wives and children on a local Sunday outing.

4. Appendix B provides a more detailed profile of the three different types of gangs and describes at greater length the problems of crime, violence, and gangs in Guayaquil.

5. For a discussion on the difference between structural causes and trigger risk factors, see Moser and Moser (2003).

6. By 2004, while basic wages were U.S.$120 a month, a taxi back from town (essential to avoid being robbed after shopping) cost U.S.$3 a ride.

7. This categorization was developed in research on urban violence and insecurity in Colombia and Guatemala, undertaken with Cathy McIlwaine (Moser and McIlwaine 2004), in which the categories of productive and perverse social capital were adapted from the work of Rubio (1997). He defined "productive" social capital as that which may generate institutional change and favor growth. In turn, "perverse" social capital referred to networks and to

the legal and reward systems that encourage rent-seeking behavior and criminal activity. While the concept was not fully developed, Rubio alluded to the fact that criminal activities might have sophisticated organizational structures that provided more viable alternatives to legitimate or "productive" activities, particularly for youth.

Chapter 12

1. Inter-American Development Bank, "Guyana. Second Low Income Settlement Program GY-L1019. Loan Proposal, 2008" (http://idbdocs.iadb.org/wsdocs/getdocument. aspx?docnum=1807169).

2. A livelihood has been defined as comprising the capabilities, assets, and activities required for a means of living. A livelihood is identified as sustainable when it can cope with and recover from stresses and shocks and maintain or enhance capabilities and assets, both now and in the future, while not undermining the natural resource base (Carney 1998, p. 1).

3. See Moser (2008) for an analysis of the power of epistemic communities to develop and drop new policy approaches, as well as an evaluation of the advantages and limitations of the sustainable livelihoods approach.

4. Social protection has been defined as those longer-term policies that aim to protect and promote the economic and social security or well-being of the poor. Social protection policies are designed to provide a buffer against short-term shocks and also to enhance the capacity of households to accumulate assets and improve their well-being so that they are better protected in times of hardship (Cook, Kabeer, and Suwannarat 2003). The World Bank's social risk management framework identifies social protection as a set of public interventions "to assist individuals, households and communities in better managing income risks" (Holtzmann and Jorgensen 1999, p. 4) by "preventing, mitigating and coping with risks and shocks" (World Bank 2000).

5. Research by Krishna (2007) has shown that health shocks, such as sickness and disease, are the most powerful force pushing people below this threshold.

6. Mahajan (2007), for instance, argues that in a globalized world, financial capital is becoming central to the other forms of capital assets, as each in turn becomes "financialized." Natural capital, connected with land in many rural areas, is no longer communally owned but tradable, with forests privatized and sold. Even air becomes financialized with carbon credits, while pollution also will be financialized in the future. In the case of social capital, this financialization includes the purchase of access to clubs and networks and membership in circles that once required kinship. Human capital costs relate to the privatization of both health care and education. Private physical capital has always been financialized, but now access to public goods is being controlled and priced.

Appendix B

1. Nieves Ortega Pérez, "Spain: Forging an Immigration Policy," February 2003 (www. migrationinformation.org/profiles/display.cfm?id=97 [May 2009]).

References

Acción Internacional Técnica. 1976. *El otro Guayaquil: Servicios sociales del suburbio intimidades y perspectivas.* Publicaciones de la Junta Cívica de Guayaquil.

Acosta, Alberto, Susana López, and David Villamar. 2004. "Ecuador: Oportunidades y amenazas económicas de la emigración." In *Migraciones: Un juego con cartas marcadas,* edited by Francisco Hidalgo, pp. 259–302. Quito: Abya-Yala/Instituto Latinoamericano de Investigaciones Sociales.

———. 2006. *La emigración en el Ecuador: Oportunidades y amenazas.* Quito: Corporación Editora Nacional.

Actis, Walter. 2005. "Ecuatorianos/as en España. Inserción(es) en un mercado de trabajo segmentado." Presented at the Conferencia Internacional Migración, Transnacionalismo e Identidades: La Experiencia Ecuatoriana. Facultad Latinoamericana de Sciencias Sociales (FLACSO) Ecuador. Quito, January 17–19.

Adams, Richard H., and John Page. 2005. "Do International Migration and Remittances Reduce Poverty in Developing Countries?" *World Development* 33, no. 10: 1645–69.

Adato, Michelle, Michael R. Carter, and Julian May. 2006. "Exploring Poverty Traps and Social Exclusion in South Africa Using Qualitative and Quantitative Data." *Journal of Development Studies* 42, no. 2: 226–47.

Agarwal, Bina. 1994. *A Field of One's Own: Gender and Land Rights in South Asia.* Cambridge University Press.

Alsop, Ruth, Mette Frost Bertelsen, and Jeremy Holland. 2006. *Empowerment in Practice: From Analysis to Implementation.* Washington: World Bank.

Alvarez, Sonia E. 1990. *Engendering Democracy in Brazil: Women's Movements in Transition.* Princeton University Press.

Anderson, Jeanine. 2003. "Accumulating Advantage and Disadvantage: Urban Poverty Dynamics." In *Urban Longitudinal Research Methodology: Development Planning Unit Working Paper 124,* edited by Caroline Moser, pp. 41–47. University College London, Development Planning Unit.

Andrade, Xavier. 1994. "Violencia y vida cotidiana en el Ecuador." In *La violencia en la región Andina: El caso de Ecuador,* edited by Julio Echeverría and Amparo Menéndez-Carrión, pp. 131–63. Quito: FLACSO.

———. 2006. "Más ciudad, menos ciudadanía: Renovación urbana y aniquilación del espacio público en Guayaquil." *Ecuador Debate* 68 (August): 161–98.

Appadurai, Arjun. 2001. "Deep Democracy: Urban Governmentality and the Horizon of Politics." *Environment and Urbanization* 13, no. 2: 23–44.

———. 2004. "The Capacity to Aspire: Culture and the Terms of Recognition." In *Culture and Public Action,* edited by Vijayendra Rao and Michael Walton, pp. 59–85. Stanford University Press.

Ariza, Marina, and Orlandina de Oliveira. 2001. "Familias en transición y marcos conceptuales en redefinición." *Papeles de Población* 28 (April–June): 9–39.

Arnett, Jeffrey. 2007. "Emerging Adulthood: What Is It, and What Is It Good For?" *Society for Research in Child Development* 1, no. 2: 68–73.

Asselin, Louis-Marie. 2002. "Multidimensional Poverty: Composite Indicator of Multidimensional Poverty." Lévis, Quebec: Institut de Mathématique Gauss.

Ballard, Roger. 2002. "A Case of Capital-Rich Under-Development: The Paradoxical Consequences of Successful Trans-National Entrepreneurship from Mirpur." University of Manchester, Center for Applied South Asian Studies.

Banco Central del Ecuador. 2005. "Coyuntura del mercado laboral agosto 2005." Quito.

Banco Ecuatoriano de Vivienda. 1975. "Informe de labores, 1972–74." Quito.

Barrientos, Armando, and David Hulme, eds. 2008. *Social Protection for the Poor and the Poorest: Concepts, Policies and Politics.* Basingstoke, U.K.: Palgrave.

Barrientos, Armando, David Hulme, and Andrew Shephard. 2005. "Can Social Protection Tackle Chronic Poverty?" *European Journal of Development Research* 17, no. 1: 8–23.

Barrig, Maruja. 1991. "Women and Development in Peru: Old Models, New Actors?" *Environment and Urbanization* 3, no. 2: 66–70.

BASIS Collaborative Research Program. 2004. "Innovative Development: BASIS CRSP Findings and Policy Recommendations." BASIS Brief 27. University of Wisconsin, Department of Agricultural and Applied Economics (November).

Baulch, Bob. 1996. "Editorial: The New Poverty Agency: A Disputed Consensus." *Institute of Development Studies (IDS) Bulletin* 27, no. 1: 1–10.

Beall, Jo. 2006. "Cities, Terrorism and Development." *Journal of International Development* 18, no. 1: 105–20.

Bebbington, Anthony. 1999. "Capitals and Capabilities: A Framework for Analyzing Peasant Viability, Rural Livelihoods and Poverty." *World Development* 27, no. 12: 2021–44.

Bebbington, Anthony, and Denise Bebbington. 2001. "Development Alternatives: Practice, Dilemmas and Theory." *Area* 33, no. 1: 7–17.

Bebbington, Anthony, and others. 2006. *The Search for Empowerment: Social Capital as Idea and Practice at the World Bank.* Hartford, Conn.: Kumarian Press.

Becker, Gary. 1965. "A Theory of the Allocation of Time." *Economic Journal* 75, no. 299: 493–517.

Beneria, Lourdes. 1991. "Structural Adjustment in the Labour Market and the Household: The Case of Mexico." In *Towards Social Adjustment: Labour Market Issues in Structural Adjustment,* edited by Guy Standing and Victor Tockman, pp. 161–83. Geneva: International Labor Organization.

Blaikie, Piers M., and Harold Brookfield. 1986. *Land Degradation and Society.* London: Methuen.

Bonilla, Frank. 1970. "Rio's Favelas: The Rural Slum within the City." In *Peasants in Cities,* edited by William Mangin, pp. 72–84. Boston: Houghton Mifflin.

Booth, David. 1994. *Rethinking Social Development: Theory, Research and Practice.* Harlow, U.K.: Longman Scientific and Technical.

Booysen, Frikkie, and others. 2008. "Using an Asset Index to Assess Trends in Poverty in Seven Sub-Saharan African Countries." *World Development* 36, no. 6: 1113–30.

Boshara, Ray, and Michael Sherraden. 2004. *Status of Asset Building Worldwide.* Washington: New America Foundation.

Bourdieu, Pierre. 1993. *Sociology in Question.* London: Sage Publications.

Bradshaw, Sarah. 1995. "Female-Headed Households in Honduras: Perspectives on Rural-Urban Differences." *Third World Planning Review* 17, no. 2: 117–32.

Broad, Robin, and John Cavanagh. 2006. "The Hijacking of the Development Debate: How Friedman and Sachs Got It Wrong." *World Policy Journal* 23 (Summer): 21–30.

Bromley, Ray. 1977. *Development Planning in Ecuador.* London: Latin American Publication Fund.

Bromley, Ray, and Chris Gerry, eds. 1979. *Casual Work and Poverty in Third World Cities.* Chichester, U.K: Wiley.

Brooks, John. 1980. *The South American Handbook.* Suffolk, U.K.: Trade and Travel Publications.

Burgwal, Gerrit. 1995. *Ecuador: SNV en la ciudad: Investigación sobre la problemática urbana.* Quito: Servicio Holandés de Cooperación de Desarrollo.

Buvinic, Mayra, and Nadia H. Youssef. 1978. *Women-Headed Households: The Ignored Factor in Development Planning.* Washington: International Center for Research on Women.

Buvinic, Mayra, and others. 1992. "The Fortunes of Adolescent Mothers and Their Children: The Transmission of Poverty in Santiago, Chile." *Population and Development Review* 18, no. 2: 269–97.

Cadena, Lenín, and Susana López. 2005. *Análisis de coyuntura económica. Una lectura de los principales componentes de la economía ecuatoriana durante el año 2005.* Quito: FLACSO Ecuador/Instituto Latinoamericano de Investigaciones Sociales (ILDIS)/Friedrich Ebert Stiftung.

Camacho, Gloria, and Kattya Hernández. 2005. *Cambió mi vida. Migración femenina, percepciones e impacto.* Quito: United Nations Development Fund for Women, Centro de Planificación y Estudios Sociales.

Carney, Diana. 1998. "Implementing the Sustainable Livelihoods Approach." In *Sustainable Rural Livelihoods: What Contribution Can We Make?* edited by Diana Carney, pp. 3–23. London: Department for International Development.

Carter, Michael R. 2007. "Learning from Asset-Based Approaches to Poverty." In *Reducing Global Poverty: The Case for Asset Accumulation,* edited Caroline O. N. Moser, pp. 51–61. Brookings.

Carter, Michael R., and Christopher B. Barrett. 2006. "The Economics of Poverty Traps and Persistent Poverty: An Asset-Based Approach." *Journal of Development Studies* 42, no. 2: 178–99.

Carter, Michael R., and Julian May. 2001. "One Kind of Freedom: Poverty Dynamics in Post-Apartheid South Africa." *World Development* 29, no. 12: 1987–2006.

Castells, Manuel. 1978. *The Urban Question: A Marxist Approach.* MIT Press.

———. 1983. *The City and the Grassroots: A Cross-Cultural Theory of Urban Social Movements.* London: Edward Arnold.

Centro de Planificación y Estudios Sociales (CEPLAES). 2005. "Migraciones internacionales: Principales implicaciones de las migraciones para el desarrollo del Ecuador." Draft document. United Nations Development Fund for Women.

Chambers, Robert. 1989. "Editorial Introduction: Vulnerability, Coping and Policy." *IDS Bulletin 20, no. 2: 1–7.*

———. 1992. "Rural Appraisal: Rapid, Relaxed and Participatory." Discussion Paper 311. University of Sussex, Institute of Development Studies.

———. 1994a. "Participatory Rural Appraisal (PRA): Analysis of Experience." *World Development* 22, no. 9: 1253–68.

———. 1994b. "Participatory Rural Appraisal (PRA): Challenges, Potentials and Paradigm." *World Development* 22, no. 10: 1437–54.

———. 1994c. "The Origins and Practice of Participatory Rural Appraisal." *World Development* 22, no. 7: 953–69.

———. 1995. "Poverty and Livelihoods: Whose Reality Counts?" Discussion Paper 347. University of Sussex, Institute of Development Studies.

———. 2007. "Poverty Research: Methodologies, Mindsets and Multidimensionality." Working Paper 293. University of Sussex, Institute of Development Studies.

Chambers, Robert, and Gordon Conway. 1992. *Sustainable Rural Livelihoods: Practical Concepts for the 21st Century.* University of Sussex, Institute of Development Studies.

Chant, Sylvia. 1991. *Women and Survival in Mexican Cities: Perspectives on Gender, Labour Markets and Low-Income Households.* Manchester University Press.

———. 1997. *Women-Headed Households: Diversity and Dynamics in the Developing World.* Basingstoke, U.K.: Macmillan.

———. 2008. "The 'Feminization of Poverty' and the 'Feminization' of Anti-Programmes: Room for Revision?" *Journal of Development Studies* 44, no. 2: 165–97.

Chant, Sylvia, and Cathy McIlwaine. 1995. *Women of a Lesser Cost: Female Labor, Foreign Exchange and Philippine Development.* London: Pluto.

Chimhowu, Admos, Jennifer Piese, and Caroline Pinder. 2003. "Report on the Development of a Framework for Assessing the Socio-Economic Impact of Migrant Workers' Remittances on Poverty Reduction." London: Department for International Development.

Cleaves, Peter Shurtleff. 1974. *Bureaucratic Politics and Administration in Chile.* University of California Press.

Coleman, James S. 1990. *Foundations of Social Theory.* Harvard University Press.

Collier, David. 1976. *Squatters and Oligarchs: Authoritarian Rule and Policy Change in Peru.* Johns Hopkins University Press.

Committee Indio Guayas. 1986. "Historia di mi organización." Mimeo. Guayaquil.

Cook, Sarah, Naila Kabeer, and Gary Suwannarat. 2003. *Social Protection in Asia.* New Delhi: Har Anand.

Corbett, Jane. 1988. "Famine and Household Coping Strategies." *World Development* 16, no. 9: 1099–112.

Corbridge, Stuart, and Gareth A. Jones. 2005. "The Continuing Debate about Urban Bias: The Thesis, Its Critics, Its Influence, and Implications for Poverty Reduction." London School of Economics and Political Science, Department of Geography and Environment.

Corkill, David, and David Cubitt. 1988. *Ecuador: Fragile Democracy.* London: Latin American Bureau.

Cornelius, Wayne A. 1973 *Political Learning among the Migrant Poor: The Impact of Residential Context.* London: Sage Publications.

Cornwall, Andrea. 2002. "Spending Power: Love, Money, and the Reconfiguration of Gender Relations in Ado-Odo, Southwestern Nigeria." *American Ethnologist* 29, no. 4: 963–80.

———. 2003. "Whose Voices? Whose Choices? Reflections on Gender and Participatory Development." *World Development* 31, no. 8: 1325–42

———. 2007. "Myths to Live By? Female Solidarity and Female Autonomy Reconsidered." *Development and Change* 38, no. 1: 149–68.

Cornwall, Andrea, Elizabeth Harrison, and Ann Whitehead. 2007. "Gender Myths and Feminist Fables: The Struggles for Interpretive Power in Gender and Development." *Development and Change* 38, no 1: 1–20.

Cortés Maisonave, Almudena. 2005. "La experiencia del codesarrollo Ecuador-España: Una aproximación inicial." Presented at the Conferencia Internacional Migración, Transnacionalismo e Identidades: La Experiencia Ecuatoriana. FLACSO Ecuador. Quito, January 17–19.

Craske, Nikki. 1999. *Women and Politics in Latin America.* Rutgers University Press.

———. 2003. "Gender, Politics and Legislation." In *Gender in Latin America,* edited by Sylvia Chant and Nikki Craske, pp. 19–45. London: Latin American Bureau.

Dani, Anis, and Caroline Moser. 2008. "Asset-Based Social Policy and Public Action in a Polycentric World." In *Assets, Livelihoods and Social Policy,* edited by Caroline Moser and Anis Dani, pp. 3–41. Washington: World Bank.

Davies, Susanna. 1993. "Are Coping Strategies a Cop Out?" *IDS Bulletin* 24, no. 4: 60–72.

Davis, Mike. 2006. *Planet of Slums.* London: Verso.

Deere, Carmen D., Cheryl Doss, and Caren Grown. 2007. "Measuring Women's Assets: A Guide to Survey Development." Paper commissioned for the World Bank project on Collecting Data on Individual Assets. Washington: World Bank (June).

De Haan, Arjan. 2006 "Migration in the Development Studies Literature: Has It Come out of Marginality?" Research Paper RP/2006/19. Helsinki: United Nations University, World Institute for Development Economics Research.

De la Rocha, Mercedes. 1994. *The Resources of Poverty: Women and Survival in a Mexican City.* Oxford: Blackwell.

———. 2007. "The Construction of the Myth of Survival." *Development and Change* 38, no. 1: 45–66.

Departamento de Planeamiento Urbano. 1975. "Esquema político de Guayaquil." Guayaquil: Municipalidad de Guayaquil.

De Soto, Hernando. 2000. *The Mystery of Capital: Why Capitalism Triumphs in the West and Fails Everywhere Else.* New York: Basic Books.

Development GAP. 1993. *The Other Side of the Story: The Real Impact of the World Bank and the IMF Structural Adjustment Programs.* Washington.

Devereux, Stephen. 1993. "Goats before Ploughs: Dilemmas of Household Response Sequencing during Food Shortage." *IDS Bulletin* 24, no. 4: 52–59.

De Waal, Alex. 1989. "Is Famine Relief Irrelevant to Rural People?" *IDS Bulletin* 20, no. 2: 63–69.

Downing, Thomas. 1991. *Assessing Socioeconomic Vulnerability to Famine: Frameworks, Concepts and Applications.* World Hunger Program, Brown University.

Drèze, Jean, and Amartya Kumar Sen. 1989. *Hunger and Public Action.* Oxford: Clarendon Press.

Dwyer, Daisy, and Judith Bruce, eds. 1988. *A Home Divided: Women and Income in the Third World.* Stanford University Press.

Easterly, William R. 2006. *The White Man's Burden: Why the West's Efforts to Aid the Rest Have Done So Much Ill and So Little Good.* New York: Penguin Press.

Eckstein, Susan. 1976. "The Rise and Demise of Research on Latin American Urban Poverty." *Studies in Comparative International Development* 11, no. 2: 107–26.

———. 1977. *The Poverty of Revolution: The State and the Urban Poor in Mexico.* Princeton University Press.

———. 2001. *Power and Popular Protest.* University of California Press.

Elder, Glen. 1998. "The Life Course as Development Theory." *Child Development* 69, no. 1: 1–12.

Elson, Diane. 1991. "Male Bias in Macro-economics: The Case of Structural Adjustment." In *Male Bias in the Development Process,* edited by Diane Elson, pp. 164–90. Manchester University Press.

Escobar, Arturo. 1995. *Encountering Development: The Making and Unmaking of the Third World.* Princeton University Press.

Estrada Ycaza, Julio. 1973. "Desarrollo historico del suburbio Guayaquilleño." *Revista del Archivo Historico del Guayas,* no. 3: 14–26.

———. 1977. *Regionalismo y migración.* Guayaquil: Publicaciones del Archivo Historico del Guayas.

Evans, Alison. 1989. "Women, Rural Development and Gender Issues in Rural Household Economics." Discussion Paper 254. University of Sussex, Institute of Development Studies.

Fan, Lilianne. 2007. "Protecting Land Rights in Post-Tsunami and Postconflict Aceh, Indonesia." In *Reducing Global Poverty: The Case for Asset Accumulation,* edited by Caroline O. N. Moser, pp. 149–66. Brookings.

Farrington, John, and Rachel Slater. 2006. "Introduction: Cash Transfers: Panacea for Poverty Reduction or Money down the Drain?" *Development Policy Review* 24, no. 5: 499–511.

Ferguson, Claire, Caroline Moser, and Andy Norton. 2007. "Claiming Rights: Citizenship and the Politics of Asset Distribution." In *Reducing Global Poverty: The Case for Asset Accumulation,* edited by Caroline O. N. Moser, pp. 273–88. Brookings.

Filmer, Deon, and Lant Pritchett. 1998. "The Effect of Household Wealth on Educational Attainment: Demographic and Health Survey Evidence." Policy Research Working Paper 1980. Washington: World Bank.

———. 2001. "Estimating Wealth Effects without Expenditure Data—or Tears: An Application to Educational Enrollments in States of India." *Demography* 38, no. 1: 115–32.

Fine, Ben. 1999. "The Development State Is Dead—Long Live Social Capital." *Development and Change* 30, no. 1: 1–19.

———. 2001. *Social Capital versus Social Theory: Political Economy and Social Science at the Turn of the Millennium.* New York: Routledge.

Floro, Maria, and Alberto Acosta. 1993. "Ecuador in the 1980s: A Review of National and Urban Level Economic Reforms." TWURD Working Paper 10. Washington: Transportation, Water, and Urban Development Department, World Bank.

Folbre, Nancy. 1986. "Hearts and Spades: Paradigms of Household Economics." *World Development* 14, no. 2: 245–55.

Ford Foundation. 2004. *Building Assets to Reduce Poverty and Injustice.* New York: Ford Foundation

Fossgard-Moser, Titus. 2005. "Social Performance: Key Lessons from Recent Experiences within Shell." *Journal of Corporate Governance* 5, no. 3: 105–18.

Fretes Cibils, Vicente, Marcelo Giugale, and Jóse Roberto López-Cálix, eds. 2003. *Ecuador: An Economic and Social Agenda in the New Millennium.* Washington: World Bank.

Friedmann, John. 1989. "The Latin American Barrio Movement as a Social Movement: Contribution to a Debate." *International Journal of Urban and Regional Research* 13, no. 3: 501–10.

Fukuyama, Francis. 1995. *Trust: The Social Virtues and the Creation of Prosperity.* London: Penguin.

———. 2001. "Social Capital, Civil Society and Development." *Third World Quarterly* 22, no. 1: 7–20.

Fussell, Elizabeth, and Alberto Palloni. 2004. "Persistent Marriage Regimes in Changing Times." *Journal of Marriage and Family* 66, no. 5: 1201–13.

Gates Foundation. 2008. "Strategy Lifecycle Overview and Guide." Seattle.

Gerlach, Allen. 2003. *Indians, Oil, and Politics: A Recent History of Ecuador.* Wilmington, Del.: SR Books.

Gilbert, Alan. 1981. "Pirates and Invaders: Land Acquisition in Urban Colombia and Venezuela." *World Development* 9, no. 7: 657–78.

Gilbert, Alan, and Josef Gugler. 1982. *Cities, Poverty, and Development: Urbanization in the Third World.* Oxford University Press.

Gilbert, Alan, and Peter M. Ward. 1978. "Housing in Latin American Cities." In *Geography and the Urban Environment,* edited by David T. Herbert and Ronald J. Johnston, pp. 285–318. New York: John Wiley.

Giménez Romero, Carlos. 2002. "Dinamización comunitaria en el ambito de la inmigración. Apuntes y propuestas sobre participaciòn, mediaciòn y codesarrollo." In *La Exclusión Social. Teoría y Práctica de la Intervención,* edited by María José Rubio and Silvina Monteros, pp. 99–128. Madrid: Editorial CCS.

Glewwe, Paul W., and Gillette Hall. 1995. "Who Is Most Vulnerable to Macroeconomic Shocks? Hypotheses Tests Using Panel Data from Peru." Living Standards Measurement Study Working Paper 117. Washington: World Bank.

Gluckman, Max. 1968. "Analysis of a Social Situation in Modern Zululand." Rhodes-Livingston Paper 28. Manchester University Press.

Green, Maia. 2006. "Representing Poverty and Attacking Representations: Perspectives on Poverty from Social Anthropology." *Journal of Development Studies* 42, no. 7: 1108–29.

Green, Maia, and David Hulme. 2005. "From Correlates and Characteristics to Causes: Thinking about Poverty from a Chronic Poverty Perspective." *World Development* 33, no. 6: 867–79.

Grootaert, Christiaan, and Thierry Van Bastelaer, eds. 2002. *Understanding and Measuring Social Capital: A Multidisciplinary Tool for Practitioners*. Washington: World Bank.

Grootaert, Christiaan, and others. 2004. "Measuring Social Capital: An Integrated Questionnaire." Working Paper 18. Washington: World Bank.

Haddad, Lawrence, John Hoddinott, and Harold Alderman. 1997. *Intrahousehold Resource Allocation in Developing Countries: Models, Methods and Policies*. Johns Hopkins University Press.

Haddad, Lawrence, and Ravi Kanbur. 1989. "How Serious Is the Neglect of Intra-Household Inequality?" Policy Research Working Paper 296. Washington: World Bank.

Hall, Anthony. 2008 "International Migration and Challenges for Social Policy: The Case of Ecuador." In *Assets, Livelihoods and Social Policy*, edited by Caroline Moser and Anis Dani, pp. 85–106. Washington: World Bank.

Harriss, John. 2002. *Depoliticizing Development: The World Bank and Social Capital*. London: Anthem Press.

———. 2007a. "Bringing Politics Back in to Poverty Analysis: Why Understanding of Social Relations Matters More for Policy on Chronic Poverty than Measurement." Q-Squared Working Paper 34. University of Toronto, Center for International Studies (April).

———. 2007b. "The Search for Empowerment: Social Capital as Idea and Practice at the World Bank." *Development in Practice* 17, no. 1: 162–64.

Harriss, John, and Paolo de Renzio. 1997. "An Introductory Bibliographic Essay. 'Missing Link' or Analytically Missing? The Concept of Social Capital." *Journal of International Development* 9, no. 7: 919–37.

Health and Life Sciences Partnership. 1989. "Urban Basic Services Evaluations. No. 1: Guayaquil, Ecuador. Evaluation of the Primary Health Care Component." Unpublished report.

Herrera, Gioconda. 2005. "Mujeres ecuatorianas en las cadenas globales del cuidado." Presented at the Conferencia Internacional Migración, Transnacionalismo e Identidades: La Experiencia Ecuatoriana. FLACSO Ecuador. Quito, January 17–19.

Hidrobo Estrada, Jorge. 1992. *Power and Industrialization in Ecuador*. Boulder, Colo.: Westview Press.

Himmelweit, Susan, and Simon Mohun. 1977. "Domestic Labour and Capital." *Cambridge Journal of Economics* 1, no. 1: 15–31.

Holzmann, Robert, and Steen Jorgensen. 1999. "Social Protection as Social Risk Management: Conceptual Understandings for the Social Protection Sector Strategy Paper." Social Protection Discussion Paper 9904. Washington: World Bank, Human Development Network, Social Protection Unit.

Hulme, David, and Andy McKay. 2005. "Identifying and Measuring Chronic Poverty: Beyond Monetary Measures." Paper presented at the Conference on Multidimensional Poverty, International Poverty Center of the United Nations Development Programme. Brasília, August 29–31.

Instituto Latinoamericano de Investigaciones Sociales (ILDIS/FES) and others. 2002. "El trabajo doméstico en la migración." Cartillas sobre Migración 2. Quito.

———. 2003. "Causas del reciente proceso migratorio ecuatoriano." Cartilla sobre Migración 3. Quito.

Isaacs, Anita. 1993. *Military Rule and Transition in Ecuador, 1972–92*. University of Pittsburgh Press.

Islam, Rizwanul. 2004. "The Nexus of Economic Growth, Employment and Poverty Reduction: An Empirical Analysis." Issues in Employment and Poverty Discussion Paper 14. Geneva: International Labor Organization.

Jackson, Cecile. 1998. "Rescuing Gender from the Poverty Trap." In *Feminist Visions of Development: Gender Analysis and Policy,* edited by Cecile Jackson and Ruth Pearson, pp. 38–65. London: Routledge.

———. 2007. "Resolving Risk? Marriage and Creative Conjugality." *Development and Change* 38, no. 1: 107–30.

Jelin, Elizabeth, ed. 1990. *Women and Social Change in Latin America.* London: Zed Books.

———. 2007. "Las familias latinoamericanas en el marco de las transformaciones globales." In *Familias y Políticas Públicas en América Latina: Una Historia de Desencuentros,* edited by Irma Arriagada, pp. 93–123. Santiago de Chile: Comision Economica para America Latina y el Caribe (CEPAL).

Jensen, Arthur R. 2002. "Psychometric *g:* Definition and Substantiation." In *The General Factor of Intelligence: How General Is It?* edited by Robert J. Sternberg and Elena Grigorenko, pp. 39–54. Mahwah, N.J: Lawrence Erlbaum Associates.

Jokisch, Brad D., and Jason Pribilsky. 2002. "The Panic to Leave: Economic Crisis and the 'New Emigration' from Ecuador." *International Migration* 40, no. 4: 75–101.

Junta Nacional de Planificación. 1967. *Proyecto de rehabilitación de terrenos, Guayaquil.* Quito.

Junta Nacional de Planificación y Coordinación Económica. 1973. *El estrato popular urbano: Informe de investigación sobre Guayaquil, Ecuador.* Quito.

Kabeer, Naila. 1994. *Reversed Realities: Gender Hierarchies in Development Thought.* London: Verso.

Kanbur, Ravi. 2003. *Q-Squared: Combining Qualitative and Quantitative Methods in Poverty Appraisal.* Delhi: Permanent Black.

———. 2007. "Globalization, Growth and Distribution: Framing the Questions." Draft document of paper prepared for the Commission on Growth and Development (the Spence Commission). Cornell University, Department of Economics (September).

Kaplan, Temma. 1982. "Female consciousness and collective action: The case of Barcelona 1910–1918." *Signs: Journal of Women in Culture and Society* 7, no. 3: 545–66.

Klasen, Stephan. 2000. "Measuring Poverty and Deprivation in South Africa." *Review of Income and Wealth* 46, no. 1: 33–58.

———. 2008. "Economic Growth and Poverty Reduction: Measurement Issues Using Income and Non-Income Indicators." *World Development* 36, no. 3: 420–45.

Kolenikov, Stanislav, and Gustavo Angeles. 2004. "The Use of Discrete Data in Principal Component Analysis: Theory, Simulations, and Applications to Socioeconomic Indices." Working Paper WP-04-85 of MEASURE/Evaluation Project. University of North Carolina, Carolina Population Center.

———. 2005. "On Reuse of Clusters in Repeated Studies." Paper presented at the American Statistical Association. Minneapolis, Minn., August.

Koonings, Kees, and Dirk Kruijt. 2007. *Fractured Cities: Social Exclusion, Urban Violence and Contested Spaces in Latin America.* London: Zed Books.

Kothari, Uma. 2005. *A Radical History of Development Studies: Individuals, Institutions and Ideologies.* London: Zed Books.

Kothari, Uma, and Martin Minogue. 2002. *Development Theory and Practice: Critical Perspectives.* Basingstoke, U.K.: Palgrave.

Krishna, Anirudh. 2007. "The Stages-of-Progress Methodology and Results from Five Countries." In *Reducing Global Poverty: The Case for Asset Accumulation,* edited by Caroline O. N. Moser, pp. 62–79. Brookings.

Kyle, David. 1999. "The Otavalo Trade Diaspora: Social Capital and Transnational Entrepreneurship." *Ethnic and Racial Studies* 22, no. 2: 422–46.

Leeds, Anthony. 1969. "The Significant Variables Determining the Character of Squatter Settlements." *America Latina* 12, no. 3: 44–86.

Levy, Santiago. 2006. *Progress against Poverty: Sustaining Mexico's Progresa-Oportunidades Program.* Brookings.

Lewis, Oscar. 1961. *The Children of Sanchez: Autobiography of a Mexican Family.* New York: Random House.

———. 1966. "The Culture of Poverty." *Scientific American* 215, no. 4: 19–25.

Lewis, Oscar, and others. 1975. *Five Families.* University of Chicago Press.

Lipton, Michael. 1977. *Why Poor People Stay Poor: A Study of Urban Bias in World Development.* Australian National University Press.

Lipton, Michael, and Simon Maxwell. 1992. *The New Poverty Agenda: An Overview.* Discussion Paper 306. University of Sussex, Institute of Development Studies.

Lipton, Michael, and Martin Ravallion. 1995. "Poverty and Policy." In *Handbook of Development Economics,* edited by Hollis Chenery and T. N. Srinivasan, pp. 2551–657. London: Elsevier.

Liu, Amy. 2007. "Hurricane Katrina: Impact on Assets and Asset-Building Approaches to Poverty Reduction." In *Reducing Global Poverty: The Case for Asset Accumulation,* edited by Caroline O. N. Moser, pp. 167–78. Brookings.

Logan, Kathleen. 1990. "Women's Participation in Urban Protest." In *Popular Movements and Political Change in Mexico,* edited by Joe Foweraker and Ann L. Craig, pp. 150–59. Boulder, Colo.: Lynne Rienner.

Lomnitz, Larissa. 1977. *Networks and Marginality: Life in a Mexican Shantytown.* New York: Academic Press.

Long, Norman. 1968. *Social Change and the Individual.* Manchester University Press.

———. 1992. "From Paradigm Lost to Paradigm Regained? The Case for an Actor-Oriented Sociology of Development." In *Battlefields of Knowledge. The Interlocking of Theory and Practice in Social Research and Development,* edited by Norman Long and Ann Long, pp. 16–43. London: Routledge.

Longhurst, Richard. 1994. "Conceptual Frameworks for Linking Relief and Development." *IDS Bulletin* 25, no. 4: 17–23.

Loor, Kleber, Lidice Aldas, and Fernando López. n.d. "Pandillas y naciones de Ecuador. Alarmante realidad, tarea desafiante: De víctimas a victimarios." Quito: Children in Organised Armed Violence.

Lutz, Thomas M. 1970. "Self-Help Neighborhood Organization, Political Orientations of Urban Squatters in Latin America: Contrasting Patterns from Case Studies in Panama City, Guayaquil and Lima." Ph.D. dissertation, Georgetown University.

Luzuriaga, C., and D. Valentine. 1988. "UNICEF Basic Urban Services Evaluation, Guayaquil, Ecuador. Content of Previous Assessments." Unpublished report. Quito: United Nations Children's Fund.

MacIntosh, Duncan. 1972. "The Politics of Primacy: Political Factors in the Development of Ecuador's Largest City, Guayaquil." M.Sc. dissertation thesis. Columbia University, Faculty of Architecture.

Mahajan, Vijay. 2007. "Beyond Microfinance." In *Reducing Global Poverty: The Case for Asset Accumulation,* edited by Caroline O. N. Moser, pp. 196–207. Brookings.

Maimbo, Samuel Munzele, and Dilip Ratha, eds. 2005. *Remittances. Development Impact and Future Prospects.* Washington: World Bank.

Maluccio, John A., Alexis Murphy, and Kathryn M. Yount. 2005. "Research Note: A Socio-economic Index for the INCAP Longitudinal Study 1969–77." *Food and Nutrition Bulletin* 26, no. 2: 120–24.

Marshall, Gordon. 1998. *A Dictionary of Sociology.* Oxford University Press.

Massolo, Alejandra. 1992. *Por amor y coraje: Mujeres en movimientos urbanos de la Ciudad de Mexico.* Mexico City: El Colegio de Mexico.

Mathie, Alison, and Gordon Cunningham. 2003. "Who Is Driving Development? Reflections on the Transformative Potential of Asset-Based Community Development." Occasional Paper 5. St. Xavier University.

Maxwell, Simon, and Marisol Smith. 1992. "Household Food Security, a Conceptual Review." In *Household Food Security, Concepts, Indicators, Measurements: A Technical Review,* edited by Timothy R. Frankenberger and Simon Maxwell, pp. 1–72. New York: United Nations Children's Fund/International Fund for Agricultural Development.

Mayo, Marjorie. 1975. "Community Development: A Radical Alternative?" In *Radical Social Work,* edited by Roy Bailey and Mike Brake, pp. 129–43. London: Edward Arnold.

McIlwaine, Cathy. 1998. "Civil Society and Development Geography." *Progress in Human Geography* 22, no. 3: 415–24.

———. 2007. "From Local to Global to Transnational Civil Society: Reframing Development Perspectives on the Non-State Sector." *Geography Compass* 1, no. 6: 1252–81.

McIlwaine, Cathy, and Caroline O. N. Moser. 2001. "Violence and Social Capital in Urban Poor Communities: Perspectives from Colombia and Guatemala." *Journal of International Development* 13, no. 7: 965–84.

———. 2007. "Living in Fear: How the Urban Poor Perceive Violence, Fear and Insecurity." In *Fractured Cities: Social Exclusion, Urban Violence and Contested Spaces in Latin America,* edited by Kees Koonings and Dirk Kruijt, pp. 117–37. London: Zed.

McNeill, Desmond. 2004. "Social Capital and the World Bank." In *Global Institutions & Development,* edited by Morten Bøås and Desmond McNeill, pp. 108–23. London: Routledge.

Menéndez-Carrión, Amparo. 1985. *La conquista del voto.* Quito: Corporacion Editora Nacional.

Milkman, Ruth. 1976. "Women's Work and the Economic Crisis: Some Lessons from the Great Depression." *Review of Radical Political Economics* 8, no. 1: 75–97.

Mitchell, J. Clyde. 1968. "The Kalela Dance." Rhodes–Livingston Paper 27. Manchester University Press.

Molyneux, Maxine. 1978. "Beyond the Domestic Labour Debate." *New Left Review* 116 (July–August): 3–27.

———. 2002. "Gender and the Silences of Social Capital: Lessons from Latin America." *Development and Change* 33, no. 2: 167–88.

Moore, Richard J. 1978. "Urban Problems and Policy Responses for Metropolitan Guayaquil." In *Metropolitan Latin America: The Challenge and the Response,* edited by Wayne A. Cornelius and Robert V. Kemper, pp. 181–203. Beverly Hills, Calif.: Sage.

Moore, Richard, and R. Caruso. 1975. *Estudio de investigación del mercado guayaquileño.* Guayaquil: Meals for Millions Foundation.

Moser, Caroline O. N. 1976. "Differentiation and Mobility in a Bogotá Retail Market." Unpublished Ph.D. thesis, University of Sussex.

———. 1978. "Informal Sector or Petty Commodity Production: Dualism or Dependence in Urban Development?" *World Development* 6, no. 9–10: 1041–64.

———. 1981. "Surviving in the Suburbios." *IDS Bulletin* 12, no. 3: 19–29.

———. 1982. "A Home of One's Own: Squatter Housing Strategies in Guayaquil, Ecuador." In *Urbanization in Contemporary Latin America: Critical Approaches to the Analysis of Urban Issues,* edited by Alan Gilbert, Jorge Enrique Hardy, and Ronaldo Ramírez, pp. 159–90. London: Wiley.

———. 1984. "The Informal Sector Reworked: Viability and Vulnerability in Urban Development." *Regional Development Dialogue* 5, no. 2: 135–78.

———. 1987. "Mobilization Is Women's Work: Struggles for Infrastructure in Guayaquil, Ecuador." In *Women, Human Settlements and Housing,* edited by Caroline O. N. Moser and Linda Peake, pp. 166–94. London: Taylor and Francis.

———. 1989a. "Community Participation in Urban Projects in the Third World." *Progress in Planning* 32, no. 2: 73–133.

———. 1989b. "Gender Planning in the Third World: Meeting Practical and Strategic Gender Needs." *World Development* 17, no. 11: 1799–825.

———. 1992. "Adjustment from Below: Low-Income Women, Time and the Triple Role in Guayaquil, Ecuador." In *Women and Adjustment Policies in the Third World,* edited by Haleh Afshar and Carolyne Dennis, pp. 87–116. Basingstoke, U.K.: Macmillan.

———. 1993. *Gender Planning and Development: Theory, Practice and Training.* London: Routledge.

———. 1996. "Confronting Crisis: A Summary of Household Responses to Poverty and Vulnerability in Four Poor Urban Communities." Environmentally Sustainable Development Studies and Monographs 7. Washington: World Bank.

———. 1997. "Household Responses to Poverty and Vulnerability. Volume 1: Confronting Crisis in Cisne Dos, Guayaquil, Ecuador." Urban Management Program Policy Paper 21. Washington: World Bank.

———. 1998. "The Asset Vulnerability Framework: Reassessing Urban Poverty Reduction Strategies." *World Development* 26, no. 1: 1–20.

———. 2001. "Insecurity and Social Protection—Has the World Bank Got It Right?" *Journal of International Development* 13, no. 3: 361–68.

———. 2003. " 'Apt Illustration' or 'Anecdotal Information?' Can Qualitative Data Be Representative or Robust?" In *Q-Squared: Combining Qualitative and Quantitative Methods in Poverty Appraisal,* edited by Ravi Kanbur, pp. 79–89. Delhi: Permanent Black.

———. 2004. "Urban Violence and Insecurity: An Introductory Roadmap." *Environment and Urbanization* 16, no. 2: 3–16.

———. 2005. "Rights, Power and Poverty Reduction." In *Power, Rights and Poverty: Concepts and Connections,* edited by Ruth Alsop, pp. 29–50. Washington: World Bank/Department for International Development.

———, ed. 2007. *Reducing Global Poverty: The Case for Asset Accumulation.* Brookings.

———. 2008. "Assets and Livelihoods: A Framework for Asset-Based Social Policy." In *Assets, Livelihoods and Social Policy,* edited by Caroline Moser and Anis Dani, pp. 43–81. Washington: World Bank.

Moser, Caroline O. N., and Oscar Antezana. 2002. "Social Protection in Bolivia: An Assessment in Terms of the World Bank's Social Protection Framework and the PRSP." *Development Policy Review* 20, no. 5: 637–56.

Moser, Caroline O. N., and Anis A. Dani. 2008. *Assets, Livelihoods, and Social Policy.* Washington: World Bank.

Moser, Caroline O. N., and Andrew Felton. 2007. "Intergenerational Asset Accumulation and Poverty Reduction in Guayaquil, Ecuador, 1978–2004." In *Reducing Global Poverty: The Case for Asset Accumulation,* edited by Caroline O. N. Moser, pp. 15–50. Brookings.

———. 2009. "The Construction of an Asset Index: Measuring Asset Accumulation in Ecuador." In *Poverty Dynamics: Interdisciplinary Perspectives,* edited by Tony Addison, David Hulme, and Ravi Kanbur, pp. 102–27. Oxford University Press.

———. Forthcoming. "The Gendered Nature of Asset Accumulation in Urban Contexts: Longitudinal Results from Guayaquil, Ecuador." In *Beyond the Tipping Point: The Benefits and Challenges of Urbanization,* edited by Jo Beall, Basudeb Guha-Khasnobis, and Ravi Kanbur. Oxford University Press.

Moser, Caroline O. N., Mike Gatehouse, and Helen Garcia. 1996. "Urban Poverty Research Sourcebook: Module I: Sub-City Level Household Survey. Module II: Indicators of Urban Poverty." Urban Management Program Working Paper 5. Washington: World Bank.

Moser, Caroline O. N., and Jeremy Holland. 1997. "Urban Poverty and Violence in Jamaica." Viewpoints. Washington, D.C.: World Bank, Latin American and Caribbean Studies.

Moser, Caroline O. N., and Cathy McIlwaine. 1999. "Participatory Urban Appraisal and Its Application for Research on Violence." *Environment and Urbanization* 11, no. 2: 203–26.

———. 2004. *Encounters with Violence in Latin America: Urban Poor Perceptions from Colombia and Guatemala.* London: Routledge.

———. 2006. "Latin American Urban Violence as a Development Concern: Towards a Framework for Violence Reduction." *World Development* 34, no. 1: 89–112.

Moser, Caroline O. N., and Annalise Moser. 2003. "Gender-Based Violence: A Serious Development Constraint." Background paper. Washington: World Bank, Gender Unit.

Moser, Caroline O. N., and Linda Peake. 1996. "Seeing the Invisible: Women, Gender and Urban Development." In *Urban Research in the Developing World,* vol. 4: *Thematic Issues,* edited by Richard E. Stren, pp. 249–347. University of Toronto, Center for Urban and Community Studies.

Moser, Caroline O. N., and Peter Sollis. 1991. "Did the Project Fail? A Community Perspective on a Participatory Primary Health Care Project in Ecuador." *Development in Practice* 1, no. 1: 19–33.

Moser, Caroline O. N., and Ailsa Winton. 2002. "Violence in the Central American Region: Towards an Integrated Framework for Violence Reduction." Working Paper 17. London: Overseas Development Institute.

Narayan, Deepa. 1997. *Voices of the Poor: Poverty and Social Capital in Tanzania.* Washington: World Bank.

Narayan, Deepa, and Lant Pritchett. 1997. "Cents and Sociability: Household Income and Social Capital in Rural Tanzania." Policy Research Working Paper 1796. Washington: World Bank.

Navarro Jiménez, Guillermo. 1976. *La concentracion de capitales en el Ecuador.* Universidad Central del Ecuador.

Navarro, Marysa. 1989. "The Personal Is Political: Las Madres de Plaza de Mayo." In *Power and Popular Protest. Latin American Social Movements,* edited by Susan Eckstein, pp. 241–58. University of California Press.

Nederveen Pieterse, Jan. 2000. "After Post-Development." *Third World Quarterly* 21, no. 2: 175–91.

Nelson, Joan. 1979. *Access to Power: Politics and the Urban Poor in Developing Nations.* Princeton University Press.

Oakley, Peter, and David Marsden. 1984. *Approaches to Participation in Rural Development.* Geneva: International Labor Organization.

O'Connor, Alice. 2001. *Poverty Knowledge: Social Science, Social Policy, and the Poor in Twentieth-Century U.S. History.* Princeton University Press.

Orozco, Manuel. 2005. "Markets and Financial Democracy: The Case for Remittance Transfers." *Journal of Payment Systems Law* 1, no. 2: 166–215.

———. 2007. "Migrant Foreign Savings and Asset Accumulation." In *Reducing Global Poverty: The Case for Asset Accumulation,* edited by Caroline O. N. Moser, pp. 225–238. Brookings.

Osmani, S. R. 2008. "When Endowments and Opportunities Don't Match: Understanding Chronic Poverty." In *Poverty Dynamics: Interdisciplinary Perspectives,* edited by Tony Addison, David Hulme, and Ravi Kanbur, pp. 247–66. Oxford University Press.

Parpart, Jane L., Shirin M. Rai, and Kathleen Staudt, eds. 2002. *Rethinking Empowerment— Gender and Development in a Global/Local World.* London: Routledge.

Paul, Samuel. 1987. "Community Participation in Development Projects: The World Bank Experience." World Bank Discussion Paper 6. Washington: World Bank.

Pearce, Jenny. 1998. "From Civil War to 'Civil Society': Has the End of the Cold War Brought Peace to Central America?" *International Affairs* 74, no. 3: 587–615.

Peattie, Lisa Redfield. 1968. *The View from the Barrio.* University of Michigan Press.

Pécaut, Daniel. 1999. "From Banality of Violence to Real Terror: The Case of Colombia." In *Societies of Fear,* edited by Kees Koonings and Dirk Kruijt, pp. 141–67. London: Zed Press.

Pedone, Claudia. 2002. "Las representaciones sociales en torno a la inmigración ecuatoriana a España." *Iconos: Revista de Ciencias Sociales,* no. 14: 56–66.

Perlman, Janice. 1976. *The Myth of Marginality: Urban Poverty and Politics in Rio de Janeiro.* University of California Press.

Perlman, Janice, and Molly O'Meara Sheehan. 2007. "Fighting Poverty and Environmental Injustice in Cities." In *State of the World. Our Urban Future,* 24 ed., Worldwatch Institute, pp. 172–90. London: Earthscan.

Plan Integrado para la Rehabilitación de las Areas (PREDAM). 1976. *Plan de rehabilitación de las areas marginales de Guayaquil. Tomo uno y segundo.* Quito: Junta Nacional de Planificación y Coordinación Económica.

Plan International Ecuador. 1985. *Manual de operaciones del programa de desarrollo familiar y comunitario correspondiente a Plan Guayas.* Guayaquil.

Portes, Alejandro. 1998. "Social Capital: Its Origins and Applications in Modern Sociology." *Annual Review of Sociology* 24: 1–24.

———. 2009. "Migration and Development: Reconciling Opposite Views." *Ethnic and Racial Studies* 32, no. 1: 5–22

Portes, Alejandro, and Patricia Landolt. 2000. "Social Capital: Promises and Pitfalls of Its Roles in Development." *Journal of Latin American Research* 32, no. 2: 529–47.

Portes, Alejandro, and John Walton. 1976. *Urban Latin America: The Political Condition from Above and Below.* University of Texas Press.

Pujadas, Joan J., and Julie Massal. 2002. "Migraciones ecuatorianas a España: Procesos de inserción y claroscuros." *Iconos: Revista de Ciencias Sociales,* no. 14: 67–87.

Putnam, Robert D. 1993. *Making Democracy Work: Civic Traditions in Modern Italy.* Princeton University Press.

Putzel, James. 1997. "Policy Arena: Accounting for the 'Dark Side' of Social Capital: Reading Robert Putnam on Democracy." *Journal of International Development* 9, no. 7: 939–49.

Quijano, Anibal. 1974. "The Marginal Pole of the Economy and the Marginalized Labour Force." *Economy and Society* 3, no. 4: 393–428.

Radcliffe, Sarah. 2004. "Geography of Development: Civil Society and Inequality—Social Capital Is (Almost) Dead?" *Progress in Human Geography* 28, no. 4: 517–27.

Rakodi, Carole. 1991. "Cities and People: Towards a Gender-Aware Urban Planning Process?" *Public Administration and Development* 11, no. 6: 541–59.

———. 1999. "A Capital Assets Framework for Analysing Household Livelihood Strategies: Implications for Policy." *Development Policy Review* 17, no. 3: 315–42.

Rao, Vijayendra. 2006. "On Inequality Traps and Development Policy." Findings 268. Washington: World Bank (November).

Ravallion, Martin. 1992. "Poverty Comparisons: A Guide to Concepts and Methods." Living Standards Measurement Study Working Paper 88. Washington: World Bank.

Razavi, Shahra. 1999. "Gendered Poverty and Well-Being: Introduction." *Development and Change* 30, no. 3: 409–33.

Ribe, Helena, and others. 1990. "How Adjustment Programs Can Help the Poor: The World Bank's Experience." World Bank Discussion Paper 71. Washington: World Bank.

Robben, Antonius, and Carolyn Nordstrom. 1995. "The Anthropology and Ethnography of Violence and Sociopolitical Conflict." In *Fieldwork under Fire: Contemporary Studies of Violence and Survival,* edited by Antonius Robben and Carolyn Nordstrom, pp. 1–24. University of California Press.

Roberts, Bryan. 1978. *Cities of Peasants.* London: Edward Arnold.

Robichaux, David. 2007. "Introducción. Diversidad familiar en América Latina: Perspectivas multidisciplinarias." In *Familia y Diversidad en América Latina. Estudios de Caso,* edited by David Robichaux, pp. 11–23. Buenos Aires: Consejo Latinoamericano de Ciencias Sociales.

Rubio, Mauricio. 1997. "Perverse Social Capital: Some Evidence from Colombia." *Journal of Economic Issues* 31, no. 3: 805–16.

Ruíz, Marta Cecilia. 2002. "Ni sueño ni pesadilla: Diversidad y paradojas en el proceso migratorio." *Iconos: Revista de Ciencias Sociales,* no. 14: 88–97.

Saavedra, Eduardo C., and Letty C. Loqui. 1976. *Estudio de la legislación de desarrollo urbano del Cantón Guayaquil.* Guayaquil: Indeca.

Sabates-Wheeler, Rachel, and Lawrence Haddad. 2005. "Reconciling Different Concepts of Risk and Vulnerability: A Review of Donor Documents." University of Sussex, Institute of Development Studies.

Sachs, Jeffrey D. 2006. *The End of Poverty: Economic Possibilities for Our Time.* New York: Penguin Press.

Sahn, David E., and David Stifel. 2000. "Assets as a Measurement of Household Welfare in Developing Countries." Working Paper 00-11. Washington University, Center for Social Development.

————. 2003. "Urban-Rural Inequality in Living Standards in Africa." *Journal of African Economics* 12, no. 4: 564–97.

Sánchez-Paramo, Carolina. 2005. "Poverty in Ecuador." En Breve 71. Washington: World Bank, Latin America and Caribbean Region.

Sandbrook, Richard. 1982. *The Politics of Basic Needs: Urban Aspects of Assaulting Poverty in Africa.* London: Heinemann.

Santos Alvite, Eduardo, 1989. "Poverty in Ecuador." *CEPAL Review* 38: 121–34.

Satterthwaite, David. 2006. "Book Review: *Planet of Slums* by Mike Davis and *Shadow Cities* by Robert Neuwirth." *Environment and Urbanization* 18, no. 2: 543–46.

Saunders, Peter. 1981. *Social Theory and the Urban Question.* London: Hutchinson.

Schneider, Ronald. 2006. *Latin American Political History.* Boulder, Colo.: Westview Press.

Scoones, Ian. 1998. "Sustainable Rural Livelihoods: A Framework for Analysis." Working Paper 72. University of Sussex, Institute of Development Studies.

Scott, Alison MacEwen. 1979. "Who Are the Self-Employed?" In *Casual Work and Poverty in Third World Cities,* edited by Ray Bromley and Chris Gerry, pp. 105–32. Chichester, U.K.: Wiley.

Sen, Amartya. 1981. *Poverty and Famines: An Essay on Entitlement and Deprivation.* Oxford University Press.

————. 1990. "Gender and Cooperative Conflicts." In *Persistent Inequalities,* edited by Irene Tinker, pp. 123–49. Oxford University Press.

————. 1997. "Editorial: Human Capital and Human Capability." *World Development* 25, no. 12: 1959–61.

————. 2006. "The Man without a Plan." *Foreign Affairs* 85 (March/April): 171–78.

Sepulveda, Juan R. 1977. *Algunos elementos de socialización política en el area suburbana de Guayaquil.* Departamento de Publicaciones de la Universidad de Guayaquil.

Serageldin, Ismail, and Andrew Steer. 1994 "Making Development Sustainable: From Concepts to Action." Environmentally Sustainable Development Occasional Paper 2. Washington: World Bank.

Shanahan, Michael J. 2000. "Pathways to Adulthood in Changing Societies: Variability and Mechanisms in Life Course Perspective." *Annual Review of Sociology* 26: 667–92.

Sherraden, Michael W. 1991. *Assets and the Poor: A New American Welfare Policy.* Armonk, N.Y.: M. E. Sharpe.

Siegel, Paul B. 2005. "Using an Asset-Based Approach to Identify Drivers of Sustainable Rural Growth and Poverty Reduction in Central America: A Conceptual Framework." Policy Research Working Paper 3475. Washington: World Bank.

Singer, Paul. 1982. "Neighborhood Movements in Sao Paulo." In *Towards a Political Economy of Urbanization in Third World Countries,* edited by Helen I. Safa, pp. 283–304. Oxford University Press.

Skinner, Ryder. 1983. *People, Poverty and Shelter.* London: Methuen.

Smith, Margo. 1973. "Domestic Service as a Channel of Upward Mobility for the Lower Class Woman: The Lima Case." In *Female and Male in Latin America,* edited by Ann Pescatello, pp. 191–207. University of Pittsburgh Press.

Solimano, Andrés. 2002. "Crisis, Dollarization, and Social Impact: An Overview." In *Crisis and Dollarization in Ecuador: Stability, Growth, and Social Equity,* edited by Paul Beckerman and Andrés Solimano, pp. 1–16. Washington: World Bank

Sollis, Peter. 1992. "Cisne Dos Health Survey." Unpublished document.

Sollis, Peter, and Caroline O. N. Moser. 1991. "A Methodological Framework for Analyzing the Social Costs of Adjustment at the Micro Level: The Case of Guayaquil, Ecuador." *IDS Bulletin* 22, no. 1: 23–30.

Sparr, Pamela, and Caroline O. N. Moser. 2007. "International NGOs and Poverty Reduction Strategies: The Contribution of an Asset-Based Approach." Global Economy and Development Working Paper 8. Brookings.

Stevens, Evelyn. 1973. "Marianismo: The Other Face of Machismo in Latin America." In *Female and Male in Latin America: Essays,* edited by Ann Pescatello, pp. 90–101. University of Pittsburgh Press.

Streeten Paul, and others. 1981. *First Things First: Meeting Basic Human Needs in Developing Countries.* Oxford University Press.

Swift, Jeremy. 1989. "Why Are Rural People Vulnerable to Famine?" *IDS Bulletin* 20, no. 2: 8–15.

Swyngedouw, Erik. 2004. *Social Power and the Urbanization of Water.* Oxford University Press.

Tilly, Charles. 1999. "Durable Inequality." In *A Nation Divided: Diversity, Inequality, and Community in American Society,* edited by Phyllis Moen, Donna Dempster-McClain, and Henry Walker, pp. 15–33. Cornell University Press.

Toye, John, and Carl Jackson. 1996. "Public Expenditure Policy and Poverty Reduction: Has the World Bank Got It Right?" *IDS Bulletin* 27, no. 1: 56–66.

Turner, John F. C. 1968. "Housing Priorities, Settlement Patterns and Urban Development in Modernizing Countries." *Journal of the American Institute of Planners* 34, no. 6: 54–63.

———. 1969. "Uncontrolled Urban Settlements: Problems and Policies." In *The City in Newly Developing Countries: Readings on Urbanism and Urbanization,* edited by Gerald Breese, pp. 507–34. Englewood Cliffs, N.J.: Prentice-Hall.

———. 1972. "Housing as a Verb." In *Freedom to Build,* edited by John F. C. Turner and Robert Fichter, pp. 148–75. New York: Collier Macmillan.

United Nations General Assembly. 2001. "Road Map towards the Implementation of the United Nations Millennium Summit." Report of the Secretary-General, A/56/326. New York.

United Nations, Department of Economic and Social Affairs, Population Division. 2008. *World Urbanization Prospects: The 2007 Revisions.* New York.

United Nations Development Program. 2002. *Human Development Report 2002: Deepening Democracy in a Fragmented World.* Oxford University Press.

———. 2004. *Human Development Report 2004.* New York.

———, International Poverty Center. 2006. "Social Protection. The Role of Cash Transfers." *Poverty in Focus* 8 (June).

United Nations Human Settlements Program. 2007. *Global Report on Human Settlements 2007: Enhancing Urban Safety and Security.* London: Earthscan.

United Nations Children's Fund (UNICEF). 1984. "Reaching Children and Women of the Urban Poor." Occasional Paper 3. New York.

———. 1985a. "Sistema de atención primaria de salud areas urbano marginales, Guayaquil, Ecuador." Paper presented to World Health Organization meeting on Primary Health Care Strategy in the Transformation of Health Services System. Santiago, Chile.

———. 1985b. "Sistema de atención primaria de salud, areas urbanas marginales, Guayaquil." Working paper (2d version). New York (July).

Van Velsen, Jaap. 1967. "The Extended-Case Method and Situational Analysis." In *The Craft of Anthropology,* edited by Arnold L. Epstein, pp. 129–49. London: Tavistock Publications.

Varley, Ann. 1993. "Gender and Housing: The Provision of Accommodation for Young Adults in Three Mexican Cities." *Habitat International* 17, no. 4: 13–30.

Vasconcelos, Pedro. 2004. "Sending Money Home: Remittance Recipients in the Dominican Republic and Remittance Senders from the U.S." Washington: Multilateral Investment Fund and Inter-American Development Bank.

Villavicencio, Gaitán. 2001. "El costo social del delito en el Ecuador y Guayaquil." Universidad de Guayaquil, Instituto Superior de Criminología y Ciencias Penalistas (December).

———. 2003. "Violencia social e inseguridad comprobada en Guayaquil: Diagnóstico de situación." In *Sumando para Guayaquil: Proyectos posibles.* Guayaquil: ILDIS/Fundación el Universo.

———. 2004. "Diagnósticos y propuestas para la seguridad ciudadana de Guayaquil." Seminario Internacional sobre Política Pública de Seguridad y Convivencia Ciudadana. Guayaquil, March 24–26.

Walton, John. 1998. "Urban Conflicts and Social Movements in Poor Countries: Theory and Evidence of Collective Action." *International Journal of Urban and Regional Research* 22, no. 3: 460–81.

Ward, Peter M. 1978. "Self-Help Housing Mexico City: Social and Economic Determinants of Success." *Town Planning Review* 49, no. 1: 38–50.

Whitehead, Ann. 1984. "I'm Hungry Mum: The Politics of Domestic Budgeting." In *Of Marriage and the Market: Women's Subordination Internationally and Its Lessons,* edited by Kate Young, Carol Wolkowitz, and Roslyn McCullagh., pp. 93–116. London: Routledge.

———. 2004. "Persistent Poverty in Upper East Ghana." BASIS Brief 26. University of Wisconsin, Department of Agriculture and Applied Economics (November).

Wisner, Ben. 1988. *Power and Need in Africa: Basic Human Needs and Development Policies.* London: Earthscan.

Woolcock, Michael. 1998. "Social Capital and Economic Development: Toward a Theoretical Synthesis and Policy Framework." *Theory and Society* 27, no. 2: 151–208.

———. 2007. "Towards an Economic Sociology of Chronic Poverty: Enhancing the Rigor and Relevance of Social Theory." Working Paper 104. University of Manchester, Chronic Poverty Research Center.

Woolf, Virginia 2002. *A Room of One's Own.* Modern Classics edition. London: Penguin Books.

World Bank. 1990. *World Development Report 1990: Poverty.* Oxford University Press.

———. 1991a. "Assistance Strategies to Reduce Poverty." World Bank Policy Paper. Washington.

———. 1991b. "Operational Directive 4.15." Washington.

———. 1992. *Poverty Reduction Handbook.* Washington.

———. 1995a. *Ecuador Poverty Report,* vols.1 and 2. Washington.

———. 1995b. "Social Impacts of Adjustment Operations: An Overview." Washington: Operations Evaluation Department.

———. 2000. *World Development Report 2000/2001: Attacking Poverty.* Oxford University Press.

———. 2004. "Ecuador Poverty Assessment." Report 27061-EC. Washington: Poverty Reduction and Economic Management Sector Unit, Latin America and the Caribbean Region.

———. 2005. *World Development Report 2006: Equity and Development.* Oxford University Press.

Index